Heath Grammar and Composition

with a Process Approach to Writing

Second Course

Authors
Carol Ann Bergman
J. A. Senn

D.C. Heath and Company
Lexington, Massachusetts / Toronto, Ontario

Series Titles

Heath Grammar and Composition: Introductory Course
Heath Grammar and Composition: First Course
Heath Grammar and Composition: Second Course
Heath Grammar and Composition: Third Course
Heath Grammar and Composition: Fourth Course
Heath Grammar and Composition: Fifth Course
Heath Grammar and Composition: Complete Course

Supplementary Materials (for each course)

Annotated Teacher's Edition
Teacher's Resource Binder
Writing Transparencies
Workbook
Tests

Contributing Writer

Florence Harris

Editorial	Christopher Johnson (Managing Editor), Barbara Brien, Kathleen Kennedy Kelley, Peg McNary, Nadia Yassa
Editorial Services	Marianna Frew Palmer (Manager), K. Kirschbaum Harvie
Design by	Dawn Ostrer Emerson
Production	Patrick Connolly

Acknowledgments: page 619

International Standard Book Number: 0-669-23503-2

12 13 14 —QUH—01 00 99 98 97

Second Course

Heath
Grammar and Composition

with a Process Approach to Writing

Series Consultant

Henry I. Christ
Former Chairman of the English Department
Andrew Jackson High School
St. Albans, New York

Reviewers

Arkansas

Joy Leatherwood
Lake Hamilton Junior High School
Pearcy, Arkansas

Elizabeth A. McDuff
Cloverdale Junior High School
Little Rock, Arkansas

California

Joan B. Greenberger
Jean Strauber
Suzanne M. Woods
Portola Junior High School
Tarzana, California

Linda Kay
Gompers Middle School
Los Angeles, California

Florida

Faithia T. Clayton
Sixteenth Street Middle School
St. Petersburg, Florida

Patricia A. Davey
Osceola Middle School
Seminole, Florida

Rebecca Hight Miller
Westridge Junior High School
Orlando, Florida

Illinois

Helen Glass Fulce
Haven Middle School
Evanston, Illinois

Iowa

Nathan James Weate
Lamoni Community School
Lamoni, Iowa

Louisiana

Diane Marusak
Campti Junior High School
Campti, Louisiana

New Jersey

Kathleen Kayser
Pequannock Valley School
Pompton Plains, New Jersey

Michael Napurano
Terrill Middle School
Scotch Plains, New Jersey

Jennifer Pasculli
Readington School
Readington, New Jersey

New York

Geraldine C. Charney
Center School
New York, New York

Carol S. Lotz
Booker T. Washington Junior High School
New York, New York

North Carolina

Ruth L. Hudson
Ligon Gifted and Talented Middle School
Raleigh, North Carolina

Wilma M. Roseboro
Kingswood Sixth Grade Center
Cary, North Carolina

Oregon

Vicki Jefferson
Briggs Middle School
Eugene, Oregon

Pennsylvania

Bonnie Burns Guarini
Saint Paul School
Norristown, Pennsylvania

Tennessee

Shelia A. Duncan
Margaret A. Moore
Central Middle School
Murfreesboro, Tennessee

Rebecca Harrelson
Brainerd Junior High School
Chattanooga, Tennessee

Washington

Steven Berry
Carmichael Junior High School
Richland, Washington

Evelyn Blatt
Islander Middle School
Mercer Island, Washington

Contents

UNIT 2   *Usage*

UNIT 3

Mechanics

UNIT 4 *Composition*

Part One

UNIT 5 Composition
Part Two

UNIT 6 Composition
Part Three

UNIT 7

Related Language Skills

Chapter 33 The Dictionary 558

Chapter 34 The Library 572

Chapter 35 Spelling 588

To the Student

This book is about communication—the act of expressing yourself. Think of how much of your day is spent speaking with your family, friends, and many others in your school and community. Speaking, however, is only one means of communication. Writing is another. Writing clearly is an important skill. In today's world more and more businesses are using computers to communicate information. The written word—whether displayed on a screen or printed on paper—is the backbone of communication.

The different units in this book have one main goal. That goal is to help you speak and write clearly. The first unit, on grammar, shows the structure of English and gives you choices for your speaking and writing. The next unit, on usage, explains ways to speak and write clearly. The third unit, on mechanics, shows the importance of punctuation and capitalization in writing. The fourth, fifth, and sixth units show how to find, organize, and communicate your ideas in writing. The seventh unit gives important study tips and other language skills that you will need in school.

The composition units in this book are unique. The chapters include all the help you need to understand and write different kinds of compositions—from single paragraphs through reports. Within chapters you are taken step by step through the four stages of the writing process. In the *prewriting* stage, you choose and limit a subject and organize your ideas. In the *writing* stage, you learn how to write a draft based on your prewriting notes that includes a topic sentence and a concluding sentence. In the *revising* stage, you learn how to improve your work and to look at it from a reader's point of view. Finally, in the *editing* stage, you learn how to polish your work by applying what you have learned in the first three units.

Going through these writing stages is like having someone steady you as you learn how to ride a bike. If you are unsure of yourself, there are many helps, including practice exercises, models, and checklists. These will show you exactly what to do, how to do it, and when to do it. Following these stages in the writing process will help you write well on your own.

As you go through each unit in this book, remember its goal: to help you speak and write clearly. Each chapter has been written with this goal in mind. The skills you build today will help you in tomorrow's world.

Special Helps

Your teacher will probably go through some of the chapters in this book with you. All of the chapters, however, have been written and organized so that you can refer to them and use them on your own throughout the year. You may find some of the following features of the book particularly helpful.

Keyed Rules All the rules are clearly marked with keyed blue arrows. An index at the back of the book tells you where to find each rule.

Tinted Boxes Throughout the text, important lists, summaries, and writing steps are highlighted in tinted boxes for easy reference.

Application to Writing These sections in the first three units of the book clearly show you how you can use the various grammatical concepts you have learned to improve your writing.

Diagnostic and Mastery Tests You can use the diagnostic and mastery tests to measure your progress. The diagnostic test at the beginning of a chapter will show you what you need to learn; the mastery test at the end of a chapter will show how well you learned it.

High-Interest Exercises Many of the exercises throughout the book are based on interesting topics. You will not only practice learning a particular skill, but you will also find the material in these exercises informative and interesting.

Composition Models Clearly marked models in the composition chapters provide interesting examples by professional writers.

Spotlight on Writing Fun activities at the end of each composition chapter give you many writing projects. Some ask you to write about a picture. Some give you information to work with. All of them give you more practice in growing as a writer.

Composition Checklists Almost all the composition chapters end with a checklist that you can follow—step by step—when you are writing a paragraph, an essay, or a report.

Standardized Tests Standardized tests, which follow all seven units, give you practice and build your confidence in taking tests.

Study Skills You will find information on note-taking, using the library, taking tests, and other topics that will help you succeed in school. A special chapter on speaking and listening will sharpen your oral skills.

Grammar

The Sentence

Diagnostic Test

Number your paper 1 to 10. Make two columns on your paper. Label the first column *subjects* and the second column *verbs*. Then under the proper heading, write each subject and each verb. (Some subjects and some verbs are compound.)

EXAMPLE Tad has gone but has left this note for you.
ANSWER <u>subjects</u>   <u>verbs</u>
Tad   has gone, has left

1. Robert E. Lee married Martha Washington's great-granddaughter.
2. An ordinary harmonica has ten holes.
3. The sun is rotating clockwise on its axis.
4. Did Paul ever explore the cave?
5. I have not made any plans yet.
6. In the middle of the road sat a shaggy dog.
7. The apple and the cherry belong to the rose family.
8. We must win the next game.
9. There is an extra blanket in the closet.
10. Kim climbed the tree and picked a coconut.

Kinds of Sentences

All sentences can be grouped according to their purpose. A sentence can make a statement, ask a question, give a command, or express strong feeling. The punctuation mark that belongs at the end of a sentence is determined by the purpose of that sentence.

1a A **declarative sentence** makes a statement or expresses an opinion and ends with a period.

Whales are the largest animals in the world today. [statement]

Whales probably are not afraid of people. [opinion]

1b An **interrogative sentence** asks a question and ends with a question mark.

Have you ever seen a live whale?

1c An **imperative sentence** makes a request or gives a command and ends with either a period or an exclamation point.

Read this book about whales. [This imperative sentence ends with a period because it is a mild request.]

Watch out for that whale approaching our boat! [This sentence ends with an exclamation point because it is a strong command.]

1d An **exclamatory sentence** expresses strong feeling and ends with an exclamation point.

What a huge animal the whale is!

EXERCISE 1 Classifying Sentences

Number your paper 1 to 10. Write each sentence, using the correct end mark. Then label each sentence *declarative, interrogative, imperative,* or *exclamatory.*

EXAMPLE   Have you heard the good news

ANSWER   Have you heard the good news?
            interrogative

Ice Hockey
at Last

1. Kelly's Pond has finally frozen over
2. Find your skates
3. Can you practice after school
4. Bring your hockey stick
5. Does anyone have an extra hockey stick
6. We need a good goalie
7. Jim could be our goalie
8. What a game this will be
9. Don't be late
10. I've waited all winter for this game

EXERCISE 2 Classifying Sentences

Number your paper 1 to 10. Write each sentence, using the correct end mark. Then label each sentence *declarative, interrogative, imperative,* or *exclamatory.*

1. Leave your books on your desk
2. What a great opportunity this is for you
3. Which joke was the funniest
4. With much enthusiasm the children climbed aboard the bus for home
5. Look out for that low branch
6. Sir Arthur Conan Doyle created the famous fictional detective Sherlock Holmes
7. Buy your tickets before school
8. The evening sun slowly disappeared below the rim of the canyon
9. Find the information in the *Almanac*
10. Cairo, the capital of Egypt, is located on the right bank of the Nile River

Subjects and Predicates

To communicate clearly, good writers learn to recognize and write complete thoughts.

A **sentence** is a group of words that expresses a complete thought.

In order to express a complete thought, a sentence must have two basic parts—a subject and a predicate. The *subject* names the person, place, or thing the sentence is about. The *predicate* tells something about the subject.

SUBJECT (*names whom or what the sentence is about*)	PREDICATE (*tells what the subject is or does*)
My best friend	lives a block away.
The new gymnasium	holds over 2,000 people.
The actors	rehearsed the scene.

EXERCISE 3 Combining Subjects and Predicates

Number your paper 1 to 10. Match a subject in column A with a predicate in column B. Then combine them to form a sentence that makes sense. Begin each sentence with a capital letter and end each one with a period.

A	B
1. the famous river in London	was first in line
2. the weary hikers	hung over his desk
3. this morning's newspaper	is easy to use
4. the clock in my room	is the Thames
5. my brand new camera	were laughing loudly
6. a box of beads	trudged up the hill
7. the flowers in the garden	is not accurate
8. the lady with the red hat	had large headlines
9. a still-life painting	are in full bloom
10. the children on the bus	spilled onto the floor

Complete Subjects

In the previous exercise, some subjects—such as *the children on the bus*—have more than one word. These subjects are *complete subjects*.

> **1f** A **complete subject** includes all the words used to identify the person, place, thing, or idea that the sentence is about.

To find a complete subject, ask yourself, *Who or what is doing something?* or *About whom or what is some statement being made?*

┌────────complete subject────────┐
The birds in our backyard ate all the bread. [Who or what is doing something in this sentence? *The birds in our backyard* is the complete subject.]

┌────────complete subject────────┐
The calendar in the kitchen is a year old. [About whom or what is some statement being made? *The calendar in the kitchen* is the complete subject.]

EXERCISE 4   *Finding Complete Subjects*

Number your paper 1 to 10. Then write each complete subject.

About Birds

1. The wingspan of an albatross averages 10 to 12 feet.
2. The nest of a golden eagle can weigh several tons.
3. The average hummingbird weighs less than a penny.
4. Small, colorful orioles nest in the same tree year after year.
5. Some eagles in South America feed on monkeys.
6. Owls in the forest see considerably better at night than most animals.
7. Some wild ducks build their nests in treetops.
8. The largest bird's egg in the world belongs to the ostrich.
9. The unusual penguin builds its nest out of rocks.
10. A female condor lays one egg every two years.

Simple Subjects

Most complete subjects include more than one word. Within each complete subject, however, there is one main word that clearly answers the question *Who or what is doing something?* or *About whom or what is some statement being made?* This main word is called the *simple subject*.

1g A **simple subject** is the main word in the complete subject.

The simple subjects in the following examples are in heavy type.

┌────── complete subject ──────┐
The **jet** above our house rattled our windows. [What is the main word in the complete subject? Who or what is doing something? The simple subject is *jet*.]

┌────── complete subject ──────┐
The **cowboys** on the ranch rounded up all the cattle. [What is the main word in the complete subject? Who or what is doing something? The simple subject is *cowboys*.]

Sometimes the simple subject can have more than one word. Usually these subjects are the names of persons or places.

┌────────── complete subject ──────────┐
Grant's Hardware Store on Brook Road is closed today. [*Grant's Hardware Store* is the simple subject even though it is three words. All three words are considered the name of one place.]

A complete subject and a simple subject can be the same.

┌ complete ┐
└ subject ┘
Katharine feeds her dog every morning.

┌ complete ┐
└ subject ┘
Everyone cheered the team.

NOTE: Throughout the rest of this book, the simple subject will be called the *subject*.

EXERCISE 5   *Finding Complete and Simple Subjects*

Number your paper 1 to 10. Write each complete subject. Then underline each simple subject.

EXAMPLE   The mountains near us are covered with snow.
ANSWER   The <u>mountains</u> near us

1. Giant icebergs once reached as far south as Mexico City.
2. The blue eyes of the old man looked cheerful.
3. No two snowflakes are exactly alike.
4. A baby whale gains about 200 pounds a day.
5. The old table in the kitchen has collapsed again.
6. The shell of a giant clam weighs up to 600 pounds.
7. Thomas Edison held over 1,300 patents.
8. That book with the leather cover is very rare.
9. Maine has 3,500 miles of coastline.
10. Only the male cricket makes a chirping sound.

*C*omplete Predicates

To express a complete thought, a sentence must have not only a subject but also a *predicate*.

> **1h** A **complete predicate** includes all the words that tell what the subject is doing, or that tell something about the subject.

To find a complete predicate, first find the subject. Then ask yourself, *What is the subject doing?* or *What is being said about the subject?*

Our dog **plays gently with the new kittens.** [The subject is *dog*. What does the dog do? *Plays gently with the new kittens* is the complete predicate.]

That car **has many special features.** [The subject is *car*. What is being said about the car? *Has many special features* is the complete predicate.]

EXERCISE 6 Finding Complete Predicates

Number your paper 1 to 10. Then write each complete predicate.

EXAMPLE Extinct dodo birds exist only in models, paintings, and stories.

ANSWER exist only in models, paintings, and stories

The
Unusual
Dodo Bird

1. The dodo bird stood about three feet tall.
2. This mostly ash-gray bird weighed 50 pounds.
3. Its face had only a few feathers.
4. A strange tuft of curly feathers served as a tail.
5. Its huge hooked beak extended as much as nine inches.
6. This flightless bird had stubby wings of three or four black feathers.
7. The dodo lived on some islands in the Indian Ocean.
8. Its dinner consisted mainly of vegetables and fruit.
9. The female laid one big white egg a year.
10. A resident of the islands saw the last dodo bird around 1681.

Simple Predicates, or Verbs

Within each complete predicate, there is one main word or phrase that tells what the subject is doing, or that tells something about the subject. This main word or phrase is called the *simple predicate*, or *verb*.

1i ▸ A **simple predicate,** or **verb,** is the main word or phrase in the complete predicate.

Verbs that tell what a subject is doing are *action verbs*. Action verbs can show physical action, mental action, or ownership. The verbs in the examples are in heavy type.

┌──complete predicate──┐
The fire engine **raced** down the street. [What is the main word in the complete predicate? What did the subject do? The verb is *raced*.]

r—————————— complete predicate ——————————┐
Lance **dreamed** about a ride in a hang glider.

r——————— complete predicate ————————┐
We **have** a new basketball hoop.

Some verbs do not show action. These verbs tell some-thing about a subject. Following is a list of some common verbs that make a statement about a subject.

Verbs That Make Statements

am   is   are   was   were

---

r———————————— complete predicate ————————┐
The answer **was** on the last page of the book.

r——————— complete predicate ————————┐
Our road **is** very narrow and bumpy.

Notice that a complete predicate and a simple predicate can be the same.

The baby **crawled.**

EXERCISE 7 *Finding Complete Predicates and Verbs*

Number your paper 1 to 10. Write each complete predicate. Then underline each verb.

EXAMPLE   Your eye works like a motion-picture camera.
ANSWER   <u>works</u> like a motion-picture camera

Like
Cameras

1. Your eyes have features like those of a camera.
2. The iris is a kind of shutter.
3. An automatic light meter controls the shutter opening.
4. The shutter opens wide in darkness.
5. The opening gets very small in bright light.
6. The lens serves as a color filter.
7. The lens filters out certain colors.
8. An eye quickly changes its focus from near to far.
9. The cornea serves as a covering for the eye.
10. The eyelids clean the cornea with the help of the tear glands.

Verb Phrases. Sometimes a verb needs the help of other verbs, which are called *helping verbs*, or auxiliary verbs. The main verb and one or more helping verbs make up a *verb phrase*. Following is a list of common helping verbs.

Common Helping Verbs	
be	am, is, are, was, were, be, being, been
have	has, have, had
do	do, does, did
other verbs	may, might, must, can, could, shall, should, will, would

The helping verbs in the following examples are in heavy type.

┌─verb phrase─┐
The squirrel **is** gathering nuts for the winter.

┌─verb phrase─┐
The captain **will be** taking the sailboat out today.

A verb phrase is often interrupted by one or more words. The verb phrases below are in heavy type.

   We **should** never **have gone** to that movie.
   Vegetables **do** not **grow** well in our backyard.

NOTE: *Not* and its contraction *n't* are never part of a verb phrase.

   Ms. Allen **did** not **hear** the bell.
   The class **did**n't **finish** the experiment.

   To find the verb phrase in a question, turn the question around to make a statement.

   Have the guests **arrived** on time? [The guests *have arrived* on time.]

NOTE: Throughout the rest of this book, a verb phrase will be called a verb.

11

EXERCISE 8 Finding Verb Phrases

Number your paper 1 to 10. Then write each verb phrase.

1. A wolf may eat as much as 20 pounds of food in one meal.
2. Almost all bears can climb trees.
3. Most residents of Calama, Chile, have never seen rain.
4. Earth's magnetic field has been constantly weakening.
5. Has Joel written his editorial about music in the cafeteria during lunch break?
6. A sperm whale could easily swallow a person in one gulp.
7. Trisha hasn't left for school yet.
8. Can a ten-gallon hat hold ten gallons?
9. Mosquitoes are strongly attracted to the color blue.
10. Niagara Falls has eroded 10 miles upstream in the past 10,000 years.

TIME-OUT FOR REVIEW • • • • •

Number your paper 1 to 10. Then write the subject and the verb in each sentence.

Insect Strength

1. Do you know about the great strength of insects?
2. An ant, for example, moved a stone 52 times its own weight.
3. A beetle carried something on its back 850 times its own weight.
4. A person with similar strength could do amazing things.
5. Such an individual could supposedly pull a 14,000-pound trailer truck.
6. Scientists haven't overlooked the other amazing feats of insects either.
7. A mosquito can carry something twice as heavy as itself.
8. Some insects can fly hundreds of miles nonstop.
9. Butterflies in large swarms have flown from the United States to the island of Bermuda.
10. Sailors in ships have also seen insects far out at sea.

Position of Subjects

A sentence is in *natural order* when the subject comes before the verb. In the following examples, each subject is underlined once, and each verb is underlined twice.

Six <u>mechanics</u> <u>restored</u> the old plane.

When the verb or part of the verb phrase comes before the subject, the sentence is in *inverted order*. To find the subject in such a sentence, turn the sentence around to its natural order.

INVERTED ORDER   From deep in the forest <u>echoed</u> a <u>screech</u>.

NATURAL ORDER   A <u>screech</u> <u>echoed</u> from deep in the forest.

Questions are usually written in inverted order. To find the subject in such a question, turn the question into a statement.

QUESTION   <u>Is</u> the <u>alarm</u> <u>set</u> for six o'clock?

STATEMENT   The <u>alarm</u> <u>is set</u> for six o'clock.

A sentence beginning with the word *here* or *there* is in inverted order. To find the subject in such a sentence, turn the sentence around to its natural order.

INVERTED ORDER   Here <u>are</u> the <u>actors</u>.

NATURAL ORDER   The <u>actors</u> <u>are</u> here.

INVERTED ORDER   There <u>is</u> some <u>soup</u> in the pot.

NATURAL ORDER   Some <u>soup</u> <u>is</u> in the pot. [Sometimes there must be dropped for the sentence to make sense.]

Understood Subjects.   The subject *you* is not stated in a command or a request. *You* is called an *understood subject*.

COMMAND   **(you)** Wait for me in the library.

OR REQUEST   **(you)** Call me tonight after dinner.

13

EXERCISE 9   Finding Subjects and Verbs

Number your paper 1 to 15. Then write the subject and the verb in each sentence.

1. Into the ring pranced three white horses.
2. Do you know the fastest route to the stadium?
3. There are wild orchids in the hot, damp jungles of northern Brazil.
4. Near the top of Mount Jefferson stands a small hut.
5. Did Peter catch that twelve-inch trout?
6. Here is your sweater.
7. Will Alma enter the race?
8. There is a line in front of the theater.
9. Out of the waves rose a huge black fin.
10. Are the Kaspers moving to Houston?
11. Around the middle of the package is a red ribbon.
12. Here are your messages on the desk.
13. Has Keith called the travel agent yet?
14. Under the bridge rushed the violent waters.
15. Have the students completed their projects?

EXERCISE 10   Finding Subjects and Verbs

Number your paper 1 to 10. Then write the subject and the verb in each sentence. If the subject is an understood *you*, write *you* in parentheses.

Early Robots

1. Are robots something new?
2. Don't answer too quickly.
3. In the 1700s, a Frenchman built a robot duck.
4. The duck would eat from a person's hand.
5. Across a small pool swam the duck each evening.
6. In Europe a man built a female piano player.
7. During a piece of music, her hands moved across the keyboard.
8. Listen to this.
9. At the end she would bow to the audience.
10. Since then there have been many more robots.

Compound Subjects

Two or more subjects joined by the conjunction *and* or *or* are called a *compound subject*.

A **compound subject** is two or more subjects in one sentence that have the same verb and are joined by a conjunction.

ONE SUBJECT   <u>Apples</u> <u>grow</u> on trees.
COMPOUND SUBJECT   <u>Apples</u> and <u>oranges</u> <u>grow</u> on trees.

A pair of conjunctions such as *either/or, neither/nor,* or *both/and* may also join the parts of a compound subject.

Neither <u>Sasha</u> nor <u>Keith</u> <u>had read</u> the letter.

EXERCISE 11   Finding Compound Subjects

Number your paper 1 to 10. Then write each compound subject.

EXAMPLE   Mark or Lee will manage the team.
ANSWER   Mark, Lee

1. Denmark and Switzerland produce numerous dairy products.
2. Both volleyball and badminton are played with a net.
3. Neither the cucumber nor the eggplant is a vegetable.
4. In the crystal punch bowl floated bright red strawberries and cherries.
5. Science or math is scheduled after lunch next term.
6. Both the gulls and the sandpipers crowded the beach.
7. Either a book or a record would make a nice birthday gift for Susan.
8. The tiger and the rhinoceros are natural enemies of the elephant.
9. Did Mario or Adam write this story?
10. Either wrens or sparrows come to our bird feeder.

*C*ompound Verbs

Two or more verbs joined by the conjunction *and, or,* or *but* are called a *compound verb*.

> **1k** A **compound verb** is two or more verbs that have the same subject and are joined by a conjunction.

ONE VERB   The <u>runner</u> <u>glanced</u> back.
COMPOUND VERB   The <u>runner</u> <u>glanced</u> back and <u>darted</u> sideways.

A sentence can include both a compound subject and a compound verb.

<u>Tourists</u> and <u>residents</u> <u>gathered</u> in the town square and <u>watched</u> the holiday festivities.

*E*XERCISE 12   *Finding Compound Subjects and Verbs*

Number your paper 1 to 10. Then write the subject and the verb in each sentence.

Bats
1. In the daytime bats hang upside down and sleep.
2. Bats then fly around and snare all kinds of insects.
3. A bat's ears and mouth guide it through the dark.
4. These amazing creatures can chase insects on the darkest nights but will not strike a single object.
5. High-frequency waves strike objects in the bat's path and echo back to the animal's ears.
6. A bat reacts instantly to the signals and swerves away from the objects.
7. Bats almost never bite or infect humans or animals.
8. Caves, hollow trees, and unused buildings are often the homes of bats.
9. Red bats live in the North during the summer but spend the winter in the South.
10. Many myths and horror stories tell about the strange activities of bats.

Exercise 13   *Writing Sentences*

Write five sentences that describe a freight train approaching a road crossing. Use at least one compound subject and one compound verb. Then underline each subject once and each verb twice.

Time-out for Review • • • • •

Number your paper 1 to 20. Then write the subject and the verb in each sentence. If the subject is an understood *you*, write *you* in parentheses. (Some subjects and some verbs are compound.)

The Ferris
Wheel

1. Listen to this true story about the famous Ferris wheel.
2. People in Chicago were planning a world's fair in 1893.
3. Politicians and the organizers of the fair envied the Eiffel Tower, the hit of the last world's fair.
4. Could Chicago ever find such an attraction?
5. There were many engineers with ideas.
6. George Ferris appeared with a strange set of plans.
7. Ferris suggested a huge wheel with seats and then explained his idea.
8. His wheel could carry people 250 feet into the air.
9. Did Ferris get instant approval for his idea?
10. People listened but ignored his plans.
11. Into the battle for his idea plunged George Ferris.
12. Eventually the organizers gave Ferris the go-ahead.
13. Many difficulties and problems arose from the start.
14. Among his worst critics were the banks and investors.
15. Finally Ferris received approval and began the work.
16. Through a bitter winter, Ferris and his workers built the huge wheel.
17. Did Ferris meet the deadline for the fair's opening?
18. After a delay of two months, the giant wheel finally opened.
19. The wheel ran for 19 weeks and carried nearly a million and a half passengers.
20. Remember this story on your next Ferris-wheel ride!

Diagraming Subjects and Verbs

A *sentence diagram* is a picture of lines that can help you find and identify all the parts of a sentence.

Subjects and Verbs. A baseline is a horizontal line that is the foundation of all sentence diagrams. A straight, vertical line separates the subject (or subjects) on the left from the verb (or verbs) on the right. Capital letters are included in the diagram, but punctuation is not. In the second example, notice that the whole verb phrase is written on the baseline.

People work.   Roy has been sleeping.

| People | work | | Roy | has been sleeping |

Questions. A question is diagramed as if it were a statement.

Has Dale arrived? (Dale has arrived.)

| Dale | Has arrived |

Understood Subjects. When the subject of a sentence is an understood *you*, as in a command or a request, place *you* in parentheses in the subject position.

Watch.   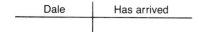 (you) | Watch

Compound Subjects and Verbs. Place the parts of a compound subject or a compound verb on parallel horizontal lines. Then put the conjunction connecting each part on a broken vertical line between them. In the first example, notice that the two conjunctions are written on either side of the broken line.

Both girls and boys attended.

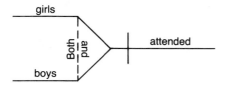

Dogs chase and play.

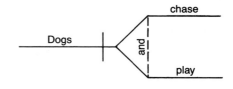

Karen and Bart dived or swam.

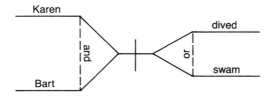

EXERCISE 14 Diagraming Subjects and Verbs

Diagram the following sentences or copy them. If your teacher tells you to copy them, draw one line under each subject and two lines under each verb. If the subject is an understood *you*, write *you* in parentheses.

1. Wolves howled.
2. Candles sputtered.
3. Clouds were appearing.
4. Listen.
5. Will Ed wait?
6. Luis is winning.
7. Aunts and uncles arrived.
8. Jeffrey sat and studied.
9. Martha will sing or will dance.
10. Cars and trucks waited and honked.

19

Application to Writing

An important goal of a writer is a smooth, flowing style. One way to achieve such a style is to eliminate some short, choppy sentences from a piece of writing. You can make this positive change in your writing in two ways.

The first way to avoid short, choppy sentences is to combine two short sentences that have the same verb but different subjects. Use a compound subject.

TWO SENTENCES	<u>Birds</u> <u>have</u> a high and fairly even body temperature. <u>Mammals</u> also <u>have</u> a similar temperature.
COMBINED SENTENCES	<u>Birds</u> and <u>mammals</u> <u>have</u> a high and fairly even body temperature. [combined with a compound subject]
TWO SENTENCES	<u>Gene</u> <u>ran</u> for Student Council president. <u>Rosa</u> also <u>ran</u>.
COMBINED SENTENCES	<u>Gene</u> and <u>Rosa</u> <u>ran</u> for Student Council president. [combined with a compound subject]

NOTE: Some repeated or unnecessary words can be dropped when the sentences are combined.

The second way to avoid short, choppy sentences is to combine two short sentences that have the same subject but different verbs. Use a compound verb.

TWO SENTENCES	<u>Stems</u> of plants <u>produce</u> food. <u>Stems</u> also <u>store</u> water.
COMBINED SENTENCES	<u>Stems</u> of plants <u>produce</u> food and <u>store</u> water. [combined with a compound verb]
TWO SENTENCES	The <u>kite</u> <u>rose</u>. <u>It</u> <u>drifted</u> over the trees.
COMBINED SENTENCES	The <u>kite</u> <u>rose</u> and <u>drifted</u> over the trees. [combined with a compound verb]

EXERCISE 15 Combining Sentences

Number your paper 1 to 15. Then combine each pair of sentences into one sentence with a compound subject or a compound verb. Use the conjunction in brackets to join the compound subject or the compound verb.

EXAMPLE   The envelopes are in the desk. The pens are there too. [and]

ANSWER   The envelopes and the pens are in the desk.

1. Sea horses cling to seaweed. They drift along with the current. [and]
2. Anna cannot go to the movies tonight. She can go on Wednesday. [but]
3. My books are locked in the car. My sneakers are there also. [and]
4. Polar bears live near the water. They feed mainly on fish. [and]
5. I want the lead part in the class play. I may get a supporting role. [but]
6. Jacob had a head start. He lost the race. [but]
7. American Indians used maple syrup for sweetening. The early settlers also used maple syrup. [and]
8. Moths have scales on their wings. Butterflies also have scales on their wings. [and]
9. Dawn mailed the letter last week. She has not received an answer yet. [but]
10. I am taking flute lessons. I prefer the guitar. [but]
11. Penguins do not fly. Ostriches don't fly either. [and]
12. The stage crew worked a week. They did not complete the sets on time. [but]
13. The spinal cord relays information between the brain and the rest of the body. It also controls reflexes. [and]
14. Rob wrote his essay. He has not edited it yet. [but]
15. Your jackets are here. Your boots are here also. [and]

Chapter Review

A **Finding Subjects and Verbs.** Number your paper 1 to 10. Then write the subject and the verb in each sentence.

1. No water exists on the moon's surface.
2. Mom doesn't know the time of the meeting of the school board.
3. On one side of the road, a fire had blackened trees and shrubs.
4. Over the airfield hung a dense fog.
5. Tops and hobbyhorses were popular toys in the twelfth century.
6. Is your sister studying art this semester?
7. There were 12,430 beans in the jar at the county fair.
8. People have rigged small, flat icebergs with sails and have piloted them more than 2,000 miles.
9. How long can a redwood live?
10. Chris has been digging for clams all day in the bay area near the beach.

B **Finding Subjects and Verbs.** Number your paper 1 to 10. Then write the subject and the verb in each sentence. If the subject is an understood *you*, write *you* in parentheses.

1. Stand beside Barbara for the picture.
2. Amanda does not have a paper route anymore.
3. Sing more softly.
4. At the aquarium one porpoise blows a horn and leaps through a hoop.
5. From behind the door jumped a clown.
6. Wade has never ridden on a subway.
7. Look for the clues in the mystery.
8. On the top of the tent lay the compass.
9. Mozart and Beethoven were famous composers.
10. Should the dogs go out now?

C **Finding Subjects and Verbs.** Number your paper 1 to 10. Then write the subject and the verb in each sentence.

Clouds

1. Warm air and moisture rise into the sky.
2. At a certain height, the warm air cools.
3. At the cooler temperatures, the air cannot hold all its moisture.
4. The extra moisture then changes into small drops of water or bits of ice.
5. From these droplets clouds will develop.
6. About 100,000,000 droplets form one large raindrop.
7. *Cirrus, stratus,* and *cumulus* are the names of the three main types of clouds.
8. Clouds are always changing their shapes.
9. Weather forecasters can look at clouds and learn much about the day's weather.
10. Do you see any clouds in the sky today?

Mastery Test

Number your paper 1 to 10. Make two columns on your paper. Label the first column *subjects* and the second column *verbs*. Then under the proper heading, write each subject and each verb. (Some subjects and some verbs are compound.)

1. Peacocks cry loudly before a storm.
2. A goose has no white meat.
3. From the auditorium came hearty laughter.
4. San Francisco and New York are large cities.
5. Chester is not pitching in the game today.
6. Benjamin Franklin is the inventor of flippers.
7. The sun has been shining all day.
8. Did your uncle grow this corn in his garden?
9. There are 200 to 400 vertebrae in a long snake.
10. A cheetah can suddenly jump and run up to 45 miles per hour in two seconds.

2

Nouns and Pronouns

Diagnostic Test

Number your paper 1 to 10. Write each underlined word. Then beside each one, label it *noun* or *pronoun*.

EXAMPLE This could be the answer to your problem.
ANSWER   this—pronoun, answer—noun

1. A tuna can swim 100 miles in a single day.
2. Is he in the auditorium now?
3. I put everything on the table.
4. Five counties in Texas are larger than Rhode Island.
5. Nobody is going to the parade.
6. Something is bothering you. What is it?
7. These are great photographs of her!
8. Maria felt great pride as she accepted the award.
9. Mr. Higgins found your dog in his garage.
10. In one year the average heart circulates over one million gallons of blood throughout the body.

*N*ouns

In English there are eight *parts of speech*. A word's part of speech is determined by the job that it does in a sentence. The same word may be used as a noun in one sentence and as an adjective in another sentence.

The Eight Parts of Speech

noun [names]
pronoun [replaces]
verb [states action or being]
adjective [describes, limits]
adverb [describes, limits]

preposition [relates]
conjunction [connects]
interjection [expresses strong feeling]

The most frequently used part of speech is the noun. Many words are nouns because many words name people, places, things, or ideas.

2a ▶ A **noun** is a word that names a person, a place, a thing, or an idea.

PEOPLE   girl, men, president, Ms. Taylor, farmers

PLACES   buildings, stadium, Denver, Atlantic Ocean

THINGS   [*that can be seen, heard, or touched*] lamp, wind, drums, cotton, Venus, Mount Rainier [*that cannot be seen, heard, or touched*] pain, flu, history, hunger, health, life

IDEAS AND QUALITIES   love, friendship, kindness, thoughtfulness, courage, patriotism, faith, ideals, ambition

A *collective noun* names a group of people or things.

COLLECTIVE NOUNS   crew, group, class, audience, troop, committee, herd, chorus

EXERCISE 1 *Finding Nouns*

Number your paper 1 to 10. Then write each noun. There are 33 nouns.

Deadly
Winds

1. A hurricane begins over the ocean in hot regions.
2. Strong winds bump together and start to whirl.
3. The sky becomes dark with circling clouds that look like a giant wheel.
4. If a hurricane hits land, it can blow down trees.
5. The hurricane also stirs up the sea into huge waves that can wreck docks along the shore.
6. Heavy rains also fall and fill creeks and rivers, making them overflow their banks.
7. In an hour a hurricane uses up enormous energy.
8. In this country one hurricane killed 6,000 people.
9. Now cities in the path of a hurricane are often given advance information.
10. Satellites, radar, and planes help to forecast these destructive storms.

Kinds of Nouns

Some nouns, called *common nouns*, can name any person, place, or thing. Other nouns, called *proper nouns*, name a particular person, place, or thing. A proper noun begins with a capital letter and may include more than one word.

COMMON NOUNS boy, state, lake

PROPER NOUNS Rob Mason, Tennessee, Lake Louise

Some common nouns, called *compound nouns*, have more than one word. A record player is *one* thing, even though it is named by two words. Compound nouns can take one of three forms. Always check the form of a compound noun in the dictionary.

SEPARATE WORDS study hall, poison ivy, water ballet

HYPHENATED WORDS mother-in-law, baby-sitter, cave-in

COMBINED WORDS skyscraper, farmhouse, sideline

EXERCISE 2 Finding Nouns

Number your paper 1 to 15. Then write each noun. There are 33 nouns. (*You* is not a noun.)

A Look into
the Future

1. In the morning you will bathe in a machine in which sound waves clean you.
2. Then you will casually and effortlessly push a button marked breakfast.
3. A short, skinny robot immediately comes out of a concealed door.
4. Quickly and perfectly, it prepares your food on a stove run by sunlight.
5. Then a moving sidewalk will take you wherever you want to go.
6. Trains and planes will travel extremely fast.
7. Consequently, you could live in New York but go to school in California.
8. A trip across the United States will take only 21 minutes.
9. All students in your classroom will have their own computers.
10. These advanced machines will instruct you and give you your assignments.
11. Once you have finished your work, it will be graded instantly.
12. Later, you find that your brother has returned from the World Medical Center.
13. His left arm has been destroyed in an accident.
14. Doctors, however, were able to grow him a new, perfect arm.
15. When you're sleepy, you will lie down on a soft mattress that floats in the air.

EXERCISE 3 Writing Sentences

Write five sentences that describe what Earth might look like from the window of an alien spaceship. Try to use some proper nouns and some compound nouns. Then underline each noun.

TIME-OUT FOR REVIEW ● ● ● ● ●

Number your paper 1 to 20. Then write each noun. (A date is a noun.) There are 50 nouns.

Beavers to
the Rescue

1. In 1981 an experiment gave hope to the future of wildlife.
2. For many years cattle had eaten all the grass and shrubs along Currant Creek in Wyoming.
3. Heavy rains constantly fell and completely washed the soil away.
4. The fast-moving creek had once been a home for many trout.
5. Now it was a muddy hole in and around which no life existed.
6. The answer was to build several dams.
7. The dams would eventually cause ponds to form behind them and spill over.
8. The muddy banks would then be covered with calm water.
9. Unfortunately, dams of concrete cost far too much money.
10. The local people looked for a different, less expensive solution.
11. Finally two interested scientists had a wonderful and practical idea.
12. They knew that beavers no longer lived in this region.
13. Consequently, they captured some in other lakes and brought them to Currant Creek.
14. Since there were no longer any trees around, men brought in logs.
15. Shortly afterward, the busy rodents had built several dams.
16. "Beavers are inexpensive and very industrious," one rancher said.
17. Soon grass and trees began to sprout.
18. As the water cleared, many fish returned.
19. Even the birds have returned and built nests.
20. Other states are now using these cooperative and hard-working animals.

Application to Writing

Choosing specific nouns will add interest and liveliness to your writing. Use a specific noun like *blue jay* or *hawk* instead of a general noun like *bird*.

EXERCISE 4   Choosing Specific Nouns

Number your paper 1 to 10. Then write at least two specific nouns for each general noun.

> EXAMPLE   state
> POSSIBLE ANSWERS   Iowa, Missouri, Kansas

1. insect   3. car   5. school   7. color   9. street
2. flower   4. book   6. animal   8. month   10. vegetable

EXERCISE 5   Using Specific Nouns

Number your paper 1 to 10. Then substitute a specific noun for each underlined word or group of words.

> EXAMPLE   That girl is a fine athlete.
> POSSIBLE ANSWER   Kate is a fine gymnast.

1. My two friends met a popular actor last night.
2. The man visited his relative on a holiday.
3. For lunch the woman ate some food.
4. The girl won a letter in a sport.
5. A silver car was parked opposite the restaurant.
6. While the boy waited for the doctor, he listened to a radio station on his headphones.
7. Our neighbors bought a new item for their room.
8. The singer held a concert in the park.
9. The student joined a club at the school.
10. That building is the tallest one in the city.

EXERCISE 6   Writing Sentences

Write five sentences that describe the main street of your city or town on a Saturday afternoon. Use specific nouns.

*P*ronouns

A pronoun is a part of speech that is a stand-in, or substitute, for a noun.

> **2b** A **pronoun** is a word that takes the place of one or more nouns.

Notice how pronouns save the following sentences from *The Call of the Wild* from being boring and repetitious.

> Camp once made, Buck lay down like a dead dog. Hungry
> as ~~Buck~~ was, ~~Buck~~ would not move to receive ~~Buck's~~ ration
>   he   he   his
> of fish that François had brought to ~~Buck.~~
>   him

Each pronoun in the example replaces the noun *Buck*. The word or group of words that a pronoun replaces, or refers to, is called its *antecedent*. An antecedent usually comes before the pronoun. It may be in the same sentence as the pronoun or in another sentence. In the following examples, arrows point to the antecedents.

The **trees** have lost their leaves.

Marcy is happy. Her dog won in a pet contest.

A pronoun can have more than one antecedent.

Allison and **Connie** have taken their eye tests.

Sometimes more than one pronoun can refer to the same antecedent.

Jason took his raincoat with him.

The antecedent of a pronoun may not always be in the same sentence: **You** can always count on **my** help.

EXERCISE 7 Finding Antecedents

Number your paper 1 to 10. Then write the antecedent for each underlined pronoun.

1. Jason moves confidently with the aid of <u>his</u> crutches.
2. In 1875, Elizabeth Blackwell opened <u>her</u> own medical college for women.
3. Most snakes never travel more than a few miles from <u>their</u> birthplace.
4. Roy entered the diving contest. <u>His</u> second dive received a perfect score.
5. Chico and Susan said <u>they</u> can't come to the party.
6. Dad took <u>his</u> toolbox with <u>him</u> to work.
7. Venus rotates around the sun at a much faster rate than <u>it</u> spins around on <u>its</u> own axis.
8. Mom bought some apples. <u>They</u> were hard and tart.
9. Stephen and Barry realized that <u>they</u> were going to be late.
10. The fireworks lit the sky as <u>they</u> exploded.

Personal Pronouns

Of all the different kinds of pronouns, *personal pronouns* are used most often. There are *first person, second person,* and *third person* pronouns. Following is a list of singular and plural forms for each person.

Personal Pronouns		
	Singular	Plural
FIRST PERSON (speaker)	I, me my, mine	we, us our, ours
SECOND PERSON (person spoken to)	you your, yours	you your, yours
THIRD PERSON (person or thing spoken about)	he, him, his she, her, hers it, its	they, them their, theirs

The following sentences show ways in which personal pronouns are used.

FIRST PERSON
PRONOUNS

I must remember to take **my** book report with **me** to school tomorrow.
We haven't seen **our** grades yet.

SECOND PERSON
PRONOUNS

You shouldn't try to walk with **your** sprained ankle.
You should sit next to each other on the plane and share **your** magazines.

THIRD PERSON
PRONOUNS

He told **her** that the book was **his.**
They have taken **their** dog with **them** on **their** vacation.

NOTE: Pronouns such as *himself* or *themselves* are formed by adding *-self* or *-selves* to some personal pronouns. However, you should never use *hisself* or *theirselves*.

EXERCISE 8   *Finding Personal Pronouns*

Number your paper 1 to 10. Then write each personal pronoun. There are 25 pronouns.

1. They couldn't find their car anywhere in the parking lot.
2. We should have taken yours instead of ours.
3. David folded his hat and put it in his pocket.
4. I think that jacket is too small for me but perfect for you.
5. Our class liked the experiment because it taught us about electricity.
6. My coat is here, but hers is lying over the chair in the back hall.
7. The book of poems is mine; the book of short stories is yours.
8. You can grow a potato plant in your home.
9. He asked them to tell him when the game was over.
10. She accepted the award that the mayor presented to her.

TIME-OUT FOR REVIEW • • • • •

Number your paper 1 to 10. Write each personal pronoun. Then beside each one, write its antecedent. There are 15 pronouns.

EXAMPLE Mike told Anne that he would walk with her.
ANSWER he—Mike, her—Anne

1. The carpenters took pride in their work.
2. Karen got confused in the subway. A police officer told her which train she should take.
3. Andrea and Steve usually do their laundry on Saturday mornings.
4. An elephant can lift with its trunk an object as large as a tree.
5. Bruce carefully folded his shirts and placed them in the suitcase.
6. The iron is hot. Don't touch it!
7. Some swallows make their nests out of mud balls.
8. Mom asked David if he had written to his grandparents about the awards banquet.
9. Richard told Mrs. Sullivan that he would help her paint the kitchen.
10. Joe told Ellen that his dog follows him to school every day.

Other Kinds of Pronouns

Personal pronouns are not the only kind of pronouns. There are, for example, indefinite pronouns, demonstrative pronouns, and interrogative pronouns.

An *indefinite pronoun* usually does not have a definite antecedent as a personal pronoun does. Instead, an indefinite pronoun refers to an unnamed person or thing.

Did **anyone** notice **something** strange?
Can **anybody** take **all** of these leftovers home?
No one knew **anything** about the mysterious letter.

33

Common Indefinite Pronouns			
all	both	few	nothing
another	each	many	one
any	either	most	several
anybody	everybody	neither	some
anyone	everyone	none	someone
anything	everything	no one	something

Demonstrative pronouns point out persons and things.

That was a great dinner! Lee already saw **those**.

Interrogative pronouns are used to ask questions.

What did you say? **Which** did he choose?

Demonstrative Pronouns			
this	that	these	those

Interrogative Pronouns				
what	which	who	whom	whose

EXERCISE 9 *Finding Pronouns*

Number your paper 1 to 10. Then write each pronoun.

1. Who was at the door?
2. Neither of my sisters won any of the prizes.
3. Whose was the most unusual?
4. No one has seen anything unusual.
5. This is the model Vince wanted.
6. Some of the people brought a few of their friends.
7. That must be the turnoff ahead.
8. Each of the contestants chose one of the doors.
9. He didn't like either of the sweaters.
10. What is Roger doing after school?

TIME-OUT FOR REVIEW • • • • •

Number your paper 1 to 20. Then write each pronoun.

1. Chun liked each of the three dogs in the pet shop.
2. The detective looked at everything and missed nothing in the investigation.
3. Whom do the students want for class president?
4. Everyone must support one of the two plans for the family's vacation.
5. This has been a very challenging campaign for the candidates.
6. Something is wrong; there doesn't seem to be anyone here yet.
7. Many of the people were cheering the team on from the sidelines.
8. Both of the boys know everybody on the soccer team from Murphysville High School in Memphis.
9. Those are free to residents of the town.
10. Would anyone like either of the seats at the back of the airplane?
11. What did the boys find in the old trunk?
12. Each of the boys can choose from any of the books on the shelf.
13. Is there anything from the nineteenth century on display at the museum?
14. Some of the apples and most of the grapes aren't really ripe.
15. Who on the farm is responsible for taking care of the chickens?
16. Several of the students in homeroom didn't know anything about the assembly.
17. Nothing would taste better than a glass of cold milk.
18. Someone correctly answered all of the questions on the math test.
19. Everyone took the elevator to the lobby.
20. Many of the television sets are for sale, but a few are for rent.

*C*hapter *R*eview

A Finding Nouns. Number your paper 1 to 10. Then write each noun. There are 25 nouns. (A date should be regarded as one noun.)

Eyes
toward the
Sky

The first woman to become an astronomer was Maria Mitchell. She was born in Nantucket, Massachusetts. For many years, even though she was working as a teacher and librarian, she spent much time studying the stars and galaxies with her father in their observatory. In 1847, the young woman sighted a new comet. Later she received a great honor. Her name was given to the comet she found. Eventually she became a professor at Vassar College. Miss Mitchell wrote about her own work and encouraged many students to study astronomy.

B Finding Pronouns. Number your paper 1 to 10. Then write each pronoun. There are 20 pronouns.

1. Those really look like the clothes they wore in *Gone with the Wind*.
2. What was your grade on the history quiz in Mr. Mason's class?
3. Has each of the puppies had its physical examination and first shots?
4. None of the wonderful homemade applesauce was left for us.
5. In my opinion the insect with the white wings is a moth, not a butterfly.
6. At our annual Girl Scout banquet, who will be the speaker?
7. Did he rent a van for their trip to the mountains last year?
8. Everyone found something on the bargain table.
9. Any of the boxes will hold most of your things.
10. Is she the person you voted for?

C **Finding Antecedents.** Number your paper 1 to 10. Write each personal pronoun. Then beside each one, write its antecedent.

1. Mozart wrote his first minuet at the age of five.
2. Jean suddenly noticed she was wearing two different sneakers.
3. Ken told his mother he didn't have any lunch money with him.
4. Mr. Jackson and Mrs. Young have announced they are running for the school board.
5. Americans stand as their national anthem is played.
6. Brenda asked Sue if they were going to be neighbors.
7. Sue told Jim she wrote her report on a computer.
8. Get the milk at the new market. It just opened today.
9. An elephant smells with its mouth, not its trunk.
10. Ask Susan if she has her notebook with her.

*M*astery *T*est

Number your paper 1 to 10. Write each underlined word. Then beside each one, label it *noun* or *pronoun*.

1. Who sent the large package to you?
2. The magician raised his hand, and the woman rose into the air.
3. There were about 50 million Indians living in the Western Hemisphere just before Columbus arrived.
4. Something should be done about this.
5. I think honesty is necessary in friendship.
6. A chicken can lay over 1,000 eggs during its life.
7. Has anyone looked in the doghouse?
8. Americans make about 350 million calls a day on their 150 million telephones.
9. That is your best poem yet!
10. When it is born, a panda is smaller than a mouse and weighs about four ounces.

3

Verbs

Number your paper 1 to 10. Write each verb or verb phrase. Then label each one *action* or *linking*.

EXAMPLE   The weather will be warmer tomorrow.
ANSWER   will be—linking

1. The oldest pet cat on record was a 36-year-old tabby.
2. Did Wally join the basketball team?
3. The noise in the hallway grew louder and louder.
4. The tadpoles in that tank have become frogs.
5. Some early American Indians printed paper money.
6. Last summer I did not go to camp.
7. The young girl in the picture is your grandmother.
8. Louise grew flowers in boxes outside the apartment windows.
9. The hayride should be fun.
10. Like a chameleon, an octopus can change the color of its body at will.

Action Verbs

Without a *verb* a group of words cannot be a sentence. Some verbs are called *action verbs* because they show action or movement.

3a ▶ An **action verb** tells what action a subject is performing.

To find an action verb, first find the subject of the sentence. Then ask yourself, *What is the subject doing?* Some action verbs show physical action.

PHYSICAL ACTION   The frog **swallowed** a fly. [The subject is *frog*. What did the frog do? *Swallowed* is the action verb.]

Some action verbs show mental action. Others show ownership or possession.

MENTAL ACTION   I **forget** his name.
OWNERSHIP   Jeffrey **has** a new bicycle.

EXERCISE 1   Finding Action Verbs

Number your paper 1 to 10. Then write each action verb.

EXAMPLE   Marilyn writes witty poems.
ANSWER   writes

1. An elephant's trunk holds six quarts of water.
2. Mavis speaks three languages.
3. Most bald eagles live in Alaska.
4. The Ramóns own a new minivan.
5. The gorilla reached for the bananas on the top branch.
6. The sun disappeared behind the mountain.
7. I thought about the math test all weekend.
8. Pecans grow on hickory trees.
9. The ostrich lays the largest bird's egg.
10. Mount St. Helens erupted in 1980.

39

EXERCISE 2 Finding Action Verbs

Number your paper 1 to 15. Then write each action verb.

How Do
Cats Keep
Cool?

1. Cats have fur coats in the winter and the summer.
2. Unlike people, cats wear their coats all year.
3. As a result, cats behave very differently during the hot days and nights of summer.
4. Most cats restrict their activities during the hottest part of the day.
5. Many cats rest in cool places like basements and dark garages.
6. A cool breeze through a window makes some cats more comfortable.
7. Cats also like the coolness of a bathroom floor on a hot day.
8. Cats drink more water in the summer than in any other season.
9. Cool water lowers their body temperature.
10. A cat's skin also changes in hot weather.
11. Their natural pores open slightly.
12. Fortunately these openings work as an air conditioner for cats.
13. A cat's fur serves as a warm coat in the winter.
14. Surprisingly, their fur coats also keep cats cool in the summer.
15. The fur acts as protective insulation from the heat of the summer.

EXERCISE 3 Writing Sentences

Number your paper 1 to 10. Then write a sentence for each of the following action verbs.

1. dug
2. owned
3. had
4. ran
5. dreamed
6. scrubbed
7. galloped
8. crawled
9. memorized
10. stretched

Linking Verbs

Verbs that do not show action are called state-of-being verbs. These verbs make statements about a subject.

The rice **is** on the top shelf.
Martin and Justin **were** here early.

State-of-being verbs are often used as *linking verbs*. This means that they join the subject to another word in the sentence.

3b A **linking verb** links the subject with another word in the sentence. The other word either renames or describes the subject.

Christopher's favorite school sport **is** basketball. [*Is* links *sport* with *basketball*. Basketball renames the subject.]

The temperatures recently **have been** very low. [*Have been* links *temperatures* with *low*. *Low* describes the temperatures—*the low temperatures.*]

Following is a list of common linking verbs. All of the verbs in the list are forms of the verb *be*.

Common Linking Verbs		
be	shall be	have been
is	will be	has been
am	can be	had been
are	could be	could have been
was	should be	should have been
were	would be	may have been
	may be	might have been
	might be	must have been

EXERCISE 4 *Finding Linking Verbs*

Number your paper 1 to 10. Write each linking verb. Then write the two words that the verb links.

EXAMPLE   The water in the kettle on the front burner is very hot.

ANSWER   is—water, hot

1. The piano is the most popular instrument in the Western world.
2. The movie must have been very short.
3. Pablo should have been the announcer for the talent show.
4. That sailboat was a schooner.
5. Wisconsin's nickname is the Badger State.
6. Because of the new exam schedule, Friday may be your last chance for extra help with math.
7. After the thunderstorm our tent was wet for the rest of the night.
8. Celery is a close relative of the carrot.
9. Someday I will be a disk jockey.
10. Circuses were common in the United States after 1830.

EXERCISE 5 *Finding Linking Verbs*

Number your paper 1 to 10. Write each linking verb. Then write the two words that the verb links.

1. Monday is a holiday.
2. The sound on our radio could be better.
3. She is a good swimmer.
4. The parade should have been longer.
5. Matthew is my cousin.
6. Some honey can be poisonous.
7. In the Middle East, turbans have been customary headgear for many centuries.
8. Your handwriting should be neater.
9. They have been careful with your tools.
10. The pearl is the birthstone for the month of June.

Additional Linking Verbs

Forms of the verb *be* are not the only words that can be used as linking verbs. The following words can also be used as linking verbs.

Additional Linking Verbs

appear	grow	seem	stay
become	look	smell	taste
feel	remain	sound	turn

Any of the verbs in the box can link a subject with a word that either renames or describes the subject.

Our candidate **became** the new governor. [*Governor* renames the subject.]

Yesterday the air **felt** very damp. [*Damp* describes the subject—the *damp air.*]

EXERCISE 6   *Finding Linking Verbs*

Number your paper 1 to 10. Write each linking verb. Then write the two words that each verb links.

1. Your homemade bread smells absolutely wonderful.
2. Of all the ideas, your idea sounds the best.
3. Chi looked very happy yesterday.
4. Pollution in big cities still remains a problem.
5. The problem continually grows worse.
6. During the storm the cable stayed secure.
7. In the wild, deer seem very shy.
8. The floor feels sticky to me.
9. Billy Franco just became a new club member.
10. The hot spicy chili in the new Mexican restaurant on Front Street tasted delicious.

43

Linking Verb or Action Verb?

Some of the additional linking verbs listed on page 43 are not always used as linking verbs. Those words can also be used as action verbs. When you come across one of those verbs, ask yourself this question: *What is the verb doing in the sentence?* If the verb links a subject to a word that renames or describes it, it is a linking verb. If the verb is used to show action, it is an action verb.

LINKING VERB	The man in that picture **looked** happy. [*Looked* links *happy* and *man. Happy* describes the subject, *man.* The sentence is about the *happy man.*]
ACTION VERB	For days the girl looked desperately for her lost dog. [*Looked* shows action. It tells what the girl did. Also, there is no word in the sentence that renames or describes the subject.]

EXERCISE 7 Distinguishing between Action Verbs and Linking Verbs

Number your paper 1 to 15. Write each verb. Then label each one *action* or *linking.*

EXAMPLE That music sounds familiar.
ANSWER sounds—linking

1. That paper feels very thin.
2. Hannah smelled the pine trees in the grove.
3. An extra charge appeared on our bill.
4. Everyone at the table eagerly tasted the Hungarian goulash.
5. She grew taller during the summer.
6. At the circus my little sister appeared tired.
7. The air in the country smells so fresh.
8. That orange tasted unusually sweet.
9. That cactus grows well in bright sunlight.

10. Feel this new material.
11. Terry looked through two computer manuals.
12. After lunch the weather turned dark and rainy.
13. At first the test looked difficult.
14. These gerbils seem content with their new home.
15. I usually feel energetic early in the day.

EXERCISE 8 Writing Sentences

Write two sentences for each of the following verbs. First use the verb as a linking verb. Then use it as an action verb. Label each one *linking* or *action*.

1. taste   2. look   3. smell   4. feel   5. sound

TIME-OUT FOR REVIEW • • • • •

Number your paper 1 to 10. Write each verb. Then label each one *action* or *linking*.

An Instant Dam

1. This is a true story about the nation's least expensive dam.
2. In 1958, a severe earthquake caused a great landslide in Montana.
3. About 43 million cubic yards of rock and earth crashed into the Madison River.
4. Within seconds the enormous mass of rock and earth formed a dam.
5. The dam was not only very high but more than a half mile long as well.
6. The earth and rock immediately blocked the flow of the river.
7. A seven-mile lake formed in the river behind the dam and became quite deep.
8. A cement dam of this size would be very expensive.
9. Crews work for years on the construction of a cement dam.
10. Today that earth-and-rock dam remains strong.

Helping Verbs

Sometimes an action verb or a linking verb is part of a *verb phrase* that includes *helping verbs,* or *auxiliary verbs.*

3c A **verb phrase** is a main verb plus one or more helping verbs.

Following is a list of common helping verbs.

Common Helping Verbs	
be	am, is, are, was, were, be, being, been
have	has, have, had
do	do, does, did
others	may, might, must, can, could, shall, should, will, would

A main verb may have one or more helping verbs.

The acrobats **are** practicing somersaults.

The actors **have been** rehearsing all evening.

One or more words may interrupt a verb phrase. *Not* and its contraction *n't,* for example, often interrupt verb phrases. The verb phrases below are in heavy type.

The ball **had** almost **hit** the mark.
Your train **is** not **leaving** for 20 minutes.

To find the verb phrase in a question, turn the question into a statement.

QUESTION   Have you called the fire department?
STATEMENT   You **have called** the fire department.

NOTE: Remember that a verb phrase is called a verb.

EXERCISE 9   Finding Verbs

Number your paper 1 to 20. Then write each verb. Remember that a verb phrase may be interrupted by one or more words.

EXAMPLE   How much do you know about insects?
ANSWER   do know

Baffling
Bugs

1. Have you ever counted the number of different bugs in a field at one time?
2. You would not have an easy job!
3. Scientists have identified about five million different species of insects.
4. From one batch of eggs, some insects can produce 2,000 identical offspring.
5. Ants have built some incredible underground cities with hundreds of tunnels.
6. Of course all ants do not work all the time.
7. Some ants will kidnap the workers from another tribe of ants.
8. A dragonfly can fly faster than 50 miles an hour.
9. Cockroaches have existed on Earth 265 million years longer than humans.
10. The insects actually have not changed very much in all that time.
11. Do you know today's temperature?
12. You can count all the chirps of a single cricket for 14 seconds.
13. Then you should add 40 to your total.
14. You will then have a nearly accurate Fahrenheit temperature.
15. A honeybee will often visit 400 flowers in 20 minutes.
16. A queen bee may lay 3,000 eggs in a single day.
17. Only female mosquitoes will bite people.
18. A flea can leap 200 times its length.
19. In the tropics, army ants will march in groups of 100,000.
20. They will completely destroy anything in their way, like humans and elephants.

TIME-OUT FOR REVIEW • • • • •

Number your paper 1 to 20. Write each verb. Then label each one *action* or *linking*.

1. Runners always called the marathon the great competitive sport.
2. Today many people across the country are racing in the "triathlon."
3. This race includes a 2.4-mile swim, a 112-mile bicycle ride, and a 26-mile run.
4. The competitors swim the 2.4 miles in the choppy waters of the ocean.
5. A 2.4-mile swim is the same distance as four times up and down the Empire State Building.
6. According to records the triathlon started in Hawaii in 1978.
7. The first name for this competition was the Iron Man Triathlon.
8. Over the years more and more women were joining the competition.
9. The organizers eventually changed the name to the International Triathlon.
10. Only 12 athletes competed in the first triathlon.
11. By 1981, the triathlon had become a major event in the United States.
12. More than 4,000 people from across the world were contestants that year.
13. Now organizers in over 1,000 American cities are holding annual triathlons.
14. People of all ages have become triathletes.
15. One triathlete is John Huckaby.
16. He was 60 years old at the time.
17. Preparation for a triathlon is often a full-time job.
18. After much training a runner's bones actually become denser.
19. Triathletes also develop very strong hearts.
20. In fact, the life expectancy of many triathletes is much longer than the average human's.

Application to Writing

Before school some day, watch how different people walk down the hall. Some walk at a leisurely pace, and others walk along as if they had already heard the last bell ring. If you were to write a description of this scene, you might include overused verbs such as *walk*. If you used your imagination or looked in a dictionary or a thesaurus, however, you might use more colorful verbs, such as *stroll* and *scurry*. For the verb *stop*, for example, you might substitute *pause* or *halt*. Colorful verbs will make your word pictures come to life for your readers.

EXERCISE 10 Choosing Colorful Verbs

Number your paper 1 to 10. Then choose the verb in parentheses that is more colorful.

EXAMPLE   Cars (swished, moved) along the slippery road.
ANSWER   swished

1. The window (broke, shattered) into tiny pieces.
2. Don't (cover, litter) the kitchen table with your books.
3. The light in the lonely house (gleamed, shone).
4. The driver (swerved, turned) the car to avoid the pothole.
5. The baby (clutched, held) her doll tightly.
6. The young boy (stood, teetered) for a moment on the fence rail and then jumped down.
7. The small squirrel (collected, stockpiled) a large number of nuts for the winter.
8. Every tree in the yard (bent, arched) in the strong wind.
9. The hummingbird (flew, darted) about.
10. The light rain (pattered, fell) steadily all night.

EXERCISE 11 Writing Sentences

Write five sentences that describe what is happening in a game as your school team wins a championship. Use as many colorful verbs as possible.

Chapter Review

A **Finding Action and Linking Verbs.** Number your paper 1 to 10. Write each verb. Then label each one *action* or *linking*.

1. The grocer weighed the cheese.
2. The waves were pounding against the shore.
3. The battery in our car is dead.
4. Over the weekend the ocean remained rough.
5. The heart of a normal adult will beat about 38 million times each year.
6. Once again the computer was correct.
7. More than 300 United States citizens have appeared on the stamps of other countries.
8. Sodium in salt can contribute to high blood pressure.
9. The roses near the house smell fragrant.
10. Benjamin Franklin was the founder of the first public library in the United States.

B **Finding Verb Phrases.** Number your paper 1 to 10. Then write each verb. Remember that words may interrupt a verb phrase.

1. Greg hasn't found a part-time job yet.
2. This piece might not be a part of that puzzle.
3. The Thompkinses will be your new neighbors.
4. Have you seen the movie about Africa at the Plaza?
5. I have always wanted a really good pair of leather hiking boots.
6. Did the new reporter for WGHT appear nervous during his report?
7. Have they taken their dog with them?
8. Hail will sometimes fall in the summer.
9. May I have that picture of you?
10. A machine can produce coins at the rate of 10,000 per minute.

C **Finding the Verb.** Number your paper 1 to 10. Write each verb. Then label each one *action* or *linking*.

The Buried City

1. The morning of August 24, A.D. 79, was normal in Pompeii, a beautiful little city in Italy.
2. Everyone was talking about that evening's sports contests.
3. Mount Vesuvius, a nearby volcano, seemed peaceful.
4. For 1,500 years the volcano had been inactive.
5. Then around noon it suddenly erupted.
6. Hot rock and ash fell like rain from the sky.
7. Huge clouds of ash, smoke, and poisonous gases grew dark and thick.
8. People could not see the sun anymore.
9. After eight days the volcano finally became quiet.
10. Pompeii, however, had disappeared under 20 feet of ash and rock.

Mastery Test

Number your paper 1 to 10. Write each verb. Then label each one *action* or *linking*.

1. The world's longest bicycle seats 20 people.
2. That small, furry animal is a chipmunk.
3. During the late spring, the lilacs along the fence smelled fragrant.
4. The President has signed the bill into law.
5. A curlew can fly nonstop for more than 2,000 miles.
6. Have you taken your math test yet?
7. Blood type is hereditary.
8. The weather has become much colder this past week.
9. The audience grew restless during the second act.
10. The apples on our tree seem ripe.

4

Adjectives and Adverbs

Diagnostic Test

Number your paper 1 to 10. Make two columns on your paper. Label the first column *adjectives* and the second column *adverbs*. Then under the proper heading, write each adjective and each adverb. (Do not list *a, an,* and *the*.)

EXAMPLE David opened the old door carefully.

ANSWER <u>adjectives</u> <u>adverbs</u>
old   carefully

1. Slowly the large ship lowered the anchor.
2. The Southern senator spoke convincingly.
3. Jeffrey worked hard on the science project.
4. Did you put that box there?
5. Tons of meteor dust fall to Earth daily.
6. Life in Hollywood always seems glamorous.
7. The cliffs, high and steep, overlooked the sea.
8. This is a very tasty sandwich.
9. Somewhere the reporter obtained much information.
10. Theresa makes friends quite easily.

*A*djectives

All writing would be dull and lifeless without words called *modifiers*. Modifiers describe other words; they add color and exactness to a sentence. One kind of modifier is an adjective.

4a An **adjective** is a word that modifies a noun or a pronoun.

An adjective answers the question *What kind? Which one? How many?* or *How much?* about nouns and some pronouns. In the following examples, an arrow points to the noun or the pronoun each adjective modifies.

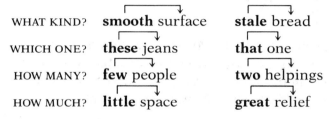

WHAT KIND?	**smooth** surface	**stale** bread
WHICH ONE?	**these** jeans	**that** one
HOW MANY?	**few** people	**two** helpings
HOW MUCH?	**little** space	**great** relief

Usually an adjective comes right before the noun or the pronoun it modifies. However, an adjective can follow the word it modifies. It can also follow a linking verb. (*See pages 41 and 43 for a list of linking verbs.*)

BEFORE A NOUN The **quiet, patient** child sat an hour in the doctor's office.

AFTER A NOUN The child, **quiet and patient,** sat an hour in the doctor's office.

AFTER A LINKING VERB The child was **quiet** and **patient.**

NOTE: The words *a, an,* and *the* form a special group of adjectives called *articles.*

Ravi dropped **a** letter into **the** mailbox.

You do not have to list articles in the exercises in this book.

Adjectives and Adverbs

EXERCISE 1   Finding Adjectives

Number your paper 1 to 10. Write each adjective. Then beside each one, write the word it modifies. There are 15 adjectives.

EXAMPLE   A helpful porpoise once guided ships.
ANSWER   helpful—porpoise

A Friend to Sailors

1. There is a channel through several islands off the coast of New Zealand.
2. The route, narrow and risky, is a shortcut for ships.
3. On a dark, stormy morning in 1871, the schooner *Brindle* approached the channel.
4. Suddenly a young and lively porpoise jumped up in front of the ship.
5. The porpoise seemed friendly.
6. It then led the ship safely through the deep waters.
7. For 41 years, the same porpoise led ships through the channel—except for one ship, the *Penguin.*
8. In 1903, a passenger on the *Penguin* shot the defenseless porpoise.
9. The porpoise survived, but it never again guided the *Penguin* through the dangerous channel.
10. In 1909, the *Penguin* sank in the channel with many casualties.

EXERCISE 2   Writing Sentences

Write three to five sentences that describe a circus clown. The clown can be one that you have seen or one that you imagine. Then underline each adjective.

Proper Adjectives

France is a proper noun. It is the name of a particular place. *French* is a *proper adjective.* It is formed from the proper noun *France,* but it is used to modify a noun or a pronoun—the *French city.* A proper adjective always begins with a capital letter.

54

PROPER NOUNS	PROPER ADJECTIVES
the **S**outh	**S**outhern hospitality
America	**A**merican trade
Queen **V**ictoria	**V**ictorian furniture

EXERCISE 3 *Finding Adjectives*

Number your paper 1 to 10. Write each adjective. Then beside each one, write the word it modifies. There are 15 adjectives.

1. The Martian spaceship landed on the mountain.
2. One of the first items exported from the American colonies was cranberries.
3. I have been reading about Roman history.
4. We will listen to the speeches of the Democratic and Republican candidates.
5. Did he have a Polish accent or a Hungarian accent?
6. Have you ever seen a Shakespearean play?
7. In 1497, John Cabot established the first British claim in North America.
8. The Atlantic coast has a rich supply of wildlife.
9. Picasso was a Spanish painter.
10. New York City began in 1612 with the arrival of Dutch ships on the Hudson River.

*A*djective or Noun?

A word's part of speech depends on how it is used in a sentence. *Street* and *winter,* for example, can be either nouns or adjectives.

NOUN   The narrow **street** was crowded.

ADJECTIVE   **Street** cleaners are working near our apartment building.

NOUN   **Winter** is my favorite season.

ADJECTIVE   **Winter** winds in Chicago are very severe.

**EXERCISE 4   Distinguishing between Adjectives
and Nouns**

Number your paper 1 to 10. Then label each underlined
word *adjective* or *noun.*

1. What <u>book</u> did you read for your report?
2. We need a new <u>television</u>.
3. Kim selected a brilliant red <u>tulip</u> for her painting.
4. The <u>Arizona</u> climate is hot and dry.
5. <u>Music</u> is one of my favorite subjects.
6. The <u>tulip</u> border in our garden is beautiful.
7. Where did you buy that <u>book</u> bag?
8. Who is your <u>music</u> teacher?
9. Have you ever been to <u>Arizona</u>?
10. The <u>television</u> program was very interesting.

EXERCISE 5   Writing Sentences

Write two sentences for each of the following words. The
first sentence should use the word as an adjective. The
second sentence should use the word as a noun. Then label
the use of each one.

1. cotton   2. tennis   3. silver   4. two   5. mystery

Adjective or Pronoun?

A word can be a pronoun in one sentence and an adjective in another sentence. For example, *this* is a pronoun if
it stands alone and takes the place of a noun. It is an adjective if it modifies a noun or a pronoun.

ADJECTIVE   **This** volleyball needs air. [*This* modifies
volleyball.]

PRONOUN   **This** needs air. [*This* takes the place of the
noun *volleyball.*]

ADJECTIVE   **Which** card did you send?

PRONOUN   **Which** did you send?

The following pronouns can be used as adjectives in a sentence.

Words Used as Pronouns or Adjectives

Demonstrative	Interrogative	Indefinite	
that	what	all	many
these	which	another	more
this	whose	any	most
those		both	neither
		each	other
		either	several
		few	some

NOTE: The possessive pronouns *my, your, his, her, its, our,* and *their* are sometimes called *pronominal adjectives* because they answer the adjective question *Which one?* Throughout this book, however, these words will be considered pronouns.

EXERCISE 6 Distinguishing between Adjectives and Pronouns

Number your paper 1 to 10. Then label each underlined word *adjective* or *pronoun*.

1. <u>What</u> type of dog do you own?
2. <u>That</u> was a delicious meal!
3. <u>Several</u> students entered the swimming race at the local pool.
4. <u>Many</u> helped clean up after the party.
5. Why did you buy <u>those</u>?
6. <u>What</u> did he say?
7. <u>Those</u> apples are quite tart.
8. Did you hear <u>that</u> strange noise coming from the engine of your car?
9. Because records were on sale, we bought <u>several</u> for Dad.
10. <u>Many</u> reporters covered the trial.

EXERCISE 7 *Writing Sentences*

Write two sentences for each of the following words. The first sentence should use the word as an adjective. The second sentence should use the word as a pronoun. Then label the use of each one.

1. this   2. which   3. both   4. some   5. these

TIME-OUT FOR REVIEW ● ● ● ● ●

Number your paper 1 to 15. Then write each adjective. There are 25 adjectives.

EXAMPLE A peculiar animal lives in eastern Australia.
ANSWER   peculiar, eastern

The
Duckbill
Platypus

1. Which animal is the oddest creature on Earth?
2. The answer is easy; it is the Australian platypus.
3. The platypus is a primitive mammal.
4. Unlike most kinds of mammals, however, the platypus lays eggs.
5. The eggs have a tough, leathery covering.
6. Baby platypuses are blind and helpless.
7. The feet of the platypus are unusual.
8. They have webs for swimming, but they also have hard claws for digging.
9. The back legs of male platypuses have daggers made of bone.
10. The daggers, narrow and hollow, are like the fangs of a rattlesnake.
11. The platypus can shoot a deadly poison through the daggers.
12. A jab from one of these daggers can instantly kill an animal.
13. A platypus pokes around in river mud with a broad bill.
14. This bill is soft and flexible.
15. A platypus eats worms, snails, and tiny shellfish.

Application to Writing

When you write, look in a dictionary or a thesaurus for fresh, specific adjectives to communicate your exact meaning.

VAGUE   We ate the food.
CLEARER   We ate the **leftover** food.
We ate the **delicious Mexican** food.

EXERCISE 8   Finding Fresh, Specific Adjectives

Number your paper 1 to 5. Find at least three specific adjectives that would describe each noun.

EXAMPLE   ship
POSSIBLE ANSWER   swift, huge, cargo, leaky

1. statue   2. car   3. book   4. insect   5. song

EXERCISE 9   Expanding Sentences

Number your paper 1 to 5. Expand each sentence by adding at least two specific adjectives. Then underline each adjective.

EXAMPLE   Waves pounded the beach.
POSSIBLE ANSWER   <u>Powerful</u> waves pounded the <u>rocky</u> beach.

1. A truck roared down the street.
2. Musicians played tunes.
3. The farmer plowed the field.
4. Photographers took pictures.
5. The bowl held apples.

EXERCISE 10   Writing Sentences

Imagine that you have landed on a distant planet. Suddenly the creatures who inhabit the planet appear and invite you to dinner. Write at least five sentences that describe what the dinner might be like. Use fresh, colorful adjectives.

Adverbs

An adverb is another kind of modifier. Adverbs make the meaning of verbs, adjectives, and other adverbs more precise.

4b An **adverb** is a word that modifies a verb, an adjective, or another adverb.

Many adverbs end in *-ly*.

Hold the rope **tightly** as you lower the bucket **slowly.**

The common adverbs in the following list, however, do not end in *-ly*.

Common Adverbs

again	even	now	somewhat
almost	ever	often	somewhere
alone	everywhere	outside	soon
already	here	quite	still
also	just	rather	there
always	late	seldom	too
away	never	so	very
down	not	sometimes	yet

NOTE: *Not* and its contraction *n't* are always adverbs.

I did **not** go because I did**n't** finish my homework.

Adverbs That Modify Verbs

Most adverbs modify verbs. To find these adverbs, ask yourself, *Where? When? How?* or *To what extent?* about each verb. A word that answers one of these questions is an adverb. When it modifies a verb, an adverb can usually be placed anywhere in the sentence.

WHERE?   Everyone gathered **outside.**

WHEN?   **Sometimes** we visit Aunt Sarah.

HOW?   Ted spoke **quietly.**

TO WHAT EXTENT?   The fog **completely** disappeared.

More than one adverb can modify the same verb.

Dad **never** drives **fast.**

When there are helping verbs in addition to the main verb, an adverb modifies the entire verb phrase.

You should answer the invitation **promptly.**

An adverb sometimes interrupts a verb phrase in a statement or a question.

STATEMENT   I have **always** earned *A*'s in math.

QUESTION   Did**n't** she hear the telephone?

EXERCISE 11   *Finding Adverbs*

Number your paper 1 to 10. Write each adverb. Then beside each one, write the word or words it modifies. There are 15 adverbs.

EXAMPLE   We have worked hard and steadily.
ANSWER   hard—have worked,   steadily—have worked

1. Roberto nearly missed the train.
2. The electrician has not repaired the elevator yet.
3. Our school should easily win the championship.
4. Carefully the fire fighter crawled toward the man.
5. The cement truck rumbled noisily down the street.
6. Our dog has always barked at strangers.
7. Mrs. Kent repeated the directions slowly and clearly.
8. Now you can put your wet boots here.
9. A hawk flew gracefully and effortlessly above the valley.
10. Suddenly the chipmunk scampered away.

EXERCISE 12 *Finding Adverbs*

Number your paper 1 to 10. Write each adverb. Then beside each one, write the word or words it modifies. There are 15 adverbs.

1. The miners had previously dug the tunnel into the side of the mountain.
2. Suddenly the large dog snarled angrily at the group on the sidewalk.
3. Doesn't the team have practice now?
4. The freight train was moving slowly and noisily.
5. The wildcat will usually hunt at night.
6. The official investigator has now found the cause of the fire.
7. Several athletes in wheelchairs were rapidly approaching the marathon's finish line.
8. Our dog will often snore loudly.
9. That rancher has always trained wild horses easily.
10. Is Mandy still baby-sitting on weekends?

Adverbs That Modify Adjectives and Other Adverbs

Almost all adverbs modify verbs. However, occasionally an adverb, such as *quite, rather, so, somewhat,* and *very,* modifies an adjective or another adverb. Such an adverb usually comes immediately before the word it modifies.

MODIFYING
AN ADJECTIVE
The evenings have become **rather** chilly. [*Chilly* is an adjective. *Rather* is an adverb that modifies *chilly*. It tells how chilly the evenings are.]

MODIFYING
AN ADVERB
Thunderstorms can strike **very** suddenly. [*Suddenly* is an adverb. *Very* is an adverb that modifies *suddenly*. It tells how suddenly thunderstorms can strike.]

EXERCISE 13   Finding Adverbs

Number your paper 1 to 10. Write each adverb. Then beside each one, write the word or words it modifies. There are 15 adverbs.

EXAMPLE   The dog watched the bone very carefully.
ANSWER   very—carefully,   carefully—watched

1. Beetles have very strong legs.
2. The old door creaked quite eerily.
3. Bob started the race too quickly.
4. Very soon he changed his mind.
5. Our old car runs surprisingly well.
6. The Chinese dinner at the Pagoda Restaurant tasted especially delicious.
7. The sandstone banks of the Connecticut River contain beautifully clear footprints of dinosaurs.
8. The players ran especially fast after the huddle in the third quarter.
9. Her performance was nearly perfect.
10. During the holiday my neighborhood seemed exceptionally empty.

EXERCISE 14   Writing Sentences

Number your paper 1 to 5. Write sentences that follow the directions below, using an adverb in each sentence. Then underline each adverb.

EXAMPLE   Describe how a train moves.
POSSIBLE ANSWER   The enormous train roared <u>swiftly</u> down the track.

1. Describe how a rooster crows.
2. Describe how rain might fall.
3. Describe how a kitten plays.
4. Describe how calm a lake might be by including an adverb that modifies the adjective *calm*.
5. Describe how quickly you can finish drying the dishes by including an adverb that modifies the adverb *quickly*.

TIME-OUT FOR REVIEW • • • • •

Number your paper 1 to 10. Then write each adverb. There are 15 adverbs.

The Yo-Yo

1. The yo-yo first came to America from the Philippines.
2. Originally yo-yos were handmade.
3. They worked rather poorly.
4. Donald F. Duncan did not like the design of the first yo-yos.
5. In 1927, he creatively redesigned the toy.
6. He quickly added a special string to the toy.
7. The new yo-yos moved faster and quite precisely.
8. Almost every child was soon buying a Duncan yo-yo.
9. Eventually experts gave demonstrations everywhere.
10. They skillfully taught children many yo-yo tricks.

Application to Writing

To add variety to your writing, begin some sentences with an adverb.

EXERCISE 15 Creating Sentence Variety

Number your paper 1 to 10. Rewrite each sentence so that it begins with the adverb.

1. A swarm of hornets angrily chased us.
2. The squirrel swiftly scurried up the tree.
3. The new swimming pool will open soon.
4. We will meet them later.
5. A distant wolf howled mournfully.
6. The detective cleverly solved the crime.
7. The old train chugged slowly out of the station.
8. The game ended abruptly when the rain started.
9. Tom considered the problem thoughtfully.
10. The motorboats roared loudly down the river.

Diagraming Adjectives and Adverbs

Adjectives and adverbs are both diagramed on a slanted line below the words they modify.

The band concert starts soon.

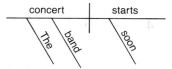

Adverbs That Modify Adjectives or Other Adverbs. This adverb is also connected to the word it modifies. It is written on a line parallel to the word it modifies.

A very costly error occurred quite recently.

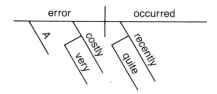

EXERCISE 16 Diagraming Adjectives and Adverbs

Diagram the following sentences or copy them. If your teacher tells you to copy them, draw one line under each subject and two lines under each verb. Then label each modifier *adjective* or *adverb*.

1. The entire class will vote.
2. We dressed quickly.
3. The full moon was shining brightly.
4. The silver tinsel sparkled.
5. Nick always works carefully.
6. The unusually fast rabbit hopped away.
7. The robot moved quite near.
8. Has the evening concert just begun?
9. Did those large red apples ripen recently?
10. The young candidate spoke very confidently.

*C*hapter *R*eview

A Identifying Adjectives and Adverbs. Number your paper 1 to 10. Make two columns on your paper. Label the first column *adjectives* and the second column *adverbs*. Then under the proper heading, write each adjective and adverb.

The Greatest Explosion of All

1. In 1883, a volcano on Krakatoa erupted suddenly.
2. This eruption was the most violent explosion of modern times.
3. Volcanic ash soared 50 miles into the atmosphere.
4. The ash constantly circled the earth.
5. The dark cloud of ash severely blocked the sun.
6. In fact, the normal amount of heat could not reach the earth during the whole next year.
7. Weather patterns changed throughout the world.
8. The northern states were unusually cold in 1884.
9. That year was "the year without a summer."
10. After 40 years Krakatoa finally became green again.

B Identifying Adjectives and Adverbs. Number your paper 1 to 10. Write each adjective and adverb. Then beside each one, write the word or words it modifies.

Animal Behavior

1. Words and actions are the main means of human communication.
2. Animals also have various ways to communicate.
3. Very often the songs of birds are messages.
4. Some animals communicate with body movements.
5. Communication is especially important in groups.
6. Animals form social groups for several reasons.
7. One reason is safety in large numbers.
8. A lion will rarely attack a whole herd of antelopes.
9. Warmth is another reason for social groups.
10. Antarctic penguins actually huddle for protection against the winds.

C **Noun, Pronoun, or Adjective?** Number your paper 1 to 10. Write each underlined word. Then label each one *noun, pronoun,* or *adjective.*

1. Which airplane hangar is off limits to the public?
2. I have math after lunch.
3. What book did this come from?
4. Party decorations were hung across the barn door.
5. Several desserts were on the lunch menu.
6. What is the answer to the second math problem?
7. I need a new picture frame for this photograph.
8. Which would you prefer to fly, a single-engine airplane or a jet?
9. Several of my friends have been invited to the party.
10. Did you paint the picture of the barn?

Mastery Test

Number your paper 1 to 10. Make two columns on your paper. Label the first column *adjectives* and the second column *adverbs.* Then under the proper heading, write each adjective and each adverb. (Do not list *a, an,* or *the.*)

1. Anthony was born in a small Italian village.
2. Recently much rain has fallen.
3. A lion, sick and dangerous, escaped from the zoo.
4. She has not returned the book yet.
5. Everyone is talking too loudly.
6. This road can be dangerous at night.
7. A loud thunderclap crashed outside.
8. Did he just take two sandwiches?
9. Weather balloons record temperatures and wind speeds.
10. Everyone in the audience was extremely quiet.

5

Other Parts of Speech

Diagnostic Test

Number your paper 1 to 10. Write each underlined word. Then label each one *preposition, conjunction,* or *interjection.*

EXAMPLE   <u>Great</u>! We can leave <u>in</u> ten minutes.
ANSWER   great—interjection, in—preposition

1. The pull of the moon <u>on</u> the earth makes the tides rise <u>and</u> fall.
2. Those wild flowers <u>along</u> the railroad tracks are common <u>throughout</u> the Midwestern states.
3. Watch the street signs carefully, <u>or</u> you will miss the turnoff <u>to</u> the turnpike.
4. <u>Ugh</u>! This milk looks good, <u>but</u> it's sour.
5. Four kinds <u>of</u> poisonous snakes live <u>in</u> the United States.
6. <u>Both</u> the coach <u>and</u> the team were excited by the final score.
7. <u>Whew</u>! We finally got all the hay <u>inside</u> the barn.
8. We looked <u>above</u> the rooftops <u>yet</u> could not see the fireworks.
9. <u>Caution</u>! You must be finished <u>before</u> midnight.
10. <u>From</u> the bottom of a well, you can see the stars <u>during</u> the day.

Prepositions

If someone gives you directions, a *preposition* such as *beside, on,* or *under* could make all the difference in whether you find what you are looking for.

Look for Kate's contact lens $\begin{cases} \textbf{beside} \\ \textbf{on} \\ \textbf{under} \end{cases}$ the sofa.

5a ▶ A **preposition** is a word that shows the relationship between a noun or a pronoun and another word in the sentence.

Following is a list of common prepositions.

Common Prepositions

about	before	during	of	toward
above	behind	except	off	under
across	below	for	on	underneath
after	beneath	from	over	until
against	beside	in	past	up
along	between	inside	since	upon
among	beyond	into	through	with
around	by	like	throughout	within
at	down	near	to	without

EXERCISE 1 Supplying Prepositions

Number your paper 1 to 10. Then write two prepositions that could fill each blank in the following sentences.

EXAMPLE She pinned the rose _____ her collar.

POSSIBLE ANSWERS on, near

1. Put your report _____ your notebook.
2. The choir will sit _____ the stage.

3. Corey is relaxing _____ the rehearsal.
4. The damaged plane landed smoothly _____ the icy runway.
5. Two huge hawks soared _____ the clouds.
6. He found his watch _____ his locker.
7. Were you able to get _____ the fence?
8. Our old neighbors, the Oteros, will visit us _____ three weeks.
9. We waded _____ the river.
10. The dog's favorite toy was lying _____ the dining room table.

Prepositional Phrases

A preposition is always part of a group of words called a *prepositional phrase*.

5b ▶ A **prepositional phrase** is a group of words made up of a preposition, its object, and any words that modify the object.

PREPOSITIONAL PHRASES

$\overset{\text{prep.}}{ }$ $\overset{\text{obj.}}{ }$
Did you speak **with them?**

$\overset{\text{prep.}}{ }$ $\overset{\text{obj.}}{ }$
Within a few months, school will be out.

$\overset{\text{prep.}}{ }$ $\overset{\text{obj.}}{ }$
The ice **on the lake** is safe.

A prepositional phrase can have more than one object. Such a phrase has a *compound object of a preposition*.

COMPOUND OBJECT OF A PREPOSITION

$\overset{\text{prep.}}{ }$ $\overset{\text{obj.}}{ }$ $\overset{\text{obj.}}{ }$ $\overset{\text{obj.}}{ }$
Boxes **of uniforms, hats, and boots** filled the band room.

A sentence can have more than one prepositional phrase.

$\overset{\text{prep.}}{ }$ $\overset{\text{obj.}}{ }$ $\overset{\text{prep.}}{ }$ $\overset{\text{obj}}{ }$
After the game we walked **to the pizza parlor.**

$\overset{\text{prep.}}{ }$ $\overset{\text{obj.}}{ }$ $\overset{\text{prep.}}{ }$ $\overset{\text{obj.}}{ }$
During the winter some beetles go **into hibernation**

$\overset{\text{prep.}}{ }$ $\overset{\text{obj.}}{ }$
under the ground.

EXERCISE 2   *Finding Prepositional Phrases*

Number your paper 1 to 10. Write each prepositional phrase.
Then underline the preposition and circle its object.

EXAMPLE   Over the years baseball equipment has
          improved.

ANSWER   *over the* (years)

Early
Baseball
Equipment

1. Baseball was originally played without any special equipment.
2. In the early days, bases were tall stakes.
3. Many players ran into the stakes and were hurt.
4. Later the stakes were replaced with rocks.
5. Unfortunately, the rocks were also dangerous to players.
6. Eventually sandbags were placed at each base.
7. Early baseball bats were adapted from sticks.
8. The first baseball glove was developed by Charles Waite.
9. It was like an ordinary winter glove.
10. Catchers did not use masks until 1877.

EXERCISE 3   *Finding Prepositional Phrases*

Number your paper 1 to 10. Then write each prepositional
phrase. There are 20 phrases.

EXAMPLE   Light from the moon shone on the lake.
ANSWER   from the moon,   on the lake

1. Since last year Carla has often baby-sat for the Man-cuso family.
2. You will find the Transportation Museum between the subway station and the park.
3. In one day the human body makes a billion red blood cells.
4. One specific end of a compass needle always points toward the north.
5. Shadows from the huge clouds moved slowly across the wheat fields.
6. With a quick volley, Tom smashed the tennis ball into the court of his opponent.

7. Air is a combination of nitrogen, oxygen, and other invisible gases.
8. I asked Ken if he would save a seat for me at the baseball game.
9. Over millions of years, the Colorado River has carved the Grand Canyon through deep rock layers.
10. During our trip to Washington, I learned much about the federal government.

Preposition or Adverb?

Some words can be a preposition in one sentence and an adverb in another sentence. *Around*, for example, is a preposition when it is part of a prepositional phrase. *Around* is an adverb, however, when it stands alone and is *not* part of a prepositional phrase.

PREPOSITION   The skaters sped **around** **the rink.** [*Around the rink* is a prepositional phrase.]

ADVERB   Albert drove **around.** [*Around* is an adverb that tells where he drove. It is not part of a prepositional phrase, and it has no object.]

EXERCISE 4   *Distinguishing between Prepositions and Adverbs*

Number your paper 1 to 10. Write each underlined word. Then label each one *preposition* or *adverb*.

1. Marianna had never seen that particular kind of word processor <u>before</u>.
2. Sally, confused by the signs, mistakenly rode <u>past</u> her bus stop.
3. Through the streets crowded with happy shoppers, Mary slowly wandered <u>along</u>.
4. Eva and Carl called here an hour ago and said they would stop <u>by</u>.

5. Is the cat <u>inside</u> the house?
6. Crowds filled the sidewalks <u>along</u> the parade route.
7. Some children just strolled <u>past</u>.
8. We drove <u>by</u> your house last night.
9. I will call you <u>before</u> Tuesday.
10. I'm afraid to look <u>inside</u>.

EXERCISE 5   Writing Sentences

Write two sentences for each of the following words. The first sentence should use the word as a preposition. The second sentence should use the word as an adverb. Then label the use of each one.

1. over   2. without   3. down   4. along   5. across

TIME-OUT FOR REVIEW • • • • •

Number your paper 1 to 10. Then write each prepositional phrase.

EXAMPLE   On summer nights fireflies drift lazily over the grass.

ANSWER   on summer nights,   over the grass

Nature's Lanterns

1. These insects live in warm areas throughout the world.
2. During the day many fireflies eat plant pollen.
3. Fireflies lay their eggs on the ground.
4. Newly hatched fireflies burrow underneath the ground or hide within old stumps.
5. The red and green lights from one kind of firefly resemble traffic signals.
6. Scientists have recently learned much about firefly light.
7. The firefly's light comes from light organs on the underside of the abdomen.
8. The light of fireflies is not hot.
9. This cool light is produced by chemical reactions inside the insect.
10. The light stops after a final chemical reaction.

Application to Writing

In the last chapter, you learned that you can create variety in your sentences by beginning some sentences with an adverb. You can create additional variety by beginning some sentences with a prepositional phrase.

REGULAR ORDER   I have saved twenty dollars **in one month.**

VARIETY   **In one month** I have saved twenty dollars.

REGULAR ORDER   They saw an unusual rock formation **inside the cave.**

VARIETY   **Inside the cave** they saw an unusual rock formation.

EXERCISE 6   Creating Sentence Variety

Number your paper 1 to 10. Find the prepositional phrase in each sentence. Then rewrite each sentence so that it begins with the prepositional phrase.

EXAMPLE   Vicky hung a picture above the fireplace.
ANSWER   Above the fireplace Vicky hung a picture.

1. The senator and his staff should arrive within the hour.
2. The astronomy club members saw many stars through the telescope.
3. The explorers discovered an ancient city beyond that ridge.
4. Betsy Rawlings met her favorite author at the bookfair.
5. I found three four-leaf clovers in my backyard.
6. Tad runs a mile before breakfast.
7. Bart could not have easily repaired the car without his mechanic.
8. Rain pelted the windows throughout the afternoon.
9. We left during the intermission.
10. Two cars collided at the intersection.

Conjunctions and Interjections

A connecting word is called a *conjunction*.

5c ▶ A **conjunction** connects words or groups of words.

There are three kinds of conjunctions. A *coordinating conjunction* is a single connecting word. The conjunctions in the following list are used to connect single words or groups of words.

Coordinating Conjunctions
and   but   or   yet

WORDS   *Pete* **and** *Terry* are good friends. [nouns]
Did you speak with *him* **or** *her?* [pronouns]
The dog *growled* **and** *barked* at me. [verbs]
The box was *long* **but** *narrow.* [adjectives]
She spoke *softly* **yet** *urgently.* [adverbs]

GROUPS OF WORDS   He looked *on the chair* **and** *under the chair.* [prepositional phrases]
Katy *began the job* **but** *did not finish.* [complete predicates]
You should remove the bread from the oven, **or** *it will burn.* [sentences]

Correlative conjunctions are pairs of conjunctions. Like coordinating conjunctions, correlative conjunctions connect words or groups of words.

Correlative Conjunctions
both/and   either/or   neither/nor

WORDS   **Both** the *temperature* **and** the *humidity* were high yesterday. [nouns]
That coat is **neither** *warm* **nor** *comfortable.* [adjectives]

GROUPS
OF WORDS   **Either** *Eva will come to our house,* **or** *we will see her at my cousin's house.* [sentences]

The third kind of conjunction is a *subordinating conjunction.* It will be covered in Chapter 9.

Words such as *ugh, whew,* and *wow* are *interjections.* All these words show strong emotion.

5d An **interjection** is a word that expresses strong feeling.

An interjection usually comes at the beginning of a sentence. It is followed by an exclamation point or a comma.

Ouch! That water is hot.
Surprise! We were waiting for you.
Oh, I just remembered the rehearsal for the dance troupe tomorrow.

NOTE: Do not use interjections too often. They lose their force when you use too many of them.

EXERCISE 7 *Finding Conjunctions*

Number your paper 1 to 10. Then write the coordinating and correlative conjunctions in the following sentences.

EXAMPLE   I would like both a baked potato and a salad with the swordfish.
ANSWER   both, and

1. Susanne quickly but accurately drew a map to her house for the group.
2. The special messenger arrived at the dock and instantly boarded the ship.
3. Trees and bushes bordered the path all the way to the house.

4. Because of the bus strike, we must either walk or ride our bicycles to school.
5. We put on lotion before the hike, yet the mosquitoes still bit us.
6. The ocean, calm but cold, was inviting because of the hot, muggy climate.
7. The kingfisher is a good hunter both in the air and under the water.
8. Should the flag-bearer walk before the major or after him?
9. Neither Jane nor her brother could coax the kitten out of the tree.
10. Seiji patiently weeded and raked all the pine needles from the garden.

EXERCISE 8 Writing Sentences

Number your paper 1 to 10. Then write sentences that follow the directions below.

1. Use *and* to connect two proper nouns.
2. Use *but* to connect two sentences. (Place a comma before *but*.)
3. Use *or* to connect two prepositional phrases.
4. Use *either/or* to connect two subjects.
5. Use *but* to connect two adjectives.
6. Use *both/and* to connect two verbs.
7. Use *or* to connect a noun and a pronoun.
8. Use *yet* to connect two sentences. (Place a comma before *yet*.)
9. Use *and* to connect two prepositional phrases.
10. Use *neither/nor* to connect two adjectives.

EXERCISE 9 Writing Sentences

Number your paper 1 to 5. Then write a sentence for each of the following interjections.

1. Oops!   2. Hey!   3. No!   4. Hurray!   5. Well!

*C*hapter *R*eview

A **Finding Prepositions, Conjunctions, and Interjections.** Number your paper 1 to 10. Make three columns on your paper. Label the first *prepositions*, the second *conjunctions*, and the third *interjections*. Then under the proper column, write these parts of speech.

1. The lawyers for the trial spoke slowly but precisely.
2. After the rain the air seemed cooler, and the grass looked greener.
3. Ugh! Did you see that worm crawl across the porch?
4. Either sleet or snow is expected today.
5. The black walnut grows widely over the eastern half of the United States.
6. Congratulations! Both your son and daughter have won.
7. The surefooted horse walked along the steep mountain trail without any difficulty.
8. Neither Sam nor Earl has been inside the old mine.
9. Gosh! She walked on the stage and forgot her lines.
10. At that moment a huge dog dashed into our yard.

B **Finding Prepositional Phrases.** Number your paper 1 to 10. Then write each prepositional phrase.

1. The seeds dropped slowly from the pinecones.
2. A four-inch abalone can grip a rock with a force of 400 pounds.
3. Did Paul sit among the celebrities at the banquet?
4. Some lizards stand up and run on their back legs.
5. Below the sink, water was gushing from a broken pipe.
6. Everyone except Julie and Tom sat on the lawn.
7. Set the oven on *Broil* and wait for the light.
8. The Hawaiian Islands are a chain of volcanic islands.
9. Without any hesitation the lifeguard jumped into the water after the swimmer.
10. Along the way to the farm, we drove past Bart's house.

C **Finding Prepositional Phrases.** Number your paper 1 to 10. Then write each prepositional phrase.

Tunes for
the Circus

At the circus you always hear the calliope. A calliope has a keyboard like the one on a small piano. The keyboard is attached to steam whistles.

The calliope first appeared in 1855. It was first used for entertainment on riverboats. After 20 years the newer steamboats no longer used the calliope. Soon, however, it found a new home under the circus tent. Even today the calliope remains the musical instrument commonly used by circuses and carnivals.

Mastery Test

Number your paper 1 to 10. Write each underlined word. Then label each one *preposition, conjunction,* or *interjection.*

1. Some messages travel <u>along</u> your nerves <u>at</u> a speed of 200 miles per hour.
2. <u>No</u>, I cannot reach the spoon <u>underneath</u> the stove.
3. A lobster <u>or</u> a crab can drop a leg at will, <u>but</u> it soon grows a replacement.
4. <u>Beyond</u> the public library, the bus moved slowly <u>through</u> the heavy traffic.
5. The game <u>of</u> lacrosse was invented <u>by</u> American Indians.
6. <u>Wonderful</u>! Ken was behind at the beginning of the last lap, <u>yet</u> he won the race.
7. <u>Neither</u> my sister <u>nor</u> my brother has a job.
8. <u>Inside</u> the old trunk, I found a stack of letters <u>under</u> some old clothes.
9. <u>Wow</u>! A huge tree limb has fallen <u>against</u> the house.
10. The United States bought Alaska <u>from</u> Russia <u>in</u> 1867.

Parts of Speech Review

Diagnostic Test

Number your paper 1 to 10. Write each underlined word. Then beside each word, write its part of speech: *noun, pronoun, verb, adjective, adverb, preposition, conjunction,* or *interjection.*

EXAMPLE   <u>Unfortunately</u> Felicia overwatered her <u>plants</u>.
ANSWER   unfortunately—adverb, plants—noun

1. Have <u>you</u> met the <u>German</u> exchange student?
2. The explorers climbed <u>steadily</u> up the <u>mountain</u>.
3. The area of the United States would fit <u>into</u> the continent of <u>Africa</u> three and a half times.
4. <u>Wow</u>! The runner was heading for a sure touchdown <u>but</u> stumbled on the five-yard line.
5. A <u>bee</u> colony consists of a queen bee, drones, <u>and</u> workers.
6. <u>That</u> is the home of a <u>squirrel</u>.
7. <u>Quickly</u> <u>she</u> stuffed the papers into her briefcase.
8. <u>That</u> team <u>has</u> two left-handed pitchers.
9. The woodchuck <u>is</u> a member of the <u>squirrel</u> family.
10. The panda has a black patch <u>over</u> <u>each</u> of its eyes.

Parts of Speech Review

This chapter reviews the eight parts of speech. It is also a reminder that a word does not become a part of speech until it is used in a sentence. Suppose, for example, that someone asked you what part of speech the word *fish* is. Before answering, you would have to see how *fish* is used in a sentence because *fish* can be used as three different parts of speech.

NOUN   I caught three **fish** yesterday.

VERB   **Fish** the spoon out of the soup.

ADJECTIVE   Carlos cooked a **fish** casserole.

To find a word's part of speech, ask yourself, *What is each word doing in this sentence?*

NOUN   Is the word naming a person, place, thing, or idea?
Ken saw two **eggs** in the **nest.**
I have **faith** in the **United States.**

PRONOUN   Is the word taking the place of a noun?
This is **my** present to **you.**

VERB   Is the word showing action?
The detective **has solved** the mystery.

Does the word link the subject with another word in the sentence?

The lights **were** very bright.

ADJECTIVE   Is the word modifying a noun or a pronoun? Does it answer the question *What kind? Which one(s)? How many?* or *How much?*

The **stray** dog seems **friendly.**
Almost everyone ran **four** miles.

ADVERB   Is the word modifying a verb, an adjective, or another adverb? Does it answer the question *How? When? Where?* or *To what extent?*

The **very** old clock ran **slightly fast.**

PREPOSITION   Is the word showing a relationship between a noun or a pronoun and another word in the sentence? Is it part of a phrase?

Before the dance I collected tickets *at the door.*

CONJUNCTION   Is the word connecting words or groups of words?

Remember to buy some eggs **and** milk.
Science is my favorite subject, **but** I also like math.

INTERJECTION   Is the word expressing strong feeling?
Ouch! That skillet is hot.

Exercise 1 *Identifying Parts of Speech*

Number your paper 1 to 10. Write each underlined word. Then beside each word, write its part of speech: *noun, pronoun, verb, adjective, adverb, preposition, conjunction,* or *interjection.*

EXAMPLE   The old fisherman *expertly* mended *his* nets.
ANSWER   expertly—adverb, his—pronoun

1. <u>After</u> more than 33 hours, Charles Lindbergh landed in <u>Paris</u>.
2. The <u>young</u> seals were pushed <u>into</u> the pool by their mother.
3. The airplane <u>carries</u> passengers <u>but</u> does not transport cargo.
4. Late in the afternoon last Friday, the storm came on <u>quite</u> <u>suddenly</u>.

5. Genuine <u>Mexican</u> jumping beans contain the caterpillars of a small <u>moth</u>.
6. What do <u>you</u> remember <u>about</u> the book?
7. Because of the sudden thunderstorm, we <u>held</u> the picnic <u>inside</u>.
8. During the first inning of the game, the pitcher <u>had</u> a little <u>trouble</u>.
9. <u>They</u> will wait for us by the fountain <u>or</u> inside the front door.
10. <u>Yes</u>! <u>I</u> will show the senator around the new school building.

EXERCISE 2   Identifying Parts of Speech

Number your paper 1 to 10. Write each underlined word. Then beside each word, write its part of speech: *noun, pronoun, verb, adjective, adverb, preposition, conjunction*, or *interjection*.

Against All
Odds

1. Wilma Rudolph was born <u>on</u> June 23, 1940, in St. Bethlehem, <u>Tennessee</u>.
2. At age four she <u>suffered</u> attacks <u>of</u> double pneumonia and scarlet fever.
3. After these illnesses she <u>totally</u> lost the use of her <u>left</u> leg.
4. For the next seven years, she could <u>not</u> walk <u>without</u> braces on her legs.
5. With enormous <u>determination</u> she <u>painfully</u> exercised every day.
6. She even <u>played</u> basketball in her <u>backyard</u>.
7. <u>Incredible</u>! By high school she <u>was</u> a very healthy champion athlete.
8. During this time she broke records in <u>both</u> track <u>and</u> basketball.
9. In college <u>she</u> set world records as a sprinter and then set her eyes on the <u>Olympics</u>.
10. In 1960, this courageous woman won <u>three</u> gold medals and set an <u>Olympic</u> record in the 100-meter dash.

EXERCISE 3   Identifying Parts of Speech

Number your paper 1 to 25. Write each underlined word. Then beside each word, write its part of speech: *noun, pronoun, verb, adjective, adverb, preposition, conjunction,* or *interjection.*

How the
Frisbee Got
Flying

The (1) Frisbee has been (2) around for over 30 years. Fred Morrison (3) made the first flying disk (4) after World War II. His early (5) metal disks (6) were too (7) heavy. (8) They didn't fly (9) very well. Then he turned to (10) plastic.

(11) No, Frisbee was (12) not the original name (13) for the disk. In the beginning (14) it was called Morrison's Flyin' Saucer. In 1955, Morrison sold the (15) toy to the Wham-O Company in (16) California. The company first called it the Pluto Platter (17) but then renamed it the Frisbee.

At first the Frisbee (18) was a loser. The Hula-Hoop was the (19) popular toy at that time. (20) Nobody cared (21) about the flying disk until 1964. (22) Then a new model came out. It could (23) really fly! Now over two million people (24) under the age of 15 (25) compete in the World Junior Frisbee Championship every year.

EXERCISE 4   Determining Parts of Speech

Number your paper 1 to 10. Write each underlined word. Then beside each word, write its part of speech: *noun, pronoun, verb, adjective, adverb, preposition, conjunction,* or *interjection.*

1. What sport do you like besides baseball?
2. We need some help inside.
3. No! I cannot join the baseball team.
4. Several valuable coins were found in that old hatbox in the attic.
5. What did you pick from the garden?
6. That was a charming town we traveled through on our way to the mountains.

7. <u>No</u> utensils could be found in the <u>apartment</u>.
8. <u>Some</u> of my friends brought <u>several</u>.
9. <u>Inside</u> the tool shed, we found some <u>garden</u> tools.
10. <u>Through</u> her <u>apartment</u> door, we could hear the radio.

EXERCISE 5 Labeling Parts of Speech

Number your paper 1 to 5. Copy the following sentences, skipping a line between each one. Then above each word, label its part of speech, using the following abbreviations. Remember that the articles *a*, *an*, and *the* are adjectives.

noun = *n.*	adjective = *adj.*	conjunction = *conj.*
pronoun = *pron.*	adverb = *adv.*	interjection = *interj.*
verb = *v.*	preposition = *prep.*	

EXAMPLE   He had been working in the old barn.

          pron. v.   v.   v.   prep. adj. adj.   n.
ANSWER   He had been working in the old barn.

1. Wow! That story really amazed me.
2. My family usually buys groceries at an Italian market.
3. You should choose a new bicycle carefully.
4. Nancy waited for him in the lobby.
5. Europeans colonized South America.

EXERCISE 6 Writing Sentences

Number your paper 1 to 10. Then write sentences that follow the directions below.

1. Use *apple* as a noun and an adjective.
2. Use *turn* as a noun and a verb.
3. Use *both* as a pronoun and an adjective.
4. Use *in* as an adverb and a preposition.
5. Use *toy* as a noun and an adjective.
6. Use *each* as a pronoun and an adjective.
7. Use *down* as an adverb and a preposition.
8. Use *plant* as a noun, a verb, and an adjective.
9. Use *record* as a noun and a verb.
10. Use *light* as a noun, a verb, and an adjective.

Chapter Review

A   **Identifying Parts of Speech.** Number your paper 1 to 10. Write each underlined word. Then beside each word, write its part of speech: *noun, pronoun, verb, adjective, adverb, preposition, conjunction,* or *interjection.*

Ten Tiny
Tongue
Twisters

1. David <u>and</u> <u>Dora</u> dawdled dreamily down the deck.
2. The <u>brisk</u> <u>breeze</u> blighted the bright blossoms.
3. Several sheep were sheared <u>swiftly</u> <u>with</u> sharp scissors.
4. The humble hermit hummed <u>happily</u> on <u>his</u> hickory harmonica.
5. The butler bought the butter, <u>but</u> he found <u>it</u> bitter.
6. <u>Ugh</u>! <u>I</u> saw a slippery slug hug a beetle bug.
7. Shellfish shells <u>seldom</u> <u>sell</u>.
8. <u>Double</u>-bubble gum <u>bubbles</u> beautifully.
9. <u>Wealthy</u> Wanda wears <u>Swiss</u> wristwatches.
10. <u>Sunshine</u> shines softly <u>on</u> scenic seashores.

B   **Determining Parts of Speech.** Number your paper 1 to 10. Write each underlined word. Then beside each word, write its part of speech: *noun, pronoun, verb, adjective, adverb, preposition, conjunction,* or *interjection.*

1. The bucket is <u>in</u> the <u>well</u>.
2. <u>These</u> are your tickets to the <u>first</u> performance of the water ballet.
3. <u>That</u> is the <u>one</u> in the catalog.
4. <u>Which</u> is the right <u>answer</u>?
5. <u>That</u> old tractor works <u>well</u>.
6. <u>Great</u>! I've wanted <u>these</u> sneakers for a long time.
7. With a pen write your name clearly at the <u>top</u> of the <u>answer</u> sheet.
8. <u>Which</u> gift should we open <u>first</u>?
9. Without hesitation the <u>great</u> athlete dived <u>in</u>.
10. <u>One</u> red <u>top</u> costs two dollars and fifty cents.

C **Determining Parts of Speech.** Number your paper 1
to 10. Write each underlined word. Then beside each
word, write its part of speech: *noun, pronoun, verb, adjective, adverb, preposition, conjunction,* or *interjection.*

1. <u>Those</u> are the candles from my <u>birthday</u> cake.
2. <u>Which</u> of your dogs jumped <u>over</u> the fence?
3. That plant <u>flowers</u> in the <u>spring</u>.
4. We put the <u>geranium</u> <u>outside</u>.
5. The <u>spring</u> dance will be held during <u>school</u> hours.
6. Karen received a <u>shell</u> necklace for her <u>birthday</u>.
7. <u>Which</u> seeds are the <u>geranium</u> seeds?
8. Did you grow <u>those</u> beautiful <u>flowers</u>?
9. That unusual <u>shell</u> is not found <u>outside</u> the Gulf of
   Mexico.
10. When will <u>school</u> be <u>over</u>?

Mastery Test

Number your paper 1 to 10. Write each underlined word.
Then beside each word, write its part of speech: *noun, pronoun, verb, adjective, adverb, preposition, conjunction,* or
interjection.

1. A <u>typical</u> tree <u>or</u> any other plant receives about 90 percent of its nutrition from the atmosphere.
2. <u>We</u> stopped near a <u>mountain</u> pool.
3. The waves tossed <u>both</u> of the boats <u>against</u> the dock.
4. In the spring of 1974, 90 tornadoes struck <u>from</u> Ohio
   to Georgia in a single <u>day</u>.
5. <u>Wow</u>! <u>These</u> are great records.
6. About 3,000 stars <u>appear</u> in the night <u>sky</u>.
7. <u>I</u> saw a strange <u>animal</u> at the zoo.
8. Baldwin apples <u>are</u> hard and <u>tasty</u>.
9. We drove <u>very</u> <u>slowly</u> through the traffic.
10. The first collection of Aesop's <u>animal</u> fables appeared
    200 years <u>after</u> his death.

7

Complements

Diagnostic Test

Number your paper 1 to 10. Then label each underlined complement *direct object, indirect object, predicate nominative,* or *predicate adjective.*

EXAMPLE   My new shoes feel <u>tight</u>.
ANSWER   predicate adjective

1. Captain Nemo set the <u>controls</u>.
2. The birthstone for May is the <u>emerald</u>.
3. The Himalayan peaks are always <u>snowy</u>.
4. Sea horses have spiny <u>shells</u>.
5. Mary gave her <u>sister</u> a bicycle ride.
6. Marty's voice sounded <u>nervous</u>.
7. Is Mr. Hall your history <u>teacher</u>?
8. Pine trees are always <u>green</u>.
9. Donald owns a Hereford <u>calf</u>.
10. The lifeguard tossed the tired <u>swimmer</u> a life preserver.

Kinds of Complements

Laura found.   Paulo seems.

These groups of words have a subject and a verb, but each one needs another word to complete its meaning. This additional word is called a *complement,* or completer.

Laura found her **dog.**
Paulo seems **tireless.**

There are four kinds of complements. *Direct objects* and *indirect objects* always follow action verbs. *Predicate nominatives* and *predicate adjectives* always follow linking verbs and are called subject complements.

Direct Objects

A direct object is always a noun or a pronoun that follows an action verb.

7a A **direct object** is a noun or a pronoun that answers the question *Whom?* or *What?* after an action verb.

To find a direct object, first find the subject and the action verb in a sentence. (*See pages 39–40 for a review of action verbs.*) Then ask yourself *Whom?* or *What?* after the verb. The answer to either question will be a direct object. In the following examples, subjects are underlined once, and verbs are underlined twice.

	d.o.

DIRECT   Mark <u>has</u> two **tickets.** [Mark has what?
OBJECTS   *Tickets* is the direct object.]

Carrie <u>invited</u> **them** to her party. [Carrie invited whom? *Them* is the direct object.]

To find the direct object in a question, change the question into a statement.

QUESTION <u>Did</u> <u>you</u> <u>memorize</u> your speech?

STATEMENT You <u>did memorize</u> your **speech.** [You did memorize what? *Speech* is the direct object.]

A *compound direct object* consists of two or more direct objects following the same verb.

COMPOUND <u>Uncle</u> <u>Luke</u> <u>sells</u> **hamsters** and **parakeets.**
DIRECT [Uncle Luke sells what? The compound
OBJECT direct object is *hamsters* and *parakeets.*]

EXERCISE 1 Finding Direct Objects

Number your paper 1 to 10. Then write each direct object.

EXAMPLE Ellen swept the sidewalk.
ANSWER sidewalk

1. White sharks have powerful teeth.
2. Last night we watched the hockey game.
3. In 1828, Noah Webster published his first dictionary.
4. Did she ever sign the petition?
5. Paul answered the phone.
6. For homework I must read the newspaper.
7. Have you ever seen a boomerang?
8. The modern harp has 46 strings.
9. For breakfast Sam ate two eggs.
10. The Colosseum in Rome held 50,000 people.

EXERCISE 2 Finding Direct Objects

Number your paper 1 to 10. Then write each direct object. (Some sentences have a compound direct object.)

1. I have read this book several times.
2. In 1867, William Cummings pitched the first curveball in a baseball game.

3. Did you see the school newspaper this month?
4. Everyone admired the decorations for the dance.
5. A common housefly may carry harmful bacteria on its legs.
6. My sister has knit a sweater and mittens.
7. On April 18, 1775, Paul Revere saw two lanterns in the Old North Church.
8. Dad will drive Brenda and me to the stadium.
9. Marcy found her wallet under the radiator.
10. Through a telescope we studied the moons of Jupiter and the rings of Saturn.

EXERCISE 3   *Writing Sentences*

Number your paper 1 to 5. Write a sentence that answers each question. Then underline each direct object.

1. What did you eat for breakfast?
2. How many classes have you had so far today?
3. What are you wearing on your feet?
4. What are two things that you have in your locker?
5. What do you want most for your next birthday?

Indirect Objects

Like a direct object, an *indirect object* is a noun or a pronoun that follows an action verb. In order to have an indirect object, a sentence must have a direct object.

7b ▶ An **indirect object** is a noun or a pronoun that answers the questions *To* or *for whom?* or *To* or *for what?* after an action verb.

To find an indirect object, first find the direct object. Then ask yourself, *To whom? For whom? To what?* or *For what?* about the direct object. The answer to any of these questions will be an indirect object. An indirect object always comes before a direct object.

INDIRECT
OBJECTS
     i.o.   d.o.
I threw the **dolphins** some fish. [*Fish* is the direct object. I threw some fish to what? *Dolphins* is the indirect object.]

     i.o.   d.o.
The guide gave **everyone** a sample. [The guide gave a sample to whom? *Everyone* is the indirect object.]

A *compound indirect object* consists of two or more indirect objects following the same verb.

COMPOUND
INDIRECT
OBJECT
    i.o.   i.o.   d.o.
I took **Mandy** and **them** some water. [You took water to whom? The compound indirect object is *Mandy* and *them*.]

An indirect object can never be part of a prepositional phrase that begins with *to* or *for*.

OBJECT
OF THE
PREPOSITION
Sam made dinner for us. [*Us* is *not* the indirect object. It is part of the prepositional phrase *for us*.]

EXERCISE 4 *Finding Indirect Objects*

Number your paper 1 to 10. Then write each indirect object.

EXAMPLE   Did you tell Joan the good news?
ANSWER   Joan

1. The director assigned Lee the lead in the play.
2. Our chorus will sing you a song.
3. The keeper gave the pandas bamboo stalks for dinner each night.
4. The guide brought me the catalogs.
5. Did the club send Mrs. Parker some flowers for her anniversary celebration?
6. The witch handed Snow White an apple.
7. Workers in a beehive bring the queen her food.
8. The guide drew us maps of the canyon.
9. Lani gives her dogs obedience training.
10. The team awarded Chris the baseball trophy.

EXERCISE 5 *Finding Indirect Objects*

Number your paper 1 to 10. Then write each indirect object. If a sentence does not have an indirect object, write *none* after the number. (Some sentences have a compound indirect object.)

1. Cindy picked her mother and her aunt some violets.
2. Mom gave a chess set to Dad for his birthday.
3. Did you feed the cat and dog their dinner?
4. The museum guide showed us the ancient armor.
5. Save Paul and me a seat in the theater.
6. The mail carrier brought Mom and Dad a special-delivery package.
7. Mr. Grange sold Buddy and me some balsa wood for a model airplane.
8. The police officer gave a lecture on safety to the class.
9. Toss Carlos or me the ball.
10. Rescue workers found temporary homes for the tornado victims.

EXERCISE 6 *Finding Direct Objects and Indirect Objects*

Number your paper 1 to 10. Write each complement. Then label each one *direct object* or *indirect object*.

EXAMPLE   David gave his friends a kite.
ANSWER   kite—direct object   friends—indirect object

1. Eli Whitney received a patent for his cotton gin on March 14, 1794.
2. Steve sketched us a picture of his new house.
3. Louis made eggs and toast for us for breakfast.
4. Mom gave Kathy a ride to school.
5. Will you lend me your bicycle?
6. Give this note to your teacher.
7. Did you find Victor and me an evening newspaper?
8. Nancy sent everyone a postcard from Dallas.
9. Have you given Jamie his badge?
10. The guidance counselor gave Al and me good advice.

Predicate Nominatives

A *predicate nominative* is a noun or a pronoun that follows a linking verb. A predicate nominative is called a subject complement because it identifies, renames, or explains the subject of the sentence.

A **predicate nominative** is a noun or a pronoun that follows a linking verb and identifies, renames, or explains the subject.

In order to find a predicate nominative, you first must be able to recognize a linking verb. (*See page 41 for a more complete list of linking verbs.*)

Common Linking Verbs	
BE verbs	is, am, are, was, were, be, being, been, shall be, will be, can be, should be, would be, may be, might be, has been, etc.
other verbs	appear, become, feel, grow, look, remain, seem, smell, sound, stay, taste, turn

To find a predicate nominative, first find the subject and the linking verb. Then find the noun or the pronoun that identifies, renames, or explains the subject. This word will be a predicate nominative.

PREDICATE NOMINATIVES

Cheryl is the **leader.** [*Leader* renames the subject *Cheryl.*]

Was that **they** on the beach? [Change a question into a statement. *That was they on the beach. They* renames the subject *that.*]

A *compound predicate nominative* consists of two or more predicate nominatives following the same verb.

94

COMPOUND
PREDICATE
NOMINATIVE
My best <u>days</u> <u>are</u> **Saturday** and **Sunday.**
[The compound predicate nominative
Saturday and *Sunday* renames the subject
days.]

EXERCISE 7 *Finding Predicate Nominatives*

Number your paper 1 to 15. Then write each predicate
nominative. (Some sentences have a compound predicate
nominative.)

EXAMPLE   Kim is a math tutor and a fine skier.
ANSWER   tutor, skier

1. Mercury is the smallest planet.
2. Is Barbara the catcher on the Wayland Junior High softball team?
3. Thomas will become an electrician or a plumber after his graduation.
4. This book is my main source of information about plants for my science report.
5. In this afternoon's play-off, the starting tackles will be Butch and I.
6. Mount McKinley is the highest peak on the continent of North America.
7. Was that she in the cafeteria line?
8. Owls are excellent mousetraps for farmers.
9. Will you remain my friend for life?
10. The only items in the drawer are pens and paper.
11. After years of lessons and many hours of practice, Lee became the first violinist of the orchestra.
12. Flint, Michigan, is a large Midwestern manufacturing town.
13. All during the gymnastics tournament, Mandy remained the top scorer.
14. The largest inland bodies of water in the United States are the Great Lakes.
15. One of the most energetic birds is the hummingbird.

EXERCISE 8 Supplying Predicate Nominatives

Number your paper 1 to 10. Then complete each sentence with a predicate nominative. If you use a pronoun, use only *I, you, he, she, it, we,* or *they.*

EXAMPLE My favorite sport is ———.
POSSIBLE ANSWER basketball

1. The most popular subject at my school is ———.
2. Two useful tools are the ——— and ———.
3. Was that ——— at the front door?
4. My best friends are ——— and ———.
5. George Washington was the first ———.
6. In another 20 years, I will be a (an) ———.
7. Two famous explorers were ——— and ———.
8. The captain of our baseball team should be ———.
9. Benedict Arnold became a ———.
10. My favorite actress is ———.

Predicate Adjectives

A *predicate adjective* is an adjective that follows a linking verb. A predicate adjective is called a subject complement because it modifies, or describes, the subject of the sentence.

7d A **predicate adjective** is an adjective that follows a linking verb and modifies the subject.

To find a predicate adjective, first find the subject and the linking verb. Then find an adjective that follows the verb and describes the subject. This word will be a predicate adjective.

PREDICATE
ADJECTIVES

Deer are usually **swift**. [*Swift* describes the subject—the *swift deer.*]

Is that coat too **small**? [Change a question into a statement. *That coat is too small. Small* describes the subject—the *small coat.*]

A *compound predicate adjective* consists of two or more predicate adjectives following the same verb.

| | p.a. | p.a. |

COMPOUND
PREDICATE
ADJECTIVE

The subway was **fast** and **clean.**
[Both *clean* and *fast* describe the subject *subway.*]

EXERCISE 9 Finding Predicate Adjectives

Number your paper 1 to 15. Then write each predicate adjective. (Some sentences have a compound predicate adjective.)

EXAMPLE   My brother is very small and energetic.
ANSWER   small, energetic

1. Surprisingly, the paint on the fence is dry.
2. The otter is extemely graceful.
3. The knees of a camel look tough and thick.
4. The lilacs smell very fragrant.
5. Is reindeer meat tough?
6. Over this past year, my brother has grown quite tall.
7. The black bears are friendly but dangerous.
8. Everyone should remain calm.
9. Guppies are very small.
10. After several hours the hikers felt weary and cold.
11. New Orleans is famous for its Mardi Gras.
12. The climate of Ireland is damp and chilly.
13. The baby appears unusually curious.
14. Last night the rain seemed so gentle.
15. The youngsters became restless during the movie.

EXERCISE 10 Supplying Predicate Adjectives

Number your paper 1 to 10. Then write predicate adjectives that complete the following sentences. (Avoid overused adjectives like *great, nice,* or *good.*)

1. The coach seemed _____ today.
2. I wrote in my journal that my best friend is _____ and _____.

3. The chicken tasted ———.
4. All during the night, the mosquito's buzz was ———
   and ———.
5. Kathleen looked rather ——— when she arrived at the
   birthday party.
6. The big house on the corner of Commonwealth Avenue
   looks ———.
7. Today the puppy became ——— and ———.
8. That German shepherd sounds ———.
9. Yesterday at the market, my neighbor Mrs. Matthews
   appeared ———.
10. The rabbit's fur felt ——— and ———.

EXERCISE 11 Finding Subject Complements

Number your paper 1 to 10. Write each complement. Then
label each one *predicate nominative* or *predicate adjective*.

1. The temperature on the surface of Venus is extremely
   hot.
2. Since graduation from art school, my brother has
   become a commercial artist.
3. After track practice today, Jo Ann looked pale and tired.
4. Brown rice is rich in minerals and vitamin B.
5. Could that be your history book in front of Maureen's
   locker?
6. A tornado is a brief but violent storm.
7. This bread seems old and stale.
8. The most popular metals in ancient times were copper
   and brass.
9. The tallest kind of tree in the world is the redwood.
10. Flamingos were once abundant throughout the world.

EXERCISE 12 Writing Sentences

Write four sentences. Each sentence should include a different complement. Then label each complement *d.o.*, *i.o*,
p.n., or *p.a.*

TIME-OUT FOR REVIEW • • • •

Number your paper 1 to 20. Write each complement. Then label each one *direct object, indirect object, predicate nominative,* or *predicate adjective.*

Fun at the Park

1. The amusement park had its start in France during the eighteenth century.
2. Originally it was a place only for relaxation.
3. Park directors soon gave these parks games and rides.
4. Around 1860, Coney Island became the biggest attraction in New York City.
5. It was fun for people of all ages.
6. Coney Island developed three parks within its borders.
7. Steeplechase Park was the most popular of all.
8. Other cities were anxious for parks of their own.
9. Soon cities across the country built new parks.
10. The introduction of the theme park gave directors of these parks new ideas.
11. Historians give Walt Disney credit for the idea of the theme park.
12. Disneyland in California was the first park of its kind in the United States.
13. Disney divided his park into Main Street, Adventureland, Frontierland, Fantasyland, and Tomorrowland.
14. The theme of each section became clear in the types of rides and other attractions.
15. Disneyland was instantly famous and successful.
16. Many other parks around the country are now imitators of Disneyland.
17. The theme park Six Flags over Texas, for example, emphasizes the history of Texas.
18. Another park, Kings Dominion in Virginia, includes copies of buildings from foreign countries.
19. Opryland, U.S.A., in Nashville is a famous center for country music.
20. Hundreds of amusement parks across the country now give visitors hours and hours of fun.

Diagraming Complements

The *sentence base* includes a subject, a verb, and sometimes a complement. Complements are diagramed on the baseline or are attached to it.

Direct Objects. A direct object is placed on the baseline after the verb. The direct object and the verb are separated by a vertical line that stops at the baseline.

I have already read that book.

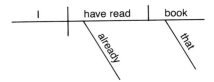

Indirect Objects. An indirect object is diagramed on a horizontal line that is connected to the verb by a slanted line.

Give me another chance.

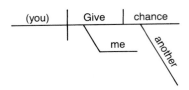

Subject Complements. A predicate nominative and a predicate adjective are diagramed in the same way. They are placed on the baseline after the verb. These subject complements are separated from the verb by a slanted line that points back toward the subject.

100

Alaska is the largest state.

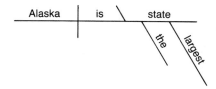

The morning air was quite damp.

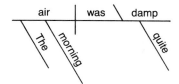

EXERCISE 13 *Diagraming Complements*

Diagram the following sentences or copy them. If your teacher tells you to copy them, draw one line under each subject and two lines under each verb. Then label each complement *d.o., i.o., p.n.,* or *p.a.*

1. The chorus sang three encores.
2. My favorite month is June.
3. Many great discoveries were accidental.
4. Mr. Tompkins gave Marsha a weekend job.
5. The first batter hit three fouls.
6. Is that stamp very valuable?
7. Diamonds are very brittle.
8. Fred gave everyone a hamburger.
9. Tell Jenny and me the directions.
10. Are his favorite books mysteries?

*A*pplication to Writing

Good writers not only select the correct words, but also place them in the right order, or in the right pattern. Following are examples of five basic sentence patterns.

PATTERN 1: S-V (subject—verb)

   S   V
Dogs bark.

       S   V
Many dogs bark at strangers.

PATTERN 2: S-V-O (subject—verb—direct object)

   S   V   O
Students enjoy sports.

      S   V   O
Most students at my school really enjoy team sports.

PATTERN 3: S-V-I-O (subject—verb—indirect object—
                                    direct object)

   S   V I O
Friends give us fruit.

       S   V   I O
Several friends often give us fruit from their trees.

PATTERN 4: S-V-N (subject—verb—predicate nominative)

    S   V   N
My collection is stamps.

       S   V   N
My biggest collection is stamps from foreign lands.

PATTERN 5: S-V-A (subject—verb—predicate adjective)

    S   V   A
Customers were restless.

      S   V   A
The customers in the restaurant were very restless.

To find the pattern of a sentence, drop all the modifiers and the prepositional phrases.

<pre>
      S   V   N
</pre>
The Pentagon is the largest office building in the world.

EXERCISE 14   Determining Sentence Patterns

Number your paper 1 to 10. Then write the sentence pattern that each sentence follows: *S-V, S-V-O, S-V-I-O, S-V-N,* or *S-V-A.*

1. The copper weather vane on the roof creaks.
2. Students in the high school annually hold an art exhibit.
3. The waterfall near our camp site sounded quite pleasant.
4. My grandfather proudly showed the dinner guests his bowling trophies.
5. The fireworks at the Fourth of July celebration brightly lit the dark sky.
6. The old bed in the attic feels very lumpy.
7. My next-door neighbor just became a reporter.
8. The wind howled like a wolf last night.
9. The autumn leaves suddenly turned very colorful.
10. My little sister bought her best friend two small goldfish.

EXERCISE 15   Expanding Sentence Patterns

Each of the following sentences follows a different sentence pattern. Expand each sentence by adding modifiers or prepositional phrases or both.

1. (S-V)   Airplanes landed.
2. (S-V-O)   Hikers found paths.
3. (S-V-I-O)   Children told visitors stories.
4. (S-V-N)   Winner was a friend.
5. (S-V-A)   Weather is uncertain.

*C*hapter *R*eview

A **Identifying Direct and Indirect Objects.** Number your paper 1 to 10. Write each complement. Then label each one *direct object* or *indirect object*. (Some sentences have a compound complement.)

1. Pitcher plants trap insects in their hollow leaves.
2. Each Mother's Day Ann serves her mother breakfast.
3. Jonathan feeds his turtle special food.
4. Will you do a favor for me?
5. Before dinner show Bruce and him the new calf in the barn.
6. On his birthday Penny gave a card and a present to Michael.
7. Orchids take their food and water from the air.
8. Brian likes most fresh vegetables.
9. Our neighbors gave us a fan during the heat wave.
10. Wish me luck.

B **Identifying Subject Complements.** Number your paper 1 to 10. Write each complement. Then label each one *predicate nominative* or *predicate adjective*. (Some sentences have a compound complement.)

1. The state flower of Alaska is the forget-me-not.
2. Chinese food is very tasty and nutritious.
3. Your fingerprints are different from everyone else's in the world.
4. Did Mark become an officer in the Honor Society last week?
5. The harpies of Greek mythology were hideous monsters.
6. The new band members are she and Carl.
7. The action in a hockey game is fast and furious.
8. That must have been Sheila on the telephone.
9. In the moonlight the swamp looked ghostly.
10. The winds of Antarctica are constant and violent.

C **Identifying Complements.** Number your paper 1 to 10. Write each complement. Then label each one *direct object, indirect object, predicate nominative,* or *predicate adjective.*

Snowflakes

1. Have you ever thrown a snowball?
2. One snowball is several thousand snowflakes.
3. Since 1940, scientists have studied snowflakes.
4. They have offered the public interesting information about snowflakes.
5. Each snowflake is unique.
6. Snowflakes generally have eight sides.
7. Their patterns, however, are always different.
8. Scientists often give these different patterns names.
9. The smallest flakes are extremely tiny.
10. Snowflakes are probably the most beautiful forms in nature.

*M*astery *T*est

Number your paper 1 to 10. Then label each underlined complement *direct object, indirect object, predicate nominative,* or *predicate adjective.*

1. A white shark has no natural <u>enemies</u>.
2. The meeting room felt very <u>warm</u>.
3. The store will send <u>you</u> a replacement.
4. Is the plant in that pot <u>new</u>?
5. Leonard proudly displayed a huge <u>tuna</u>.
6. Rhode Island is the smallest <u>state</u> in the Union.
7. Show <u>Lee</u> the pictures of the lambs.
8. The city issued <u>Mr. Murphy</u> a new license.
9. Porcupines are rather slow <u>animals</u>.
10. The road over the mountain looks <u>dangerous</u>.

8

Phrases

Diagnostic Test

Number your paper 1 to 10. Then label each underlined phrase *prepositional* or *participial*.

EXAMPLE   <u>Racing across the snow</u>, the sled dogs headed for the trading post.
ANSWER   participial

1. The pilot <u>of the jumbo jet</u> radioed the control tower.
2. <u>Located on Pennsylvania Avenue</u>, the White House is about a mile and a half from the Capitol.
3. The plant <u>on the windowsill</u> should be watered.
4. El Paso and Juárez are cities <u>separated by a river</u>.
5. The skaters glided <u>over the smooth ice</u>.
6. <u>Galloping wildly across the field</u>, the horse appeared terrified.
7. The ball rolled <u>beneath the car</u>.
8. <u>Before lunch</u> we took a quick swim.
9. A mackerel sky is made up of little fleecy clouds <u>arranged in even rows</u>.
10. Mr. Jenkins owns that old barn <u>near the road</u>.

Prepositional Phrases

A phrase is a group of related words that acts like a single part of speech. It does not have a subject and a verb. One kind of phrase is a *prepositional phrase.*

A **prepositional phrase** is a group of words that begins with a preposition, ends with a noun or a pronoun, and is used as an adjective or an adverb.

PREPOSITIONAL PHRASES   The man **with the papers** is my coach.
She threw the ball **over the fence.**

Following is a list of the most common prepositions.

Common Prepositions				
about	before	during	of	toward
above	behind	except	off	under
across	below	for	on	underneath
after	beneath	from	over	until
against	beside	in	past	up
along	between	inside	since	upon
among	beyond	into	through	with
around	by	like	throughout	within
at	down	near	to	without

EXERCISE 1   Finding Prepositional Phrases

Treetops Hotel

Number your paper 1 to 15. Then write the prepositional phrases in the following paragraph.

A most unusual hotel is located in Africa. The hotel is not built on the ground. It is 40 feet above the ground in the branches of a giant tree. Underneath the tree is a large salt deposit. During the evening the animals from the jungle come to the salt deposit for a lick. The guests at the hotel sit on the screened porch above the salt deposit. From their easy chairs, in comfort and safety, they watch the wild animals.

107

Adjective Phrases

An *adjective phrase* is a prepositional phrase. It is used like a single adjective.

SINGLE ADJECTIVE   Ray Street is a **wide** road.

ADJECTIVE PHRASE   Ray Street is a road **with six lanes.**

8b   An **adjective phrase** is a prepositional phrase that is used to modify a noun or a pronoun.

An adjective phrase answers the question *Which one?* or *What kind?* just as a single adjective does.

WHICH ONE?   The picture **on the right** is hers.

                I like the apples **in the salad.**

WHAT KIND?   Dad bought a car **with four-wheel drive.**

                This is a chest **without any drawers.**

A sentence can have more than one adjective phrase.

    The basket **of fruit** is for a friend **of the family.**

Once in a while, an adjective phrase will modify a noun or a pronoun in another phrase.

    The movie *about* the food *of* the future was amazing.

EXERCISE 2 *Finding Adjective Phrases*

Number your paper 1 to 10. Write each adjective phrase. Then beside each one, write the word it modifies.

EXAMPLE   I embroidered the pillow on the sofa.
ANSWER   on the sofa—pillow

  1. The mushrooms under that tree are poisonous.
  2. The key inside the box will unlock the old trunk.

3. The area along the river has riding trails.
4. Mrs. Jordan issued badges with members' names.
5. That novel about colonial days is fascinating.
6. The microphone above the stage recorded their duet.
7. The maximum length of a total solar eclipse is 7 minutes and 31 seconds.
8. A Navaho wove that rug with the beautiful design.
9. The period after English is my study hall.
10. The car took the road toward the canyon.

EXERCISE 3 Finding Adjective Phrases

Number your paper 1 to 10. Write each adjective phrase. Then beside each one, write the word it modifies. Some sentences have more than one phrase.

1. The house around the corner is being sold.
2. Our time without a TV passed quite quickly.
3. The mountains beyond that valley are the Rockies.
4. All the cabins throughout the camp are occupied.
5. Waves with huge white crests pounded the rocks on the shore.
6. The photograph on the desk shows the cotton fields beside our house.
7. The sign between those two posts contains information about the summer concert program.
8. The girl at the piano is my cousin from Pittsburgh.
9. Those trees near the house across the street will blossom soon.
10. Their trip into the jungles of Africa could be dangerous.

EXERCISE 4 Writing Sentences

Number your paper 1 to 5. Write a sentence that uses each of the following prepositional phrases as an adjective phrase. Remember to place each phrase directly after the noun or the pronoun it modifies.

1. beside the chair
2. at the front
3. near the road
4. under the porch
5. of corn

*A*dverb Phrases

An *adverb phrase* is a prepositional phrase. It is used like a single adverb.

SINGLE ADVERB   The nurse spoke **softly.**

ADVERB PHRASE   The nurse spoke **in a whisper.**

8c ▷ An **adverb phrase** is a prepositional phrase that is used mainly to modify a verb.

An adverb phrase answers the question *Where? When?* or *How?* just as a single adverb does. Occasionally an adverb phrase will answer the question *Why?*

WHERE?   The Volkers moved **to San Francisco.**

WHEN?   **On Monday** he begins his new job.

HOW?   Jasmín swam **with sure, strong strokes.**

WHY?   He wrote **for more information.**

An adverb phrase modifies the whole verb phrase.

For three hours the snow has been falling heavily.

Two adverb phrases can modify the same verb. Notice that an adverb phrase can appear anywhere in a sentence.

Before Friday I must send a letter **to my cousin.**

We waited **by the main entrance** *for* 15 minutes.

Once in a while, an adjective phrase will modify the object of the preposition of an adverb phrase.

Ben carelessly dropped his book *in* a **puddle** *of* water.

110

EXERCISE 5 *Finding Adverb Phrases*

Number your paper 1 to 10. Write each adverb phrase. Then beside each one, write the word or words it modifies.

EXAMPLE   I will soon phone you about the party.
ANSWER   about the party—will phone

1. The pitcher threw a curveball past the batter.
2. The Memorial Day parade will begin at noon.
3. In one day bamboo can grow 35 inches.
4. The campers rowed to the deserted island.
5. By next week we will be harvesting squash.
6. The sea gull searched the beach for food.
7. The plane flew above the storm.
8. After breakfast we cleaned our rooms.
9. The first nickel did not appear until 1886.
10. You should find the fertilizer inside the barn.

EXERCISE 6 *Finding Adverb Phrases*

Number your paper 1 to 10. Write each adverb phrase. Then beside each one, write the word or words it modifies.

1. A baby blue whale gains 200 pounds daily during its first year.
2. The sleek white boat sailed up the river past the rocky island.
3. The Mason-Dixon line runs between Pennsylvania and Maryland.
4. No one can go into the stadium until six o'clock.
5. The French flag flew over New Orleans for 45 years.
6. Since early morning Mom has worked in the garden.
7. At the signal run with all your might.
8. Glenda sat among the TV reporters throughout the press conference.
9. Over the last decade, many changes have occurred within the United States.
10. Across the desert two huge trucks rumbled down the highway.

Punctuation with Adverb Phrases

If a short adverb phrase begins a sentence, usually no comma is needed. However, a comma should be placed after an introductory adverb phrase of four or more words or after two or more introductory phrases.

NO COMMA **During intermission** you can call home.

COMMA **During the first intermission,** you can call home.

COMMA **During the intermission between the acts,** you can call home.

EXERCISE 7 *Writing Sentences*

Write five sentences describing a holiday you have spent with family or friends. Use an adverb phrase in each sentence. Begin at least two sentences with adverb phrases. Use commas where needed.

TIME-OUT FOR REVIEW • • • •

Number your paper 1 to 10. Write each prepositional phrase. Then label each one *adjective* or *adverb*. There are 20 phrases.

Super-
heroes

1. Superhuman people in the comics have entertained readers throughout the years.
2. The real name of Superman is Kal-el.
3. He came from Krypton in outer space.
4. On Earth he is a reporter for the *Daily Planet*.
5. Superman can fly and leap over tall buildings.
6. With his X-ray vision, he can see through walls.
7. All of his powers come from the sun.
8. In the real city of Metropolis in Illinois, there is a Superman Square.
9. A huge mural of Superman hangs on a water tower.
10. Many other superheroes with great powers have appeared on the pages of comic books.

Participles and Participial Phrases

A *participle* is a word that is formed from a verb but acts like an adjective. In the following examples, the participles are in heavy type. An arrow points to the word each participle modifies.

The **dripping** faucet annoyed Pablo.

The **respected** scientist explained her research.

> **8d** A **participle** is a verb form that is used as an adjective.

Present participles end in *-ing*. *Past participles* usually end in *-ed* or *-d*. Some, however, have irregular endings, such as *-n*, *-t*, or *-en*.

Verb	Present Participle	Past Participle
cook	cooking	cooked
tear	tearing	torn
send	sending	sent
freeze	freezing	frozen

PRESENT PARTICIPLE Everyone cheered the **winning** team.

PAST PARTICIPLE The **broken** vase was an heirloom.

Since a participle is used as an adjective, it modifies a noun or a pronoun. It also answers the adjective question *Which one?* or *What kind?*

WHICH ONE? The **ringing** bells filled the air with sound.

The **damaged** tree will live.

WHAT KIND? These **blooming** plants need special care.

The **bent** branches made a lovely centerpiece.

113

EXERCISE 8 Finding Participles

Number your paper 1 to 10. Write each participle. Then beside each one, write the word it modifies.

EXAMPLE   The falling leaves covered the driveway.
ANSWER   falling—leaves

1. The rising sun shines through my window.
2. All of the invited guests will attend the ceremony.
3. No one should disturb the sleeping cat.
4. Glowing candles lighted the windows of the old house at the end of the lane.
5. Make sure that you clean up the splattered paint.
6. Those drifting logs could be dangerous.
7. Did you ever walk on this winding road before?
8. Eventually Sharon found the lost watch.
9. Did you throw out those worn jeans?
10. Please stack the split wood.

Participial Phrases

Because a participle is a verb form, it has some of the features of a verb. It can have one or more complements. In addition, it can be modified by an adverb or an adverb phrase. A participle and any modifiers and complements form a *participial phrase*.

8e A **participial phrase** is a participle with its modifiers and complements—all working together as an adjective.

PARTICIPLE WITH AN ADVERB	**Working quickly,** we decorated the room in an hour.
PARTICIPLE WITH A PREPOSITIONAL PHRASE	Ted, **fishing from the pier,** caught three flounder.
PARTICIPLE WITH A COMPLEMENT	With fascination we watched the spider **spinning its web.**

EXERCISE 9 Finding Participial Phrases

Number your paper 1 to 10. Write each participial phrase.
Then underline each participle.

Facts and
Figures

EXAMPLE   A hailstone weighing almost two pounds once
fell in Kansas.

ANSWER   <u>weighing</u> almost two pounds

1. In the United States, there are about 1.3 million people
named Smith.
2. Of all the symbols appearing on national flags, the star
is the most common.
3. The *Skylab* scientific space mission carried out 25
experiments designed by students.
4. Measuring about 64 million square miles, the Pacific
Ocean is the world's largest body of water.
5. Working continuously, the human heart beats more than
2.5 billion times in a lifetime.
6. The Panama Canal, completed in 1914, cost about $350
million.
7. A person weighing 100 pounds on Earth would weigh
38 pounds on Mars.
8. The Shell Oil Company started out as a novelty shop
selling seashells.
9. The world's oldest gloves, discovered in King Tut's tomb,
are over 3,300 years old.
10. The polar regions contain over half of Earth's fresh
water, trapped in ice.

EXERCISE 10 Finding Participial Phrases

Number your paper 1 to 10. Write each participial phrase.
Then beside each one, write the word it modifies.

1. I haven't seen the picture drawn by David.
2. Taking a deep breath, Andy began his speech.
3. Mike lifted the backpack, loaded with supplies.
4. Weighing about 1,000 pounds, the saltwater crocodile
is the biggest reptile on Earth.

5. The snake made of leather looked almost real.
6. The evidence presented by the lawyer was impressive.
7. *Voyager I*, passing by Jupiter, took many photographs.
8. Sitting in the front row, we could hear very well.
9. The bread filled with cranberries was delicious.
10. I talked to the woman giving the lecture.

Punctuation with Participial Phrases

A participial phrase that comes at the beginning of a sentence is always followed by a comma.

Listening carefully, Debra wrote down the directions.

EXERCISE 11 *Writing Sentences*

Write a sentence for each participial phrase. The phrase should come at the beginning of the sentence.

1. Breaking the track record
2. Hired at the market
3. Rearing on its hind legs
4. Running swiftly
5. Locked inside a safe

TIME-OUT FOR REVIEW • • • •

Number your paper 1 to 10. Then write each phrase and label it *prepositional* or *participial.*

1. We discovered the small house behind some trees.
2. The rowboat carrying the supplies had broken loose.
3. The box office will give a refund to everyone.
4. The gymnast straddling the beam is my sister.
5. We watched the street artists painting the mural.
6. Amy noticed the banner above the doorway.
7. The actor is a large man resembling Mark Twain.
8. Sitting quietly, we enjoyed the sunrise.
9. I watched the workers repaving our street.
10. Do you know the name of the Wright brothers' first airplane?

116

Misplaced Modifiers

When you write, place a prepositional phrase or a participial phrase as close as possible to the word it modifies.

The lifeguard called to the people **swimming beyond the markers.** [In this sentence the people are swimming beyond the markers.]

Swimming beyond the markers, the lifeguard called to the people. [In this sentence the lifeguard, not the people, is swimming beyond the markers.]

These examples have different meanings, but they both make sense.

Sometimes when a phrase is not close to the word it modifies, the whole meaning of the sentence can be changed. A phrase that is placed too far away from the word it modifies is called a *misplaced modifier*. The danger of a misplaced modifier is that a reader will misunderstand the meaning of the sentence.

To correct a misplaced modifier, first decide what the intended meaning of the sentence is. Then find the word being modified. Place the phrase near that word.

MISPLACED	The children laughed at the clowns **in the audience.** [The position of the phrase in this sentence makes it seem as if the clowns are in the audience.]
CORRECT	The children **in the audience** laughed at the clowns.
MISPLACED	**Hanging on the wall of the old house,** Ben saw a beautiful painting. [This sentence suggests that Ben, not the painting, is hanging on the wall.]
CORRECT	Ben saw a beautiful painting **hanging on the wall of the old house.**

117

EXERCISE 12 Correcting Misplaced Modifiers

Number your paper 1 to 10. Then rewrite each sentence by placing the prepositional phrase closer to the word it modifies. Remember to use commas where needed.

1. At the bottom of the pond, Tim described the plant life.
2. Under the sofa Sue watched the mouse scamper.
3. Todd fed the nuts to the squirrel in the jar.
4. The record belongs to Jerry on the table.
5. The speaker told us about gorillas at the assembly.
6. I read that book to the children on the shelf.
7. Take that box to Mrs. Glynn with the red bow.
8. Maps were handed to the convention members of the city.
9. Meg told us about her exciting vacation in the auditorium.
10. A trick-or-treater in a mask bumped into a tree with tinted goggles.

EXERCISE 13 Correcting Misplaced Modifiers

Number your paper 1 to 10. Then rewrite each sentence, placing the participial phrase closer to the word it modifies. Remember to use commas where needed.

1. We saw some geese driving along the lake.
2. We could hear a bear lying in bed in our tent.
3. Filled with helium, each child was given a balloon.
4. Performing with a flaming baton, the spectators applauded the majorette.
5. We could see the church sitting on our porch.
6. Sliding into home plate, the crowd cheered the runner.
7. Buried in the snow, Martin found the bicycle.
8. Ben dropped all his books jumping over the puddle in the middle of the road.
9. Shattered into dozens of tiny pieces, Marcy gingerly stepped over the vase.
10. They welcomed the hot cocoa exhausted from the hike.

Diagraming Phrases

In a diagram both prepositional phrases and participial phrases are connected to the words they modify.

Adjective Phrases.   An adjective phrase is connected to the word it modifies. The preposition is placed on a connecting slanted line. The object of the preposition is placed on a horizontal line that is attached to the slanted line.

Your recipe for chicken is delicious.

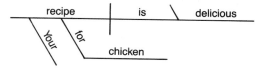

Sometimes an adjective phrase modifies the object of a preposition of another phrase.

Juanita waited by the swings in the park.

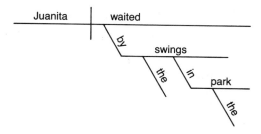

Adverb Phrases.   An adverb phrase is connected to the verb it modifies.

During the night we heard some strange noises.

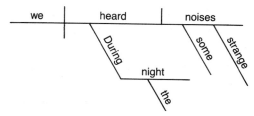

Participial Phrases. A participial phrase is diagramed under the word it modifies. It is written in a curve. If the participial phrase has a complement, it is diagramed after the participle. A vertical line separates the complement from the participle.

Everyone watched the robin making its nest.

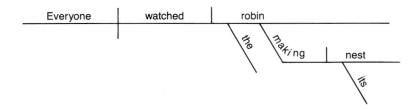

EXERCISE 14 Diagraming Phrases

Diagram the following sentences or copy them. If your teacher tells you to copy them, draw one line under each subject and two lines under each verb. Then put parentheses around each phrase and label it *adjective (adj.), adverb (adv.),* or *participle (part.).*

1. Each of the infielders made one error.
2. She put the package by the back door.
3. This book about boats is informative.
4. The museum in town displayed several prints of famous artists.
5. During the summer Sheila works at a dairy with sixty-four cows.
6. The cows in the pasture are heading for the barn.
7. Did you write to your friend in Tampa?
8. Playing his electric guitar, Michael did not hear the doorbell.
9. The principal congratulated the students accepting the athletic awards.
10. The student delivering the speech is the class president.

120

Application to Writing

You can create variety in the length of your sentences by using phrases to combine short, choppy sentences.

TWO SENTENCES	Our neighbors are having a garage sale. They live across the street.
ONE SENTENCE	Our neighbors **across the street** are having a garage sale. [adjective phrase]
TWO SENTENCES	Jack climbed the cliff. He had a rope.
ONE SENTENCE	Jack climbed the cliff **with a rope.** [adverb phrase]
TWO SENTENCES	We could see a small boat. It was tossing in the high waves.
ONE SENTENCE	We could see a small boat **tossing in the high waves.** [participial phrase]

EXERCISE 15 Combining Sentences

Number your paper 1 to 10. Then combine each pair of sentences into one sentence. Put the information in one sentence into a prepositional phrase or a participial phrase. Remember to add commas where needed.

1. Please get the fan. It is in the basement.
2. The batter hit the ball. It went into left field.
3. We watched a bird. It was building a nest in the tree.
4. We had a picnic. We held it at Hillside Park.
5. We live on a street. It is lined with tall buildings.
6. Brenda and Pauline found shelter in the barn. They stayed there during the unexpected storm.
7. My aunt sent this old clock. It was made in Germany.
8. The elephant is a large animal. It has a long trunk and large, floppy ears.
9. Tony has written a song. It is based on travels.
10. This evening, in a blaze of color, the sun set. It set behind those mountains.

*C*hapter *R*eview

A **Finding Prepositional Phrases.** Number your paper 1 to 10. Write each prepositional phrase. Then beside each one, write the word or words it modifies.

1. The rain beat against our windows.
2. The water below the cliff is deep and icy.
3. During the first inning, Curt made a home run.
4. At the museum we saw models of Indian homes.
5. With great speed she walked past the old house.
6. In the cave we searched for unusual crystals.
7. The decision will affect many areas within the city.
8. After their rapid climb up the hill, the hikers rested awhile.
9. The Choy family has moved into the new house with a two-car garage.
10. In one day a large oak tree expels approximately seven gallons of water through its leaves.

B **Finding Prepositional Phrases.** Number your paper 1 to 10. Write each prepositional phrase. Then label each one *adjective* or *adverb*.

The Pony Express

1. A private company started the Pony Express in 1860.
2. The company established a network of relay stations that were 10 or 15 miles apart.
3. Pony Express riders carried United States mail by horseback between California and Missouri.
4. At each station the rider transferred the mail to a fresh horse.
5. Each of the riders rode three horses.
6. Then a new rider at the next station took over.
7. The usual time for delivery was eight days.
8. The cost of this service was very high.
9. The Pony Express lasted for only 18 months.
10. The completion of the first transcontinental telegraph line abruptly ended the service.

C **Finding Participial Phrases.** Number your paper 1 to 10. Write each participial phrase. Then beside each one, write the word or words it modifies.

1. Facing the bull, the matador waved his red cape.
2. The temperature, rising since noon, is now 98 degrees.
3. These mittens, knit by my aunt, are now too small.
4. Using a telescope, Galileo could see the rings around Saturn.
5. Sitting up, Ginger begged for a dog biscuit.
6. The first steam locomotive in the United States was the *Tom Thumb*, built in 1830.
7. We had a wonderful campsite overlooking a lake.
8. Drumming on the telephone pole, the woodpecker dug a hole for its nest.
9. The sun's rays focused through glass can start a fire.
10. The spaniel, barking ferociously, raced through the tall grass after the rabbit.

Mastery Test

Number your paper 1 to 10. Then label each underlined phrase *prepositional* or *participial.*

1. On Friday we must go to the store.
2. The amount of gold dissolved in the oceans is nearly nine million tons.
3. There is a subway stop beyond that tall office building.
4. This is the quickest route to Maynard High School.
5. The African eagle, flying at over 100 miles per hour, can brake to a halt in 20 feet.
6. Do you ever walk in your sleep?
7. I have been making a model of a World War II plane.
8. The barge headed down the river.
9. Fully grown, a polar bear can be nine feet tall and weigh 1,000 pounds.
10. We watched the planes taking off down the runway.

Compound and Complex Sentences

*D*iagnostic *T*est

Number your paper 1 to 10. Then label each sentence *simple*, *compound*, or *complex*.

EXAMPLE   If you take the subway, get off at Park Avenue.
ANSWER   complex

1. Last Saturday my uncle appeared on television.
2. The sirens screeched, and the cars pulled over to the curb.
3. Redwoods produce bark that is more than a foot thick.
4. A penguin's wings are useless on land, but in the water they become effective paddles.
5. Before we can enter the theater, we must buy our tickets.
6. Greg ran down the court and dunked the ball into the basket.
7. The rings that surround Saturn are not solid.
8. The earth's crust burst open, and huge chunks of lava shot into the air.
9. Ruffy and Muffy growled at the stuffed panda.
10. After a butterfly egg ripens and hatches, out comes a caterpillar.

Independent and Subordinate Clauses

This chapter will explain three kinds of sentences: *simple*, *compound*, and *complex*. Before you can fully understand the different kinds of sentences, you must first learn about *clauses* and how they are used.

9a A **clause** is a group of words that has a subject and a verb.

There are two kinds of clauses: *independent clauses* and *subordinate clauses*.

9b An **independent (or main) clause** can stand alone as a sentence because it expresses a complete thought.

9c A **subordinate (or dependent) clause** cannot stand alone as a sentence because it does not express a complete thought.

In the following examples, each subject is underlined once, and each verb is underlined twice.

┌─independent clause─┐ ┌──independent clause──┐
He pulled the cord, and the stage curtains closed.

┌──subordinate clause──┐ ┌─independent clause─┐
After the storm passed, the air became cooler.

┌──independent clause──┐ ┌─subordinate clause─┐
I like the blue sweater that you bought me.

EXERCISE 1 Distinguishing between Clauses

Number your paper 1 to 10. Then label each underlined clause *independent* or *subordinate*.

Field Hockey

1. Panels that were carved by the ancient Greeks show players using crooked sticks to hit a small object.
2. Field hockey was played in Europe during the Middle Ages, but the game was once outlawed in England.

3. Field hockey interfered with archery training, <u>which was the basis of the national defense</u>.
4. <u>Even though field hockey was played worldwide after 1850</u>, it was never popular in the United States.
5. Although it became part of the Olympics in 1908, <u>field hockey was not organized in the United States until 1926</u>.
6. In that year Henry Greer arranged matches between teams <u>that were made up of men from New York</u>.
7. <u>While it is not certain</u>, the first men's field hockey match in the United States probably occurred in 1928.
8. <u>Because the U.S. Olympic committee wanted an American team</u>, it organized the men's hockey teams.
9. <u>The teams formed the Field Hockey Association of America in 1930</u>, and a team was sent to the 1932 Olympics.
10. <u>Field hockey is now very popular among women</u>, and many high schools and universities have a women's team.

*A*djective Clauses

A subordinate clause can be used the way a single adjective or an adjective phrase is used. Such a clause is called an *adjective clause.*

9d	An **adjective clause** is a subordinate clause that is used to modify a noun or a pronoun.

An adjective clause answers the adjective question *Which one?* or *What kind?* It usually modifies the word directly in front of it.

WHICH ONE? Ken's address book, **which is small and black,** is lost.

WHAT KIND? Cathy likes hamburgers **that are cooked on a charcoal grill.**

Relative Pronouns. Most adjective clauses begin with a relative pronoun. A *relative pronoun* relates an adjective clause to the noun or the pronoun the clause modifies.

Relative Pronouns				
who	whom	whose	which	that

I just met Cindy, **who is from Dallas, Texas.**

Barbara, **whose picture won first prize,** hopes to be an artist one day.

EXERCISE 2 *Finding Adjective Clauses*

Number your paper 1 to 10. Write each adjective clause. Then underline the relative pronoun.

EXAMPLE   I need the book that explains ecosystems.
ANSWER   <u>that</u> explains ecosystems

1. Many roads that the Romans built are still in use.
2. Ms. Morgan, whom you have not met, is the coach of the soccer team.
3. John F. Kennedy was the president who predicted a landing on the moon by United States astronauts.
4. Galileo, whose observations of the stars made history, eventually went blind.
5. The Boston Marathon, which is almost a 27-mile course, occurs each year in April.
6. Our mail carrier, whom we like so much, is retiring.
7. The beaver is one of the few animals that grow fat in the winter.
8. The composer who wrote this music comes from Italy.
9. The first Super Bowl game, which was played in 1967, was held at the Los Angeles Coliseum.
10. The hummingbird is a fearless fighter whose needle-sharp bill can drive off crows and hawks.

EXERCISE 3   Finding Adjective Clauses

Number your paper 1 to 10. Write each adjective clause and the word it modifies.

EXAMPLE   I enjoy the painting that hangs in the hall.
ANSWER   that hangs in the hall—painting

 1. Refined sugar is a food that has no nutrition.
 2. The boy whom you saw in the play is my brother.
 3. Sarah, whose essay won first prize, also paints.
 4. Volleyball, which was originally called *mintonette*, was invented in 1895.
 5. Ted, who is on the lacrosse team, is class president.
 6. The only thing that I need is my notebook.
 7. An elephant's trunk is really a big nose, which contains 40,000 muscles.
 8. My sister, whom I really admire, is a bookkeeper.
 9. The author whose books I enjoy most is Betsy Byars.
10. Beth, who is an architect, is also studying law.

Punctuation with Adjective Clauses

No punctuation is used with an adjective clause that contains information that is essential to identify a person, place, or thing in the sentence.

ESSENTIAL   A dog **that has black-and-white spots** was found in the park.

A comma or commas, however, should set off an adjective clause that is nonessential. A clause is nonessential if it can be removed from the sentence without changing the basic meaning of the sentence. A clause is usually nonessential if it modifies a proper noun.

NONESSENTIAL   The Janninos, **who moved here years ago,** are our best friends.

The relative pronoun *that* is used in an essential clause, and *which* is usually used in a nonessential clause.

EXERCISE 4 *Writing Sentences*

Add an independent clause to each adjective clause to make a complete sentence. Use commas where needed.

1. who finally arrived
2. which was performed by the seventh graders
3. whose dog was lost
4. that lasted two hours
5. whom I saw at the game

Misplaced Modifiers

Place an adjective clause as near as possible to the word it modifies. A clause that is too far away from the word it modifies is called a *misplaced modifier*.

MISPLACED   Mindy sold the dog **who runs a pet store.**

CORRECT   Mindy, **who runs a pet store,** sold the dog.

EXERCISE 5 *Correcting Misplaced Modifiers*

Number your paper 1 to 10. Then write the following sentences, correcting each misplaced modifier. Use commas where needed.

1. My mom now teaches my niece who taught me to read.
2. The Atlas Mountains are named after a strong mythological character which the Greeks discovered.
3. The bike is on the lawn that I got for my birthday.
4. The doctor saw me whom you recommended.
5. The skyscraper's windows reflected many buildings which were light blue.
6. The workers talked to my parents who were on strike.
7. Everyone swam in the lake who had hiked all day.
8. The ranger saw the bear who had the binoculars.
9. I bought a computer from Computer World which I paid for in installments.
10. Today I mowed the lawn and washed Mom's car which was almost half a foot high.

*A*dverb Clauses

A subordinate clause can be used the way a single adverb or an adverb phrase is used. Such a clause is called an *adverb clause.*

9e An **adverb clause** is a subordinate clause that is used mainly to modify a verb.

An adverb clause answers the adverb question *How? When? Where? Under what condition?* or *Why?*

HOW?	She walked **as though she had hurt her foot.**
WHEN?	**When the bell rings,** we will go into the auditorium.
WHERE?	We will meet **wherever we can find a room.**
UNDER WHAT CONDITION?	**If you have lost your schedule,** come to the office immediately.
WHY?	We missed the first act **because Anthony's watch had stopped.**

Subordinating Conjunctions. Adverb clauses begin with a *subordinating conjunction.*

Common Subordinating Conjunctions			
after	as soon as	in order that	until
although	as though	since	when
as	because	so that	whenever
as far as	before	than	where
as if	even though	though	wherever
as long as	if	unless	while

EXERCISE 6   Finding Adverb Clauses

Number your paper 1 to 10. Write each adverb clause. Then underline each subordinating conjunction.

1. Fish cannot close their eyes because they have no eyelids.
2. Before he invented the telegraph, Samuel F. B. Morse was a successful painter.
3. The Texas Rangers were organized while Texas was still a part of Mexico.
4. When the *Apollo 12* astronauts landed on the moon, the moon's surface vibrated for 55 minutes.
5. The barrel cactus has saved many lives in the desert, since the water in it is drinkable.
6. Although most people think of dinosaurs as huge monsters, some dinosaurs were quite small.
7. Zoos were originally opened so that people could see animals from faraway places.
8. Bees do not sting unless they are provoked.
9. If the earth were the size of a quarter, the sun would be the size of a nine-foot ball.
10. A fox's tail keeps the animal steady as it runs.

EXERCISE 7   Finding Adverb Clauses

Number your paper 1 to 10. Write each adverb clause. Then beside each one, write the word or words it modifies.

1. After you went inside, a shooting star appeared.
2. We will go to the station as soon as you call.
3. While he was at work, we decorated the hall.
4. Ted Williams began his professional career with the San Diego Padres when he was 16 years old.
5. David is acting as though nothing had happened.
6. We will meet you in the park unless it rains.
7. Whenever you hear the bell, you must leave quickly.
8. If you strung a pound of spider's threads end to end, they would circle the earth.
9. Speak loudly so that everyone can hear you.
10. Alan enjoyed the race even though he placed tenth.

Punctuation with Adverb Clauses

Always place a comma after an adverb clause that comes at the beginning of a sentence.

Since several members are absent, we cannot vote.

EXERCISE 8 *Writing Sentences*

Write a sentence for each adverb clause. Begin three sentences with an adverb clause. Use commas where needed.

1. as it rose in the air
2. if you phone before noon
3. although I will miss you
4. until I hear from you
5. when the game starts

TIME-OUT FOR REVIEW • • • •

Number your paper 1 to 10. Write each subordinate clause. Then label each clause *adjective* or *adverb*.

An Amazing Feat

1. Many swimmers have crossed the English Channel, which is 22 miles wide.
2. In 1961, Antonio Abertondo attempted something that no one else had ever done before.
3. Abertondo, who was 42 years old, swam across the English Channel and back again without a stop!
4. When he arrived at Dover Beach, he was covered with grease for protection against the cold water.
5. He swam steadily for the next 18 hours and 50 minutes until he reached the French coast.
6. After he sipped a hot drink, he headed back to England.
7. Because Abertondo eventually became extremely tired, he had hallucinations.
8. During the hallucinations, he saw huge sharks, which were swimming all around him.
9. When he finally reached the English coast, he had been swimming for 43 hours and 15 minutes.
10. The last mile, which had taken him two hours, had been the hardest.

Kinds of Sentence Structure

The ability to recognize independent and subordinate clauses will help you understand sentence structure. There are three kinds of sentences: *simple, compound,* and *complex.*

9f ▶ A **simple sentence** consists of one independent clause.

Terry caught several fish in the mountain stream.
The cat pounced on the ball of yarn.

A *compound sentence* is two or more sentences that are usually joined by the conjunction *and, but, or,* or *yet.*

9g ▶ A **compound sentence** consists of two or more independent clauses.

Each independent clause in a compound sentence can stand alone as a separate sentence.

┌── independent clause ──┐   ┌── independent clause ──┐
Lori pitched the ball, and Albert hit a home run.

┌── independent clause ──┐   ┌── independent clause ──┐
The actors are ready, but the director is not here.

EXERCISE 9 Recognizing Simple and Compound Sentences

Number your paper 1 to 10. Copy each sentence. Draw one line under each subject and two lines under each verb. Then label each sentence *simple* or *compound.*

People and
Animal
Facts

1. Color-blind people cannot distinguish between the colors red and green.
2. Moths usually fly at night, and butterflies fly during the day.
3. A lobster may easily replace a lost claw.
4. The brown pelican dives for fish, but the white pelican scoops the fish from the water's surface.

5. The earthworm has no lungs.
6. The fastest land animal is the cheetah.
7. The walrus is a marine animal like a seal.
8. Most insects have feelers and wings, but spiders do not have either.
9. A grain of sand in the shell of an oyster may eventually become a pearl.
10. The human brain is smarter, but the computer works faster.

Compound Sentence or Compound Verb?   Sometimes a compound sentence is mistaken for a simple sentence that has a compound verb.

COMPOUND SENTENCE   The <u>captain</u> <u>blew</u> the whistle, and the <u>boat</u> <u>moved</u> away from the dock.

COMPOUND VERB   The <u>captain</u> <u>blew</u> the whistle and <u>steered</u> the boat away from the dock.

EXERCISE 10   Distinguishing between Simple and Compound Sentences

Number your paper 1 to 15. Then label each sentence *simple* or *compound*.

1. The Jamestown colonists dug a well and cleared land for their spring gardens.
2. Mom works every day and travels occasionally.
3. Dogs are the most popular American pets, but cats run a close second.
4. The flowers of the peanut are formed above the ground, but the peanuts ripen below the surface.
5. The stalks actually bend downward, and the peanuts grow under the ground.
6. Chief Powhatan and his warriors spared Captain John Smith's life and adopted him into their tribe.
7. A chipmunk scampered across the road and disappeared into the woods.

8. Evergreen trees have cones, but other seed plants have flowers.
9. The ranger tied his horse to a tree and started down the hill toward the wounded fawn.
10. Suddenly the clock struck four, but many of the workers needed more time for their tasks.
11. The children left the school fair and went to the playground near their homes.
12. At the party the guests took slips of paper, and everyone went on a scavenger hunt.
13. He read his paragraph, crossed out several lines, and rewrote the ending.
14. The crowd cheered the team and tossed their hats into the air.
15. Jennie had made plans for the movies, but then her aunt invited her to dinner.

Punctuation with Compound Sentences

There are several ways to connect the independent clauses in a compound sentence. One way is to join them with a comma and a conjunction. (*See page 252.*)

I left school at 3:30, **but** Anne stayed for softball practice until 6:00.

You can also join independent clauses with a semicolon and no conjunction. (*See page 281.*)

The Rangers won the pennant; the Blue Jays lost first place in the league for the first time in three years.

EXERCISE 11 *Writing Sentences*

Write five compound sentences about your favorite sport. Use the conjunctions *and, but, or,* and *yet.* Then write a compound sentence without a conjunction. Remember to use the proper punctuation.

Complex Sentences

If you can recognize independent and subordinate clauses, you can also recognize complex sentences.

9h ▶ A **complex sentence** consists of one independent clause and one or more subordinate clauses.

```
      ┌──── adverb clause ────┐ ┌──── independent clause ────┐
      Since we have extra time, we can walk to the movies.
```

```
      ┌───── independent clause ─────┐ ┌──── adjective clause────┐
      I have already finished my report that is due on Friday.
```

EXERCISE 12   Distinguishing between Sentences

Number your paper 1 to 10. Then label each sentence *compound* or *complex*.

Things That Move

1. The first steam-driven cars were unpopular because they were noisy and dirtied the air with smoke.
2. The first postal trucks were made so that a mule could replace a failed engine.
3. An electric car gets its power from a battery, but the battery must constantly be recharged.
4. Electric cars were popular in the 1890s and 1900s, but cars with gasoline engines soon replaced them.
5. Although people had hired vehicles for thousands of years, the word *taxicab* wasn't used until the 1800s.
6. The longest bicycle, which was built for 35, was made in Denmark in 1976.
7. The bicycle weighed more than a ton, and it was 72 feet long.
8. Some astronauts who went to the moon traveled in a lunar rover.
9. A lunar rover looks something like a jeep, but a rover's top and sides are completely open.
10. Since a lunar rover has no engine, it runs on power from a battery.

EXERCISE 13 Writing Sentences

Number your paper 1 to 5. Write five sentences that follow the directions below. Use punctuation where needed.

1. Write a simple sentence with a compound verb.
2. Write a compound sentence that contains the conjunction *but*.
3. Write a compound sentence that contains a semicolon.
4. Write a complex sentence that includes one adverb clause.
5. Write a complex sentence that includes one adjective clause.

TIME-OUT FOR REVIEW • • • • •

Number your paper 1 to 10. Then label each sentence *simple, compound,* or *complex.*

A Great
Artist

1. Charles Willson Peale never saw a painting until he was a grown man.
2. He was a saddlemaker by trade and lived in Annapolis, Maryland.
3. One day Peale went to Norfolk for supplies and saw paintings for the first time.
4. He did not like any of the paintings; they did not look realistic.
5. When he returned home, he took up painting with a great deal of energy and talent.
6. He took lessons in Boston and even went to London for more lessons.
7. After he had made some money from his paintings, he became a full-time painter.
8. Peale loved painting, but his enjoyment was not enough for him.
9. He taught his skills to his 17 children and all his relatives and created a family of artists.
10. Charles Willson Peale became the famous patriot painter who painted George Washington's portrait.

Diagraming Sentences

All simple sentences have one baseline. Diagrams for compound and complex sentences, however, have two or more baselines. Each clause has its own baseline.

Compound Sentences.   These sentences are diagramed the way two simple sentences are. The baselines of the separate sentences, however, are joined by a broken line on which the conjunction is placed. The broken line connects the verbs.

Dad enjoys movies, but Mom prefers the theater.

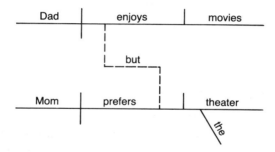

Complex Sentences.   In a complex sentence, an adverb clause is diagramed beneath the independent clause. The subordinating conjunction belongs on a broken line that connects the verb in the adverb clause to the word the clause modifies.

After I watch the news, I am going to bed.

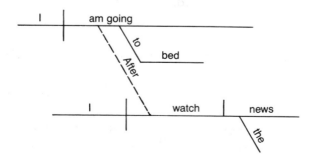

138

An adjective clause is also diagramed beneath the independent clause. The relative pronoun is connected by a broken line to the noun or the pronoun the clause modifies. A relative pronoun can be the subject of the clause.

The dancer who appeared in the lead role is my friend.

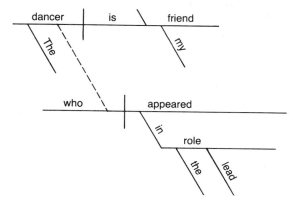

EXERCISE 14   Diagraming Sentences

Diagram the following sentences or copy them. If your teacher tells you to copy them, draw one line under each subject and two lines under each verb. Put parentheses around each subordinate clause. Then label each subordinate clause *adverb* or *adjective*.

1. A snail has no legs, but it does have a foot.
2. Stan will collect tickets, and Diane will usher.
3. I have an opal in my ring, and it cracked.
4. The house was dark, but we heard music in the backyard.
5. Before the rain started, I closed the car windows.
6. We stayed at a cabin that stood under the redwood trees.
7. When an explosion damaged the ship, the captain radioed for help.
8. Mrs. O'Reilly, who just moved here, will teach the new computer course.
9. You can go to the concert if your work is finished.
10. The movie, which is playing at Cinerama, is very funny.

Application to Writing

In the editing stage of your writing, look at the kinds of sentences you have written. If most of your sentences are simple sentences, combine some of them into compound or complex sentences. Then your writing will have more variety and be more interesting to read.

TWO SIMPLE SENTENCES
We practiced until five o'clock. Then the coach talked about next week's game.

A COMPOUND SENTENCE
We practiced until five o'clock, **and** then the coach talked about next week's game. [The two sentences have been joined by a comma and the conjunction *and*.]

TWO SIMPLE SENTENCES
We finally reached the dock. Then the storm broke.

A COMPLEX SENTENCE
When we finally reached the dock, the storm broke. [The first sentence has been changed into an adverb clause.]

TWO SIMPLE SENTENCES
Otters love the water. They do not feel at home in dry places.

A COMPLEX SENTENCE
Otters, **which love the water,** do not feel at home in dry places. [Part of one sentence has been changed into an adjective clause.]

EXERCISE 15   Combining Sentences

Number your paper 1 to 10. Then combine each pair of sentences into a compound sentence. Use a comma or a semicolon where needed.

1. Morning glories are open wide at sunrise. Strong light often closes the blossoms before noon.
2. After the play we went backstage. Some of the actors gave us their autographs.
3. Moths don't eat your clothes. Some moth caterpillars do.

4. The pitcher threw the ball high. The batter slammed it.
5. The collie is a nervous dog. It is a good companion.
6. Monkeys, apes, and humans are primates. Human primates have the most highly developed brain.
7. I enjoyed our visit to Minnesota. Adam preferred our visit to Wisconsin.
8. John Adams was the second president. Thomas Jefferson was his vice-president.
9. The Tigers wanted the state championship. The Bears were too good for them.
10. Sprains occur in the ligaments. Strains occur in the muscles.

EXERCISE 16 Combining Sentences

Number your paper 1 to 10. Then combine each pair of sentences into a complex sentence. Use commas where needed.

1. We were walking by the river. We skimmed stones across the surface of the water.
2. Spanish missionaries settled in California. They planted the first orchards in America.
3. Clay feels very smooth. It actually is powdered rock.
4. Madison High will close this year. It is across town.
5. Bees can see ultraviolet rays. The rays are invisible to the human eye.
6. In colonial days mail was carried by a postrider. He rode horseback from city to city.
7. Adobe consists of clay and sand. It dries without a crack.
8. I tracked mud across the kitchen floor. Mom handed me the mop.
9. Judy Mason is a student at Kendall Middle School. She takes gymnastic lessons with me.
10. W. D. Boyce visited the English Boy Scouts. Then he organized the Boy Scouts of America.

Chapter Review

A **Finding Subordinate Clauses.** Number your paper 1 to 10. Write each subordinate clause. Then next to each clause, write the word or words it modifies.

1. As soon as the bell rings, I will eat lunch.
2. My ankle, which I sprained last month, still hurts.
3. We must find the people whose car is blocking ours.
4. Steve can't eat now because he has a swim meet.
5. I swam a mile before I felt tired.
6. I know Mr. Myers, whom you mentioned in your note.
7. When my dog doesn't recognize a visitor, she barks.
8. Anne, who raises beagles, won three blue ribbons.
9. Don't put the glass where it will get broken.
10. The first baseball game that was a tie occurred in 1854.

B **Finding Adjective and Adverb Clauses.** Number your paper 1 to 10. Write each subordinate clause. Then label each one *adjective* or *adverb*.

Unusual and Unused Inventions

1. Because chickens peck at each other, someone invented chicken glasses.
2. The glasses, which extend to the back of a chicken's neck, protect its eyes.
3. An alarm clock was invented for people who don't get up in the morning.
4. The clock has 60 little wooden blocks that hang over a person's head.
5. When the alarm rings, the blocks drop down and hit the sleeping person.
6. If you are ever caught in a burning building, you will want the following invention.
7. You can buy a hat which is attached to a parachute.
8. It comes with padded shoes that soften the landing.
9. A twirling spaghetti fork's handle has a small wheel that you can move with your thumb.
10. As the fork spins around, it rolls up the spaghetti.

C **Identifying Simple, Compound, and Complex Sentences.** Number your paper 1 to 10. Then label each sentence *simple, compound,* or *complex*.

1. If the ice on the south polar cap melted, the water would cover the Statue of Liberty up to her nose.
2. The waves crashed, and the sandpipers ran toward them.
3. Al climbed over the stone wall that bordered the farm.
4. The sphinx moth curls up its tongue and uses it as a pillow.
5. The center lost the ball, and five players fell on it.
6. We left for the train station but had a flat tire.
7. A fly can walk upside down on a ceiling because it has special pads on each of its six feet.
8. Although the weather was bad, we kept playing.
9. Eskimos buy refrigerators so that food won't freeze.
10. A spider spins a web of silk that it makes inside its body.

*M*astery *T*est

Number your paper 1 to 10. Then label each sentence *simple, compound,* or *complex*.

1. If you cut a starfish into pieces, each piece will grow into a whole starfish.
2. Santa Fe is one of the oldest capital cities in the United States, but New Mexico is one of the youngest states.
3. Even though he snacks often, Matt always seems hungry.
4. We rode to Belmont Park and ate our lunch there.
5. The second president who came from Virginia is Thomas Jefferson.
6. The sky was gray, and a light rain started.
7. Soccer, which is my best sport, is popular at school.
8. The World Series begins Monday, and I have four tickets.
9. The team put on helmets and entered the rink.
10. People like the praying mantis because it eats many harmful insects.

Sound Sentences

Diagnostic Test

Number your paper 1 to 10. Then label each group of words *sentence, fragment,* or *run-on.*

EXAMPLE · An exciting book about wild horses.
ANSWER   fragment

1. Mike dribbled the ball down the court, suddenly the referee blew his whistle.
2. Anderson Ranch Dam in Idaho controls floods and produces electrical power.
3. The huge red sun behind the High Sierra at sunset.
4. In the dentist's quiet office.
5. Jean jumped off the float within six minutes she was on the beach.
6. As we drove through the long, dark tunnel.
7. Playing a trumpet on the roof of the apartment building.
8. In Washington, D. C., we visited the White House and attended a session of Congress.
9. Brazil is the largest country in South America it is larger than the continent of Australia.
10. Thomas wading through waist-high water at the pool.

Sentence Fragments

When you edit your writing, the first thing you should do is look for any sentence errors. One common sentence error is called a *sentence fragment*.

10a   A **sentence fragment** is a group of words that does not express a complete thought.

To express a complete thought, a sentence must have a subject and a verb. Study the sentence fragments below.

NO SUBJECT   <u>Made</u> a model of a ship. [Who made a model?]

SENTENCE   <u>Fred</u> <u>made</u> a model of a ship.

NO VERB   The <u>players</u> on our baseball squad. [What do they do?]

SENTENCE   The <u>players</u> on our baseball squad <u>practice</u> every afternoon.

Occasionally a phrase will look long enough to be a sentence. Because a phrase has no subject or verb, however, it must not be written as a sentence.

PREPOSITIONAL PHRASE   Near the white fence.

SENTENCE   <u>We</u> <u>waited</u> **near the white fence.**

PARTICIPIAL PHRASE   Hiding in the tree.

SENTENCE   <u>I</u> <u>saw</u> the cat **hiding in the tree.**

A subordinate clause may also look like a sentence because it has a subject and a verb. When it stands alone, however, it is a fragment because it does not express a complete thought.

ADVERB CLAUSE   Before <u>class</u> <u>began</u>.

SENTENCE   **Before <u>class</u> <u>began</u>,** <u>Jed</u> <u>hid</u> the gift.

ADJECTIVE CLAUSE   That <u>she</u> <u>bought</u>.

SENTENCE   <u>I</u> <u>love</u> the hat **that <u>she</u> <u>bought</u>.**

EXERCISE 1 *Recognizing Sentence Fragments*

Number your paper 1 to 10. Then label each group of words *sentence* or *fragment*.

1. Visited my cousins Marianna and Roberto.
2. A dachshund with short, fat legs.
3. Modern shorthand was invented in 1837.
4. Which was discovered in Yellowstone National Park.
5. Salt was once used for money.
6. Under the back porch.
7. On the top of the refrigerator perched our cat.
8. After lightning struck the chestnut tree.
9. Watching the start of the Boston Marathon.
10. We lost.

Ways to Correct Sentence Fragments

You can correct a sentence fragment in one of two ways. You can attach it to the sentence before or after it. You can also make a sentence fragment into a separate sentence by adding the words needed to make a complete thought.

SENTENCE AND FRAGMENT	I live in an apartment building. Near the Mystic River.
ATTACHED	I live in an apartment building **near the Mystic River.**
SEPARATE SENTENCES	I live in an apartment building. **It is located near the Mystic River.**
SENTENCE AND FRAGMENT	We watched the ship. Sailing into the harbor.
ATTACHED	We watched the ship **sailing into the harbor.**
SEPARATE SENTENCES	We watched the ship. **It was sailing into the harbor.**
SENTENCE AND FRAGMENT	The students responded immediately. When the fire alarm rang.
ATTACHED	The students responded immediately **when the fire alarm rang.**

EXERCISE 2 Correcting Sentence Fragments

Number your paper 1 to 10. Correct each sentence fragment. Add punctuation where needed.

EXAMPLE   Tim stopped. And picked up the trash.
POSSIBLE ANSWER   Tim stopped and picked up the trash.

1. Some starfish have small bodies. With long arms.
2. After he finished dinner. Mark walked for a mile.
3. We were driving down Temple Street. When suddenly a truck pulled out from a driveway in front of us.
4. The gymnast jumped the highest. And won first place.
5. Riding the waves. The surfer approached the shore.
6. Ray watched the birds. That perched on the feeder.
7. I found Skippy's biscuits. In the last grocery bag.
8. Since Bruce bought a face mask. He enjoys snorkeling.
9. Moving slowly through the fog. The boat reached the shore.
10. We saw many wild flowers. On our walk through the woods.

EXERCISE 3 Writing Sentences

Number your paper 1 to 10. Make each fragment a complete sentence by adding any necessary words. Add capital letters, commas, and end marks where needed.

EXAMPLE   The new hotel in town
POSSIBLE ANSWER   The new hotel in town has a ballroom.

1. a small restaurant on the corner
2. caught a fish in the pond
3. at the outdoor swimming pool
4. loudly cheered the victorious football players
5. from a favorite relative
6. the comics in the Sunday newspaper
7. walking the dog each evening
8. because rain, sleet, or snow is predicted
9. that he saw in the store window
10. after the truck came to an abrupt halt

Run-on Sentences

Another kind of sentence error is called a *run-on sentence*.

10b A **run-on sentence** is two or more sentences that are written as one sentence. They are separated by a comma or no mark of punctuation at all.

Run-on sentences can be confusing to read because it is not clear where one idea ends and another idea begins.

RUN-ON SENTENCE	The <u>tide</u> <u>is rising</u>, <u>it</u> <u>will reach</u> its highest level at 6:37.
RUN-ON SENTENCE	<u>Danny</u> <u>missed</u> the shot a <u>member</u> of the other team <u>got</u> the rebound.

EXERCISE 4   Recognizing Run-on Sentences

Number your paper 1 to 10. Then label each group of words *sentence* or *run-on*.

1. Normally your heart beats 70 to 80 times a minute that comes to more than 36 million beats a year.
2. The club members raised money and held a picnic.
3. Some hawks nest on high cliffs, a few have even nested on the ledges of tall buildings.
4. The woman hailed a cab and arrived in the city on time.
5. My sister's birthday is this month, next month is my birthday.
6. Lions rest during the day and hunt for food at night.
7. Make a fist with your hand, that's about the size of your heart.
8. The baseball soared over the fence and landed in the bleachers.
9. A hornet is a kind of wasp, it is related to the bee family.
10. Our school colors are blue and orange I prefer blue and white.

Ways to Correct Run-on Sentences

Basically there are three ways to correct a run-on sentence. You can change a run-on sentence into separate sentences or into a compound or a complex sentence.

RUN-ON SENTENCE   A few actors forgot their lines the play was still a success.

SEPARATE SENTENCES   A few actors forgot their lines. The play was still a success.

COMPOUND SENTENCE   A few actors forgot their lines, but the play was still a success.

NOTE: If the run-on sentence already has a comma, simply add the proper conjunction.

COMPLEX SENTENCE   Although a few actors forgot their lines, the play was still a success.

EXERCISE 5   Correcting Run-on Sentences

Number your paper 1 to 10. Correct each run-on sentence. Either write each one as separate sentences or write each one as a compound sentence, using a conjunction and a comma. Remember to add capital letters and end marks where needed.

EXAMPLE   A crocodile and an alligator look similar a crocodile has a narrower nose.

POSSIBLE ANSWER   A crocodile and an alligator look similar, but a crocodile has a narrower nose.

1. I dropped the bag of groceries the eggs and jars did not break.
2. Ostriches cannot fly they can run almost as fast as a horse.
3. The temperature was in the nineties, everyone went for a swim.
4. Camels are excellent desert animals, some can hold more water than the gasoline tank of an average car.

149

5. Jennifer gave her sister Sarah a long blue sweater it fit her perfectly.
6. I will be home after school at three o'clock, I may decide to stay for band practice.
7. Koalas aren't bears, they belong to the same family as kangaroos.
8. Lynn came to the party she was unable to stay longer than two hours.
9. Thanksgiving was fun, we had 18 people for dinner.
10. Pam collects china animals she likes miniatures best.

EXERCISE 6   Correcting Run-on Sentences

Number your paper 1 to 10. Correct each run-on sentence. Write each one as a complex sentence by adding a subordinating conjunction or a relative pronoun. Add capital letters and punctuation as needed.

EXAMPLE   We camped last weekend the tent collapsed.
POSSIBLE   When we camped last weekend, the tent
ANSWER   collapsed.

1. The alarm clock rang at 6:00 A.M. Jim pulled the covers over his head.
2. The brontosaurus weighed as much as ten elephants it ate only plants.
3. The hikers followed a narrow trail it brought them to a mysterious cave.
4. We were late for the concert, we waited in the lobby.
5. My sister Janet is a lawyer she specializes in international law.
6. Highway 80 was closed power lines were down from the storm.
7. Spiders are not true insects, they look like insects.
8. Christopher ate his supper he walked the dog and finished his science report.
9. The Nineteenth Amendment gave women the right to vote it was approved in 1920.
10. I am wearing a locket it belonged to my grandmother.

TIME-OUT FOR REVIEW • • • • •

Number your paper 1 to 15. Then correct each sentence fragment or run-on sentence. Add capital letters, conjunctions, and punctuation marks where needed.

EXAMPLE   The octopus is a mollusk. Which belongs to a group of shellfish including snails and clams.

ANSWER   The octopus, which belongs to a group of shellfish including snails and clams, is a mollusk.

The Octopus

1. There are 50 kinds of octopuses most are no bigger than a person's fist.
2. An octopus has three hearts. That pump blood through its body.
3. An octopus has a big head. With hardly any neck.
4. The word *octopus* comes from two Greek words. That mean "eight feet."
5. An octopus has eight arms, an eye is in each arm.
6. Under each arm an octopus has little suction cups, with them it can climb and hold on to things.
7. An octopus has no real bones in its body. And can easily change its shape.
8. Stretching itself out like a piece of rubber. An octopus can squeeze between cracks in the rocks.
9. Octopuses live in the rocks. On the ocean floor.
10. An octopus is a shy creature. That avoids its enemies in several ways.
11. An octopus squirts out a black ink, then it hides in the dark, cloudy water.
12. The skin of an octopus contains small bags of pigments. That connect with its nervous system.
13. When an octopus is in danger. It can change its color from shades of pink to gray.
14. Some octopuses inject a poison. That paralyzes their prey.
15. The octopus sees well it has the most highly developed brain of any animal without a backbone.

*A*pplication to Writing

When you are looking for sentence errors in your writing, always read your work *aloud*. Your natural voice rhythms will help you find most sentence fragments and run-on sentences.

When you correct sentence errors, do not always write them as separate sentences. Instead, attach some fragments to other sentences and turn some run-on sentences into compound or complex sentences. Good writing includes different kinds of sentences.

EXERCISE 7 *Editing for Sentence Errors*

Rewrite the following paragraphs, correcting each sentence fragment and each run-on sentence. Add capital letters, conjunctions, and punctuation marks where needed.

Burr!

During the earth's long history. Much of the world has been covered with ice. The last ice age occurred about 2,500,000 years ago. Four times great sheets of ice advanced over the land, four times the ice melted and drew back.

Covering a large part of North America. The last advance ended about 18,000 years ago. Giant ice sheets reached as far south as the present site of New York City. Then the ice gradually disappeared. Some of it evaporated directly into the air, some melted. About 6,000 years ago. The continents of the Northern Hemisphere were almost free of ice.

Great changes on the earth during the advances of the ice. Air and ocean temperatures fell. Places that are now deserts were well watered. And covered with plant life. Since great quantities of water were trapped in glaciers on land. Sea levels fell hundreds of feet. Is another ice age coming? Scientists do not know the answer to this question. Because they still must discover the causes of ice ages.

*C*hapter *R*eview

A **Correcting Sentence Fragments.** Number your paper 1 to 10. Then correct each sentence fragment. Add capital letters and punctuation marks where needed.

1. Beginning in the nineteenth century. Ice hockey was first played in eastern Canada.
2. We found a battered trunk. In the old red barn.
3. Before you go to bed. Please lock the front door.
4. Dad was in the yard. When the phone rang.
5. We could see the horses. Jumping over the fence.
6. Swimming for hours. We enjoyed our day at the beach.
7. I lost my purse. But found the car keys on the lawn.
8. The score was tied. Between Weston and Newton High.
9. In the museum. We saw our first mummy.
10. Six-day bicycle races were a fad. In the early 1900s.

B **Correcting Run-on Sentences.** Number your paper 1 to 10. Then correct each run-on sentence. Add capital letters, conjunctions, and punctuation marks where needed.

1. Duluth is about 2,000 miles from the Atlantic, its harbor is reached through the St. Lawrence Seaway.
2. I always buy mysteries I love to read them.
3. The winter Olympics were held in Japan in 1972, this was the first time these games had been held in Asia.
4. The American Revolution began in 1775 it ended in 1783.
5. Most of the snakes in the United States are harmless, many of them benefit farmers.
6. I am on a diet I eat salads, fish, and vegetables.
7. Alexander Hamilton's picture is on the ten-dollar bill, Andrew Jackson's is on the twenty.
8. Bill lifts weights, he trains every day.
9. The first Academy Awards ceremony was held in 1927 only 250 people attended.
10. Martin takes Latin he studies an hour a night.

C **Correcting Sentence Errors.** Rewrite the following paragraphs, correcting each sentence fragment and run-on sentence. Add capital letters, conjunctions, and punctuation marks where needed.

When
Space
Travel
Began

The world gasped on the morning of October 4, 1957. When Russia's *Sputnik 1* was successfully launched. Launched a month later. *Sputnik 2* carried a little dog named Laika. With increased pressure on the United States, *Explorer 1* finally got off the ground at Cape Canaveral. On January 31, 1958.

Under the direction of President John F. Kennedy. The newly organized National Aeronautics and Space Administration set a ten-year goal, it was to place a man on the moon. The first phase of this goal was the Mercury program. Which included John Glenn's first orbital flight in 1962. Then in 1968, the first Apollo crew circled the moon, seven months later the *Eagle* landed on the moon.

Mastery Test

Number your paper 1 to 10. Then label each group of words *sentence*, *fragment*, or *run-on*.

1. Whiskers sat at the back door, her feet were covered with mud.
2. Although the mountain peaks seem miles away.
3. Inside the yellow school bus.
4. The herd of cattle stretching out over the hillside.
5. The Nile Valley is rich farmland, there farmers grow cotton and other crops.
6. Red, white, and blue fireworks over the water.
7. It was almost dark when we reached the foothills.
8. Impatiently we awaited the ferry, suddenly it appeared through the thick fog.
9. Leaping suddenly over the pasture fence.
10. The first patent for a bicycle was issued in 1866.

Standardized Test

Directions: Decide which description best fits each group of words. In the appropriate row on your answer sheet, fill in the circle containing the same letter as your answer.

SAMPLE   Looking for a book about China.

   A fragment   **B** run-on   **C** sentence

ANSWER   Ⓐ Ⓑ Ⓒ

1. Finding a pair of glasses.

   A fragment   **B** run-on   **C** sentence

2. He is leaving now.

   A fragment   **B** run-on   **C** sentence

3. The lamp with the pink shade.

   A fragment   **B** run-on   **C** sentence

4. The banana isn't ripe yet.

   A fragment   **B** run-on   **C** sentence

5. Frank carried the suitcases, I carried the dog.

   A fragment   **B** run-on   **C** sentence

6. In the eighth week of the drought.

   A fragment   **B** run-on   **C** sentence

7. Three people called Anna was not one of them.

   A fragment   **B** run-on   **C** sentence

8. In the top of the ninth inning, everything changed.

   A fragment   **B** run-on   **C** sentence

9. Flora rode her bicycle, Jess jogged behind her.

   A fragment   **B** run-on   **C** sentence

10. A rare photograph of a gorilla with its baby.

    A fragment   **B** run-on   **C** sentence

Directions: Decide which underlined part is the subject in each sentence. On your answer sheet, fill in the circle containing the same letter as your answer.

SAMPLE   The <u>thunder</u> <u>frightened</u> the <u>horses</u>.
                  A   B   C

ANSWER   Ⓐ Ⓑ Ⓒ

11. The <u>chef</u> <u>grilled</u> the <u>steak</u>.
         A   B   C

12. The <u>quiet</u> <u>audience</u> waited for the <u>announcement</u>.
         A   B   C

13. <u>Have</u> <u>you</u> solved the <u>puzzle</u>?
     A   B   C

14. A <u>box</u> of <u>cereal</u> had fallen on the <u>floor</u>.
       A   B   C

15. <u>On</u> her <u>head</u> sat a peculiar flat <u>hat</u>.
     A   B   C

Directions: Decide which underlined part is the verb in each sentence. On your answer sheet, fill in the circle containing the same letter as your answer.

SAMPLE   Andrew <u>lifted</u> the <u>box</u> <u>carefully</u>.
                     A   B   C

ANSWER   Ⓐ Ⓑ Ⓒ

16. Laurie <u>found</u> the <u>road</u> <u>easily</u>.
                A   B   C

17. <u>They</u> <u>are</u> <u>skillful</u> carpenters.
     A   B   C

18. Our math <u>teacher</u> <u>always</u> <u>gives</u> homework.
                  A   B   C

19. <u>Around</u> the track <u>jogged</u> twelve <u>runners</u>.
     A   B   C

20. <u>Are</u> <u>you</u> definitely in the <u>race</u>?
     A   B   C

UNIT 2

Usage

11

Using Verbs

Diagnostic Test

Number your paper 1 to 10. Then write the correct verb form for each sentence.

EXAMPLE   Mom and Dad (came, come) to the baseball
          game.
ANSWER   came

1. We (saw, seen) bears at Yellowstone National Park.
2. My science class has (went, gone) to the Museum of Natural History twice this year.
3. The winds had (blowed, blown) the balloonists to a small island.
4. Have you (wrote, written) your poem yet?
5. Mozart (began, begun) giving concerts at the age of six.
6. Has Mary Lou (spoke, spoken) to you about the party?
7. Overnight the milk had (froze, frozen) outside.
8. Matthew (give, gave) some freshly picked blackberries to Mr. Jameson.
9. Mayard (did, done) an interesting experiment in science class yesterday.
10. Have you ever (fell, fallen) off a horse?

158

The Principal Parts of Verbs

A verb not only shows action or tells something about its subject, but it also tells when something happened.

PRESENT ACTION	Every day I **give** Bowser his food.
PAST ACTION	Yesterday I **gave** Bowser his food.
FUTURE ACTION	Tomorrow I **will give** Bowser his food.

Different forms of a verb can express different times. These different forms of a verb are called the *tense* of a verb. From the four main forms of a verb, called the *principal parts*, all of the different tenses of a verb are developed.

> **11a** The **principal parts** of a verb are the *present*, the *present participle*, the *past*, and the *past participle*.

Regular Verbs

Most verbs form their past and past participle the same way. These verbs are called *regular verbs*.

> **11b** A **regular verb** forms its past and past participle by adding *-ed* or *-d* to the present.

Following are the principal parts of the regular verbs *wish* and *skip*. Notice that the *p* is doubled when *-ing* and *-ed* are added to *skip*.

PRESENT	wish	skip
PRESENT PARTICIPLE	(is) wish**ing**	(is) skip**ping**
PAST	wish**ed**	skip**ped**
PAST PARTICIPLE	(have) wish**ed**	(have) skip**ped**

NOTE: When the present or past participle is used as a main verb, it is always joined with a helping verb. (*See page 46 for a list of helping verbs.*)

EXERCISE 1 Writing the Principal Parts of Regular Verbs

Make four columns on your paper. Label them *present, present participle, past,* and *past participle.* Then write the four principal parts of each of the following regular verbs. Use *is* with the present participle and *have* with the past participle.

1. talk	3. move	5. use	7. drop	9. knock
2. ask	4. jump	6. stop	8. play	10. suppose

EXERCISE 2 Writing Sentences

Write the principal parts of the regular verbs *start, row,* and *wrap.* Then write a sentence for each of those principal parts.

Irregular Verbs

A few verbs, called *irregular verbs,* form their past and past participle differently from regular verbs.

11c An **irregular verb** does not form its past and past participle by adding *-ed* or *-d* to the present.

Irregular verbs can be divided into groups according to the way they form their past and past participles.

Group 1

These irregular verbs have the same form for the present, the past, and the past participle.

PRESENT	PRESENT PARTICIPLE	PAST	PAST PARTICIPLE
burst	bursting	burst	(have) burst
cost	costing	cost	(have) cost
hit	hitting	hit	(have) hit
put	putting	put	(have) put
let	letting	let	(have) let

160

Group 2

These irregular verbs have the same form for the past and the past participle.

PRESENT	PRESENT PARTICIPLE	PAST	PAST PARTICIPLE
bring	bringing	brought	(have) brought
buy	buying	bought	(have) bought
catch	catching	caught	(have) caught
make	making	made	(have) made
say	saying	said	(have) said
leave	leaving	left	(have) left
lose	losing	lost	(have) lost
teach	teaching	taught	(have) taught

EXERCISE 3 Using the Correct Verb Form

Number your paper 1 to 10. Then label each underlined verb form *past* or *past participle*. Remember that a helping verb is used with a past participle.

1. I <u>made</u> the honor roll last term.
2. Who <u>let</u> the dog out of the house?
3. Have you <u>brought</u> an umbrella?
4. The door <u>burst</u> open.
5. Greg has <u>lost</u> the name tags for the open house.
6. I have <u>taught</u> my younger sister to swim.
7. The repairs <u>cost</u> two hundred dollars.
8. Mom has <u>said</u> that several times before.
9. Who <u>left</u> the living room windows open?
10. Kenneth has <u>caught</u> a bad cold.

Group 3

These irregular verbs form the past participle by adding -*n* to the past.

PRESENT	PRESENT PARTICIPLE	PAST	PAST PARTICIPLE
break	breaking	broke	(have) broken
choose	choosing	chose	(have) chosen
freeze	freezing	froze	(have) frozen
speak	speaking	spoke	(have) spoken
steal	stealing	stole	(have) stolen

Group 4

These irregular verbs form the past participle by adding *-n* to the present.

PRESENT	PRESENT PARTICIPLE	PAST	PAST PARTICIPLE
blow	blowing	blew	(have) blown
draw	drawing	drew	(have) drawn
drive	driving	drove	(have) driven
give	giving	gave	(have) given
grow	growing	grew	(have) grown
know	knowing	knew	(have) known
rise	rising	rose	(have) risen
see	seeing	saw	(have) seen
take	taking	took	(have) taken
throw	throwing	threw	(have) thrown

EXERCISE 4 Determining the Correct Verb Form

Number your paper 1 to 10. Then write the correct verb form for each sentence.

EXAMPLE   Carlos has (took, taken) the subway.
ANSWER   taken

1. The temperature has (rose, risen) five degrees in the past hour.
2. By accident Linda (threw, thrown) the newspaper away.
3. Has David (gave, given) his speech yet?
4. No one has (stole, stolen) your books; you've just misplaced them.
5. The wind (blowed, blew) down our small apple tree.
6. My older brother has (grew, grown) rapidly this past year.
7. Have you ever (froze, frozen) fresh strawberries?
8. I once (know, knew) all the state capitals.
9. My father has (drove, driven) me to school and hockey practice all week.
10. You should have (spoke, spoken) to me first.

EXERCISE 5 Using the Correct Verb Form

Number your paper 1 to 10. Write the past or the past participle of each verb in parentheses.

EXAMPLE   I have (speak) to him recently.
ANSWER   spoken

1. To our horror the crocodile slowly (rise) to the surface of the river.
2. Mary Ellen (draw) a bucket of fresh water from the well in the garden.
3. Andy hasn't (take) his test yet.
4. I had never (see) a ballet until the performance last night.
5. For his first ride, Roberto (choose) the largest horse in the entire stable.
6. Has the dog (break) another screen?
7. I nearly (freeze) waiting for the bus during the recent snowstorm.
8. Francis has (draw) a picture of you.
9. One of the actors in the chorus (steal) the show because of his talent as a dancer.
10. Should you have (throw) the receipt for your new jacket away?

Group 5

These irregular verbs form the past and past participle by changing a vowel.

PRESENT	PRESENT PARTICIPLE	PAST	PAST PARTICIPLE
begin	beginning	began	(have) begun
drink	drinking	drank	(have) drunk
ring	ringing	rang	(have) rung
sing	singing	sang	(have) sung
sink	sinking	sank	(have) sunk
swim	swimming	swam	(have) swum

NOTE: In these verbs the *i* in the present changes to an *a* in the past and a *u* in the past participle.

Group 6

These irregular verbs form the past and past participle in other ways.

PRESENT	PRESENT PARTICIPLE	PAST	PAST PARTICIPLE
come	coming	came	(have) come
do	doing	did	(have) done
eat	eating	ate	(have) eaten
fall	falling	fell	(have) fallen
go	going	went	(have) gone
ride	riding	rode	(have) ridden
run	running	ran	(have) run
wear	wearing	wore	(have) worn
write	writing	wrote	(have) written

EXERCISE 6 Determining the Correct Verb Form

Number your paper 1 to 10. Then write the correct verb form for each sentence.

1. The church bells (rang, rung) after the wedding.
2. Has the boat completely (sank, sunk)?
3. I (began, begun) my speech just as class ended.
4. Jed has (wrote, written) a report on Japan.
5. Everyone (swam, swum) several laps of the pool.
6. I have (went, gone) to every home game this season.
7. The young boy (ran, run) across the finish line.
8. Have you ever (rode, ridden) on a Ferris wheel?
9. You should have (came, come) with us to the fair.
10. Eric (drank, drunk) a large glass of ice water.

EXERCISE 7 Using the Correct Verb Form

Number your paper 1 to 10. Write the past or the past participle of each verb in parentheses.

1. I have (do) my best.
2. Jennifer (sing) the national anthem at the assembly.
3. The late bell has already (ring).
4. Have you ever (run) five miles?

5. No one (eat) the last hamburger.
6. I (write) ten thank-you notes after my birthday.
7. All the cheerleaders (wear) new uniforms at the first game.
8. Lee and I (go) to the mall with Mom and Dad.
9. The pebble skimmed the water and instantly (sink).
10. We (ride) to Atlantic City on a bus.

*T*IME-OUT FOR REVIEW ● ● ● ● ●

Number your paper 1 to 15. Write the past or the past participle of each verb in parentheses.

EXAMPLE   Children once (instruct) other children.
ANSWER   instructed

Students Who Were Teachers

1. Over 150 years ago, some children in England (go) to a very different kind of school.
2. Following an unusual system, children (know) how to read and write within two months.
3. Joseph Lancaster (develop) this system.
4. His system (use) the older children as teachers.
5. Each student monitor (teach) 10 to 20 younger children.
6. The subjects (include) reading, writing, mathematics, spelling, and moral values.
7. The monitors (give) merit tickets to good students.
8. Then students (exchange) the tickets for prizes.
9. Strict discipline (make) the system work.
10. Lancaster's system (grow) out of a need to teach large numbers of children inexpensively.
11. A few cities in the United States (choose) to keep his system for many more years.
12. Educators as far west as Michigan eagerly (bring) his system into their schools.
13. Soon after Lancaster's death in 1838, most schools (drop) his system.
14. People (believe) that his system was too strict.
15. New York City (choose) to keep his system for another 13 years.

Problem Verbs

Lie/lay and *sit/set* often cause confusion.

Lie and Lay

Lie means "to recline or rest." This verb is never followed by a direct object. Its principal parts are *lie, lying, lay,* and *(have) lain.*

PRESENT	Each day I **lie** in the hammock.
PRESENT PARTICIPLE	Mom is **lying** on the sofa.
PAST	Yesterday Marge **lay** in the sun.
PAST PARTICIPLE	The dog has **lain** here for hours.

Lay means "to put or place (something) down." This verb is usually followed by a direct object. Its principal parts are *lay, laying, laid,* and *(have) laid.*

PRESENT	I **lay** my clothes out each evening.
PRESENT PARTICIPLE	The men are **laying** the bricks.
PAST	Mandy **laid** the baby in his crib.
PAST PARTICIPLE	He has **laid** the foundation.

EXERCISE 8 Using Lie and Lay

Number your paper 1 to 10. Then write the correct form of *lie* or *lay.*

1. Rip Van Winkle (lay, laid) asleep for 20 years.
2. The towels are (lying, laying) on the ground.
3. Who (lay, laid) your books on my desk?
4. Mom has (lain, laid) the grocery list on the table.
5. Where have you (lain, laid) the keys?
6. (Lie, Lay) the tomatoes in the sun to ripen.
7. Penny (lay, laid) on the grass for a short nap.
8. A rabbit sometimes (lies, lays) in the grass.
9. Mr. Robb is (lying, laying) our reports on his desk.
10. The ship has (lain, laid) under the sea for years.

Sit *and* Set

Sit means "to occupy a seat" or "to rest in a seated position." This verb is never followed by a direct object. Its principal parts are *sit, sitting, sat,* and *(have) sat.*

PRESENT	We always **sit** in the last row.
PRESENT PARTICIPLE	The twins are **sitting** on the grass.
PAST	The dog **sat** by the table.
PAST PARTICIPLE	I have **sat** in this seat before.

Set means "to put or place (something) down." This verb is usually followed by a direct object. Its principal parts are *set, setting, set,* and *(have) set.*

PRESENT	I **set** the vase on the desk.
PRESENT PARTICIPLE	He is **setting** his hat on the chair.
PAST	Jason **set** the groceries here.
PAST PARTICIPLE	She has **set** her glasses down.

EXERCISE 9   Using Sit *and* Set

Number your paper 1 to 10. Then write the correct form of *sit* or *set.*

1. Please (sit, set) your application forms on the desk in that room.
2. Joel and his brother (sat, set) on the 50-yard line during the last Super Bowl game.
3. Let's (sit, set) here and enjoy the cool air.
4. Have you (sit, set) the packages on the table?
5. All during the first half, Lionel (sat, set) on the bench in the dugout.
6. Please (sit, set) here and wait for me.
7. Bart (sat, set) the can of wax on the fender.
8. The campers are (sitting, setting) around the campfire and telling ghost stories.
9. Martha is (sitting, setting) the props on the stage in preparation for the rehearsal.
10. (Sit, Set) down beside me.

Verb Tense

Tense is the form a verb takes to show time. The six tenses are *present, past, future, present perfect, past perfect,* and *future perfect.* The principal parts of a verb help form the tenses.

PRESENT	Every day I **walk** five miles.
PAST	I **walked** five miles yesterday.
FUTURE	I **will walk** again tomorrow.
PRESENT PERFECT	For two years I **have walked** each day.
PAST PERFECT	I **had** not **walked** much before that.
FUTURE PERFECT	I **will have walked** 800 miles by May.

Conjugation of a Verb

A *conjugation* lists all the singular and plural forms of a verb in its six tenses. Following is a conjugation of the irregular verb *spin.*

Conjugation of *Spin*

PRINCIPAL PARTS

Present	Present Participle	Past	Past Participle
spin	spinning	spun	spun

Present

This tense expresses action that is going on now.

SINGULAR	PLURAL
I spin	we spin
you spin	you spin
he, she, it spins	they spin

Past

This tense expresses action that took place in the past.

SINGULAR	PLURAL
I spun	we spun
you spun	you spun
he, she, it spun	they spun

168

Future

This tense expresses action that will take place in the future. It is formed by adding *shall* or *will* to the present.

SINGULAR	PLURAL
I shall/will spin	we shall/will spin
you will spin	you will spin
he, she, it will spin	they will spin

Present Perfect

This tense expresses action that was completed at some indefinite time in the past or action that started in the past and is still going on. It is formed by adding *has* or *have* to the past participle.

SINGULAR	PLURAL
I have spun	we have spun
you have spun	you have spun
he, she, it has spun	they have spun

Past Perfect

This tense expresses action that took place before some other action. It is formed by adding *had* to the past participle.

SINGULAR	PLURAL
I had spun	we had spun
you had spun	you had spun
he, she, it had spun	they had spun

Future Perfect

This tense expresses action that will be completed by some given time in the future. It is formed by adding *shall have* or *will have* to the past participle. (This tense is seldom used.)

SINGULAR	PLURAL
I shall/will have spun	we shall/will have spun
you will have spun	you will have spun
he, she, it will have spun	they will have spun

EXERCISE 10 *Conjugating a Verb*

Using the conjugation of *spin* as a model, write the conjugation of the verb *drive.*

EXERCISE 11   Identifying Verb Tenses

Number your paper 1 to 10. Decide whether the tense of each underlined verb is *present, past, future, present perfect, past perfect,* or *future perfect.* Then write the tense.

1. For the past year, we <u>have lived</u> in an old farmhouse.
2. Brad <u>dances</u> as well as my father.
3. In 1922, Warren Harding <u>made</u> the first presidential radio broadcast.
4. Band members <u>will meet</u> outside the stadium.
5. Ellen Church <u>had trained</u> as a nurse before she became the first airline stewardess in 1930.
6. By Friday we <u>will have studied</u> Africa for a month.
7. The Ice Capades shows <u>have occurred</u> since 1940.
8. We <u>will know</u> the test results by next Monday.
9. The Malayan crocodile <u>fears</u> no other creature.
10. The British explorer John Speke <u>found</u> the source of the Nile River.

TIME-OUT FOR REVIEW • • • • •

Number your paper 1 to 10. Then write each underlined verb in the tense that is indicated in parentheses.

EXAMPLE   We <u>take</u> (*past*) a picnic lunch with us.
ANSWER   took

1. Dan <u>set</u> (*future*) the books there.
2. Steve said that he <u>see</u> (*past perfect*) a meteor.
3. William Penn <u>sign</u> (*past*) a treaty with the Indians.
4. The snow <u>lie</u> (*present perfect*) here for days.
5. I <u>start</u> (*future*) my science project this weekend.
6. Stephanie <u>learn</u> (*present perfect*) to ski and skate.
7. At seven o'clock Bryan remembered that he <u>promise</u> (*past perfect*) to baby-sit for the Nelsons.
8. By tomorrow I <u>finish</u> (*future perfect*) the painting.
9. Hank Aaron <u>make</u> (*past*) his 715th home run in a game against the Los Angeles Dodgers.
10. I <u>collect</u> (*present perfect*) old coins for two years.

Active and Passive Voice

In addition to tense, a verb can have *active voice* or *passive voice*. Writers can use either the active or the passive voice to tell about an action.

11d ▸ The **active voice** indicates that the subject is performing the action.

11e ▸ The **passive voice** indicates that the action of the verb is being performed upon the subject.

ACTIVE VOICE   Four people **made** decorations for the Halloween party.

PASSIVE VOICE   The decorations for the Halloween party **were made** by four people.

ACTIVE VOICE   The governor **signed** the bill.

PASSIVE VOICE   The bill **was signed** by the governor.

A verb in the passive voice consists of a form of the verb *be* plus a past participle. The forms of *be* used for the passive voice are *is, are, was, were, has been, have been,* and *had been.* Study the following example.

ACTIVE VOICE   The camera club **raised** money for a trip.

PASSIVE VOICE   Money **was raised** by the camera club for a trip. [*Was* is a form of the verb *be,* and *raised* is the past participle of *raise.*]

It is important to learn to avoid the passive voice in your writing. Passive voice verbs are weak and wordy. When you write, remember to use the active voice as much as possible. The active voice is more forceful and adds life to your writing.

The only time the passive voice is useful is when the doer of the action is unknown or unimportant.

PASSIVE VOICE   That book **was printed** ten years ago.

EXERCISE 12 Recognizing Active and Passive Voice

Number your paper 1 to 10. Then write each verb and label it *active* or *passive*.

1. A squirrel buries about 20 bushels of food before each winter.
2. Parts of that movie about the old West were filmed in Spain.
3. Benjamin Franklin owned the first bathtub in the colonies.
4. This model of a Viking ship was made by my brother during his vacation.
5. These trees were planted more than 100 years ago.
6. Thomas Jefferson kept a grizzly bear on the grounds of his Virginia home.
7. The bear was given to him by his friend Meriwether Lewis.
8. The piano has been tuned.
9. At the deli I ordered a roast beef sandwich on rye.
10. Henry Welles of Waterloo, New York, instituted Memorial Day in 1866.

EXERCISE 13 Recognizing Active and Passive Voice

Number your paper 1 to 10. Then write each verb and label it *active* or *passive*.

1. The windows have not been washed since spring.
2. That small sailboat is named *Sea Mist*.
3. After school, Louella will wash the car.
4. The part in the play has been given to Jack.
5. The soccer player kicked the ball toward the goal.
6. The ducks will soon begin their winter migration.
7. Food and clothing have been collected for the victims of the flood.
8. Have you seen Jeremy lately?
9. During vacation the school will be closed.
10. Will the typewriter be repaired by tomorrow?

EXERCISE 14 Writing Sentences

Number your paper 1 to 5. The following sentences all contain passive verbs. Change each verb to the active voice. Then use each active verb in a new sentence.

EXAMPLE The jewel was found in a wastebasket.
POSSIBLE ANSWER The clever detective found the jewel in a wastebasket.

1. The last piece of the pizza was eaten.
2. A strange black car was seen on the corner around seven o'clock.
3. The horses on that farm are exercised daily.
4. Yesterday a ten-dollar bill was found on the field.
5. A new solar system has been discovered.

Application to Writing

Editing is an important part of anything you write. This final step in the writing process gives you a chance to polish your work—to find any mistakes. As you edit your written work, always look for any verb errors. One way to find some of these errors is to read your work aloud.

EXERCISE 15 Editing for Verb Errors

Read the following paragraph. Then write the paragraph, correcting each incorrect verb.

Paul Revere's Ride

Paul Revere's services to the colonies begun long before his famous ride in 1775. Before that he had rode from Boston to New York to Philadelphia many times. He use to take secret messages to the Sons of Liberty. His motives for all these trips, however, were not entirely patriotic. He once run his horse hard from Boston to New York to tell New Yorkers about the Boston Tea Party. After this trip he give a bill to the Continental Congress for his services.

Chapter Review

A **Using the Correct Verb Form.** Number your paper 1 to 10. Then write the correct verb form for each sentence.

1. On our trip to Florida, we (saw, seen) several models of cities of the world at Epcot Center.
2. Luis (threw, throwed) the ball to home plate.
3. I had never (swam, swum) in salt water before today.
4. Mom (knowed, knew) Dad in high school.
5. Have you ever (rode, ridden) in a helicopter?
6. Mom always (lies, lays) the mail by the door.
7. During the last three days I (teached, taught) my sister how to ride a bike.
8. Several students have (wrote, written) poems for the school's 50th anniversary.
9. Have you (chose, chosen) a name for your dog yet?
10. I have already (ate, eaten) lunch.

B **Using the Correct Verb Form.** Number your paper 1 to 10. Find and correct each verb form that is incorrectly used in the following sentences. If a sentence is correct, write *C* after the number.

1. The sun finally come out in the afternoon.
2. You should have seen the large audience at our play.
3. These vines have growed three feet in one week.
4. Hurricane-force winds have sank several boats at the town marina.
5. Who drunk all the milk?
6. I should have took a book with me to the doctor's office.
7. That basketball player has stole the ball from the opposing team several times.
8. Yesterday we begun math class with a surprise quiz.
9. Have you gave a donation to that charity?
10. The stock market has fallen six points since yesterday.

C **Identifying Verb Voice.** Number your paper 1 to 10. Then write each verb and label it *active* or *passive*.

1. After the play the curtain was slowly lowered.
2. Dr. Jonas Salk discovered the polio vaccine.
3. Air-conditioning was invented in 1902 by Willis H. Carrier.
4. Darrell painted the garage last summer.
5. Neil Armstrong made his historic walk on the moon in 1969.
6. In right-handed people, motor control is ruled by the left half of the brain.
7. Cindy auditioned for the school play.
8. Altitude is measured by an altimeter.
9. The beaver's den was constructed in one evening.
10. Reds, greens, and blues form the picture in color television.

Mastery Test

Number your paper 1 to 10. Then write the correct verb form for each sentence.

1. Justine has (wore, worn) Peter's jacket all day.
2. Everyone has (went, gone) to the movies except me.
3. Has your wet bathing suit (lain, laid) on the floor all night?
4. Chuck (did, done) the right thing.
5. Kim (catched, caught) the high fly to center field.
6. Has she ever (sang, sung) in a musical before?
7. The alarm (rang, rung) 15 minutes early.
8. We have (sat, set) here long enough!
9. My brother has (drove, driven) for three years now.
10. The balloons have (rose, risen) above the clouds.

12

Using Pronouns

*D*iagnostic *T*est

Number your paper 1 to 10. Then write the correct word in parentheses.

EXAMPLE   Sandy and (I, me) have tickets to the concert.
ANSWER   I

1. Mr. Martin helped Franklin and (we, us) with our science projects.
2. That's (they, them) in the rowboat.
3. Pam and (I, me) are the new class representatives.
4. A few of the girls have finished (her, their) homework.
5. (Who, Whom) painted that picture?
6. Would you like to study with Sara and (I, me)?
7. Dad proudly showed Daniel and (she, her) his new fishing rod.
8. Neither of the boys has seen (his, their) grades.
9. Should I give the note to the principal or (he, him)?
10. I saw (their, they're) dog down by the lake.

*T*he Cases of Personal Pronouns

Personal pronouns have different forms, called *cases*, depending on whether they are subjects, objects, or possessives in a sentence.

He helped **her.**   **She** helped **him.**   Rob helped **his** aunt.

Case is the form of a noun or pronoun that indicates its use in a sentence.

In English there are three cases: the *nominative case*, the *objective case*, and the *possessive case*.

Nominative Case

(Used for subjects and predicate nominatives)

	Singular	Plural
FIRST PERSON	I	we
SECOND PERSON	you	you
THIRD PERSON	he, she, it	they

Objective Case

(Used for direct objects, indirect objects, and objects of prepositions)

	Singular	Plural
FIRST PERSON	me	us
SECOND PERSON	you	you
THIRD PERSON	him, her, it	them

Possessive Case

(Used to show ownership or possession)

	Singular	Plural
FIRST PERSON	my, mine	our, ours
SECOND PERSON	your, yours	your, yours
THIRD PERSON	his, her, hers, its	their, theirs

177

The Nominative Case

The personal pronouns in the following box are in the nominative case. (*See pages 31–32 for a review of person.*)

Nominative Case		
	Singular	Plural
FIRST PERSON	I	we
SECOND PERSON	you	you
THIRD PERSON	he, she, it	they

Pronouns in the nominative case are used in two ways.

12b The **nominative case** is used for subjects and predicate nominatives.

Pronouns Used as Subjects. A subject names the person, place, or thing the sentence is about. Because the pronouns in the following sentences are used as subjects, the nominative case is used.

SUBJECTS   **I** decorated my bedroom.
Do **they** live in that apartment? [*They* do live in that apartment.]

When a sentence has only one subject, choosing the correct pronoun is usually not a problem. If there is a compound subject, however, people sometimes make a mistake.

COMPOUND SUBJECT   Mom and (I, me) painted the fence.

To find the correct pronoun, say the sentence as if each pronoun stood alone.

CORRECT   **I** painted the fence.
INCORRECT   **Me** painted the fence
CORRECT   Mom and **I** painted the fence.

EXERCISE 1 Using Pronouns in the Nominative Case

Number your paper 1 to 10. Then write the correct pronoun in parentheses.

EXAMPLE   My aunt and (they, them) have arrived.
ANSWER   they

1. My parents and (I, me) went to Virginia Beach.
2. Tim and (he, him) found seats in the last row.
3. Did the Changs and (they, them) go to the block party?
4. Last week León and (I, me) hiked into the mountains.
5. Leroy and (he, him) are excellent cooks.
6. Should the Turners and (we, us) wait for you?
7. By Friday she and (I, me) must know our lines for the play.
8. Do you and (she, her) like squash?
9. Are Beverly and (he, him) running for Student Council president?
10. Maura and (they, them) are going to the fair.

Pronouns Used as Predicate Nominatives. A predicate nominative is a word that follows a linking verb—such as *is, were,* or *has been*—and identifies or renames the subject. (*See pages 41 and 43 for lists of common linking verbs.*) A pronoun used as a predicate nominative is in the nominative case.

PREDICATE NOMINATIVE   The best dancer was **he.**

Check for the correct case of a pronoun in a compound predicate nominative by turning the sentence around to make the predicate nominatives the subjects. Then say each pronoun separately to find out which one is correct.

The bridesmaids will be Gladys and (she, her).
Gladys and (she, her) will be the bridesmaids.

CORRECT   **She** will be a bridesmaid.
INCORRECT   **Her** will be a bridesmaid.
CORRECT   Gladys and **she** will be the bridesmaids.

NOTE: Expressions like "It's me" or "That's her" are usually acceptable in informal speech. When you write, however, the correct expressions are "It is I" and "That is she" because *I* and *she* are predicate nominatives.

EXERCISE 2   Using Pronouns in the Nominative Case

Number your paper 1 to 10. Then write the correct pronoun in parentheses.

1. That was (I, me) in the bus.
2. Today's group leader will be George or (she, her).
3. The man in the brown suit is (he, him).
4. Is that (they, them) coming up the driveway?
5. The two art teachers are Ms. Jordon and (he, him).
6. That was (I, me) on the phone last night.
7. The new cocaptains are (we, us).
8. That's (they, them) at the front door.
9. The greatest skaters are Willis and (she, her).
10. The contest winners were Isaac and (she, her).

EXERCISE 3   Supplying Pronouns in the Nominative Case

Number your paper 1 to 10. Then complete each sentence by writing an appropriate pronoun for each blank. (Do not use *you* or *it*.)

EXAMPLE   Are Cora and _____ your cousins?
POSSIBLE ANSWER   he

1. Jamie or _____ will mail the package.
2. Did Barry and _____ see you at the beach?
3. The only redheads in our class are you and _____.
4. That's _____ in the red sports car.
5. Are Barbara and _____ entering the relay race?
6. The Chongs and _____ will cook a Chinese meal.
7. Was that _____ with you at the dance?
8. Is that Laurie or _____ on the white horse?
9. Amy and _____ are writing a report on music videos.
10. May Mario and _____ sit here for a while?

EXERCISE 4 Finding Errors in Case

Number your paper 1 to 10. If an underlined pronoun is in the wrong case, write it correctly. If it is in the correct case, write *C* after the number.

1. You and <u>me</u> have been friends for four years now.
2. After the intermission Laura and <u>they</u> went home.
3. Is that <u>him</u> on second base?
4. Scott and <u>me</u> often cook outside on the gas grill.
5. Andrew and <u>him</u> will be tour guides this summer.
6. The best gymnast is either Chris or <u>she</u>.
7. The Taylors and <u>us</u> will rent a cottage together.
8. Aren't you and <u>her</u> in the same school?
9. Was that Mark or <u>he</u> playing the trumpet?
10. Neither Chester nor <u>her</u> could figure out the puzzle.

EXERCISE 5 Writing Sentences

Number your paper 1 to 5. Then write sentences that follow the directions below.

1. Use *they* as a subject.
2. Use *Rosa and I* as a compound subject.
3. Use *Bud and he* as a compound subject in a question.
4. Use *he* and *I* as a compound predicate nominative.
5. Use *she* as a predicate nominative in a question.

The Objective Case

The personal pronouns below are in the objective case.

	Objective Case	
	Singular	Plural
FIRST PERSON	me	us
SECOND PERSON	you	you
THIRD PERSON	him, her, it	them

12c ▸ The **objective case** is used for direct objects, indirect objects, and objects of prepositions.

Pronouns Used as Direct and Indirect Objects. A direct object follows an action verb and answers the question *Whom?* or *What?*

DIRECT OBJECT   The Walkers invited **me** to dinner.

An indirect object comes before a direct object and answers the questions *To or for whom?* or *To or for what?*

INDIRECT OBJECT   Ms. Green gave **us** the assignment.

Check for the correct case of a compound object the same way you checked for the correct case of a compound subject. Say the nominative and objective case pronouns separately.

DIRECT OBJECT	Did Nancy thank Karen and (he, him)?
INCORRECT	Nancy did thank **he.**
CORRECT	Nancy did thank **him.**
CORRECT	Did Nancy thank Karen and **him?**
INDIRECT OBJECT	Mom handed Kim and (I, me) a gift.
INCORRECT	Mom handed **I** a gift.
CORRECT	Mom handed **me** a gift.
CORRECT	Mom handed Kim and **me** a gift.

EXERCISE 6   *Using Pronouns in the Objective Case*

Number your paper 1 to 10. Then write the correct pronoun in parentheses.

1. A huge wave knocked Leslie and (I, me) down.
2. Bruce sent Hans and (he, him) a postcard from Texas.
3. No one told Jon or (I, me) about the meeting.
4. Did the farmer give Gary and (she, her) some pears?
5. Rachel kept the DaSilvas and (they, them) waiting for an hour.
6. Francine beat her and (I, me) in the diving contest.

7. Thomas gave Willie and (he, him) two movie tickets.
8. Have the students elected Joe and (she, her)?
9. My grandparents made our relatives and (we, us) a wonderful Thanksgiving dinner.
10. The coaches praised Charles and (he, him).

Pronouns Used as Objects of Prepositions. A prepositional phrase begins with a preposition, such as *with, to, by,* or *for.* (*See page 69 for a list of common prepositions.*) A prepositional phrase ends with the object of a preposition. A pronoun used as an object of a preposition is in the objective case.

OBJECT OF   Did David talk to **them?** [*To them* is
A PREPOSITION   the prepositional phrase.]

Check for the proper case of a compound object of a preposition by saying the nominative and objective case pronouns separately.

COMPOUND OBJECT   This package of books is for Tim and
OF A PREPOSITION   (he, him).
INCORRECT   This package is for **he.**
CORRECT   This package is for **him.**
CORRECT   This package is for Tim and **him.**

EXERCISE 7 Using Pronouns in the Objective Case

Number your paper 1 to 10. Then write the correct pronoun in parentheses.

1. Mom got several letters from Mark and (she, her).
2. How did the boat leave without you and (he, him)?
3. Mr. Margolis assigned the cleanup duties to some ninth graders and (we, us).
4. Please save some milk for her and (I, me).
5. No one except Chen and (he, him) has passed the swimming test.
6. People like you and (I, me) need more sleep.
7. The new student walked toward Scott and (he, him).

183

8. You can stay with the Jeffersons or (they, them).
9. Between you and (I, me), we'll soon finish the job.
10. Is there an empty seat beside Pam or (she, her)?

EXERCISE 8 Supplying Pronouns in the Objective Case

Number your paper 1 to 10. Then complete each sentence by writing an appropriate pronoun for each blank. (Do not use *you* or *it*.)

1. My brother often drives Louis and ———— to school.
2. Rob cooked dinner for the Barkers and ————.
3. The principal spoke to the Freys and ————.
4. My aunt and uncle showed Pat and ———— their slides of Disneyland.
5. Beth invited Cliff and ———— to her party.
6. Will you give this message to Ella or ————?
7. This agreement is between Steve and ————.
8. Did you see Sara and ———— at the baseball game?
9. Mom and Dad bought Ben and ———— new jeans.
10. Paulo showed Pete and ———— his science project.

EXERCISE 9 Finding Errors in Case

Number your paper 1 to 10. If an underlined pronoun is in the wrong case, write it correctly. If it is in the correct case, write *C* after the number.

1. Aunt May prepared a special treat for Andy and I.
2. Has the doctor given Mom and her the test results?
3. Do you remember Betty and he from grade school?
4. Daniel called to Beth and she from the porch.
5. A guide took Cindy and me through the museum.
6. Grandma sent Uncle Bob and they a bushel of oranges from Florida.
7. Mike accidentally turned the hose on Sal and we.
8. Has anyone seen he or Peg since last Monday?
9. Danny told his teachers and us the good news.
10. Did you go to the movies with Diane and he?

184

EXERCISE 10   *Writing Sentences*

Number your paper 1 to 5. Then write sentences that follow the directions below.

1. Include *Dad and me* as a compound direct object.
2. Include *Sarah and us* as a compound direct object in a question.
3. Include *Lionel or him* as a compound indirect object.
4. Include *the Student Council members and them* as a compound indirect object in a question.
5. Include *Susan and her* as a compound object of a preposition.

The Possessive Case

The personal pronouns in the following box are in the possessive case.

Possessive Case		
	Singular	Plural
FIRST PERSON	my, mine	our, ours
SECOND PERSON	your, yours	your, yours
THIRD PERSON	his, her, hers, its	their, theirs

12d ▶ The **possessive case** is used to show ownership or possession.

A possessive pronoun can be used before a noun or alone.

BEFORE A NOUN	This is **their** collie.
BY ITSELF	This collie is **theirs.**

An apostrophe is used with possessive nouns but is never used with the possessive form of a personal pronoun.

POSSESSIVE NOUN	This coat is **Ruth's.**
POSSESSIVE PRONOUN	This coat is **hers.** [not "her's"]

185

Sometimes people also confuse a possessive pronoun with a contraction. *Its, your, their,* and *theirs* are possessive pronouns. *It's* (it is), *you're* (you are), *they're* (they are), and *there's* (there is) are contractions.

POSSESSIVE PRONOUN   **Their** doorbell is broken.

CONTRACTION   **They're** (they are) out of town.

EXERCISE 11   *Using Pronouns in the Possessive Case*

Number your paper 1 to 10. Then write the correct word in parentheses.

EXAMPLE   Do you know whether (its, it's) cold outside?
ANSWER   it's

1. How did you get those grease stains on (your, you're) new jacket?
2. (Their, They're) moving to Wisconsin at the end of March.
3. Is this picnic basket (ours, our's)?
4. (Theirs, There's) the bus that will take us to Kathleen's house.
5. The cat is chasing (its, it's) tail again.
6. (Your, You're) the only person who knows how to get to the state park.
7. I don't know which house is (theirs, there's).
8. (Its, It's) time for Andrew and Jamie to leave for the train station.
9. This black coat must be (hers, her's).
10. (Their, They're) apartment is on the corner of 67th and Allison streets.

EXERCISE 12   *Writing Sentences*

Number your paper 1 to 10. Then write a separate sentence for each of the following possessive pronouns.

1. my	3. yours	5. his	7. its	9. theirs
2. hers	4. their	6. our	8. mine	10. your

TIME-OUT FOR REVIEW • • • • •

Number your paper 1 to 20. Then write and correct any error. If a sentence is correct, write *C* after the number.

EXAMPLE   Mr. Foster helped Paul and I build a kayak.
ANSWER   I—me

1. Aunt Grace gave Ben and she tickets to the final game of the play-offs.
2. You're turn at bat comes after Lance's turn.
3. Carmen is standing between Harry and he.
4. Susan didn't tell my sister or me about the surprise birthday party.
5. Is that her in this photograph?
6. Sharon still hasn't packed her suitcase, but our's is already in the car.
7. The Walkins and us are organizing a picnic to celebrate the Fourth of July.
8. The rabbit has escaped from it's pen!
9. Her and I are constructing a bookcase in our wood-working class.
10. Did Mr. Lanewski recognize Melissa and them in their Pilgrim costumes?
11. That's them on the library steps.
12. Have you heard about they're plans to visit friends and relatives in Puerto Rico?
13. Athletes like him are rare.
14. Omar told Barbara and I the ending of the mystery story.
15. Could you spend a few minutes with Stephen and I so a decision can be made?
16. The most valuable player will be either Dan or he.
17. Uncle Ted hadn't seen Warren and he for two years.
18. We found mine but not theirs.
19. The math team needs another five students like Aretha and she.
20. Dad and me challenged them to a game of horseshoes in the back meadow.

Who and Whom

Who and *whom* can be used as interrogative pronouns. Like personal pronouns these pronouns also have case.

Who is in the nominative case and can be the subject.

SUBJECT   **Who** wrote this poem?

Whom is in the objective case and can be used as a direct object or an object of a preposition.

DIRECT OBJECT   **Whom** did you see? [You did see whom.]
OBJECT OF THE   From **whom** did you receive that large
PREPOSITION   package of magazines?

NOTE: *Whose* can also be used as an interrogative pronoun.

EXERCISE 13   Using Who and Whom

Number your paper 1 to 10. Then write the correct pronoun in parentheses.

1. (Who, Whom) made this delicious dessert?
2. (Who, Whom) did you see at the game?
3. (Who, Whom) is using the telephone?
4. For (who, whom) are you knitting that pair of socks?
5. (Who, Whom) have you invited?
6. About (who, whom) did you write your report?
7. (Who, Whom) do you know at the new school?
8. To (who, whom) have you spoken?
9. (Who, Whom) will mow the lawn on Saturday?
10. From (who, whom) did you get the assignment?

EXERCISE 14   Writing Sentences

Number your paper 1 to 3. Then write questions that follow the directions below.

1. Include *who* as the subject.
2. Include *whom* as the direct object.
3. Include *whom* as the object of a preposition.

*P*ronouns and Their Antecedents

The word or group of words that a pronoun refers to, or replaces, is called the pronoun's *antecedent.* In the following sentences, *Maria* is the antecedent of *her,* and *Waltons* is the antecedent of *they.*

PRONOUNS AND
ANTECEDENTS

Maria was the first to raise **her** hand and volunteer.

The **Waltons** are our neighbors. **They** are planning a garage sale.

Because a pronoun and its antecedent are referring to the same person, place, or thing, there must be agreement between them.

12e ▸ A pronoun must agree in number and gender with its antecedent.

Number is the term used to indicate whether a noun or pronoun is singular (one) or plural (more than one). A pronoun must be singular if its antecedent is singular. It must be plural if its antecedent is plural.

SINGULAR **Ken** is preparing **his** campaign speech for the meeting.

PLURAL The **teachers** have turned in **their** grades for the semester.

NOTE: The personal pronouns *you, your,* and *yours* can be either singular or plural.

Gender is the term used to indicate whether a noun or a personal pronoun is *masculine, feminine,* or *neuter.* A personal pronoun must also agree with its antecedent in gender. Following is a list of personal pronouns according to their gender.

189

Masculine	Feminine	Neuter
he, him, his	she, her, hers	it, its

NOTE: Things and places are neuter in gender. Unless animals are given a proper name, they are also considered neuter.

MASCULINE **Richard** forgot **his** sneakers.

FEMININE **Janet** had to give **her** cat a bath.

NEUTER Wash the **car** and wax **it.**

Plural pronouns such as *them* and *their* have no gender. They can have masculine, feminine, or neuter antecedents. Their antecedent can also be a combination of masculine and feminine.

The **singers** have taken **their** places on stage.

EXERCISE 15 Making Pronouns and Antecedents Agree

Number your paper 1 to 10. Then write the pronoun that correctly completes each sentence.

1. Arlene told us about _____ visit to the dentist to have braces put on.
2. The Clarks planted a garden in _____ backyard.
3. That bird must have hurt _____ wing.
4. Has Jonathan been measured for _____ band uniform yet?
5. This rose has lost all _____ petals.
6. My sister sent in _____ application for the job.
7. All swimmers should be in _____ bathing suits 20 minutes before the meet begins.
8. Mr. Mason is taking _____ students to the aquarium.
9. Rob read the recipe and put _____ in the file.
10. My mother has started _____ own business.

Indefinite Pronouns as Antecedents

An indefinite pronoun can be the antecedent of a personal pronoun. Some indefinite pronouns are singular, and others are plural. Still other indefinite pronouns can be either singular or plural.

When one of the following indefinite pronouns is the antecedent of a personal pronoun, the personal pronoun must be singular.

Singular Indefinite Pronouns			
anybody	either	neither	one
anyone	everybody	nobody	somebody
each	everyone	no one	someone

SINGULAR   **One** of the boys can't open **his** locker.

Someone in the girls' chorus forgot **her** music.

Sometimes the gender of a singular indefinite pronoun is not indicated in the sentence. Standard English solves this problem by using *his* or *his or her*.

Everyone must wash **his** own dishes.

Everyone must wash **his or her** own dishes.

When one of the following indefinite pronouns is the antecedent of a personal pronoun, the personal pronoun must be plural.

Plural Indefinite Pronouns			
both	few	many	several

PLURAL   **Several** of the women offered **their** help.

Both of my brothers lost **their** keys.

191

When one of the following indefinite pronouns is the antecedent of a personal pronoun, that pronoun could be either singular or plural.

Singular or Plural Indefinite Pronouns

all   any   most   none   some

Agreement with one of these indefinite pronouns depends upon the number and the gender of the object of the preposition that follows it.

SINGULAR   **All** of the **house** was restored to **its** original beauty.

PLURAL   **All** of the **players** wore **their** uniforms.

EXERCISE 16   *Making Personal Pronouns Agree with Indefinite Pronouns*

Number your paper 1 to 10. Then write the pronoun that correctly completes each sentence.

1. Each of the girls on the field hockey team wore _____ school sweater to the game.
2. Everyone at the Boys' Club volunteered _____ help.
3. Both of my uncles like _____ jobs very much.
4. Neither of my sisters remembered _____ bus pass.
5. Several of these dogs do not have _____ collars.
6. None of the brass has lost _____ shine yet.
7. Someone on the girls' basketball team has left _____ locker open.
8. Most of the coaches were sitting with _____ teams at the awards banquet.
9. Either of my brothers will give you _____ baseball glove.
10. Few of the boys on the team have taken _____ physical examinations yet.

Application to Writing

As you edit your written work, check for any pronoun shifts. Did you shift to the pronoun *you* when you should have used a pronoun of the same person as the subject?

PRONOUN Sue doesn't like the roller coaster because
SHIFT **you** might fall from the seat.

CORRECT Sue doesn't like the roller coaster because
she might fall from the seat.

Also check for missing antecedents. Occasionally people will use *it* or *they* without an antecedent.

MISSING Although I had never skated before, I really
ANTECEDENT enjoyed **it**. [*It* has no antecedent.]

CORRECT Although I had never skated before, I really
enjoyed **skating**.

EXERCISE 17 *Editing for Pronoun Shifts and Missing Antecedents*

Number your paper 1 to 10. Then rewrite each sentence to make its meaning clear.

1. I knew Leslie was a good cook, but I had never tasted any of it before yesterday.
2. Cathy likes the summer because you can go swimming.
3. After a long day of fishing, they tasted delicious.
4. My parents like carpooling because you save money.
5. I have never bowled a strike, but I still enjoy it.
6. I usually get up early on Saturdays because you have more time to play.
7. Mom got a new telephone so that you can hear better.
8. Ken emptied the bucket and let it run into the plant.
9. I enjoy watching the news on TV because you find out what's happening around the world.
10. Her nose was sunburned, but now it has completely disappeared.

*C*hapter *R*eview

A **Using Pronouns in the Correct Case.** Number your paper 1 to 10. Then write the correct word in parentheses.

1. Althea and (she, her) are equal partners in the delivery service.
2. During the Boston Tea Party, some of the ships in the harbor lost (its, their) cargo.
3. Should the tickets be sent to you or (he, him)?
4. (Who, Whom) did you just introduce to Ryan?
5. Was that (he, him) on the subway?
6. Give Daniel or (she, her) the money from the car wash.
7. The director chose David and (she, her) for the leads in the play.
8. (They're, Their) work on the project was excellent.
9. Either of the women will give (her, their) report at the meeting.
10. The volleyball game will be played between our relatives and (they, them).

B **Correcting Pronoun Errors.** Number your paper 1 to 10. Then write and correct any error. If a sentence is correct, write *C* after the number.

1. The final decision must be made by Ellen and he.
2. Who did you choose for the lead in the play?
3. Clara and him will be school monitors this term.
4. Isn't that she by the side of the pool?
5. Tell Ana and they about the play.
6. Mr. Brown and his wife have sold they're farm.
7. Ruth gave Lily and she matching sweaters.
8. To whom am I speaking?
9. With Roscoe and he as my helpers, we cleaned the entire house.
10. You must sign you're name on this line.

C **Making Pronouns Agree with Antecedents.** Number your paper 1 to 10. Then write the pronoun that correctly completes each sentence.

1. Both of the girls must give _____ speeches today.
2. Amanda has gone to the movies with _____ friends.
3. Mr. and Mrs. Ruiz are away on _____ vacation.
4. One of the women lawyers will plead _____ case before the state supreme court.
5. All of the beach has white sand covering _____.
6. The pony ran quickly to _____ mother.
7. Most of the apples have worms in _____.
8. Lloyd couldn't find _____ hockey stick anywhere.
9. Several of the chorus members will sing _____ own arrangement of "Oklahoma!"
10. Everyone on the boys' relay team must have _____ racing time clocked this afternoon.

Mastery Test

Number your paper 1 to 10. Then write the correct word in parentheses.

1. In 1976, each of the 50 states had (its, their) own flag printed on a postage stamp.
2. (Your, You're) bicycle has a flat tire.
3. Penny visited the Alamo in San Antonio, Texas, with Ellis and (I, me).
4. Last night Uncle Earl surprised Mom and (we, us) with tickets to the circus.
5. The winners of the contest were Bridget and (he, him).
6. The twins are having a birthday party for David and (she, her).
7. (Who, Whom) won the basketball game?
8. (He, Him) and Charles have jobs as lifeguards.
9. Both of the sisters forgot (her, their) gloves.
10. Please show Becky and (I, me) the new horses.

13

Subject and
Verb Agreement

Diagnostic Test

Number your paper 1 to 10. Then write the verb form in parentheses that agrees with each subject.

EXAMPLE   The songs on that album (is, are) excellent.
ANSWER   are

1. Umbrellas (has, have) changed very little in over 2,000 years.
2. The instructions for the model (comes, come) with the kit.
3. At the top of the stairs (was, were) a huge door.
4. The members of the track team (is, are) often training on the weekend.
5. One of my friends (plays, play) the violin.
6. There (is, are) yellow, brown, blue, green, and even black diamonds.
7. A horse and a cow (has, have) strayed into the far pasture.
8. I (was, were) at the hockey rink after school.
9. The California condor (doesn't, don't) migrate.
10. The bark of white birch trees (looks, look) ghostly in the moonlight.

Agreement of Subjects and Verbs

You would never think of wearing two shoes that did not match. Subjects and verbs must go together, just like two shoes. The subject and verb in *a dog barks* and *dogs bark* go together, but in *dogs barks* they do not. Subjects and verbs match when there is *agreement* between them.

13a A verb must agree with its subject in number.

Number

As you know, *number* is the term used to indicate whether a word is *singular* ("one") or *plural* ("more than one"). Nouns, pronouns, and verbs all have number.

Number of Nouns and Pronouns. The plural of most nouns is formed by adding *-s* or *-es* to the singular form. A few nouns, however, form their plural in other ways. A dictionary always lists an irregular plural.

SINGULAR monkey   church   mouse
PLURAL   monkey**s**   church**es**   **mice**

Pronouns also have number. For example, *I, he, she,* and *it* are singular, and *we* and *they* are plural.

EXERCISE 1   Determining the Number of Nouns and Pronouns

Number your paper 1 to 20. Label each word *singular* or *plural.*

1. we	6. feet	11. boxes	16. colors
2. it	7. star	12. birds	17. teacher
3. men	8. she	13. teeth	18. sweater
4. day	9. they	14. cities	19. glasses
5. he	10. pearl	15. calves	20. elevator

Number of Verbs.   Most present tense verbs ending in -*s* or -*es* are singular. Plural forms in the present tense do not end in -*s* or -*es*.

SINGULAR   **PLURAL**

A bird $\begin{cases} \text{eats.} \\ \text{sleeps.} \\ \text{flies.} \end{cases}$ Birds $\begin{cases} \text{eat.} \\ \text{sleep.} \\ \text{fly.} \end{cases}$

   Be, have, and *do* have special singular and plural forms in the present tense. *Be* also has special forms in the past tense.

Forms of *Be*, *Have*, and *Do*		
	Singular	Plural
be	is (present)	are (present)
	was (past)	were (past)
have	has	have
do	does	do

In the following examples, each subject is underlined once, and each verb is underlined twice.

SINGULAR   He is a hard worker.
           Bonnie has a cold.
   PLURAL   They are hard workers.
           My sisters have colds.

EXERCISE 2 *Determining the Number of Verbs*

Number your paper 1 to 10. Then label each item *singular* or *plural*.

1. bats are
2. dogs guard
3. he is
4. telephones ring
5. it was

6. we were
7. lights flash
8. they do
9. Andy has
10. she thinks

Singular and Plural Subjects

Since nouns, pronouns, and verbs all have number, the number of a verb must agree with the number of its subject (a noun or a pronoun).

13b ▸ A singular subject takes a singular verb.

13c ▸ A plural subject takes a plural verb.

To make a verb agree with its subject, ask yourself two questions: *What is the subject?* and *Is the subject singular or plural?* Then choose the correct verb form.

SINGULAR   That <u>man walks</u> every day.
PLURAL   Those <u>men walk</u> every day.

SINGULAR   <u>She was</u> in the play.
PLURAL   <u>They were</u> in the play.

EXERCISE 3 *Matching Subjects and Verbs*

Number your paper 1 to 10. Then write each word in the Subjects column that agrees in number with the verb in the Verbs column.

EXAMPLE   dogs, children, boy, Tom   are
ANSWER   dogs, children

Subjects	Verbs
1. stores, house, monuments, shed	stands
2. friends, Rosa, Dad, leader	talks
3. minerals, rocks, metal, gem	is
4. planes, kites, pilot, flag	fly
5. puppy, kittens, baby, men	sleeps
6. cars, boat, bicycle, train	moves
7. leaves, bark, plants, tree	grow
8. Mother, artists, guard, teachers	study
9. stars, diamonds, light, silver	twinkle
10. tadpoles, Keith, rabbits, child	hop

EXERCISE 4 *Making Subjects and Verbs Agree*

Number your paper 1 to 10. Write each subject and label it *singular* or *plural*. Then write the verb form in parentheses that agrees with the subject.

EXAMPLE   Frogs (hibernates, hibernate) in cold weather.
ANSWER   frogs, plural—hibernate

Frogs

1. Frogs (was, were) on the earth 50 million years before dinosaurs.
2. A close relative of the frog (is, are) the toad.
3. These funny creatures (has, have) huge appetites.
4. A toad (eats, eat) about 100 insects every day.
5. They (catches, catch) insects with their long, sticky tongues.
6. The longest leap by a frog (was, were) over 17 feet.
7. Every year Kermit the Frog (appears, appear) as a huge balloon in the Macy's Thanksgiving Day Parade.
8. Then he (is, are) 63 feet tall and 24 feet wide!
9. People (runs, run) frog farms in marshes and swamps.
10. Frogs' legs (is, are) popular in some restaurants.

You *and* I *as Subjects*

The pronouns *you* and *I* do not follow the two rules for agreement that you just learned. *You* is *always* used with a plural verb—whether *you* refers to one person or more than one person.

PLURAL   Chester, <u>you</u> <u>are</u> a good friend.
VERBS   Girls, <u>you</u> <u>sing</u> beautifully.

Although *I* refers to one person, it takes a plural verb. The only exceptions are the *be* verb forms *am* and *was.*

PLURAL   <u>I</u> <u>write</u> poems.
VERBS   <u>I</u> <u>have</u> extra work tonight.

SINGULAR   <u>I</u> <u>am</u> a brunette.
VERBS   <u>I</u> <u>was</u> very tired yesterday.

EXERCISE 5 *Making Verbs Agree with* **You** *and* I

Number your paper 1 to 10. Then write the verb form in parentheses that agrees with each subject.

1. You (was, were) the best act in the variety show last night.
2. You (is, are) an excellent athlete.
3. I (has, have) a present for you.
4. I (was, were) never there.
5. You always (walks, walk) so rapidly.
6. I (works, work) every day after school baby-sitting for my neighbor's twins.
7. You (has, have) a nice voice.
8. You (dances, dance) well.
9. I (was, were) the leader in the relay races in gym yesterday.
10. You (dries, dry) the dishes tonight.

Verb Phrases

A *verb phrase* is the main verb plus one or more helping verbs. If a sentence has a verb phrase, the helping verb must agree in number with the subject.

13d The helping verb must agree in number with its subject.

Following is a list of singular and plural forms of common helping verbs.

Common Helping Verbs	
SINGULAR	**PLURAL**
am, is, was, has, does	are, were, have, do

SINGULAR   Mom **is** driving us.

PLURAL   We **have** been taking the early bus.

EXERCISE 6   Making Subjects and Verb Phrases Agree

Number your paper 1 to 10. Write each subject. Then write the helping verb in parentheses that agrees with the subject.

1. Pumpkins (has, have) been growing in this country for 3,500 years.
2. Nearly 75,000 umbrellas (is, are) lost each year on London's bus and subway systems.
3. Archaeologists (has, have) found prehistoric hairpins and combs.
4. The largest marching band (was, were) composed of 1,976 musicians.
5. Siamese cats (has, have) lived in the United States since 1895.
6. A 1930 Cadillac (was, were) powered by a 16-cylinder engine.
7. The first pencil (was, were) patented in 1858.
8. Penguins (has, have) swum underwater as fast as 22 miles per hour.
9. The earth (is, are) revolving at a speed of 1,000 miles per hour.
10. Mexico's east coast (is, are) sinking into the sea at the rate of one to two inches per year.

EXERCISE 7   Writing Sentences

Number your paper 1 to 5. Choose the correct verb form in parentheses that agrees with each subject. Then complete each sentence.

EXAMPLE   The students (works, work) . . .
POSSIBLE   work—The students work very hard each year
ANSWER   on the floats for the parade.

1. The lion (roars, roar) . . .
2. You (was, were) . . .
3. I (has, have) . . .
4. The rain (is, are) pouring . . .
5. The children (was, were) playing . . .

202

TIME-OUT FOR REVIEW • • • • •

Number your paper 1 to 10. Write each subject. Then write the verb form in parentheses that agrees with each subject.

1. A housefly (beats, beat) its wings about 20,000 times a minute.
2. The Badgers (was, were) leading 9 to 5.
3. I (has, have) a free ticket to the amusement park.
4. Apples (is, are) grown in many states.
5. You (was, were) the best singer in the concert.
6. Approximately 750,000 pianos (is, are) produced worldwide each year.
7. The blue backpack (holds, hold) my lunch and books.
8. You (is, are) a fine athlete.
9. Every morning my friends (walks, walk) to school.
10. The monkeys (was, were) jumping from tree to tree.

Interrupting Words

Words, such as a prepositional phrase, can come between a subject and its verb. When this happens, a mistake in agreement can easily be made. Sometimes the verb is made to agree with a word that is closer to it, rather than with the subject.

13e   The agreement of a verb with its subject is not changed by any interrupting words.

In the following examples, notice that the subject and the verb in each sentence agree in number—in spite of the words that come between them.

The <u>juice</u> from these oranges <u>is</u> sour. [*Is* agrees with *juice*—not with the object of the preposition, *oranges*.]

The <u>candidates</u> for class president <u>are</u> Allison and Leon. [*Are* agrees with *candidates*—not with the object of the preposition, *president*.]

EXERCISE 8 Making Interrupted Subjects and Verbs Agree

Number your paper 1 to 10. Write each subject. Then write the verb form in parentheses that agrees with the subject.

1. Waves during a storm at sea rarely (reaches, reach) a height of more than 50 feet.
2. Jo's choice of words (makes, make) her story funny.
3. In skywriting the average height of the letters (is, are) nearly two miles.
4. The roots of a tree (absorbs, absorb) water and minerals from the soil.
5. All the dogs in the kennel (was, were) barking.
6. The earliest book about checkers (was, were) published in 1547.
7. The peaches in the orchard (has, have) become ripe.
8. Games like softball (requires, require) teamwork.
9. Many pages in the book (has, have) photographs.
10. The hills of Virginia (was, were) hazy.

Inverted Order

In a sentence's natural order, the subject comes before the verb. However, in a sentence having *inverted order,* the verb or part of the verb phrase comes before the subject. A verb always agrees with its subject, whether the sentence is in its natural order or in inverted order.

13f The subject and the verb of an inverted sentence must agree in number.

To find the subject in an inverted sentence, turn the sentence around to its natural order. Following are examples of inverted sentences.

INVERTED ORDER   On the glacier <u>were</u> two <u>penguins</u>.
NATURAL ORDER   Two <u>penguins</u> <u>were</u> on the glacier.

QUESTION	<u>Is</u> your <u>homework</u> <u>finished</u>?
NATURAL ORDER	Your <u>homework</u> <u>is finished</u>.
SENTENCE BEGINNING WITH *HERE*	Here <u>is</u> the perfect <u>picture</u> for your room.
NATURAL ORDER	The perfect <u>picture</u> for your room <u>is</u> here.
SENTENCE BEGINNING WITH *THERE*	There <u>were</u> only three <u>bands</u> in the Fourth of July parade.
NATURAL ORDER	Only three <u>bands</u> <u>were</u> in the Fourth of July parade. [Sometimes *here* or *there* must be dropped for the sentence to make sense.]

EXERCISE 9 *Agreement with Subjects in Inverted Order*

Number your paper 1 to 10. Write each subject. Then write the verb form in parentheses that agrees with the subject.

1. There (is, are) 75 different kinds of whales in the world's oceans.
2. Alongside the stream in the Everglades (was, were) two alligators.
3. (Was, Were) the dishes on the shelf broken during the tremor?
4. (Is, Are) wild horses still roaming on the Western plains?
5. Here (is, are) the subscription form for the science magazine.
6. There (is, are) 50 students in the school band.
7. On the rocks (was, were) traces of oil from a spill off the coast.
8. How nervous (was, were) you before your first piano recital?
9. Outside the harbor around the bay (was, were) several sailboats.
10. There (is, are) meteorite craters in Arizona, Texas, and Kansas.

EXERCISE 10 Writing Sentences

Number your paper 1 to 5. Then write five sentences that follow the directions below.

1. Write a sentence that includes *the apples on that tree* as the subject. Use a present tense verb.
2. Write a sentence that includes *the boy on the beach* as the subject. Use a present tense verb.
3. Write a sentence in inverted order that includes the verb *were shining.*
4. Write a question that begins with *have.*
5. Write a sentence that begins with *there are.*

TIME-OUT FOR REVIEW • • • • •

Number your paper 1 to 10. Write each subject. Then write the verb form in parentheses that agrees with the subject.

EXAMPLE (Was, Were) the subways crowded last night?
ANSWER Were

1. Accidents in the home (is, are) frequently caused by carelessness.
2. There (is, are) orange, green, cinnamon, and yellow canaries.
3. The parks in our city (is, are) generally in good condition due to the efforts of many volunteers.
4. In the aquarium (was, were) three swordtails.
5. (Does, Do) that windmill really work?
6. In Yellowstone National Park, there (is, are) 200 active geysers.
7. On the highest shelf in the garage (is, are) some cans of paint.
8. (Has, Have) any cardinals ever come to the bird feeder on your windowsill?
9. The noise of the gulls near the dump by the harbor (was, were) deafening.
10. Here (is, are) the list of books for summer reading.

Common Agreement Problems

Certain subjects and verbs require special rules in order to make them agree.

Compound Subjects

A compound subject is two or more subjects that have the same verb. A compound subject is usually joined by the conjunction *and* or *or*, but a compound subject can also be joined by the pairs of conjunctions *both/and*, *either/or*, or *neither/nor*. When you write a sentence with a compound subject, you need to remember two agreement rules.

13g When subjects are joined by *and* or *both/and*, the verb is usually plural.

And indicates more than one. When a subject is more than one, it is plural. The verb, therefore, must also be plural to agree with the subject.

PLURAL   <u>Sam</u> **and** <u>Jed</u> **are** <u>fishing</u> from the pier.
VERBS   **Both** the <u>hammer</u> **and** the <u>nails</u> <u>belong</u> here.

When a compound subject is joined by *or*, *either/or*, or *neither/nor*, agreement between the subject and the verb follows a different rule.

13h When subjects are joined by *or*, *either/or*, or *neither/nor*, the verb agrees with the closer subject.

SINGULAR   **Either** <u>Mom</u> **or** <u>Dad</u> **is** <u>driving</u> us to school.
VERB   [The verb is singular because *Dad*, the subject closer to it, is singular.]
PLURAL   <u>Apples</u> **or** <u>pears</u> <u>are</u> tasty snacks. [The verb is
VERB   plural because *pears*, the subject closer to it, is plural.]

207

This rule applies especially when one subject is singular and the other is plural.

SINGULAR **Neither** my <u>cousins</u> **nor** my <u>aunt</u> <u>likes</u>
VERB airplanes. [The verb is singular because *aunt*, the subject closer to it, is singular.]

PLURAL **Neither** my <u>aunt</u> **nor** my <u>cousins</u> <u>like</u>
VERB airplanes. [The verb is plural because *cousins*, the subject closer to it, is plural.]

EXERCISE 11 *Making Verbs Agree with Compound Subjects*

Number your paper 1 to 15. Then write the verb form in parentheses that agrees with each subject.

1. In animated films only three fingers and a thumb (appears, appear) on each character's hand.
2. Both peaches and oranges (was, were) cultivated in China 4,000 years ago.
3. The dictionary or a thesaurus (is, are) a good source of fresh adjectives and verbs.
4. Whales, dolphins, and porpoises (is, are) sea mammals.
5. Neither Sue nor Donna (was, were) with us yesterday morning.
6. Blueberries and blackberries (grows, grow) on bushes.
7. The canoe or the sailboat (is, are) for rent.
8. Neither the oranges nor the pineapple (was, were) eaten at breakfast.
9. Fog, smoke, and harmful gases (forms, form) smog, a type of air pollution.
10. Neither my uncle nor my grandparents (is, are) coming to our Fourth of July barbecue.
11. Both Jacinta and her family (lives, live) in San Francisco.
12. A sandwich or soup (makes, make) a nice lunch.
13. Either the instructor or her students (has, have) completed this mural.
14. Tomatoes and lettuce (is, are) needed for the salad.
15. The twins or Sally (cleans, clean) this room weekly.

Indefinite Pronouns

An indefinite pronoun can be the subject of a sentence. Some indefinite pronouns are singular, some are plural, and some can be either singular or plural.

13i A verb must agree in number with an indefinite pronoun used as a subject.

Following is a list of common indefinite pronouns.

Common Indefinite Pronouns	
SINGULAR	anybody, anyone, each, either, everybody, everyone, neither, nobody, no one, one, somebody, someone
PLURAL	both, few, many, several
SINGULAR/PLURAL	all, any, most, none, some

SINGULAR   <u>Someone</u> **has** <u>called</u> you three times. [*Has* agrees with *someone*.]
<u>Either</u> of the movies <u>is</u> fine. [*Is* agrees with *either*—not with *movies*.]

PLURAL   <u>Both</u> of my parents <u>have</u> a job. [*Have* agrees with *both*.]
<u>Few</u> of these tomatoes <u>are</u> ripe. [*Are* agrees with *few*.]

All, any, most, none, and *some* can be either singular or plural. The number of each of these pronouns is determined by the object of the preposition that follows it.

SINGULAR   <u>All</u> of the **bread** <u>is</u> fresh. [Since *bread* is singular, *is* is also singular.]

PLURAL   <u>All</u> of these **books** <u>are</u> from the library. [Since *books* is plural, *are* is also plural.]

209

EXERCISE 12 Making Verbs Agree with Indefinite Pronouns

Number your paper 1 to 15. Then write the verb form in parentheses that agrees with each subject.

1. Everyone in my homeroom (was, were) present each day last week.
2. All of my sisters (has, have) the measles.
3. Each of the crossing guards (wears, wear) a badge.
4. Neither of the fishing boats by the dock (seems, seem) seaworthy.
5. All of the broken glass (is, are) sharp.
6. Several of the apples (has, have) bruises on them.
7. None of Sunday's newspaper (has, have) been read.
8. One of the lily's closest biological relatives (is, are) asparagus.
9. Many of the test questions (was, were) difficult.
10. Anyone with good grades (is, are) applying.
11. None of the current movies (has, have) received a good review.
12. (Is, Are) anybody making the costumes for the play?
13. One of the stores in the shopping mall (sells, sell) records and tapes.
14. Few of the seats on the bus (has, have) been taken.
15. Most of our water supply (comes, come) from a reservoir in central Massachusetts.

EXERCISE 13 Writing Sentences

Number your paper 1 to 5. Then write five sentences that follow the directions below.

1. Use a compound subject with the verb *are*.
2. Use a compound subject with the verb *has*.
3. Use an indefinite pronoun as the subject of the verb *is*.
4. Use an indefinite pronoun as the subject of the verb *are riding*.
5. Use *most of the students* as the subject of the verb *has taken* or *have taken*, whichever one is correct.

Doesn't *and* Don't

When contractions are used, agreement with a subject can be confusing. To check for agreement, always say the individual words of any contraction.

13j The verb part of a contraction must agree in number with the subject.

INCORRECT   This <u>piece</u> **do**n't <u>fit</u> into the puzzle. [This piece *do not* fit into the puzzle.]

CORRECT   This <u>piece</u> **does**n't <u>fit</u> into the puzzle. [*Does* agrees with *piece*.]

INCORRECT   **Does**n't <u>they</u> <u>understand</u> the rules? [They *does not* understand the rules.]

CORRECT   **Do**n't <u>they</u> <u>understand</u> the rules? [*Do* agrees with *they*.]

The previous rule applies to all contractions.

EXERCISE 14 Making Subjects and Contractions Agree

Number your paper 1 to 10. Then write the contraction in parentheses that agrees with each subject.

1. This clock (doesn't, don't) keep time very well.
2. The rice (isn't, aren't) in the glass jar.
3. The boats (hasn't, haven't) started to race yet.
4. Several of my friends (isn't, aren't) here.
5. Timothy (hasn't, haven't) always lived in Florida.
6. (Doesn't, Don't) your cat like catnip?
7. This soup (wasn't, weren't) made with fresh vegetables from our garden.
8. Most of the football players (hasn't, haven't) missed a single game all season.
9. (Wasn't, Weren't) you at the game?
10. Everyone (isn't, aren't) here yet.

TIME-OUT FOR REVIEW • • • • •

Number your paper 1 to 20. Then write the verb form in parentheses that agrees with each subject.

1. Your hands and feet (contains, contain) nearly half the bones in your entire body.
2. Both of my pencils (has, have) an eraser.
3. Most of the newspaper (is, are) wet.
4. Phobos and Deimos (is, are) the two moons of Mars.
5. Rain or sleet (is, are) predicted for tomorrow.
6. Few of the apartments (is, are) ever vacant at this time of year.
7. Neither the lion tamer nor the clowns (is, are) signing any autographs tonight.
8. Any of those nails (is, are) fine.
9. Gold coins and silver bars (was, were) found in the sunken pirate ship.
10. Everybody at the Fourth of July parade (was, were) carrying an American flag.
11. My mother and my sister (doesn't, don't) watch TV except for the evening news.
12. Either string beans or broccoli (is, are) my favorite vegetable.
13. All of the guests (has, have) gone to the concert in the park.
14. The books and the magazine (was, were) placed on the table.
15. Some of the forest (contains, contain) patches of poison ivy.
16. Several of the field hockey players also (belongs, belong) to the track team.
17. Each of the Girl Scouts (does, do) a community service project.
18. Trumpets or a flute (creates, create) excitement in music.
19. Someone at the stables (grooms, groom) the horses every morning.
20. (Doesn't, Don't) he have the directions?

Application to Writing

As you edit your written work, always look for correct subject and verb agreement.

EXERCISE 15 Editing for Subject and Verb Agreement

Read the following paragraphs and find the 15 verbs that do not agree with their subjects. Then rewrite the paragraphs correctly.

Icebergs

Icebergs begin their existence in the polar regions. Enormous masses of ice breaks from glaciers. The new icebergs fall into the ocean and are carried far by ocean currents. An average-sized iceberg don't appear very large. However, only a very small part of it shows above the water. Icebergs from the Antarctic Regions is generally larger than those in the North Atlantic. One of the huge masses were actually twice as big as the state of Connecticut!

The fringes of Greenland's great ice cap is the major source of the icebergs in the North Atlantic. In early spring huge chunks of ice breaks off the ends of the ice cap. Then hundreds of icebergs float into the ship routes.

Icebergs and fog is the greatest natural dangers to ships. One of the world's worst sea disasters were the collision of the *Titanic* with an iceberg. Because of the work of the International Ice Patrol, there is fewer hazards to ships.

Neither fog nor darkness prevent the detection of icebergs. Even in the densest fog, the location of icebergs are registered by radar. The course of all icebergs are broadcast to ships in the area.

Eventually the North Atlantic icebergs flow farther south, and icebergs from the Antarctic is carried northward. Then bright sunshine and warm ocean water melts them. However, this process can take a long time. Some giant icebergs has even lasted ten years.

*C*hapter *R*eview

A **Making Subjects and Verbs Agree.** Number your paper 1 to 10. Then write the verb form in parentheses that agrees with each subject.

1. The weight of those rocks (is, are) about 500 pounds.
2. None of these instructions (makes, make) sense.
3. The common length of most lightning bolts (is, are) about half a mile.
4. (Is, Are) you trying out for the track team?
5. The boys in the shop (plays, play) baseball at lunchtime.
6. You (hasn't, haven't) received mail today.
7. The intercom (isn't, aren't) working today.
8. Some swans and other water birds (carries, carry) their young across the water on their backs.
9. A few of my friends (has, have) responded to the invitation.
10. There (is, are) 12 letters in the Hawaiian alphabet.

B **Making Subjects and Verbs Agree.** Number your paper 1 to 10. Find and write the verbs that do not agree with their subjects. Then write each sentence correctly. If a sentence is correct, write *C* after the number.

1. The rich mud of drained swamps make good farmland.
2. Neither Don nor Chris were chosen as an actor.
3. No one on the front steps was waiting for a bus.
4. Have one of the actors forgotten his lines?
5. There are 35 million digestive glands in the stomach.
6. Don't Jerry have his jacket with him?
7. You was smiling in the photograph.
8. Each of the Miller children have a calf and a pig.
9. Do all of your relatives want tickets?
10. The grandfather clock and the cuckoo clock chimes together.

C **Editing for Subject and Verb Agreement.** Write the following paragraphs, correcting each verb that does not agree with its subject.

Trees

Trees are green plants. A tree, like other green plants, have roots, stems, leaves, and seeds. Trees, however, are the oldest of all plants. Some of the sequoia trees of the Northwestern United States is more than 4,000 years old. These giants were here before Columbus.

The age of trees are recorded in their rings. There is rings in the cross section of most kinds of tree trunks. Each of the rings represent one year of the tree's life. The rings of a tree appears not only in the trunk but also in the branches and twigs.

Trees are also the biggest of all green plants. The giant redwoods of California is the tallest trees on Earth. One of those trees are 364 feet high! This huge tree with its enormous branches grow in Humboldt National Forest.

Mastery Test

Number your paper 1 to 10. Then write the verb form in parentheses that agrees with each subject.

1. The brain of sperm whales (is, are) the largest in the world.
2. It (weighs, weigh) as much as 20 pounds.
3. There (is, are) hundreds of Pueblo ruins in Chaco Canyon, New Mexico.
4. Everybody in these lines (has, have) a ticket.
5. That dogwood (doesn't, don't) flower until May.
6. At the edge of the field (was, were) two woodchucks.
7. I (was, were) there on time yesterday.
8. Some of the candles (has, have) already burned down.
9. Either Chung or Betsy (sits, sit) at this desk.
10. The normal pulse rate for children (is, are) 90 to 120 beats per minute.

14

Using Adjectives and Adverbs

Diagnostic Test

Number your paper 1 to 10. Then write the correct modifier in parentheses.

EXAMPLE   Joel is the (shorter, shortest) triplet.
ANSWER   shortest

1. Which of the three cars do you think is the (better, best) looking?
2. Who plays the violin (more, most) skillfully, Alana or Raymond?
3. I haven't (ever, never) learned to play chess.
4. Because the wood was green, our fire didn't burn very (good, well).
5. Although it is beautiful in all four seasons, the moon is (more, most) beautiful in the autumn.
6. I don't know who of the three was (happier, happiest).
7. Is a retriever puppy (friendlier, more friendlier) than a terrier puppy?
8. Which of the Donleavy twins is the (better, best) gymnast?
9. The milk doesn't taste (good, well).
10. Which is harvested (earlier, earliest), asparagus or squash?

Comparison of Adjectives and Adverbs

When you write, you often compare one thing with another. Adjectives and adverbs generally have three forms that are used for comparisons. These forms are called degrees of comparison.

14a   Most adjectives and adverbs have three degrees of comparison: the *positive*, the *comparative*, and the *superlative*.

The *positive* degree is used when no comparison is being made.

ADJECTIVE   The tiger is **big.**
ADVERB   A giraffe runs **swiftly.**

The *comparative* degree is used when two people, things, or actions are being compared.

ADJECTIVE   An elephant is **bigger** than a tiger.
ADVERB   A zebra runs **more swiftly** than a giraffe.

The *superlative* degree is used when more than two people, things, or actions are being compared.

ADJECTIVE   The blue whale is the **biggest** animal of all.
ADVERB   Of all animals the cheetah runs the **most swiftly.**

Regular Comparison

Most adjectives and adverbs form the comparative and superlative degrees in a regular manner. The form often depends on the number of syllables in the modifier.

14b   Add *-er* to form the comparative degree and *-est* to form the superlative degree of one-syllable modifiers.

	POSITIVE	COMPARATIVE	SUPERLATIVE
ADJECTIVE	bright	brighter	brightest
	sad	sadder	saddest
ADVERB	soon	sooner	soonest

NOTE: A spelling change sometimes occurs when -er or -est is added to certain modifiers, such as *sad.*

Many two-syllable modifiers are formed exactly like one-syllable modifiers. A few two-syllable modifiers, however, would be difficult to pronounce if -er or -est was added. "Usefuler" and "usefulest," for instance, sound awkward. For such two-syllable modifiers, *more* and *most* should be used to form the comparative and superlative forms. Also, *more* and *most* are usually used with adverbs ending in -*ly.*

14c Use -*er* or *more* to form the comparative degree and -*est* or *most* to form the superlative degree of two-syllable modifiers.

	POSITIVE	COMPARATIVE	SUPERLATIVE
ADJECTIVE	funny	funnier	funniest
	cheerful	more cheerful	most cheerful
ADVERB	early	earlier	earliest
	quickly	more quickly	most quickly

NOTE: A spelling change occurs in modifiers that end in *y,* such as *funny* and *early.*

All modifiers with three or more syllables form their comparative and superlative degrees by using *more* and *most.*

14d Use *more* to form the comparative degree and *most* to form the superlative degree of modifiers with three or more syllables.

	POSITIVE	COMPARATIVE	SUPERLATIVE
ADJECTIVE	difficult	more difficult	most difficult
ADVERB	frequently	more frequently	most frequently

EXERCISE 1 Forming the Comparison of Regular Modifiers

Number your paper 1 to 20. Copy each modifier. Then write its comparative and superlative forms.

EXAMPLE cozy
ANSWER cozy, cozier, coziest

1. restless
2. safe
3. narrow
4. wonderful
5. carefully
6. smart
7. loudly
8. late
9. pretty
10. dark
11. happy
12. athletic
13. slowly
14. obedient
15. hard
16. fast
17. often
18. high
19. easily
20. lovely

EXERCISE 2 Using the Correct Form of Modifiers

Number your paper 1 to 10. Then write the correct modifier in parentheses.

EXAMPLE Suki is the (taller, tallest) of the twins.
ANSWER taller

1. Which of the two Dakotas is (larger, largest), North Dakota or South Dakota?
2. Do tornadoes occur (more, most) frequently in the Midwest or in New England?
3. Steve is the (more, most) helpful of the two clerks in the market.
4. Who drives the (more, most) carefully, Mom, Dad, or Andrew?
5. We need the (stronger, strongest) kind of rope available.
6. Which has the (larger, largest) population, Dallas or Houston?
7. Of the 20 questions on the test, the last one was the (more, most) difficult.
8. Which of these two peaches is (riper, ripest)?
9. Which bridge is (longer, longest), the Golden Gate, the George Washington, or the Brooklyn Bridge?
10. Anne writes the (more, most) creatively of the four.

Irregular Comparison

A few adjectives and adverbs are compared in an irregular manner. The comparative and superlative forms of the following modifiers should be memorized so that you can use them correctly in your writing.

Irregularly Compared Modifiers		
POSITIVE	**COMPARATIVE**	**SUPERLATIVE**
bad/badly	worse	worst
good/well	better	best
little	less	least
much/many	more	most

POSITIVE	The storm yesterday was **bad.**
COMPARATIVE	It was **worse** than the storm last week.
SUPERLATIVE	In fact, it was the **worst** storm of the summer.

EXERCISE 3 Using the Correct Form of Modifiers

Number your paper 1 to 5. Read the first sentence in each group. Then write the comparative and superlative forms of each word that is underlined in the first sentence.

EXAMPLE   I made too <u>much</u> popcorn.
It was _____ popcorn than I needed.
It was the _____ popcorn I have ever made.

ANSWERS   more, most

1. Terry's meatloaf tastes <u>good</u>.
Paul's meatloaf tastes even _____ than Terry's.
However, Mom's meatloaf tastes _____ of all.

2. Dad feels <u>bad</u>.
Last night he felt _____.
Two nights ago, however, he felt the _____.

3. Sometimes I have <u>little</u> free time.
   I have _____ free time than my brother.
   I have the _____ free time of anyone in my family.
4. Bart sings <u>well</u>.
   He sings _____ than I sing.
   He sings the _____ of everyone in the chorus.
5. <u>Many</u> people on the subway listen to radios.
   _____ people read books or newspapers.
   However, _____ people just sit.

EXERCISE 4 Writing Sentences

Suppose you are given a choice of what time period you would like to live in—right now, 100 years ago, or 100 years in the future. Choose one of these time periods and write at least five sentences explaining why you think that time period would be better than the other two. Use comparative and superlative forms of adjectives and adverbs.

TIME-OUT FOR REVIEW • • • • •

Number your paper 1 to 10. Find and write each incorrect modifier. Then write it correctly. If a sentence is correct, write *C* after the number.

EXAMPLE   Who is the best pitcher, Ken or David?
ANSWER   better

1. That was the worse football game I've ever seen.
2. Of the last five days, I am busier today.
3. Is Route 2 or Ridge Road the best route home?
4. Chuck lifted the heaviest carton of the four.
5. Who writes most neatly, you or Keith?
6. When did you feel best, today or yesterday?
7. Jeanne is the most intelligent of the two sisters.
8. Who ate the shrimp more eagerly, Carmen or you?
9. Which weighs least, a pint of oil or a pint of water?
10. Of the three available apartments, we like the one in Building D better.

Problems with Modifiers

Once you know how to form the comparative and super-lative forms of modifiers, there are a few problems you should watch out for when you write them.

Double Comparisons

Use only one method to form the comparative or the superlative of a modifier. Using *-er* and *more* together, for example, would result in a *double comparison*.

14e Do not use both *-er* and *more* to form the comparative degree, or both *-est* and *most* to form the superlative degree.

DOUBLE COMPARISON	Can you work **more quicklier?**
CORRECT	Can you work **more quickly?**
DOUBLE COMPARISON	The cactus is the **most strangest** plant I've ever seen.
CORRECT	The cactus is the **strangest** plant I've ever seen.

EXERCISE 5 Correcting Double Comparisons

Number your paper 1 to 10. Then write the following sentences, correcting each error.

1. Kay made the most smartest decision of all the girls.
2. Mow the grass more closelier than you did before.
3. The common orange garden spider is the most skill-fulest of web builders.
4. Eclipses of the moon occur more oftener than eclipses of the sun.
5. Few animals are more playfuler than wolf pups.
6. The earthquake damaged the more older buildings.
7. Is it more easier to row a rowboat than to paddle a canoe?

8. That car runs more smoothlier than the other one.
9. The red boat is more speedier than the blue one.
10. This exercise is the most hardest one so far.

Double Negatives

Following is a list of common negative words.

Common Negatives		
no	nobody	none
not	no one	never
-n't	nothing	hardly

Two negative words should not be used together to express the same idea. When they are, the result is a *double negative.*

14f   Avoid using a double negative.

DOUBLE NEGATIVE   We did**n't** swim **no** laps today.
CORRECT   We did**n't** swim any laps today.
CORRECT   We swam **no** laps today.

DOUBLE NEGATIVE   Sue did**n't hardly** stop for breath.
CORRECT   Sue **hardly** stopped for breath.

EXERCISE 6   Correcting Double Negatives

Number your paper 1 to 10. Then write the following sentences, correcting each error.

1. The mechanic can't find nothing wrong with the car.
2. Don't you have no film for this camera?
3. They hadn't hardly finished dinner when I arrived.
4. I can't never hit a home run.
5. I haven't done none of my homework yet.
6. After the fog settled in, I couldn't hardly see three inches in front of me.

7. No one couldn't find Tim's notebook.
8. Kathy didn't write nothing for this issue of the school newspaper.
9. Sometimes I don't have no fun at parties.
10. Nobody hasn't fixed the broken streetlight at the corner of Elm and Grove.

Good *and* Well

Good is always used as an adjective. *Well* is usually used as an adverb. When *well* means "in good health," it is used as an adjective. Remember that adjectives can follow linking verbs. (*See pages 41 and 43 for lists of linking verbs.*)

ADJECTIVE   That story was **good.** [*Good* is a predicate adjective that describes *story*.]

ADVERB   Michael read the story **well.** [*Well* is an adverb that tells how Michael read.]

ADJECTIVE   I don't feel **well** today. [In this sentence *well* means "in good health."]

EXERCISE 7   Using Good *and* Well

Number your paper 1 to 10. Then write either *good* or *well* to complete each sentence correctly.

1. Since Ted has taken lessons, he swims _____.
2. The cool day felt _____ after the heat wave.
3. Rock music really sounds _____ to me.
4. Dad's cold is gone, and he finally feels _____.
5. Scott writes very _____.
6. Our car doesn't work _____ anymore.
7. Hot soup tastes _____ on a cold winter day.
8. After eating the strange Earth food, the space creature did not feel very _____.
9. I'm glad that I studied hard, because I did _____ on the test.
10. The freshly baked bread smelled so _____.

TIME-OUT FOR REVIEW • • • • •

Number your paper 1 to 20. Then write the following sentences, correcting each error. If a sentence is correct, write *C* after the number.

EXAMPLE   The tacos really tasted well.
ANSWER   The tacos really tasted good.

1. That car was going more faster than yours.
2. The fish were biting good yesterday.
3. Paul didn't say nothing to us about rescheduling the meeting.
4. Those plums are juicy, but the peaches from the orchard were more juicier.
5. That is the most funniest story I have ever heard him tell.
6. Louis doesn't need no help with his packing.
7. The Cougars played very well against the Chargers.
8. That short nail won't hold good in the wall.
9. Which dog is most biggest, a spaniel, a German shepherd, or a Great Dane?
10. Susan's baby sister hardly ever cries.
11. Pearl had a sore throat on Friday, but she feels good today.
12. You shouldn't never start an electrical appliance when your hands are wet.
13. The comedy at the Cinema Showcase sounds good.
14. My grandmother lives in the most oldest house in Valleyton.
15. No one could tell me anything about the bus schedules to the West Coast.
16. The human brain is more complexer than the brain of any other animal.
17. Chen's chances of winning the race seemed well.
18. Mercury is the planet most closest to the sun.
19. Sharon is more eager than Lillian to learn ballet.
20. Mrs. Nguyen hadn't hardly arrived when she had to leave again.

*A*pplication to Writing

When you write comparisons, always edit your work to make sure you have used the correct forms of comparison. Also check to see if you have avoided the problems with modifiers.

EXERCISE 8 *Editing for the Correct Use of Modifiers*

Read the following paragraphs and find the ten errors. Then write the paragraphs correctly.

Toads and Frogs

Toads and frogs are the most commonest amphibians. A toad is usually a chubby creature with rough, bumpy skin. A frog, on the other hand, is thinnest and has more smoother skin. A toad is more clumsier than a frog.

Toads usually jump more shorter distances than frogs do. Both toads and frogs, however, can move quickly. Of these two amphibians, frogs have the longest hind legs. Some people think frogs' legs taste well for dinner.

All toads and frogs are born in water. They aren't never born on land. Once they are grown, most toads live on land, but frogs usually must live near water. Some frogs, however, live in unusual places, such as treetops. These frogs have toe pads, which help them climb good.

There is another important thing you should know about toads and frogs. They don't cause no warts.

EXERCISE 9 *Writing Sentences*

The appearance of most places changes from morning to evening. Choose some location, such as your neighborhood, a park, or a forest. Write at least five sentences comparing the way the place looks in the morning to the way it looks in the evening. When you have finished, edit your writing to correct any mistakes in modifiers.

*C*hapter *R*eview

A **Using the Correct Form of Modifiers.** Number your paper 1 to 10. Then write the correct modifier in parentheses.

1. Your book report sounded (good, well).
2. Which shines (more, most) brightly, gold or silver?
3. Craig didn't know (nothing, anything) about the broken window.
4. My three aunts held the baby, but Aunt Carrie was the (more, most) nervous.
5. Is Daniel (taller, more taller) than you?
6. Ruth is doing (good, well) at the police academy.
7. There aren't (no, any) seats left in the theater.
8. Can you tell which of these three snakes is (deadlier, deadliest)?
9. Who made the (wiser, wisest) choice, Jerry or Pat?
10. Which television set has the (worse, worst) picture, mine or yours?

B **Correcting Errors with Modifiers.** Number your paper 1 to 10. Then write the following sentences, correcting each error. If a sentence is correct, write *C* after the number.

1. Which of the six New England states is smaller?
2. There aren't no oars in this boat.
3. In some science-fiction stories, spaceships travel more faster than the speed of light.
4. I don't know who was coldest, you or I.
5. Of the two cars, this one is more reliable.
6. Haven't you seen none of my pictures?
7. Which of the three days was hotter?
8. Our 12-year-old dog doesn't see very good.
9. This coat looks more better on you than the other one did.
10. I did well on my lifesaving test at the YMCA.

C **Forming the Comparison of Modifiers.** Write the form indicated below for each modifier. Then use that form in a sentence.

1. the comparative of *wisely*
2. the comparative of *keen*
3. the superlative of *good*
4. the comparative of *useful*
5. the comparative of *scary*
6. the superlative of *much*
7. the superlative of *smooth*
8. the comparative of *cautiously*
9. the superlative of *dangerous*
10. the comparative of *comfortable*

Mastery Test

Number your paper 1 to 10. Then write the correct modifier in parentheses.

1. During years of good weather, trees grow (good, well).
2. Which of the two stories did you like (better, best)?
3. This kind of model plane is (more difficult, more difficulter) to make than that kind.
4. Because of a headache, I didn't feel (good, well) yesterday morning.
5. After looking at the two bicycles, I learned that the red one was (cheaper, cheapest).
6. Of the three comedians, I think the last one was the (funnier, funniest).
7. Which one of the two carpenters is (more, most) energetic?
8. Our baseball team hasn't (never, ever) won the state championship.
9. Of the three jackets, which one did you think was made (better, best)?
10. This is the (more, most) dangerous intersection in town.

Standardized Test

Directions: Choose the word or words that best complete each sentence. In the appropriate row on your answer sheet, fill in the circle containing the same letter as your answer.

SAMPLE   Donna _____ a tuna sandwich.

      A ate   **B** eaten   **C** eated

ANSWER   Ⓐ Ⓑ Ⓒ

1. David _____ three inches in six months.

   A grew   **B** growed   **C** grown

2. Why are the sneakers _____ than the sandals?

   A cheaper   **B** more cheap   **C** more cheaper

3. Diana had never _____ at night before.

   A driven   **B** drived   **C** drove

4. The missing kitten had been _____ in the bathtub.

   A laying   **B** lying   **C** lain

5. Ramona _____ by the telephone and waited.

   A set   **B** sit   **C** sat

6. Which do you like _____, summer or winter?

   A best   **B** better   **C** more better

7. The storm grew _____ as it approached the mountain.

   A worst   **B** worse   **C** worser

8. Of the three flowers, which do you think is _____?

   A most beautiful   **B** beautifulest   **C** more beautiful

9. Edgar Allan Poe _____ a poem called "The Raven."

   A written   **B** writed   **C** wrote

10. Sheila has never looked _____ than she did today.

   A happyer   **B** more happy   **C** happier

229

Directions: Decide which underlined part in each sentence contains an error in usage. On your answer sheet, fill in the circle containing the same letter as the incorrect part. If there is no error, fill in *D*.

SAMPLE She <u>don't</u> have <u>any</u> more paper. <u>No error</u>
       A **B**   **C**   **D**

ANSWER Ⓐ ⒝ Ⓒ Ⓓ

11. <u>Has</u> you <u>been</u> <u>there</u> lately? <u>No error</u>
    A   **B** **C**   **D**

12. <u>Her</u> and Richard <u>were</u> surprised when Iris <u>won</u>. <u>No error</u>
    A   **B**   **C** **D**

13. The coach <u>hasn't</u> <u>given</u> us <u>no</u> instructions yet. <u>No error</u>
          A   **B**   **C**   **D**

14. Mr. Wexler <u>set</u> his alarm clock and <u>put</u> it in <u>it's</u> usual
           A   **B**   **C**

    place next to his bed. <u>No error</u>
                   D

15. Each of the girls <u>has</u> <u>bringed</u> <u>her</u> own sleeping bag.
                 A   **B**   **C**

  <u>No error</u>
    D

16. A dog or a raccoon <u>has</u> <u>stolen</u> the chicken that we <u>left</u>
                A   **B**   **C**

    on the picnic table! <u>No error</u>
                  D

17. <u>Have</u> you or <u>you're</u> brother <u>seen</u> the exhibit on volcanoes
    A   **B**   **C**

    at the Science Museum? <u>No error</u>
                     D

18. Marvin may look <u>good</u>, but he <u>doesn't</u> feel <u>well</u>. <u>No error</u>
               A   **B**   **C**   **D**

19. Talented musicians like Vivian and <u>he</u> <u>have</u> <u>made</u> the
                               A **B**   **C**

    band famous. <u>No error</u>
               D

20. Which of the two athletes <u>swam</u> and <u>ran</u> <u>fastest</u>? <u>No error</u>
                       A   **B**   **C**   **D**

Mechanics

15

Capital Letters

Diagnostic Test

Number your paper 1 to 10. Then write each word that should begin with a capital letter.

EXAMPLE   is friday the last day of october?
ANSWER   Is, Friday, October

1. koalas are found wild only in australia.
2. many explorers drew maps of the west.
3. next year i'm taking spanish.
4. harvard college, the first college in the united states, was established in 1636.
5. many dutch settlers made their homes near the hudson river.
6. do you have a soccer team at reed junior high?
7. have you ever read the story "wolves in the forest"?
8. king john of england signed the magna charta.
9. a friend of mine just bought a commodore computer.
10. the mississippi river begins in minnesota.

*F*irst Words and the Word *I*

Capital letters can be as important to writing as the words themselves. The correct use of capital letters makes what you write easy to follow and understand.

A capital letter, for example, clearly marks the beginning of a sentence or a new line of poetry.

15a ▶ Capitalize the first word in a sentence or a line of poetry.

SENTENCE **T**oday the temperature reached 97 degrees.

LINES OF   **O**f Jonathan Chapman
POETRY   **T**wo things are known,
          That he loved apples,
          That he walked alone.
                    —ROSEMARY BENÉT

The pronoun *I* is always capitalized when it stands alone and when it is part of a contraction.

15b ▶ Capitalize the pronoun *I*, both alone and in contractions.

ALONE   Yesterday **I** painted my bedroom orange.
CONTRACTION   If you leave after class, **I**'ll go with you to
            the pizza parlor.

*E*XERCISE 1 *Capitalizing First Words and* I

Number your paper 1 to 15. Then write each word that should begin with a capital letter.

A Day Off | there is no school today. i wonder what i should do. for several days i've been meaning to write to my grandparents. i think i will do that. sooner or later, though, i'll have to give the dog a bath. there's also that new magazine i've been wanting to read. oh, well, i think i will just sit down for a while and rest until i make up my mind.

*P*roper Nouns

A *proper noun* is the name of a particular person, place, thing, or idea.

COMMON NOUNS boy, park, car
PROPER NOUNS **D**aniel, **E**lizabeth **P**ark, **F**ord

15c ▶ Capitalize proper nouns and their abbreviations.

Study the following groups of rules for capitalizing proper nouns. Refer to them when you edit your writing.

Names of Persons and Animals. Capitalize the names of particular persons and animals.

PERSONS **R**obyn; **E. W. L**uther; **J**ames **R. B**utler, **J**r.
ANIMALS **S**pot, **F**luffy, **T**hunderhead, **M**iss **F**eathers

Geographical Names. Capitalize the names of particular places and bodies of water.

STREETS, HIGHWAYS	**A**very **R**oad (**R**d.), **O**hio **T**urnpike, **R**oute 128, **F**ifty-sixth **S**treet (**S**t.)
CITIES, STATES	**L**os **A**ngeles, **C**alifornia
COUNTRIES	**E**gypt, **N**ew **Z**ealand, **C**hina, **I**ndia
CONTINENTS	**N**orth **A**merica, **A**frica, **A**ntarctica
MOUNTAINS	**B**lue **R**idge **M**ountains, **M**ount **H**ood
PARKS	**B**ryce **C**anyon **N**ational **P**ark
ISLANDS	**V**ancouver **I**sland, **C**ape **H**atteras
BODIES OF WATER	**M**ississippi **R**iver, **L**ake **O**ntario, **P**acific **O**cean, **G**ulf of **M**exico

Sections of the country, such as the *Southwest* and the *East*, are also capitalized. (The word *the* is often used in naming a section of the country.) Simple compass directions, however, are not capitalized.

SECTION OF THE COUNTRY I once lived in *the* **S**outh.
COMPASS DIRECTION Go **s**outh for six miles.

234

Planets and Stars. Capitalize the names of planets and stars. Do not capitalize *sun* and *moon*.

PLANETS   Mercury, Uranus, Neptune, Pluto
STARS   the North Star, Sirius, Canopus

NOTE: Do not capitalize *earth* if *the* comes before it.

CAPITAL   Is Venus bigger or smaller than Earth?
NO CAPITAL   Many satellites are orbiting *the* earth.

EXERCISE 2 Capitalizing Proper Nouns

Number your paper 1 to 10. Then write the following items, adding capital letters only where needed.

1. a park in denver
2. moosehead lake
3. niagara falls
4. my friend sarita
5. the frozen north
6. mercury and the sun
7. a horse named blue streak
8. a store on commons road
9. the capital of nevada
10. a boat on lake michigan

EXERCISE 3 Capitalizing Proper Nouns

Number your paper 1 to 10. Then write each word that should begin with a capital letter.

1. geysers are found only in iceland, new zealand, and yellowstone national park in wyoming.
2. the star called sirius is blue in color.
3. laramie, wyoming, is near the medicine bow mountains.
4. our museum has a display of rocks from the moon.
5. from denver our plane headed east, passing over some of the most populous cities in the midwest.
6. elroy lives at state street and route 67.
7. roller skates were invented by james l. plimpton of medfield, massachusetts, in 1863.
8. the nile river flows northward from the center of africa to the mediterranean sea.
9. since 1965, mars has been photographed by spacecraft sent from earth.
10. niagara falls in canada produces great waterpower.

EXERCISE 4 *Writing Sentences* ✒

Write five sentences about an imaginary planet. Explain its location in the solar system. Then describe some of its geographical characteristics, such as specific mountain ranges and bodies of water.

Nouns of Historical Importance. Capitalize the names of historical events, periods, and documents.

EVENTS	the French Revolution, the Battle of Hastings, the War of 1812
PERIODS	the Victorian Era, the Space Age
DOCUMENTS	the Declaration of Independence

NOTE: Prepositions, such as the *of* in *Declaration of Independence*, are not capitalized.

Names of Groups and Businesses. Capitalize the names of organizations, businesses, institutions, and government bodies.

ORGANIZATIONS	the National Organization for Women, the Red Cross, the Chicago White Sox
BUSINESSES	the Douglas Equipment Company; R. F. Foster and Sons, Inc.; Casper's Market
INSTITUTIONS	Glover Memorial Hospital, Wayne Middle School, the University of Florida
GOVERNMENT BODIES	the Senate, the House of Lords, the Department of Commerce, Congress

Specific Time Periods and Events. Capitalize days of the week, months of the year, civil and religious holidays, and special events. Also capitalize the abbreviations used in giving dates and the time of day: A.D., B.C., A.M., and P.M.

DAYS, MONTHS	Monday, Tuesday, February, March
HOLIDAYS	Martin Luther King Day, New Year's Day, Washington's Birthday
SPECIAL EVENTS	the New York Marathon, Tulip Festival
ABBREVIATIONS	The alarm is set for 6:30 A.M.

NOTE: Do *not* capitalize the seasons of the year unless they are part of a specific name.

NO CAPITAL Each **f**all the squirrels prepare for winter.
CAPITAL Are you going to the next dance, the one called the **F**all Fling?

EXERCISE 5 *Capitalizing Proper Nouns*

Number your paper 1 to 10. Then write the following items, adding capital letters only where needed.

1. battle of britain
2. hillside high school
3. spring and fall
4. middle ages
5. fourth of july
6. house of representatives
7. louisiana purchase
8. jenson's department store
9. department of defense
10. from june to august

EXERCISE 6 *Capitalizing Proper Nouns*

Number your paper 1 to 15. Then write each item that should be capitalized.

1. on june 1, 1954, congress changed the name of armistice day to veterans day.
2. the great pianist frederic chopin studied at the warsaw conservatory.
3. sometime after 5000 b.c., groups of farmers settled along the nile river in egypt.
4. hancock street in boston was named for a patriot famous during the american revolution.
5. the first ten amendments to the constitution are called the bill of rights.
6. the ringling brothers and barnum & bailey circus hired its first woman clown in 1970.
7. on june 28, 1919, the treaty of versailles ended world war I.
8. the first hot meal served on a plane was provided by pan american airways in 1935.
9. the industrial revolution began in england.

10. the house of commons is located in london, england.
11. a well-known school called the high school for the performing arts is located in new york city.
12. martin luther king day is a legal holiday observed on january 15.
13. in 1873, 300 men formed the group known later as the royal canadian mounted police.
14. on one sunday of each year, people take part in a fund-raising event called the walk for hunger.
15. john f. kennedy attended harvard university.

*E*XERCISE 7 *Writing Sentences*

Write five sentences that describe some historical event. Include such things as the name of the event and where the event took place.

Nationalities, Races, and Religions. Capitalize the names of nationalities, races, and religions. Also capitalize religious references.

NATIONALITIES	an **A**frican, a **S**eminole, a **C**anadian
RACES	**C**aucasian, **O**riental
RELIGIONS	**C**atholicism, **J**udaism, **B**uddhism
RELIGIOUS REFERENCES	**G**od, the **A**lmighty, the **O**ld **T**estament, the **T**almud, the **K**oran, the **V**edas

NOTE: The word *god* is not capitalized when it refers to mythological gods. Their names, however, are capitalized.

The god who gave fire to mortals was **P**rometheus.

Languages and Specific School Courses. Capitalize the names of languages and of courses followed by a number.

LANGUAGES	**E**nglish, **T**urkish, **R**ussian
NUMBERED COURSES	**A**rt II, **T**yping I, **C**horus II

NOTE: Course names such as *history, math, science,* and *physical education* are not capitalized.

Other Proper Nouns. Capitalize all other proper nouns.

AWARDS	The **N**obel **P**eace **P**rize, the **W**orld **C**up
BRAND NAMES	**D**ixie cups, **D**ove soap, **C**hrysler sedan [The product itself is *not* capitalized.]
BUILDINGS	the **E**mpire **S**tate **B**uilding, the **S**ears **T**ower
MONUMENTS, MEMORIALS	the **G**ateway **A**rch, the **P**earl **H**arbor **M**emorial, the **L**incoln **M**emorial
VEHICLES	the *Queen Mary*, *Apollo V*, *Air Force One* [Italicize, or underline, vehicles' names.]

EXERCISE 8 Capitalizing Proper Nouns

Number your paper 1 to 10. Then write the following items, adding capital letters only where needed.

1. the *mayflower II*
2. planter's peanuts
3. a chapter in genesis
4. typing and french
5. a friendly canadian
6. a ford convertible
7. a presbyterian
8. the world trade center
9. *explorer I*
10. the davis cup

EXERCISE 9 Capitalizing Proper Nouns

Number your paper 1 to 10. Then write each word that should begin with a capital letter.

1. walt disney won 31 oscars—more than anyone else.
2. the sister ship of the *titanic* was named the *olympic*.
3. the washington monument sinks six inches each year.
4. my sister, who is a translator at the united nations, can speak greek, russian, and german.
5. did you buy me a new bic pen?
6. a group of cambodians have a small business in town.
7. the last book of the old testament is malachi.
8. my electives next year will be woodworking I, gymnastics, and drawing II.
9. the romans thought neptune was the god of the sea.
10. begun in 1500 b.c., hinduism is one of the oldest religions still practiced.

TIME-OUT FOR REVIEW ● ● ● ● ●

Number your paper 1 to 20. Then write each word that should begin with a capital letter.

Who's
Who?

1. who wrote the declaration of independence?
2. who wins the stanley cup, a football or hockey team?
3. who was the first person to fly solo across the atlantic ocean?
4. who was in the white house when the emancipation proclamation was issued in 1863?
5. who won the nobel peace prize in 1964, martin luther king, jr., or john f. kennedy?
6. who was the first american to orbit the earth, john glenn or alan shepard?
7. who won the first world series, new york or boston?
8. who invented the kodak camera, thomas edison or george eastman?
9. who was the two-faced mythical god that the month of january was named after?
10. who led the soviet union during world war II, joseph stalin or karl marx?
11. who once ruled peru, the aztecs or the incas?
12. who accomplished important health reforms during the crimean war?
13. who lives at 10 downing street in london?
14. who in the bible was swallowed by a whale?
15. who led the confederate army during the civil war, robert e. lee or ulysses s. grant?
16. who is honored every year on the third sunday in june, mothers or fathers?
17. who was the founder of the mormons, joseph smith or brigham young?
18. who won a gold medal for women's gymnastics in the 1984 olympics in los angeles, california?
19. who were defeated at the battle of waterloo, the french or the english?
20. who replaced walter cronkite as anchor for the evening news broadcast on the columbia broadcasting system?

Other Uses for Capital Letters

Some proper adjectives are capitalized. So are the titles of certain people and works of art.

Proper Adjectives

Like proper nouns, most proper adjectives begin with a capital letter.

Capitalize most proper adjectives.

PROPER NOUNS	Asia, South America
PROPER ADJECTIVES	Asian art, South American rivers

EXERCISE 10 Capitalizing Proper Adjectives

Number your paper 1 to 10. Then write the following items, adding capital letters only where needed.

1. new england seafood
2. australian films
3. napoleonic wars
4. italian scientists
5. american history
6. congressional committee
7. british ships
8. southern traditions
9. european countries
10. alaskan winters

Titles

Capital letters are used in the titles of people, written works, and other works of art.

Capitalize the titles of people and works of art.

Titles Used with Names of People. Capitalize a title showing office, rank, or profession when it comes *before* a person's name. The same title is usually not capitalized when it follows a name.

241

BEFORE A NAME	The speaker will be **Governor** Blake.
AFTER A NAME	Would Todd like to be the **governor**?
BEFORE A NAME	That woman is **Colonel** Hanks.
AFTER A NAME	When was Ann promoted to **colonel**?

Titles Used in Direct Address. A noun of *direct address* is used to call someone by name. Capitalize a title used alone, instead of a name, in direct address.

DIRECT ADDRESS   What is your opinion, **Professor**?

Titles Showing Family Relationships. Capitalize titles showing family relationships when the titles come before people's names. Capitalize the titles, also, when they are used instead of names or used in direct address.

BEFORE A NAME	Is **Uncle** David staying for dinner?
USED AS A NAME	Yesterday **Mom** fixed my lunch.
IN DIRECT ADDRESS	Thanks for the ride, **Dad**.

When a possessive noun or pronoun comes before a title showing a family relationship, do not capitalize the title—unless it is considered part of the person's name.

NO CAPITAL	*My* aunt is talking to *Linda's* brother.
CAPITAL	Is *your* **Aunt** Harriet from Arizona visiting?

EXERCISE 11   Capitalizing Titles of People

Number your paper 1 to 10. Then write each word that should begin with a capital letter.

1. who is the governor of your state?
2. yesterday grandma solano called from seattle.
3. i think, sis, that you should call the dentist.
4. my grandfather was a captain in world war II.
5. first we should phone dad.
6. my grandmother was born in poland.
7. is ambassador long lecturing at the university?
8. carmen's uncle is visiting from puerto rico.
9. is general clark related to you?
10. fred morrison is the president of the eighth grade.

Titles of Written Works and Other Works of Art. Capitalize the first word, the last word, and all important words in the titles of books, newspapers, magazines, stories, poems, movies, plays, musical compositions, and other works of art. Do not capitalize a preposition, a coordinating conjunction, or an article unless it is the first or last word in a title.

WRITTEN WORKS   I liked the chapter "**P**eople and **L**and" in our textbook *The Geography of the World.*

The article "**S**tarvation around the **W**orld" on the front page of the *Hartford Courant* was very sad. [Generally the word *the* before a newspaper or magazine title is not capitalized.]

MUSICAL COMPOSITIONS   The song "**T**omorrow" is from the musical *Annie.*

EXERCISE 12   Capitalizing Titles

Number your paper 1 to 10. Then write each word that should begin with a capital letter.

1. charles dickens wrote the novel *bleak house.*
2. i just read a humorous article, "a bulldog with the name of petunia," in the *reader's digest.*
3. the movie *the grey fox* starred richard farnsworth.
4. have you ever read the short story "the legend of sleepy hollow" by washington irving?
5. we saw a ballet film called *backstage at the kirov.*
6. "the gift outright" was the poem read at president john f. kennedy's inauguration.
7. "the role of the united nations" was the lead story in the *washington post* yesterday.
8. the play *twelve angry men* was made into a movie.
9. "i left my heart in san francisco" was adopted as the official song of that city in 1969.
10. what was archie's wife's name in the television program *all in the family?*

TIME-OUT FOR REVIEW • • • • •

Number your paper 1 to 20. Then write each word that should begin with a capital letter.

What's
What?

1. what were lewis and clark sent to explore, the mississippi river or the louisiana territory?
2. what famous singer starred in the movie *love me tender*, frank sinatra or elvis presley?
3. what is the name of the author of *dr. jekyll and mr. hyde*, mark twain or robert louis stevenson?
4. what time is it in los angeles when it is 1:00 p.m. in new york city?
5. what is the name of dorothy's dog in the movie *the wizard of oz?*
6. what city has the same name as a city in china: nashua, new hampshire, or canton, ohio?
7. what constellation, the great bear or the little bear, has the seven stars that form the big dipper?
8. was the famous painter picasso french or spanish?
9. what fictional rabbit was the friend of bambi?
10. what ship fought the *monitor* during the civil war, the *merrimac* or the *constitution?*
11. what river flows between texas and mexico?
12. in what state are the golden gate bridge and yosemite national park?
13. who was the japanese emperor during world war II?
14. what state is directly north of kansas, north dakota or nebraska?
15. what do the two initials stand for in the name washington, d.c.?
16. in what city does the orange bowl take place, miami or atlanta?
17. was tonto's horse in the *lone ranger* radio series named silver or scout?
18. what south american country was named after simón bolívar?
19. in what city is wrigley field, denver or chicago?
20. where are the finger lakes, in michigan or new york?

Application to Writing

When you edit your writing, always check to see if you have included all necessary capital letters.

EXERCISE 13 Editing for Proper Capitalization

Number your paper 1 to 25. Then write all the words that should begin with a capital letter.

Conan Doyle's Other Novels

you may recognize the name of sir arthur conan doyle. he wrote the books and short stories about the fictional british detective sherlock holmes. did you know that conan doyle wrote other kinds of books? *the lost world* is a novel about atlantis, a vanished continent. another novel, *the white company*, was set in the middle ages. its brawny, comical hero was known as hordle john.

EXERCISE 14 Editing for Proper Capitalization

Number your paper 1 to 25. Then write all the words that should have been capitalized.

China

The third largest country in the world is china. the himalaya mountains form its southern boundary. The soviet union forms its western and northern boundaries; and korea, japan, and the pacific ocean are east of it. The philippine islands, which are located between the south china sea and the philippine sea, are southeast of china.

The history of china goes far back in time. Actual records began during a period before the eleventh century b.c. China was the earliest nation, as well as the earliest civilization, to develop in asia. It was a country before rome became an empire or before nations appeared in europe. Other ancient civilizations like that of egypt have changed or ended, but chinese people still follow traditions begun thousands of years ago.

Chapter Review

A **Using Capital Letters.** Number your paper 1 to 10. Then write each word that should begin with a capital letter.

1. saturn has 20 moons, but earth has only 1.
2. the supertanker *seawise giant* can carry a total load of over 560,000 tons.
3. do your mom and dad subscribe to the *tribune?*
4. the aardvark, an african mammal, eats termites.
5. the month of july was named after julius caesar.
6. does haver's hardware store rent clark tools, uncle ed?
7. the united states air force academy is located in colorado springs.
8. tasmania, a small island, is south of australia.
9. the song "happy birthday to you" was written by two sisters in 1936.
10. the red sea separates egypt from saudi arabia.

B **Using Capital Letters.** Number your paper 1 to 10. Then write each word that should begin with a capital letter.

1. if all the world's ice melted, cities such as london and paris would be underwater.
2. is your brother taking algebra II or geometry?
3. medieval knights were specially trained soldiers.
4. my uncle george and aunt martha live in the south.
5. the temperature on venus is hotter than it is on mercury, the planet closest to the sun.
6. i memorized "casey at the bat," a poem by earnest l. thayer.
7. the headquarters for the north atlantic treaty organization is located in brussels, belgium.
8. my aunt may flew from france on the *concorde.*
9. a mosque is a place of worship for muslims.
10. vikings landed in north america about a.d. 1000.

C **Editing for Proper Capitalization.** Number your paper 1 to 20. Then write each word that should begin with a capital letter. Do not include words that are already capitalized.

A Great Discovery

Late at night on monday, april 15, 1912, the *titanic,* a great ocean liner, struck an iceberg and sank off the coast of newfoundland. The ship was on a voyage from england to new york city.

In 1985, the ship was discovered on the floor of the atlantic ocean. Finding the ship had been a joint effort of the united states and france. Using sonar, a french research ship scanned the ocean bottom. When the wreck was found, scientists from the woods hole oceanographic institution in massachusetts sent down a submersible robot named *argo.* Attached to the robot were lights and television cameras. After 73 years the great ship had been found in its resting place.

Mastery Test

Number your paper 1 to 10. Then write each word that should begin with a capital letter.

1. six coins are presently minted by the united states treasury department.
2. february 14 is valentine's day.
3. wolfgang amadeus mozart wrote the opera *don giovanni* in one sitting.
4. please tell the major that i'm here, sergeant.
5. will the new high school be built on ross road?
6. what movie won the academy award last year?
7. nepal is a small country southwest of china.
8. the mouth of the statue of liberty is three feet wide.
9. in 1805, jefferson asked lafayette to become the governor of louisiana.
10. the famous french hero refused.

16

End Marks and Commas

Diagnostic Test

Number your paper 1 to 10. Write each sentence, adding a comma or commas where needed. Then write an appropriate end mark.

EXAMPLE   Before I go to bed I must finish my report
ANSWER   Before I go to bed, I must finish my report.

1. Well I never saw two people run so fast
2. Please close the door Andrew
3. When school is out how will you get home
4. What important event in American history took place on October 19 1781
5. The Komodo lizard a native of Indonesia often reaches ten feet in length
6. Mom come here at once
7. As a matter of fact peanuts grow underground
8. Oh we're lost in the middle of nowhere
9. Half of the world's population lives in China India the Soviet Union and the United States
10. John Quincy Adams was born near Boston Massachusetts on July 11 1787

End Marks

The purpose of a sentence determines its end mark. (*See pages 133–136 for a review of kinds of sentences.*)

16a Place a **period** after a statement, after an opinion, and after a command or request made in a normal tone of voice.

PERIODS   I want to be a forest ranger. [statement]
The wilderness is peaceful. [opinion]
Sign up for the career workshop. [command]

16b Place a **question mark** after a sentence that asks a question.

QUESTION MARK   Wouldn't you like to work in the woods?

16c Place an **exclamation point** after a sentence that expresses strong feeling and after a command or request that expresses great excitement.

EXCLAMATION POINTS   The fire is spreading throughout the woods!
Listen to that roar! [command]

EXERCISE 1   Using End Marks

Number your paper 1 to 10. Then write the correct end mark for each sentence.

The Train

1. Should we take the train or the bus to Rock Island
2. Buses are better than trains
3. The train, however, is faster
4. Where do I buy a ticket
5. Go over to that booth
6. The line has 25 people in it
7. We'll miss the train
8. Don't panic
9. The train doesn't leave for another hour
10. That's a relief

---

*P*eriods with Abbreviations

Abbreviations are brief ways of writing words. They are handy shortcuts when you are writing messages or taking notes in class. Most abbreviations, however, should not be used in formal writing such as a letter, a story, or a report.

| 16d | Use a period with most abbreviations. |

Following is a list of some abbreviations that are correct to use in formal writing. For the spelling and the punctuation of other abbreviations, look in a dictionary.

| TITLES WITH NAMES | Mr. | Ms. | Rev. | Sgt. | Jr. |
| | Mrs. | Dr. | Gen. | Lt. | Sr. |

TIMES WITH NUMBERS	6:45 A.M. [*ante meridiem*—before noon]
	9:00 P.M. [*post meridiem*—after noon]
	2000 B.C. [before Christ]
	A.D. 650 [*anno Domini*—in the year of the Lord]

If a sentence ends with an abbreviation, only one period is used. It serves as the period for the abbreviation and as the end mark for the sentence.

The man in the brown suit is Allen Rogers, Jr.

*E*XERCISE 2 *Writing Abbreviations*

Number your paper 1 to 10. Then write the abbreviations that stand for the following items. If you are unsure of the spelling of a particular abbreviation, look it up in the dictionary.

1. Monday
2. September
3. inch
4. Street
5. quart
6. post meridiem
7. Route
8. Mister
9. before Christ
10. Lieutenant

Commas That Separate

Commas keep similar items from running into each other and prevent misunderstanding by the reader.

Items in a Series

A series is three or more similar words or groups of words listed one after another. Commas are used to separate the items in a series.

16e Use commas to separate items in a series.

WORDS	We have eggs, bread, and cheese. [nouns]
	Their new sailboat is lean, sleek, and swift. [adjectives]
GROUPS OF WORDS	We will sweep the floor, dust the furniture, and vacuum the rug. [complete predicates]
	The extra house key is in the drawer, on the rack, or on its hook. [prepositional phrases]

If a conjunction such as *and* or *or* connects all the items in a series, no commas are needed.

Peaches **or** raisins **or** bananas taste good on cereal.

EXERCISE 3 Using Commas in a Series

Number your paper 1 to 10. Then write each sentence, adding commas where needed. If a sentence does not need any commas, write *C* after the number.

1. Washington California Alaska and Hawaii are the only four states with active volcanoes.
2. Prince sniffed his empty dish dashed to the cupboard and scratched at the door.
3. The cat could be under a bed in a closet or in a box.

4. The Nile and the Congo and the Zambezi are major rivers of Africa.
5. The audience cheered clapped and whistled.
6. Should we leave now or wait another half hour or stay until the end of the party?
7. Jack is mature dependable and trustworthy.
8. The planet Jupiter is far larger than Mercury Venus Earth and Mars put together.
9. Do zebras really bark like dogs grunt like pigs and whistle like birds?
10. The air is crisp clear and cold.

*C*ompound *Sentences*

A comma and a conjunction often separate the independent clauses in a compound sentence. *And, but, or, nor,* and *yet* are commonly used conjunctions. (*See pages 133–135 for a review of compound sentences.*)

16f Use a comma to separate the independent clauses of a compound sentence if the clauses are joined by a conjunction.

Notice in the following examples that the comma comes before the conjunction.

The newspaper is wet, but you can still read it.
Tommy cooked the dinner, and it was very good.

Keep in mind the difference between a compound sentence and a simple sentence that has a compound verb.

COMPOUND SENTENCE	Paul hit the ball into left field, but Michael caught it. [A comma is needed because there are two sets of subjects and verbs.]
COMPOUND VERB	Paul hit the ball into left field and ran to first. [No comma is needed with a compound verb.]

EXERCISE 4   Using Commas in Compound Sentences

Number your paper 1 to 10. Then write each sentence, adding a comma where needed. If a sentence does not need a comma, write *C* after the number.

Plants That
Eat Meat

1. Over 500 species of plants eat bugs and the Venus's-flytrap is one of those plants.
2. This plant eats mostly ants yet it is called a flytrap.
3. Its leaves smell sweet and attract insects.
4. On the ends of the leaves are traps and each trap contains three hairs.
5. An insect can touch one hair and be safe.
6. Two hairs act as a trigger and the trap snaps shut in a quarter of a second.
7. The insect's body is instantly crushed and acid from the Venus's-flytrap eats away at it.
8. Venus's-flytraps eat mostly insects but also consume an occasional frog.
9. One meat-eating plant has sticky red hairs but another oozes a strange liquid.
10. An insect lands on the liquid and is instantly glued to the leaf.

Introductory Elements

A comma follows certain words and groups of words at the beginning of a sentence.

16g ▶ Use a comma after certain introductory elements.

A comma sometimes separates an interjection from the rest of a sentence. Words like *no, now, oh, well, why,* and *yes* can be used as interjections.

WORDS   Yes, I can be ready in ten minutes.
Well, that was a very enjoyable movie.

NOTE: An interjection can also be followed by an exclamation point. (*See page 76.*)

A comma follows two or more introductory prepositional phrases or one that has four or more words.

PREPOSITIONAL   With a map in my pocket, I started out.
    PHRASES   Near the old barn, several cows grazed.

A comma follows a participial phrase that comes at the
beginning of a sentence. (*See pages 113–114 for a review of
participial phrases.*)

PARTICIPIAL   Looking out into the audience, Kelly
    PHRASE   could see her parents in the first row.

A comma follows an adverb clause when it comes at the
beginning of a sentence. (*See pages 130–132 for a review of
adverb clauses.*)

ADVERB   If you take this bus, you will arrive in
  CLAUSE   Pittsburgh at 6:45 P.M.

EXERCISE 5 *Using Commas with Introductory Elements*

Number your paper 1 to 10. Then write each sentence, adding a comma where needed. If a sentence does not need a
comma, write *C* after the number.

1. When chop suey was first made here the dish was completely unknown in China.
2. Yes I think your plan will work.
3. Oh must you leave so soon?
4. From the peak of Mount Izaru in Costa Rica you can
   see both the Atlantic and Pacific oceans.
5. Among India's 700 million people 880 different languages and dialects are spoken.
6. Running off the field the dog escaped with the ball.
7. From the mountaintop we could see the airport.
8. Found in every state in the Union the skunk is truly an
   all-American animal.
9. Although the dragonfly has six legs it never walks.
10. Without heat and light from the sun no life would exist
    on the earth.

EXERCISE 6 Writing Sentences

Write five sentences that follow the directions below.

1. Include a series of nouns.
2. Write a compound sentence using the conjunction *and*.
3. Begin a sentence with a long prepositional phrase.
4. Begin a sentence with a participial phrase.
5. Begin a sentence with an adverb clause.

Dates and Addresses

Commas are used between the parts of a date or an address. A comma is also used to separate a date or an address from the rest of the sentence.

Use commas to separate elements in dates and addresses.

DATE   On Tuesday, May 7, 1985, the journey began.
ADDRESS Write to Bowler Enterprises, 101 Glenn Road, Shawano, Wisconsin 54166, for a free catalog.

EXERCISE 7 Using Commas in Dates and Addresses

Number your paper 1 to 10. Then write each sentence, adding commas where needed.

1. San Francisco's famous cable cars were first put into service on August 1 1873.
2. You can write to my uncle at 5428 14th Avenue Minneapolis Minnesota 55417.
3. On December 25 1777 Captain Cook landed on Christmas Island.
4. The picnic will be held Friday June 7 at Rolley Park.
5. Write to the McCord Company 357 Jefferson Street Springfield Illinois 62703 for more information.
6. Before August 1 1958 the fee for sending a letter first-class was three cents.
7. On May 30 1793 the first daily newspaper in America was published in Philadelphia Pennsylvania.

8. Write to *Horse Illustrated* P.O. Box 6040 Mission Viejo California 92690 for a subscription.
9. On June 14 1777 the Continental Congress adopted a national flag with 13 stars and 13 stripes.
10. In Spokane Washington on June 19 1910 Father's Day began as a result of a suggestion by Mrs. Dodd.

EXERCISE 8   *Writing Sentences*

Write each sentence, adding a city and state or a month, day, and year in each blank. Use commas where needed.

1. The letter was dated _____.
2. _____ is where I'd like to spend a vacation.
3. We stopped at _____ on our way to Washington, D.C.
4. On _____ I was born in _____.

TIME-OUT FOR REVIEW • • • • •

Number your paper 1 to 10. Then write each sentence, adding a comma or commas where needed. If a sentence is correct, write *C* after the number.

1. Before tea was served as a beverage in China it was used as a medicine.
2. A fake coin often has uneven edges and feels greasy.
3. Thunderbolt reared in terror jumped the pasture fence and galloped into the woods.
4. Before the baseball game against Rudley Middle School we had extra practice sessions.
5. The pony express began on April 3 1860 between St. Joseph Missouri and Sacramento California.
6. By Friday I must finish my book report.
7. Built of mud the oldest house in the United States stands in New Mexico.
8. Kansas City Missouri was a starting point for gold seekers adventurers farmers and ranchers.
9. Well you're up early this morning.
10. The plants are lovely but my cat eats them.

Commas That Enclose

Commas are used to enclose some expressions that interrupt the main idea of a sentence. When you read a sentence aloud, you naturally pause before and after an interrupting expression. Commas are placed where these pauses would occur. Interrupters enclosed by commas could be taken out of a sentence, and the sentence would still make sense.

Parenthetical Expressions

One type of interrupter is called a *parenthetical expression*. The following parenthetical expressions should be enclosed in commas.

Common Parenthetical Expressions		
after all	for instance	of course
at any rate	generally speaking	on the contrary
by the way	I believe (guess,	on the other hand
consequently	hope, know)	moreover
however	in fact	nevertheless
for example	in my opinion	to tell the truth

16i   Use commas to set off parenthetical expressions.

The math test, in fact, was very long. [The parenthetical expression, *in fact,* could be removed without affecting the meaning of the sentence.]

In the following examples, only one comma is needed because the parenthetical expression comes at the beginning or at the end of the sentence.

In my opinion, we should hold a car wash.
The food at the restaurant was tasty, at any rate.

EXERCISE 9 *Using Commas with Parenthetical Expressions*

Number your paper 1 to 10. Then write each sentence, adding a comma or commas where needed.

1. Charles Goodyear to tell the truth was never connected with the company that bears his name.
2. The price is very high of course.
3. Some owls in fact can see well in the daylight.
4. Generally speaking a thousand new species of insects are discovered each year.
5. The movie was too violent in my opinion.
6. An otter by the way reacts remarkably quickly in a dangerous situation.
7. On the contrary a heavy dew is a sign of good weather.
8. We'll be there in time I hope.
9. The United States for example paid only two cents per acre for Alaska.
10. The Virgin Islands on the other hand cost about three hundred dollars per acre.

Direct Address

In conversation people are often addressed by name. This kind of interrupter is called a noun of *direct address*. Since nouns of direct address interrupt the flow of a sentence, they should be set off by commas.

16j ▶ Use commas to set off nouns of direct address.

The sixth inning, Brian, was the turning point. [The noun of direct address, *Brian*, could be removed.]

In the following examples, only one comma is needed because the noun of direct address comes at the beginning or at the end of the sentence.

Mom, have you seen my history book?
When will we know the results, Doctor?

EXERCISE 10   Using Commas with Direct Address

Number your paper 1 to 10. Then write each sentence, adding a comma or commas where needed.

1. The American Indians Tad invented toboggans.
2. Did you get today's assignment Mei-ling?
3. Otis where did you put my catcher's mitt?
4. These ripe tomatoes Jenny should be eaten as soon as possible.
5. Please set the table Sis.
6. Yes Marie an ostrich stride covers 25 feet.
7. Are we all going to California Dad?
8. Why Dana you're such a good cook!
9. Did you know Lani that wolves are good parents?
10. Captain please take a seat on the stage.

Appositives

An *appositive* renames or explains a noun or a pronoun in the sentence. Usually an appositive comes immediately after that noun or pronoun. Most appositives are written with modifiers. Because they interrupt the sentence, appositives should be set off by commas.

16k Use commas to set off most appositives and their modifiers.

Mrs. Gregson, our math teacher, lived in Minnesota. [The appositive, *our math teacher*, could be removed.]

In the following example, only one comma is needed because the appositive comes at the end of the sentence.

Have you been to Hartford, the capital of Connecticut?

Commas are *not* used if an appositive identifies a person or thing by telling which one or ones. Usually these appositives are names.

My brother Elroy has his own apartment. [The appositive is *Elroy*.]

EXERCISE 11 Using Commas with Appositives

Number your paper 1 to 10. Then write each sentence, adding a comma or commas where needed. If a sentence does not need any commas, write C after the number.

1. The race runner a North American lizard has a brown body with six yellow stripes.
2. The end of summer vacation is signaled by Labor Day the first Monday in September.
3. The zinnia the most popular flower in North American gardens comes in almost every color.
4. My cousin Betsy collects old stamps.
5. Have you ever met Mr. Martin my next-door neighbor?
6. Noah Webster the dictionary writer worked on his famous dictionary for 21 years.
7. I just finished reading *White Fang* a book by Jack London.
8. Mr. O'Malley my father's boss is thinking of buying a radio station.
9. The wheel one of the greatest inventions of all time came into use in the Bronze Age.
10. Many ancient weapons were made of bronze a mixture of copper and tin.

EXERCISE 12 Writing Sentences

Number your paper 1 to 5. Then write sentences that follow the directions below.

1. Include *in fact* as a parenthetical expression in the middle of a sentence.
2. Include *however* as a parenthetical expression in the middle of a sentence.
3. Include *Mr. Johnson* as a noun of direct address at the beginning of a sentence.
4. Include *my favorite kind of dog* as an appositive at the end of a sentence.
5. Include an appositive of the type that does not need any commas.

TIME-OUT FOR REVIEW • • • • •

Number your paper 1 to 10. Then write each sentence, adding a comma or commas where needed.

1. The goby a small tropical fish can change color.
2. Wait Lee for just a few more minutes.
3. The wild turkey moreover was once abundant.
4. Mr. Lee a teacher at Hyde School plays in a band.
5. Are you going to camp this summer Richard?
6. Ellen my twin sister works at the bank.
7. The decorations for example were all blue.
8. Sit here Aunt Kay out of the sun.
9. We have a library of course where we can study.
10. Joe Bud's brother called and left a message for him.

Application to Writing

Always edit your written work for the correct use of commas.

EXERCISE 13 Editing for the Correct Use of Commas

Write the following paragraphs, adding commas where needed.

Noise

Noise can be harmful to your health. Loud sounds can cause earaches and can give some people headaches. Worst of all however some people have actually lost their hearing because of too much noise.

Measured in units called decibels noise can be monitored. The sound of conversation creates about 60 decibels but rock music can reach 110 decibels. Any noise over 70 decibels by the way can be dangerous.

For more information about noise write to the Environmental Protection Agency a government agency. Address your letter to the Environmental Protection Agency Washington D.C. 20460 and enclose a self-addressed envelope.

Chapter Review

A **Using Commas Correctly.** Number your paper 1 to 10. Then write each sentence, adding a comma or commas where needed. If a sentence does not need any commas, write *C* after the number.

1. The magician Houdini was born in Wisconsin.
2. Queens workers and drones are three classes of bees.
3. On the calendar several dates were circled.
4. The game began at seven but our team reported early.
5. Before Columbus discovered America strawberries and corn were unknown in Europe.
6. On August 1 1918 the Pirates and the Braves played 20 scoreless innings.
7. The first cold spell of course killed our plants.
8. Mark collects editions of the novel *Robin Hood*.
9. Of course Pam those horses are gentle.
10. Pluto the smallest planet in the solar system is slightly smaller than the moon.

B **Using Commas Correctly.** Number your paper 1 to 10. Then write each sentence, adding a comma or commas where needed. If a sentence does not need any commas, write *C* after the number.

1. A star of course shines for millions of years.
2. Writing quickly Amanda finished her test before us.
3. On the beach at Atlantic City we found unusual shells.
4. My brother Sam pitches for the varsity team.
5. *Black Beauty* is about a horse and is set in England.
6. Air contains three gases: oxygen nitrogen and argon.
7. Write to Pride and Sons 4290 Peach Tree Parkway Atlanta Georgia 30341 for a free catalog.
8. Philadelphia Benjamin Franklin's birthplace is one of the country's major convention centers.
9. Standing on the stage the mayor read the proclamation.
10. Liz brought eggs milk cheese and English muffins.

C **Using Commas Correctly.** Write the following paragraphs, adding commas where needed.

A Tough
Race

On February 12 1908 one of the most difficult automobile races on record was in progress. Six cars left New York for Paris. The complete route included the United States Japan Russia Poland Germany and part of France. Confronted by blizzards and other dangers the racers nevertheless kept to the course.

The German entry reached Paris over 5 months later and the American entry followed 4 days later. Although the German car came in first it was not the winner. The German car was given a 15-day penalty on technicalities. As a result of this decision the American car was declared the winner. The champion car a Thomas Flyer had covered 13,400 miles in 168 days.

Mastery Test

Number your paper 1 to 10. Write each sentence, adding a comma or commas where needed. Then write an appropriate end mark.

1. Constellations were named for animals heroes or gods
2. Earthquakes in fact strike without any warning
3. Pete you missed the exit on the turnpike
4. Searching through the crowd he found his family
5. John Adams and Thomas Jefferson our second and third presidents both died on July 4 1826
6. When an ostrich sticks its head into the sand is it looking for something or hiding
7. A pipe burst and now the cellar is flooded
8. Dana will you wait for us by the gate that is closest to the parking lot
9. That was by the way the best game I've ever pitched
10. Near the empty lot at the end of our street an abandoned warehouse burned down

17

Underlining and Quotation Marks

Diagnostic Test

Number your paper 1 to 10. Then write each direct quotation, adding quotation marks, other punctuation marks, and capital letters where needed.

EXAMPLE   is the dog outside Mom asked
ANSWER   "Is the dog outside?" Mom asked.

1. a flying squirrel can glide as far as 150 feet he stated
2. Arlene asked do you want a cheese sandwich
3. I dropped the oars into the water Roy cried out
4. the doctor remarked one out of every four Americans suffers from a back problem
5. do you know how to use this computer Tracy asked
6. that book said the librarian is already checked out
7. watch out for that motorbike Chris screamed
8. Mrs. Thompson announced tomorrow is Friday your book reports are due then
9. have you ever seen a bristlecone pine tree she asked some are 4,000 years old
10. I'll arrive on Tuesday Frank said I'll meet you at six o'clock at the train station

Underlining

When certain titles, letters, numbers, and words appear in a book, they are printed in italics. *Italic print, a special kind that slants to the right, is the kind used in this sentence.* Since you cannot write in italics, you should substitute underlining wherever italics are needed.

17a Underline the titles of long written or musical works that are published as a single unit. Also underline the titles of paintings and sculptures and the names of vehicles.

Long, separately published written works include books, magazines, newspapers, full-length plays, movies, and very long poems. Long musical compositions include operas, symphonies, ballets, and albums. Vehicles include airplanes, ships, trains, and spacecraft. The titles of radio and TV series are also underlined. (*See pages 241–243 for the capitalization of titles.*)

I just finished reading the book <u>Robinson Crusoe</u>.

Where is today's copy of the <u>Chicago Tribune</u>?

The setting for one of Agatha Christie's mystery novels is the train the <u>Orient Express</u>.

Italics or underlining is also used in certain situations for letters, numbers, and words.

17b Underline letters, numbers, and words when they are used to represent themselves.

His <u>3</u>'s looked like backward <u>E</u>'s.

The word <u>paint</u> can be used as a noun, an adjective, or a verb.

NOTE: In the first example, only the *3* and the *E* are underlined, not the apostrophe and the *s*.

EXERCISE 1 Using Underlining

Number your paper 1 to 20. Then write each sentence, underlining each title, letter, number, or word that should be italicized.

EXAMPLE People in Europe cross their 7's.

ANSWER People in Europe cross their <u>7</u>'s.

1. I enjoyed reading the book The Outsiders.
2. Our local newspaper, the Terrytown Crier, is delivered each Thursday.
3. The word zymurgy is the last word in my dictionary.
4. When were the newly discovered episodes of The Honeymooners put on TV?
5. The movie Avalanche was filmed in Colorado.
6. The word lasso has two s's and one o.
7. The smallest plane ever built was called the Stits Skybaby; it was half as long as an average car.
8. Does your family subscribe to Newsweek or Time?
9. There are five 5's in her telephone number.
10. We are going to see the opera Madame Butterfly.
11. My little sister likes the number 3 because she is proud of being three years old.
12. Is that letter an i or an e with a circle over it?
13. Queen Elizabeth and Prince Philip crossed the Atlantic on their yacht, the Britannia.
14. During the Old English period, musician-storytellers called scops recited long poems like Beowulf.
15. A capital q looks like the number 2.
16. What Sandy thought were 7's on the gloves she bought were actually upside-down L's.
17. Sorry, Wrong Number became a classic radio mystery play.
18. Long epic poems such as the Odyssey offer readers more than just an adventure story.
19. Words like murmur and mumble sound like the noises they refer to.
20. The musical titled Man of La Mancha is based on the Spanish novel Don Quixote.

Quotation Marks

Quotation marks (" ") always come in pairs. They are used to enclose certain titles, and they are used to enclose a person's exact words. Quotation marks are very important. Without them, for example, a conversation between people in a story would be impossible to read or understand.

Quotation Marks with Titles

Many titles are underlined, but some titles are enclosed in quotation marks. Long works are underlined. Most of these long works, however, are made up of smaller parts. A book, for example, might include many short stories or poems. The titles of these smaller parts are enclosed in quotation marks.

17c Use quotation marks to enclose the titles of chapters, articles, stories, one-act plays, short poems, and songs.

I am writing a short story that I plan to call "Nebula."
I like the poem "Four Little Foxes" in our textbook The World of Literature.
The old song "There Is Love" is my mother's favorite.

EXERCISE 2 Using Quotation Marks with Titles

Number your paper 1 to 10. Then write each sentence, adding quotation marks and underlining where needed.

1. Wild Stallion is a poem by Alma Higbee.
2. The Star-Spangled Banner was adopted as our national anthem on March 3, 1931.
3. The main character in the short story The Redheaded League is Sherlock Holmes.
4. The one-act play Stranger with Roses takes place in the future.

5. The article Breaking the Records was in the September issue of Sports Illustrated.
6. Escape from the Sea is the first chapter in the novel Agents of Destiny.
7. Have you read the article The Bravest Dog in America in the most recent Reader's Digest?
8. In our textbook Discovering Literature, we read the poem The Base Stealer by Robert Francis.
9. Drought Predicted was today's lead story in our newspaper, the Des Moines Register.
10. Those Were the Days was the theme song for the long-running television series All in the Family.

Quotation Marks with Direct Quotations

Quotation marks are used to enclose only a *direct quotation*, the exact words of a person.

17d Use quotation marks to enclose a person's exact words.

Scott said, "I rowed across the lake."

"The lake was very calm," he added.

Quotation marks do not enclose an *indirect quotation*, a rephrasing of a person's exact words.

Scott said he rowed across the lake.

He added that the lake was very calm.

NOTE: The word *that* is often used with an indirect quotation. In the first example above, *that* is understood—Scott said *that* he rowed across the lake.

A direct quotation that is a single sentence can be written in various ways. It can appear before or after a speaker tag such as *she answered* or *he stated*. A speaker tag can also interrupt a direct quotation. In each case, however, quotation marks enclose only the person's exact words—not the speaker tag.

BEFORE	"The sun sets tonight at six," he said.
AFTER	He said, "The sun sets tonight at six."
INTERRUPTED	"The sun sets tonight," he said, "at six." [Because a speaker tag interrupts the direct quotation, two sets of quotation marks are needed: one before and one after the speaker tag.]

Only one set of quotation marks is needed around two or more sentences in a direct quotation if the sentences are not interrupted by a speaker tag.

> He said, "The sun sets tonight at six. I wish it stayed light longer." [Quotation marks come only before *the* and after *longer*.]

Capital Letters with Direct Quotations. You know that a capital letter begins a sentence. It is natural, therefore, for a capital letter to begin a direct quotation.

17e ▷ Begin each sentence of a direct quotation with a capital letter.

> "**T**his painting of mine won an award," she said.
>
> She said, "**T**his painting of mine won an award."
>
> "**T**his painting of mine," she said, "won an award."

In the last example, notice that *won* does not begin with a capital letter. It is not capitalized because it is in the middle of a one-sentence direct quotation. Notice in the examples below, however, that a capital letter is used to begin a new sentence.

> She said, "**T**his painting of mine won an award. **M**y mother framed it."
>
> "**T**his painting of mine won an award," she said. "**M**y mother framed it."

In each of the two examples above, the word *My* begins with a capital letter because it starts a new sentence.

EXERCISE 3   Using Quotation Marks and Capital Letters

Number your paper 1 to 10. Then write each direct quotation, adding quotation marks and capital letters where needed. In this exercise place a comma or an end mark that follows a quotation *inside* the closing quotation marks.

EXAMPLE   who was the first poster bear? asked Ms. Hall.
ANSWER   "Who was the first poster bear?" asked Ms. Hall.

Poster Bears

1. wasn't Smokey a cartoon character? Peter inquired.
2. no, he was a real bear, she said.
3. rangers rescued him, she continued, in New Mexico.
4. Tony asked, why did he have to be rescued?
5. she answered, he was orphaned in a forest fire. the rangers found him clinging to a charred tree.
6. that's terrible! Susan exclaimed.
7. when his burns healed, Ms. Hall continued, he was taken to the National Zoo in Washington, D.C.
8. this young bear became the international symbol in a campaign to fight forest fires, she added.
9. at age 26 Smokey died, Ms. Hall stated. he was buried near the place where he had been found.
10. she concluded, the new Smokey is another cub from New Mexico.

Commas with Direct Quotations. Commas are used to separate direct quotations from speaker tags.

17f Use a comma to separate a direct quotation from a speaker tag. Place the comma inside the closing quotation marks.

"The prize was a camera," he said.

He said, "The prize was a camera."

"The prize," he said, "was a camera." [Two commas are needed to separate the speaker tag from the direct quotation: one before the speaker tag and one after it.]

End Marks with Direct Quotations. A period is used at the end of a sentence—whether it is a regular sentence or a direct quotation. The period goes *inside* the closing quotation marks when the quotation ends the sentence.

17g ▷ Place a period inside the closing quotation marks when the end of the quotation comes at the end of the sentence.

> She said, "Rain is predicted for tonight."
>
> "Rain," she said, "is predicted for tonight."

Usually question marks and exclamation points, like periods, go inside the closing quotation marks.

> He yelled, "Watch out for the falling tree!"
>
> She asked, "Who cut the tree down?" [In both of these examples, the end marks go *inside* the closing quotation marks.]

When a question or an exclamation comes before a speaker tag, the question mark or the exclamation point is still placed inside the closing quotation marks.

> "That's a great idea!" Chris exclaimed.
>
> "Was that your idea?" she asked.

EXERCISE 4   *Using Commas and End Marks*

Number your paper 1 to 10. Then write each direct quotation, adding commas and end marks where needed.

EXAMPLE   "Some old legends tell about dragons" Mr. Jacobs stated

ANSWER   "Some old legends tell about dragons," Mr. Jacobs stated.

Real Live
Dragons

1. "Are you talking about fire-breathing dragons" Kate asked
2. "Yes" Mr. Jacobs answered "and there is an iguana that closely resembles that kind of dragon"
3. He added "This iguana is about four feet long"

4. "I hope I never run into one in my neighborhood" Jeffrey exclaimed
5. Mr. Jacobs said reassuringly "I'm sure that won't happen, Jeffrey"
6. "Did a dragon really breathe fire" Terry asked
7. Mr. Jacobs replied "No, but from its nostrils it spouted clouds of vapor, which looked like smoke"
8. Jerry asked "Is the vapor of an iguana poisonous"
9. "It's totally harmless" Mr. Jacobs stated "but the iguana uses the smoke to scare off its enemies"
10. Terry exclaimed "That's the most unusual animal I've ever heard about"

TIME-OUT FOR REVIEW • • • • •

Number your paper 1 to 10. Then write each direct quotation, adding quotation marks, other punctuation marks, and capital letters where needed.

EXAMPLE   Mr. Ames announced our topic today, class, will be oceans

ANSWER   Mr. Ames announced, "Our topic today, class, will be oceans."

The
Oceans

1. Mr. Ames asked how much of the earth is covered by ocean water
2. probably more than half of the earth is covered Tracy answered
3. you're right Mr. Ames said ocean water covers three fourths of the earth's surface
4. that doesn't leave much room for land Brad exclaimed
5. how deep is the deepest ocean Julie asked
6. the average depth of the world's oceans Mr. Ames replied is about three miles
7. he added at the depth of 3,500 feet, waves are not felt
8. Brad asked how high can waves get
9. Mr. Ames answered in a severe storm, some waves are 49 feet high they travel at 50 miles an hour
10. Julie exclaimed that's amazing

Quotation Marks with Dialogue

A *dialogue* is a conversation between two or more persons. The way it is written shows who is speaking.

When writing dialogue, begin a new paragraph each time the speaker changes.

In the following dialogue between Barry and Lisa, a new paragraph begins each time the speaker changes.

> Barry asked, "How long have you been a member of the computer club?"
> "I joined last year," Lisa answered.
> "I'm thinking about joining," he told her.
> Lisa answered, "Oh, I think you should. It's fun."

EXERCISE 5 Writing Dialogue

Correctly write the following dialogue between Barry and Lisa. Add any needed punctuation.

Barry asked do you need to have a computer at home to be a member? You don't have to Lisa answered. That's good because I don't have one. I am going to get one soon for my birthday he told her. Lisa added I don't have one of my own. I use my sister's.

Application to Writing

Including dialogue in a story makes the story more realistic. After all, people talk all the time. When you include dialogue in something you write, make sure that you punctuate it correctly. Otherwise your readers may be confused.

EXERCISE 6 Writing Dialogue

Write a short imaginary dialogue between a teenager and a popular singer. Punctuate the dialogue correctly.

*C*hapter *R*eview

A **Punctuating Titles.** Number your paper 1 to 10. Then write each sentence, adding only quotation marks and underlining where needed.

1. Is Phantom of the Opera a classic horror film?
2. In our textbook New Poetry, I read the poem Dreams.
3. The word typewriter uses only the top row of letters on a typewriter.
4. The short story The Ransom of Red Chief is a humorous story by O. Henry.
5. Charles Lindbergh's plane Spirit of St. Louis had no radio receiver or transmitter.
6. I read the article Sports Greats in this issue of Life.
7. The shortest word containing all five vowels is eunoia.
8. Twelve Angry Men, a three-act play, is now a movie.
9. The Rain in Spain is one song from My Fair Lady.
10. Sarah Bernhardt, a French actress, once played the prince's part in Shakespeare's play Hamlet.

B **Punctuating Direct Quotations.** Number your paper 1 to 10. Then write each direct quotation, adding capital letters, quotation marks, and other punctuation marks where needed.

1. what time do you want to get up Mom asked
2. a baby gazelle can outrun a horse he explained
3. this book Mom said must be returned to the library
4. you're out shouted the umpire
5. Dad asked do we have another gallon of paint
6. the coach asked which is the third most popular sport
7. the humpback whale Mr. Keating said often covers more than 4,000 miles in a single year
8. Karen cried out I've burned my finger
9. Mr. Andrews said the bell just rang everyone is dismissed
10. I just finished lunch she said it was delicious

C **Writing Dialogue.** Correctly rewrite the following dialogue. Add capital letters, quotation marks, and other punctuation marks where needed.

Speaking of Crickets

Peggy said I studied crickets for my science project and learned that they are like grasshoppers. Well, I always thought said Carl that crickets and grasshoppers were the same. No Peggy replied but they are related kinds of insects. Does that mean there are different kinds of crickets Carl asked. Peggy replied I want to explain first that female crickets *don't* sing. There are four main types of crickets, though, and you can probably name at least two kinds. Carl thought for a moment and said yes, I can. I've heard people mention house crickets and field crickets. Yes Peggy agreed those are the kinds we know best.

Mastery Test

Number your paper 1 to 10. Then write each direct quotation, adding quotation marks, other punctuation marks, and capital letters where needed.

1. a female whale weighs as much as 30 elephants he stated
2. have you ever visited New York City Pat asked
3. Ms. Marsh said the piano pieces by Mozart were composed for pianos with only five octaves
4. I smell smoke Shelley screamed
5. Mrs. Jones asked who is going on the field trip
6. lobsters are so small at birth he explained that hundreds could fit in the palm of your hand
7. Andrew exclaimed I just won a free trip to Mexico
8. work on your book reports they are due on Friday Mrs. Keaton stated
9. Thomas Edison invented the electric voting machine she said it was never used until 23 years later
10. Ben asked are you cold shall I turn up the heat

18

Other Punctuation

Diagnostic Test

Number your paper 1 to 10. Then write each sentence, adding apostrophes, semicolons, colons, and hyphens where needed.

EXAMPLE   Where is my horses saddle?
ANSWER   Where is my horse's saddle?

1. The childrens puppet theater performs each Friday.
2. Faint rings around Uranus were discovered in 1977 rings were found around Jupiter in 1979.
3. Next we will hear the treasurers report.
4. Whos the coach of the swim team?
5. Seals sometimes appear on land dolphins and whales never leave the water.
6. Their plane arrives at 7 23 P.M.
7. Several cars motors got overheated on the highway.
8. Harriet Tubman led other black people to freedom moreover, she campaigned for the rights of women.
9. My dinner will include the following foods pot roast, corn, and a salad.
10. Forty five constellations can be seen from most of the Northern Hemisphere.

Apostrophes

An apostrophe is used to show possession. It is also used to form a contraction.

Apostrophes with Possessive Nouns

Use the possessive form of a noun to show that someone or something owns or possesses something else.

web *of a spider* = a spider's web
vacation *of two weeks* = a two weeks' vacation

The Possessive Form of Singular Nouns. To form the possessive of a singular noun, write the noun but do not add or omit any letter. Then add an apostrophe and an *s*.

> **18a** Add 's to form the possessive of a singular noun.

Beth + 's = Beth's   I like Beth's new haircut.
clock + 's = clock's   Listen to the clock's chimes.

EXERCISE 1   *Forming the Possessive of Singular Nouns*

Number your paper 1 to 10. Then rewrite the following expressions, using the possessive form.

1. core of an apple
2. song of a bird
3. toy of a child
4. job of my mother
5. edge of a river
6. uniform of a sailor
7. handbook of a scout
8. book bag of Charlotte
9. chair of a dentist
10. paycheck of a week

EXERCISE 2   *Writing Sentences*

Number your paper 1 to 5. Then write sentences that use five of the answers for Exercise 1.

The Possessive Form of Plural Nouns. There are two rules to follow when forming the possessive of plural nouns.

18b Add only an apostrophe to form the possessive of a plural noun that ends in *s*.

boys + ' = boys'   The boys' shirts are new.
horses + ' = horses'   The horses' hay got wet.

18c Add '*s* to form the possessive of a plural noun that does not end in *s*.

women + 's = women's   Women's shoes are on sale.
mice + 's = mice's   Here are the mice's tracks.

EXERCISE 3 *Forming the Possessive of Plural Nouns*

Number your paper 1 to 10. Then rewrite the following expressions, using the possessive form.

1. work of students
2. toys of children
3. lease of two years
4. farm of grandparents
5. handbags of women
6. barking of dogs
7. honks of geese
8. worth of six dollars
9. wool of sheep
10. ideas of both girls

EXERCISE 4 *Writing Sentences*

Number your paper 1 to 5. Then write sentences that use five of the answers for Exercise 3.

EXERCISE 5 *Forming the Possessive of Nouns*

Number your paper 1 to 10. Then add an apostrophe and an *s* or just an apostrophe to each underlined word.

EXAMPLE   I had a two <u>weeks</u> vacation at my <u>uncle</u> farm.
ANSWER   weeks', uncle's

1. Our nails have the same kind of cells as a <u>cow</u> horns.
2. <u>Peoples</u> hair rarely grows longer than four feet.

278

3. Have you ever read any of <u>O. Henry</u> stories?
4. In the Middle Ages, <u>women</u> clothes were fancy.
5. The twin <u>sisters</u> picture was in <u>Saturday</u> paper.
6. Are <u>men</u> tennis rackets heavier than <u>women</u>?
7. <u>Pete</u> fastball made him the <u>coach</u> choice to pitch.
8. My <u>grandparents</u> ranch is an <u>hour</u> drive from Houston.
9. The <u>children</u> orchestra is planning a two <u>weeks</u> tour.
10. Do you want a <u>year</u> subscription to a <u>boys</u> magazine?

*A*postrophes with Contractions

Besides showing possession, an apostrophe is used in contractions. Two or more words are combined to form a contraction. The apostrophe replaces one or more missing letters.

is + not = isn't let + us = let's
who + is = who's there + is = there's
I + am = I'm of + the + clock = o'clock

18d Use an apostrophe in a contraction to show where one or more letters have been omitted.

Do not confuse contractions with possessive pronouns, which have no apostrophe. Say the individual words of a contraction separately: It's (*it is*) time for action.

CONTRACTIONS	it's	you're	they're	there's	who's
PRONOUNS	its	your	their	theirs	whose

*E*XERCISE 6 Using Apostrophes with Contractions
Number your paper 1 to 20. Then write the contraction for each pair of words.

1. have not	6. is not	11. we will	16. you have
2. did not	7. let us	12. I have	17. would not
3. that is	8. I am	13. it is	18. you are
4. are not	9. she is	14. do not	19. we are
5. who is	10. was not	15. they are	20. there is

EXERCISE 7 *Distinguishing between Contractions and Possessive Pronouns*

Number your paper 1 to 10. Then write the correct word in each set of parentheses.

1. (Who's, Whose) pitching in the first half? (Who's, Whose) bat is this?
2. (It's, Its) building (it's, its) nest in the bush.
3. (They're, Their) not cheering because (they're, their) team isn't winning.
4. (You're, Your) parents worry when (you're, your) late.
5. (There's, Theirs) a strange boat docked next to (there's, theirs).
6. Because of (it's, its) multiple eyes, (it's, its) hard to swat a fly.
7. (They're, Their) keeping all (they're, their) books.
8. If (you're, your) not careful, the dog may stain (you're, your) new shirt.
9. I can't see (who's, whose) car is behind us or (who's, whose) driving.
10. I'm sure this house is (there's, theirs), but (there's, theirs) no one home.

TIME-OUT FOR REVIEW • • • • •

Number your paper 1 to 10. Then correctly write each word that needs an apostrophe.

1. Muscles make up about half of your whole bodys weight.
2. Please buy me two dollars worth of birdseed.
3. Theres a letter in your mailbox.
4. Dont get so close to the fire!
5. You cant sneeze with your eyes open.
6. Please take Jasons books to his home after school.
7. All workers suggestions were given to the manager.
8. Lindas brother goes to college.
9. I wonder how much an elephants brain weighs.
10. The mens locker room closes at six oclock.

Semicolons and Colons

A semicolon (;) can signal a pause between the parts of a compound sentence. A colon (:) looks similar to a semicolon but is used for other purposes.

Semicolons

A compound sentence has two or more independent clauses. They can be joined by a comma and a conjunction or by a semicolon. (*See pages 133–135 for a review of compound sentences.*)

18e Use a semicolon between the clauses of a compound sentence that are not joined by a conjunction.

My sister has blond hair; I have red hair.

The factory closed; hundreds of people are out of work.

Semicolons with Transitional Words. A semicolon can be used to combine two independent clauses joined by any of the following transitional words.

Common Transitional Words		
accordingly	furthermore	moreover
consequently	hence	nevertheless
for example	however	otherwise
for instance	instead	therefore

18f Use a semicolon between clauses in a compound sentence that are joined by certain transitional words.

Kim practiced repeatedly; *therefore,* he made the team.

He was a leader; *hence,* he was elected captain.

Notice that a comma follows the transitional word.

EXERCISE 8 *Punctuating Compound Sentences*

Number your paper 1 to 10. Then write each sentence, adding a semicolon.

EXAMPLE   Al missed his bus otherwise, he'd be here.
ANSWER   Al missed his bus; otherwise, he'd be here.

1. The new bank building is 87 stories tall therefore, it is the largest building in the city.
2. Our car is very fuel-efficient for example, we get 27 miles to a gallon.
3. President Harry S Truman used a middle initial however, it did not stand for a middle name.
4. Arteries carry blood from the heart to the tissues veins carry blood back to the heart.
5. December 21 is the first day of winter June 21 is the first day of summer.
6. Butterflies do not spin cocoons moths do.
7. Mary McCauley carried water to thirsty soldiers therefore, the soldiers called her Molly Pitcher.
8. Rabbits raise their young in burrows hares raise their young in the open.
9. Don't wait at the gym instead, wait at your house until seven o'clock.
10. "River horse" is the meaning of *hippopotamus* however, the hippopotamus is related to the pig.

Colons

A colon is used mainly to introduce a list of items.

18g Use a colon before most lists of items, especially when the list comes after an expression like *the following*.

The test will cover the following parts of speech: nouns, pronouns, adjectives, and adverbs.

I have three brothers: Jonathan, Harry, and Roger.

A colon is not needed between a verb and its complement or directly after a preposition.

INCORRECT	In the trunk I found: old records, a diary, and photograph albums.
CORRECT	In the trunk I found the following items: old records, a diary, and photograph albums.
INCORRECT	On your walk look out for: poison ivy, poison oak, and thorny bushes.
CORRECT	On your walk, look out for three hazards: poison ivy, poison oak, and thorny bushes.

A colon is also used between the hour and the minute in writing the time of day.

Please wake me at 6:30 A.M.

EXERCISE 9 Using Colons

Number your paper 1 to 10. Then write each sentence, adding a colon where needed. If a sentence is correct, write C after the number.

1. In the last ten years, my family has lived in three cities Memphis, Charlottesville, and Atlanta.
2. The movie at Cinema II starts at 7 20 P.M.
3. There are four main types of blood A, B, AB, and O.
4. Animals with horns include these six giraffes, deer, cattle, antelopes, sheep, and goats.
5. California borders three other states Arizona, Nevada, and Oregon.
6. By 1944, Americans could buy the following frozen foods meats, vegetables, fish, and dairy products.
7. We are waiting for Pat, Dylan, Chico, and Charlene.
8. I enjoy many water sports swimming, waterskiing, and fishing.
9. The bus stops here at 2 30 and 4 30.
10. The three most heavily consumed food items in the United States are milk, potatoes, and beef.

EXERCISE 10 *Writing Sentences* ✎

Number your paper 1 to 5. Then write sentences that follow the directions below.

1. Write a compound sentence joined by a comma and the conjunction *and*.
2. Write a compound sentence joined by a semicolon.
3. Write a compound sentence joined by *however*. (Place a comma after *however*.)
4. Write a simple sentence with a colon before a series.
5. Write a compound sentence joined by *therefore*. (Place a comma after *therefore*.)

TIME-OUT FOR REVIEW ● ● ● ● ●

Number your paper 1 to 10. Then write each sentence, adding a semicolon or a colon where needed.

EXAMPLE Fish come in many shapes some look like snakes.

ANSWER Fish come in many shapes; some look like snakes.

Fishy Facts

1. A shark has an exceptional sense of smell it can sense odors from a distance of almost a mile.
2. Fish come in the following colors red, yellow, purple, gray, green, orange, blue, and brown.
3. All fish have bones all live in water.
4. Fish have no lungs however, their gills take in oxygen.
5. The lungfish can breathe air therefore, it can live without water in times of drought.
6. Fish eat all kinds of things insects, worms, plants, and even other fish.
7. Some fish swim very fast for example, the sailfish swims at more than 60 miles per hour.
8. The batfish does not swim it walks underwater.
9. A fish has very few nerves around its mouth consequently, a hooked fish feels very little pain.
10. The following deep-sea fish have light-producing organs lantern fish, viperfish, and hatchetfish.

Hyphens

A hyphen (-) is part of the spelling of certain words and is also used to divide words.

Hyphens with Divided Words

Occasionally it is necessary to divide a word at the end of a line to keep the right margin even.

Use a hyphen to divide a word at the end of a line.

Following are several guidelines for dividing a word at the end of a line. If you are not certain about where each syllable in a word ends, look the word up in a dictionary.

Dividing Words

1. Divide words only between syllables.
   pro duc tion: pro-duction or produc-tion

2. Never divide a one-syllable word.
   DO NOT BREAK   dine   meant   note

3. Do not divide a word after the first letter.
   DO NOT BREAK   omit   agree   oboe

EXERCISE 11   Using Hyphens to Divide Words

Number your paper 1 to 15. Then add a hyphen or hyphens to show where each word can be correctly divided. If a word should not be divided, write *no* after the number.

1. occasion
2. summer
3. evict
4. milk
5. sponge
6. prince
7. around
8. middle
9. question
10. silent
11. repeat
12. fleet
13. amazement
14. ocean
15. aboard

Other Uses of Hyphens

A hyphen is used in spelling certain words as well as in certain numbers, fractions, and compound nouns.

Hyphens with Certain Numbers.   A hyphen is used in most numbers when they are written out—for example, when a number is the first word in a sentence.

> **18i** ▸ Use a hyphen when writing out the numbers *twenty-one* through *ninety-nine.*

"Sixty-four" is the answer to the math problem.

Twenty-two pieces were missing from the puzzle.

Hyphens with Certain Fractions.   When a fraction is used as an adjective, it is written with a hyphen.

> **18j** ▸ Use a hyphen when writing out a fraction that is used as an adjective.

HYPHEN   A three-fourths majority is needed to pass the amendment. [*Three-fourths* is an adjective that describes *majority.*]

NO HYPHEN   Three fourths of the members were present. [The noun *three fourths* is the subject.]

Hyphens with Some Compound Nouns.   A compound noun is a noun that is made up of two or more words. The words in a compound noun may be written together or written separately. Others are written with a hyphen.

> **18k** ▸ Use a hyphen to separate the parts of some compound nouns.

Kenneth is his son-in-law.

The baby-sitter will arrive in ten minutes.

EXERCISE 12 Using Hyphens

Number your paper 1 to 10. Then correctly write each word that should be hyphenated. If no word in the sentence needs a hyphen, write C after the number. (You may use a dictionary for help.)

1. Seventy seven years usually pass between sightings of Halley's comet.
2. Yesterday there was a traffic tie up on the highway.
3. Dennis has finished only one third of his report.
4. We took dancing lessons to learn the two step.
5. I contributed a one tenth share of the expenses.
6. Several bird watchers were in the park on Sunday.
7. Eighty eight coins were found on the driveway.
8. The will stated that Marianna would inherit a two thirds share of the farm.
9. The stand in for the sick actress was talented.
10. "Seventy six Trombones" is the name of a song.

TIME-OUT FOR REVIEW ● ● ● ● ●

Number your paper 1 to 10. Then write each sentence, adding semicolons, colons, and hyphens where needed. If a sentence is correct, write C after the number.

1. Stems act as elevators water and food move up them to the leaves.
2. There are four commonwealths in the United States Kentucky, Massachusetts, Pennsylvania, and Virginia.
3. Our vegetable garden measures three fourths of an acre.
4. Lichens play an important role in nature some break down rocks to make soil.
5. My great grandmother lives with us.
6. The grass is mowed it must be raked.
7. We need detergent, dog food, and napkins.
8. Thirty five species of coconuts are known.
9. Jacques Cousteau's accomplishments are many the Aqualung, the diving saucer, and travel films.
10. A two thirds vote favoring the new bridge was expected.

Application to Writing

Editing your written work for correct punctuation is as important as editing for correct spelling or proper capitalization. Sentences and paragraphs that are not punctuated correctly can be difficult to read. Paying attention to details such as proper punctuation marks is part of communicating successfully in writing.

EXERCISE 13 Editing for Proper Punctuation

Read the following paragraphs. Then write them, adding apostrophes, semicolons, and colons where needed.

Looking Back

Streetcars were once a very common sight in the early 1900s. Maybe youve seen them in photographs or films. Perhaps youve actually ridden on one. The early streetcars were different from trackless trolleys they ran on tracks in the street.

A streetcars power came from electricity. Europes streetcars were powered by two overhead wires however, most early streetcars in the United States were powered by one wire and one electrified track. Europe got its first streetcar system in 1881 the United States followed four years later.

Streetcars began to disappear in the 1930s because of competition from cars and buses. A changeover was quickly made to trackless trolleys. These vehicles looked like buses. They used overhead power lines but didnt run on tracks. The first trackless trolley service began in 1910 in Los Angeles, once the home of the nations finest streetcar system.

Today streetcars are still used in the following countries Germany, Austria, and Switzerland. They are almost extinct in the United States nevertheless, you can still see some in various museums throughout the country and, very occasionally, in carbarns.

*C*hapter *R*eview

A **Punctuating Correctly.** Number your paper 1 to 10. Then write each sentence, adding apostrophes, semicolons, colons, and hyphens where needed.

1. Some restaurants serve frogs legs.
2. Theirs cant be the house with the shutters.
3. Turtles have no teeth instead, they have sharp beaks.
4. A honeybees stinger has a hook at the end.
5. A one fifth share of the profits sounds good to me.
6. We steamed twenty five ears of corn.
7. Dad sells many things computers, printers, software, and office supplies.
8. Vermont was not one of the original 13 colonies it became the 14th state in 1791.
9. Womens coats are on sale at the mall.
10. Do you know the following computer terms *bit, byte,* and *bug?*

B **Punctuating Correctly.** Number your paper 1 to 10. Then write each sentence, adding apostrophes, semicolons, colons, and hyphens where needed.

1. Thirty five billion pounds of potatoes are consumed by Americans each year.
2. An elephants trunk is actually its nose and upper lip.
3. After eight hours work, Mom finished her painting.
4. Tendons connect muscles to bones ligaments link the bones of ankles, knees, and elbows.
5. Well have to take the early train.
6. I missed the bus otherwise, I had a wonderful day.
7. My parents birthday present to me was a down vest.
8. The sun rises tomorrow at 6 17.
9. A small plane has three main controls a throttle lever, a control column, and a rudder bar.
10. The mens soccer team is practicing for the Olympics.

C **Punctuating Correctly.** Number your paper 1 to 10. Then write each sentence, adding all needed punctuation. If a sentence is correct, write *C* after the number.

Creatures in the Cold

1. After the twenty third day of September, the nights become longer than the days.
2. Wild creatures become aware of these signs shorter days, colder air, and less available food.
3. A house cat may begin its daily naps earlier.
4. Scientists study outdoor creatures methods of survival.
5. Some birds migrate others do not.
6. Most insects survive a long winter a few die.
7. An insects survival partly depends on burrowing under the earth or beneath the bark of trees.
8. The ability to survive the cold by sleeping most of the time exists in insects, birds, and animals.
9. Some hibernators temperatures become very low.
10. Bears also hibernate however, their temperature stays near normal.

Mastery Test

Number your paper 1 to 10. Then write each sentence, adding apostrophes, semicolons, colons, and hyphens where needed.

1. The puppy needs discipline it chews Dad's shoes.
2. The teachers room is next to the main office.
3. I went to the market however, it was closed.
4. Youre next at bat.
5. Her mother in law is Dr. Julia Ortiz.
6. Our older sister has joined a womens exercise class.
7. Twenty three inches of snow fell on the ski slopes.
8. One of Jupiters moons has volcanoes on its surface.
9. Childrens clothes are on the second floor.
10. Benjamin Franklin was many things a painter, a writer, a scientist, an inventor, and a statesman.

Standardized Test

Directions: Decide which numbered part in each sentence contains an error in capitalization or punctuation. In the appropriate row on your answer sheet, fill in the circle containing the same number as the incorrect part. If there is no error, fill in *4*.

SAMPLE   Is Marthas | favorite city | San Francisco? | None
            1   2   3   4

ANSWER   ① ② ③ ④

1. A new record store | has opened on | Grove street. | None
       1   2   3   4

2. St. Patrick's | Cathedral is | in New York City. | None
      1   2   3   4

3. If uncle Ben | makes the lasagna, | I'll make the salad. |
      1   2   3
   None
   4

4. At the meeting | the mayor announced | his plan. | None
       1   2   3   4

5. Tess's uncle, | an auto mechanic | fixed her old car. | None
       1   2   3   4

6. The opera | "The Magic Flute" | was written in German. |
      1   2   3
   None
   4

7. "Whose is this | red feather" the | detective asked. | None
        1   2   3   4

8. Can't you go | to the library | before 3:30 | None
       1   2   3   4

9. While they slept | the plane landed | and then left. | None
        1   2   3   4

10. Didn't she play | the princess in | *Star Wars*? | None
         1   2   3   4

11. Ed yelled | "The senator has | been re-elected!" | None
       1   2   3   4

12. My mother ordered | eggs: I asked for | French toast. | None
    1   **2**   **3**   **4**

13. I'm writing | a report on | Queen Elizabeth II. | None
    1   **2**   **3**   **4**

14. The Chicago bus, | I believe, | leaves at 2 42. | None
    1   **2**   **3**   **4**

15. Yes, doctor, | the article is called | "Surgery Today." | None
    1   **2**   **3**   **4**

Directions: Choose the answer that shows the correct way to write the underlined part in each sentence. On your answer sheet, fill in the circle containing the same number as your answer.

SAMPLE   He rushed to the <u>window but</u> the car was gone.
     1. window but
     2. window, but
     3. window: but

ANSWER   ① ❷ ③

16. The telephone rang at <u>6 42 AM</u>.
     1. 6 42 AM.
     2. 6:42 A.M.
     3. 6:42 AM.

17. Was Sharon born on <u>July 3, 4 or 5</u>?
     1. July 3, 4, or 5?
     2. july 3, 4, or 5?
     3. July 3, 4 or 5?

18. Charlotte Brontë wrote the <u>novel Jane Eyre</u>.
     1. novel: <u>Jane Eyre</u>.
     2. novel <u>Jane Eyre</u>.
     3. novel, "Jane Eyre."

19. Ted <u>complained "My</u> feet hurt."
     1. complained "My
     2. complained "my
     3. complained, "My

20. After the rooster <u>crowed everyone</u> went back to sleep.
     1. crowed everyone
     2. crowed. Everyone
     3. crowed, everyone

Composition

Part One

19

Words and Sentences

Exact words and well-shaped sentences can breathe life into writing. In the following passage, notice how you can experience the scene as if you were in it yourself.

It was a soft, reposeful summer landscape, as lovely as a dream and as lonesome as Sunday. The air was full of the smell of flowers and the buzzing of insects and the twittering of birds. There were no people, no wagons, no stir of life, nothing going on. The road was mainly a winding path with hoof-prints in it and now and then a faint trace of wheels on either side in the grass.   —MARK TWAIN, *A CONNECTICUT YANKEE IN KING ARTHUR'S COURT*

This chapter will help you bring your writing to life with fresh words and smooth, varied sentences.

Your Writer's Notebook

Think about a summer scene that brings back pleasant memories. Then re-create the scene in your journal. Include sights, sounds, feelings, smells, and tastes. Read your description aloud. Does it flow smoothly? Your ear can help you smooth out any rough spots.

*W*ord Choice

Mountain climbers need secure footholds to keep from slipping. In the same way, readers need something concrete to hold on to when they are trying to understand a passage. Specific words will give your readers a firm footing.

*S*pecific Words

Read the following movie reviews. Which one gives you a better idea of the film?

The movie was very good. The actors were good. The special effects were great. The story was interesting.

Star Base was thrillingly entertaining. The young cast performed sensitively. The special effects were dazzling. The story throbbed with action and conflict and concluded with a surprise ending.

The first review uses only general words. Because general words can mean different things to different people, they do not communicate precisely. The second review replaces the general words with specific words that call a precise image to mind. The examples below show general and specific words for different parts of speech.

	GENERAL	SPECIFIC
NOUNS	dog	Great Dane
	tree	Dutch elm
ADJECTIVES	cute	fresh-faced
	good	inspiring
VERBS	bother	nag
	ran	raced
ADVERBS	well	expertly
	quietly	mutely

19a Use **specific words** to convey your exact meaning.

EXERCISE 1 Choosing Specific Words

Number your paper 1 to 20. Then write two specific words for each of the following general words.

EXAMPLE   shoes
POSSIBLE ANSWERS   sneakers, sandals

1. clothing	6. pretty	11. said	16. slowly
2. car	7. nice	12. walked	17. sadly
3. house	8. sad	13. ate	18. quickly
4. train	9. fine	14. laughed	19. bravely
5. book	10. old	15. flew	20. playfully

EXERCISE 2 Replacing General Words with Specific Words

Number your paper 1 to 10. Then write a specific word to replace the underlined word or words in each sentence.

EXAMPLE   Every year I go to scout camp.
POSSIBLE ANSWER   July

Summer Camp

1. Camp Manilokin is in another state.
2. The counselors plan many things to do.
3. On nature walks we sometimes see a deer running for cover.
4. Once a day we can pair up with a partner and take boats out on the lake.
5. The rules require partners because going swimming or boating without a companion is bad.
6. The counselors teach us how to make a fire and put it out well.
7. At night we sometimes cook marshmallows over the glowing embers.
8. We don't stay up late because a bell at 6:30 A.M. calls us to our meal.
9. Sometimes, however, we do talk past bedtime with our tent-mates.
10. After spending two weeks in the woods, I return home feeling good.

296

Denotation and Connotation

Most words have two kinds of meaning. One, called *denotation*, is the meaning found in the dictionary. The other, called *connotation*, is an extra level of meaning. Connotation is the feeling or attitude a word expresses. For example, *violin* and *fiddle* have the same denotation, but the feelings they convey are different.

Samuel plays the **violin.**   Robert plays the **fiddle.**

The word *violin* is associated with classical music, the kind you would hear at symphony hall. The word *fiddle*, on the other hand, calls folk music and square dances to mind.

Some words carry positive or negative connotations. *Thrifty* and *stingy* both mean "careful with money." *Thrifty*, however, suggests a good quality. *Stingy* conveys a negative quality.

POSITIVE CONNOTATION   Rosa is thrifty.
NEGATIVE CONNOTATION   Rosa is stingy.

19b Choose specific words with appropriate **connotations** to match your meaning.

EXERCISE 3 *Finding Words with Similar Denotations*

Number your paper 1 to 10. Then match each word in Group 1 with the word in Group 2 that has the same denotation.

Group 1		Group 2	
1. saw	6. young	brainy	officers
2. hungry	7. warning	immature	tardy
3. tidy	8. intelligent	spied	jogged
4. late	9. note	message	starving
5. ran	10. police	neat	alarm

EXERCISE 4 *Choosing Connotations*

Number your paper 1 to 10. Then write the word with the connotation called for in brackets.

EXAMPLE   We went hiking on a (sunny, scorching) day. [negative]

ANSWER   scorching

1. Paul (snickered, giggled) at Jody's story. [positive]
2. The beef stew Barbara made for dinner was (thick, gooey). [negative]
3. In the summer Robert wears a (distinctive, peculiar) straw hat. [positive]
4. The dance floor was (crammed, filled) with couples. [positive]
5. The alarm clock (hummed, screeched) its wake-up call. [positive]
6. During the student council meeting on Friday, Kathy (firmly, stubbornly) refused to follow the wishes of the majority. [negative]
7. After winning the election, Sandra became more (confident, conceited). [negative]
8. All of a sudden, a stranger stepped (boldly, brazenly) onto the speaker's platform. [positive]
9. Ted has (bushy, curly) blond hair. [positive]
10. The waves (pounded, washed) against the rocky Maine coast. [negative]

Appealing to the Senses

Most of the impressions you gather come to you through your five senses. Your experiences are based on what you see, hear, smell, taste, or touch. You can share these experiences in writing by using words that appeal to your reader's senses. Read the following two sentences.

Josie felt **sad.**

Josie **slumped** in the big, **overstuffed** chair, resting her **downcast** head on her **fist** and **sighing.**

The first sentence *tells* a reader that Josie is sad. The second sentence *shows* the sadness. A reader can see Josie's posture and hear her sighing. These sensory details communicate more clearly than does the adjective *sad* in the first sentence.

19c Use words that appeal to your reader's senses.

Following are some sensory words that could add interest to your writing.

Sight	Sound	Smell	Taste	Touch
foggy	whisper	moldy	salty	rough
shiny	screech	cedar	honey	dank
crimson	pound	musty	maple	velvety
pale	hiss	fishy	yeasty	glassy
tilted	sizzle	sour	spicy	gritty
shallow	crackle	smoky	fruity	gooey
emerald	swish	floral	sugary	silky
drab	giggle	lemony	chewy	clammy
lanky	chatter	stale	bland	sticky
sheer	thud	oily	sweet	smooth
petite	roar	burned	tart	cool
golden	squeak	piney	creamy	frosty
rusty	rattle	soapy	juicy	soft
curved	squish	clean	tangy	spongy

EXERCISE 5   Using Sensory Words

Rewrite each of the following sentences. Use details that appeal to the senses to *show* rather than *tell*.

EXAMPLE   Bill was happy.
POSSIBLE ANSWER   Bill whistled as he raced home.

1. My dog is beautiful.
2. Katrina was angry.
3. The pancake breakfast was delicious.
4. Mary seemed nervous.
5. The beach was breathtaking.

EXERCISE 6   Listing Sensory Words

Copy the following five headings on your paper. Then add ten sensory words to each list. Two examples have been given in each column.

Sight	Sound	Smell	Taste	Touch
dim	clang	minty	cinnamon	icy
blue	gurgle	fresh	bitter	slimy

EXERCISE 7   Writing Sentences with Sensory Words

Write five sentences that describe a group of cowhands in the days of the Old West. Create a vivid scene by using words that would appeal to a reader's senses. When you have finished your description, underline each sensory word.

EXERCISE 8   On Your Own

Think of a specific food that you particularly like. Then copy the following five headings on your paper. Under each heading, list as many sensory words as you can that describe the food you chose. Next use your list to write five sentences that describe the food without naming it. When you have finished, exchange papers with a classmate. Try to guess the kind of food your partner has described.

Sight	Sound	Smell	Taste	Touch

riting Extra

Sometimes the best way to describe something is to compare it with something else.

His eyes are **like lasers.**
The moon is a **pearl** in the velvet night sky.
Flowers are the **embroidery** of the earth.

When you write a comparison, choose two things that are alike in only one way. For example, eyes and lasers are very different things, but they share a piercing quality. The moon and a pearl are also very different, but they both resemble shining white spheres. Flowers and embroidery are also alike in only one way. They both make very beautiful and colorful decorations.

When writing comparisons, be original. An unusual comparison will add life to a description. Avoid overused comparisons like the clichés and trite expressions below. Worn-out expressions like these add nothing to a description. They have become so commonplace that they have lost their power to call any clear image to a reader's mind.

Clichés and Trite Expressions

felt like two cents   busy as a bee
cheeks like roses   white as snow
worked like a horse   deep as the ocean
sparkled like diamonds   old as the hills
waddled like a duck   loud as thunder

Choose five of the overused comparisons from the list above. For each one write a fresh comparison. Then use each one in a complete sentence.

EXAMPLE   felt like two cents

POSSIBLE   felt like a plastic pen that had run out of ink
ANSWER   When I forgot my lines during the play, I felt
            like a plastic pen that had run out of ink.

Sentence Combining

If too many sentences in a row follow the same pattern, writing can sound as tedious as a broken record. A good mix of sentence types and structures will help keep your readers interested. Sentence combining is one way to vary the length and structure of your sentences.

19d ▶ Combine short sentences into longer, more interesting ones.

Combining with Specific Details

Writing that contains specific details creates a clear image in the mind of the reader. A series of short sentences giving details, however, can be tiresome to read. Notice how the specific details in the following sentences can be combined into one more interesting sentence.

CHOPPY SENTENCES   The robot squeaked.
                           The robot was **metallic.**
                           It squeaked **continually.**
                           It squeaked **at its hinges.**

COMBINED SENTENCE   The **metallic** robot squeaked **continually at its hinges.**

If your combined sentence contains two or more adjectives in a row, remember to separate the adjectives with commas. Study the following example. (*You may want to review the rules for using commas on page 251.*)

CHOPPY SENTENCES   The museum has a robot.
                           It is **metallic.**
                           It is **squeaky.**

COMBINED SENTENCES   The museum has a **metallic, squeaky** robot.

When you revise your writing, eliminate short sentences containing only details by combining them with other sentences.

302

EXERCISE 9 Combining Sentences with Specific Details

Number your paper 1 to 10. Then combine each group of short sentences into one longer one.

The Viking Mission

1. The Viking spacecraft was a robot. It was enormous. It was sophisticated.
2. Viking was sent on a mission. The mission was to the surface of Mars.
3. Viking relayed information. The information went to Earth.
4. Viking also took photographs. They were of the surface of Mars. The surface was red and dusty.
5. Viking had instruments aboard. The instruments were complex. They were for measuring Marsquakes.
6. Over a period of years, Viking sent back information. The information was useful.
7. One day a command was sent to Viking. The command was incorrect. It was sent from Earth by mistake.
8. It made Viking erase information. It erased it instantaneously. The information was important.
9. Viking needed this information to send its reports. The reports went to receivers on Earth.
10. Viking is still up in space collecting information. Space is deep. Space is dark.

Combining by Coordinating

Another way to smooth out short, choppy sentences is to combine them into one longer sentence by coordinating. Coordinating means linking ideas of equal importance. Use the coordinating conjunctions *and*, *but*, *or*, and *yet* to show the exact relationship between ideas.

One way to use coordination is to join two or more verbs that share the same subject. The result is a simple sentence with a compound verb.

CHOPPY SENTENCES
Scientists <u>have observed</u> the walrus for many years. Scientists <u>have recorded</u> much information.

COMPOUND VERB
Scientists <u>have observed</u> the walrus for many years and <u>have recorded</u> much information.

In other sentences two subjects may share the same verb. When you combine these sentences into one, the result is a compound subject.

CHOPPY SENTENCES
Two huge <u>tusks</u> <u>are</u> one characteristic of the walrus. A mustached upper <u>lip</u> <u>is</u> another characteristic.

COMPOUND SUBJECT
Two huge <u>tusks</u> and a mustached upper <u>lip</u> <u>are</u> characteristics of the walrus.

Sometimes two entire sentences can be joined with a coordinating conjunction. The result of this combination is a compound sentence.

CHOPPY SENTENCES
Many mysteries about these fascinating sea animals have been solved. Scientists still have much to learn about them.

COMPOUND SENTENCE
Many mysteries about these fascinating sea animals have been solved, **but** scientists still have much to learn about them.

NOTE: See compound subjects, compound verbs, and compound sentences on pages 15–16 and 133–135.

EXERCISE 10 Combining Sentences by Coordinating

Number your paper 1 to 10. Then combine each pair of sentences into one longer sentence. Use the conjunctions given in brackets to form a compound subject, a compound verb, or a compound sentence. Use commas where needed.

EXAMPLE Walruses belong to the seal family. Walruses differ from seals in many ways. [but]

ANSWER Walruses belong to the seal family but differ from seals in many ways.

The Walrus

1. The air sacs in its neck make the walrus unique. Its huge tusks make the walrus unique. [and]
2. The inflatable air sacs in its neck keep its head above water. These air sacs allow the walrus to take a nap in the ocean. [and]
3. Their huge ivory tusks are helpful tools in the ice. These long, curved teeth can become dangerous weapons during a fight. [but]
4. Walruses have a clumsy appearance. These sea animals can move over land as fast as a person. [yet]
5. In the water the walrus swims easily with its four flippers. It also slides effortlessly along the ocean bottom with its two strong tusks. [or]
6. A walrus consumes 60 pounds of clams a day. A herd of them eats over 6 million clams daily. [and]

305

7. Walruses can survive alone. Walruses can live in herds. [or]
8. Polar bears are enemies of the walrus. Killer whales are enemies too. [and]
9. The walrus is a timid animal. It will fight for the protection of its young. [yet]
10. In the 1960s walruses were in danger of extinction. Today many laws protect them. [and]

Combining by Subordinating

If the ideas in two short sentences are of unequal importance, you can combine them by subordinating. The result will be a complex sentence. (*See page 136.*)

One way to subordinate is to change the less important idea into an adjective clause. The relative pronouns *who, whom, whose, which,* and *that* begin an adjective clause.

CHOPPY SENTENCES Body language communicates clearly. Body language is used by people around the world.

COMBINED SENTENCE Body language, **which is used by people around the world,** communicates clearly.

NOTE: You may want to review the rules for using commas with adjective clauses on page 128.

Another way to subordinate is to change the less important idea into an adverb clause. Subordinating conjunctions, such as *after, although, because, unless, if,* and *until,* are used to begin adverb clauses.

CHOPPY SENTENCES Some movements have more than one meaning. Most are readily understood.

COMBINED SENTENCE **Although some movements have more than one meaning,** most are readily understood.

NOTE: You may want to review the list of subordinating conjunctions and the rules for using commas with adverb clauses on pages 130 and 132.

*E*XERCISE 11 *Combining Sentences by Subordinating*

Number your paper 1 to 10. Then combine each pair of sentences into one longer sentence. Use the suggestions in brackets. Use commas where needed.

EXAMPLE   Lifting an eyebrow may show disbelief. It may also show surprise. [adverb clause: *although*]

ANSWER   Although lifting an eyebrow may show disbelief, it may also show surprise.

Body Talk

1. Shrugging the shoulders can mean a lack of knowledge. Shrugging the shoulders is a common body signal. [adjective clause: *which*]
2. The head houses memory. Many people touch their foreheads to show forgetfulness. [adverb clause: *because*]
3. Proxemics can tell us more about body language. Proxemics is the study of distances people keep between themselves and others. [adjective clause: *which*]
4. Some people stand very close to others during a conversation. Their cultures are not uncomfortable with close spaces. [adverb clause: *because*]

307

5. The handshake was once a sign that a person carried no weapons. The handshake's purpose today is to show friendliness. [adjective clause: *whose*]
6. In Japan you have a high status. You must bow lower than the person you are greeting. [adverb clause: *unless*]
7. You are sitting alone at a cafeteria table. Your eyes can signal to a new arrival that you want to be left alone. [adverb clause: *if*]
8. You look down. The new arrival will assume you want some company and conversation. [adverb clause: *unless*]
9. The nod means no in some other cultures. The nod means yes in our culture. [adjective clause: *which*]
10. Understanding others is aided by understanding body language. Understanding others is a goal of human societies. [adjective clause: *which*]

Exercise 12 *On Your Own*

Write 10 simple sentences (one subject and one verb) about the picture below. Then look over the sentences that you have written and combine those that seem to go together.

Sentence Variety

You have learned how to use sentence combining to vary the length and structure of your sentences. Another way to add variety to your writing is to begin your sentences in different ways.

Sentence Beginnings

The most natural way to begin a sentence is with the subject. For variety, however, experiment with other sentence beginnings.

SUBJECT **Chi Cheng** was a very fast runner in her high school days.

PHRASE **In her high school days,** Chi Cheng was a very fast runner.

The following sentences show just a few of the ways you can begin your sentences.

PHRASE **At the age of 16,** she represented Taiwan in the 1960 Olympics. [prepositional phrase]

Training vigorously, she also qualified for the 1964 Olympics. [participial phrase]

ADJECTIVE **Steadfast,** she kept up her running even though she hurt her leg during the second Olympic match.

ADVERB **Altogether** Cheng broke or matched seven world records during the next five years.

CLAUSE **Although serious leg problems put an end to her running career,** Cheng took up coaching and is now helping others. [adverb clause]

NOTE: For a review of phrases and clauses, see Chapters 8 and 9. You may also wish to review the rules for punctuating introductory elements on pages 253–254.

EXERCISE 13 *Varying Sentence Beginnings*

All of the following sentences begin with the subject. Add variety by beginning each sentence with the opener suggested in brackets. Remember to follow the rules for using commas with introductory elements.

EXAMPLE   William J. Watson went to work for the National Cash Register Company in 1894. [prepositional phrase]

ANSWER   In 1894, William J. Watson went to work for the National Cash Register Company.

Think!

1. Watson sold many, many machines, surprising his bosses. [participial phrase]
2. Watson became the sales manager of the National Cash Register Company at 35 years of age. [prepositional phrase]
3. Watson left NCR and became president of the Computer-Tabulating-Recording-Company after five years. [prepositional phrase]
4. Watson worked tirelessly year after year to build up the struggling company. [adverb]
5. Watson changed the company's name to International Business Machines (IBM) when the company took on business from foreign countries. [adverb clause]
6. IBM grew steadily under Watson's direction. [prepositional phrase]
7. One reason for the company's huge success was undoubtedly Watson's belief in the value of expert sales people. [adverb]
8. Watson impressed the importance of careful thought on those who worked for him, printing up signs that said "THINK." [participial phrase]
9. The words READ, LISTEN, DISCUSS, OBSERVE, and THINK are written in gold on the steps of his sales training school in New York. [prepositional phrase]
10. Watson believed first and foremost in the importance of his workers, although he had sold machines during his whole life. [adverb clause]

EXERCISE 14 On Your Own

Describe the scene in the following picture by doing Steps 1 through 4 below.

STEP 1 Write 10 short sentences in subject-verb order.

STEP 2 Expand your sentences by adding adjectives, adverbs, and phrases. Remember to use specific words and words that appeal to the senses.

STEP 3 Vary the length of your sentences by combining sentences that contain related ideas.

STEP 4 Vary the beginnings of your sentences by starting some with an adverb, a phrase, or a clause.

Concise Sentences

When you shop, you want the most value for your dollar. When you write, you want the most value for each word you use. Be economical in your writing. Avoid using words that add no real meaning.

19e ▸ Express your meaning in as few words as possible.

Rambling Sentences

Sometimes too many ideas are piled into one long sentence. The result, called a *rambling sentence*, is hard to read and difficult to understand.

RAMBLING SENTENCE
> About seven million people in the United States do not eat meat, **but** they find protein in other types of food, **and** they combine certain kinds of food such as rice and beans to make sure they eat complete proteins, **or** they sometimes eat such dairy products as cheese, milk, and yogurt for protein.

To break up rambling sentences, eliminate some of the conjunctions and place the ideas in sentences of their own.

REVISED SENTENCES
> About seven million people in the United States do not eat meat. They find protein in other types of food. They also combine certain kinds of food such as rice and beans to make sure they eat complete proteins. Others sometimes eat such dairy products as cheese, milk, and yogurt for protein.

When revising your writing to eliminate rambling sentences, strive for a mix of long and short sentences to achieve sentence variety.

312

EXERCISE 15   *Revising Rambling Sentences*

Revise the following paragraph to eliminate the rambling sentences.

Dusty Skies

Sunlight passing through and reflecting dust particles explains the sometimes brilliant colors we see in the sky, and one of the sources of this dust is volcanic explosion, and a single blast can send tons of dust into the air. Another source of dust is the ocean, from which salt is sprayed and then evaporated into salty dust, and plants also give off billions of grains of pollen and spores. Dust particles by the ton also enter Earth's atmosphere from outer space, but no one knows exactly where these come from. Around the house dust looks gray and dingy, but in the skies dust glimmers with some of the most beautiful colors ever seen.

*R*epetition

Sometimes without thinking you may unnecessarily repeat an idea. Check your sentences to be sure you have not included needless words.

REPETITION	I resolved to **try again** and **not give up.**
CONCISE	I resolved to **try again.**
REPETITION	Sam's face looked **pale** and **colorless.**
CONCISE	Sam's face looked **pale.**
REPETITION	The **hungry** guests were **eager to eat.**
CONCISE	The guests were **eager to eat.**

EXERCISE 16   *Eliminating Repetition*

Number your paper 1 to 10. Then revise each sentence to omit words that repeat ideas.

1. The weary worker was bone-tired.
2. Marilyn is two inches taller than I am in height.
3. The farmer hollered loudly to warn his neighbors of the fire.
4. My aunt has a spare room in her house that she doesn't use.
5. At the break of day, we set out at sunrise.
6. We could hear the sound of stampeding hoofbeats in the distance.
7. The huge, gargantuan monster in the movie was really a miniature placed in a scaled-down set.
8. What was your question that you wanted me to answer?
9. Some people repeat themselves over and over again when they talk.
10. Lifeguards protecting swimmers must be certified.

Empty Expressions

Empty expressions are another kind of wasted words. These are expressions that slow the reader down and add no meaning to a sentence. Notice how they can be replaced with a single word or eliminated altogether.

EMPTY   **What I mean is,** I learned a difficult lesson.
CONCISE   I learned a difficult lesson.

EMPTY   **There was** a big truck jackknifed on the highway.
CONCISE   A big truck was jackknifed on the highway.

EMPTY   The Girl Scouts met their fund-raising goal **due to the fact that** cookie sales were high.
CONCISE   The Girl Scouts met their fund-raising goal because cookie sales were high.

Avoid the following empty expressions in your writing.

Empty Expressions

I think that	the thing that
on account of	what I mean is
the point is that	there is/there was
the reason is that	as a matter of fact
the reason being	because of the fact that

EXERCISE 17   Eliminating Empty Expressions

Number your paper 1 to 10. Then revise each sentence to omit the empty expression. You may need to change the wording slightly. Use commas where needed.

EXAMPLE   Housing for senior citizens should allow pets because of the fact that pets are good companions.

ANSWER   Housing for senior citizens should allow pets because pets are good companions.

Pets and Health

1. As a matter of fact, stroking an animal can even reduce blood pressure.
2. People who own dogs exercise regularly due to the fact that dogs need to go outside for walks.
3. Because of the fact that pets help sick people recover, pets are sometimes brought to hospitals.
4. The thing of it is that pets can bring severely isolated children out of their shells.
5. It is my belief that dogs are good alarm systems.
6. There is this natural instinct that dogs have to protect their territories.
7. It is this instinct that triggers a dog to bark when a stranger nears the house.
8. The truth is, pets can even save lives.
9. In the Chicago area, there was this young boy who wandered away from his house in winter.
10. Due to the fact that his three puppies traced him, he was kept alive during the night by their warm bodies surrounding him.

Spotlight on Writing

A **Using Specific Words.** Read the following radio advertisement for a new product called Sport Soap. Then number your paper 1 to 20. Write a specific word for each word missing in the advertisement. Choose words that would make your listeners want to buy this product.

Introducing Sport Soap! A new deodorant soap made for __(1)__ Americans. Sport Soap gets you __(2)__ and __(3)__ than regular soap because it's __(4)__ made for __(5)__ people. Sport Soap smells __(6)__ too. It is available in three __(7)__ outdoor scents: __(8)__ Mountains, __(9)__ Woods, and __(10)__ Breeze. Whether you __(11)__ , __(12)__ , or __(13)__ , Sport Soap will __(14)__ away the __(15)__ dirt and __(16)__ . So pick up some Sport Soap __(17)__ and be one of the millions of athletes who feel __(18)__ , look __(19)__ , and smell __(20)__ !

B **Combining Sentences by Coordinating.** Number your paper 1 to 10. Then combine each group of short sentences into one longer one. Use the conjunction *and, but, or,* or *yet* to form a compound subject, a compound verb, or a compound sentence. Use commas where needed.

1. Fran bought the groceries. They were for the picnic. She forgot the hamburger rolls.
2. Gary can mow the lawn on Saturday. Gary can paint the house on Saturday. He can mow the front lawn.
3. We went to the Topsfield Fair. My sister won two prizes. The fair was Friday night.
4. The warm rays of the sun feel good. The radiation can be harmful. The radiation can be harmful to your skin.
5. Bruce wanted to write a report about weight lifting. Chris had already picked that topic. The report was for science.
6. Andrea might become the captain of the basketball team. Ann might become the captain. It is the junior varsity team.

7. Bob fished silently out of the rowboat. The rowboat was old and weather-beaten. Adam fished silently out of the rowboat too.

8. I laughed at Sarah's story. She didn't mean it to be funny. I laughed out loud.

9. The New York Jets play their home games at the Meadowlands in New Jersey. The New York Giants play their home games at the Meadowlands in New Jersey too. Both play football.

10. The basketball player's foot was clearly out of bounds. The referee was inexperienced. The referee did not make the call.

C **Combining Sentences by Subordinating.** Number your paper 1 to 10. Then combine each pair of sentences using the connecting word given in brackets. Use commas where needed.

1. Seat belts may be uncomfortable at first. They do save lives. [although]

2. Bill has learned much about animals. His father is a forest ranger. [whose]

3. The Flyers won the hockey championship. They took a victory lap around the ice. [after]

4. Amy was the last person in line. She still got tickets for the show. [even though]

5. Harold paraded in front of the auditorium. Harold won the best athlete award. [who]

6. The pan balanced on the grill. The pan was filled with corn. [which]

7. The ski conditions on Wildcat Mountain were excellent over the weekend. It had snowed heavily all day on Friday. [because]

8. The mayor spoke at graduation. Her daughter goes to our school. [whose]

9. The library is closed. We'll have to study for the test at home. [since]

10. The students painted the scenery for the play. They are the best artists in the school. [who]

D **Writing Concise Sentences.** Number your paper 1 to 10. Then revise each sentence by correcting the error given in brackets.

1. The movie had a surprise ending that I never expected. [repetition]
2. I have a babysitting job tonight on account of the fact that I want to earn some money. [empty expression]
3. The boulder was huge in size and heavy in weight. [repetition]
4. It is my opinion that our volunteer group should try to raise the money. [empty expression]
5. The point is that commercials are sometimes broadcast louder than the shows. [empty expression]
6. In the first thaw of winter, the world turns to a mushy gray, and everywhere you turn you step in a puddle, and sometimes roads flood and make travel hazardous, but you know, however, that spring is on its way and before long all the water will have seeped into the ground or evaporated. [rambling sentence]
7. While he was away at camp, the homesick child missed his family. [repetition]
8. The reason that I am running is to get ready for the ten-kilometer road race next week. [empty expression]
9. The temperature usually drops after sunset when the sun goes down. [repetition]
10. On our vacation we saw the Grand Canyon, and we were overwhelmed by its size and natural beauty, especially at sunset, and the bright reds and oranges looked painted on the canyon walls, and none of us will ever forget the incredible experience of being in the Grand Canyon. [rambling sentence]

E **Writing from Your Writer's Notebook.** Choose one of the scenes that you wrote about in your writer's notebook. Then describe the scene using specific words and words that appeal to the senses. (*See the model on page 294.*) Exchange papers with a partner. Use the Chapter Summary on page 319 to revise your partner's sentences.

Chapter Summary
Words and Sentences

Word Choice

1. Use specific words to convey your meaning exactly. (*See page 295.*)
2. Choose words whose connotations match your meaning. (*See page 297.*)
3. Use descriptive words that appeal to your reader's senses. (*See page 299.*)

Sentence Combining

4. Combine short sentences into longer, more interesting ones. (*See pages 302–306.*)
5. Use the coordinating conjunctions *and, but, or,* and *yet* to combine ideas of equal importance. (*See page 304.*)
6. Use relative pronouns or subordinating conjunctions to combine ideas of unequal importance. (*See page 306.*)

Sentence Variety

7. Use sentence combining to vary the lengths of your sentences. (*See pages 302–306.*)
8. Vary the beginnings of your sentences. (*See page 309.*)

Concise Sentences

9. Break up long, rambling sentences into shorter ones by removing some of the conjunctions. (*See page 312.*)
10. Avoid unnecessary repetition. (*See page 313.*)
11. Eliminate empty expressions. (*See pages 314–315.*)

Paragraph Structure

A paragraph is a unit of thought. It can be part of a long composition, or it can stand alone as a short composition, complete within itself. However it is used, a paragraph always sticks to one main idea.

20a A **paragraph** is a group of related sentences that present and develop one main idea.

Most paragraphs that stand alone consist of three main types of sentences. These are the topic sentence, the supporting sentences, and the concluding sentence. Each type of sentence performs a special function in a paragraph.

20b

Paragraph Structure	
topic sentence	states the main idea
supporting sentences	expand on the main idea with specific facts, examples, details, or reasons
concluding sentence	provides a strong ending

In the following paragraph, notice how all the other sentences relate directly to the main idea stated in the topic sentence.

The Man Who Rode the Thunder

TOPIC
SENTENCE

SUPPORTING
SENTENCES

CONCLUDING
SENTENCE

Marine pilot William Rankin made history in 1959 when he survived a 9-mile fall from the sky. Over Norfolk, Virginia, Rankin had engine trouble and had to eject himself from his plane. After he had fallen for about 8 minutes, his parachute opened perfectly. To his dismay, however, he found himself in the middle of a thunderstorm. The strong winds kept driving him up instead of down toward earth. For 40 minutes Rankin was tossed by fierce winds and surrounded by blasts of thunder and sheets of lightning. Finally he reached the ground, frostbitten and injured, but alive. Soon after, newspapers all around the world honored "the man who rode the thunder."

Your Writer's Notebook

To help you think of ideas for paragraphs of your own, make an entry in your journal every day. Include one or more of the following ideas.

- unusual or exciting events during the week
- interesting ideas or facts you learned from books, television, magazines, or school that you could explain to others
- opinions you support or reject
- typical scenes of your everyday life that you would like to capture in words and remember in future years

You do not need to write complete sentences. Just write enough so that later you can refer back to your notes for writing ideas.

Topic Sentence

Because the topic sentence states the main idea, it is usually more general than the other sentences in a paragraph. It may be at the beginning, at the end, or in the middle of a paragraph. No matter where it appears, the purpose of the topic sentence is to focus the reader's attention on the main idea.

20c ▶ The **topic sentence** states the main idea of a paragraph.

Although a topic sentence is usually more general than the other sentences, it also serves to limit a paragraph to one specific subject. The following paragraph, for example, begins with a very general sentence about the climate of Antarctica. The second sentence, which is the topic sentence, limits the broad subject to one specific aspect.

The Emperor's Feet

TOPIC SENTENCE

The bitterly cold climate of Antarctica is hostile to many forms of life. Even the emperor penguin, which thrives in the cold, has had to develop unusual behaviors to hatch a chick. If the egg were allowed to touch the frozen ground, the developing chick inside would not survive. To protect the chick, the male penguin carries the egg on his feet, tucking it under the feathers on his body. For two months, while the female penguin is away storing food in her belly, the male goes nowhere without the egg on his feet. Cuddled securely in the male's warmth, the chick can survive until hatching. At that time the mother returns and takes over the care of her newborn chick. Even then the down-covered chick needs its mother's feet and feathers to shield it from the frigid weather of Antarctica.

*E*XERCISE 1   *Identifying Topic Sentences*

Number your paper 1 to 3. Read each paragraph to determine the main idea. Then write each topic sentence.

1. Warming by Rubbing

When our hands get cold, we can warm them up by rubbing them together. The more we rub them, the warmer they
become. Many everyday experiences illustrate that an
increase in temperature can be produced by rubbing. When
an automobile moves, the rubbing of the tires against the
ground makes the tires hot. When you hit a nail with a ham-
mer, the nail becomes hot. If you bend a stiff wire back and
forth many times, it is like rubbing the wire against itself.
The wire then becomes hot at the bend. If you drill a hole
in wood, the drill bit becomes so hot it can give you a bad
burn.   —IRVING ADLER, *HOT AND COLD*

2. Taking the Temperature of the Past

A geologist can look at a rock that was formed hundreds
of millions of years ago and tell what its temperature was
at the time of its formation. This is because the rock itself
has a built-in record of the temperature. Laboratory experiments show that the type of crystals formed in a hardening
magma, or melted rock, is determined by its temperature.
By identifying the type of crystals formed in a rock, therefore, a geologist can tell what the temperature was when
the crystal was formed.   —IRVING ADLER, *HOT AND COLD*

3. Cooling by Radiation

When you leave a hot dish of food to cool off, you use a
particular method of cooling. Every hot body loses energy
by sending out heat rays. It also gains energy by receiving
heat rays from the things surrounding it. Hot bodies, however,
send out more heat rays than cooler bodies. A hot body,
therefore, will lose more energy than it gains and will
gradually cool off until it is the same temperature as the
things around it. The simplest way to cool something that
is hotter than the things around it is to leave it alone.

—IRVING ADLER, *HOT AND COLD*

EXERCISE 2 *Choosing a Topic Sentence*

Read each paragraph. Then write the sentence that would be the best topic sentence.

1. Moving People

A city train system can move 60,000 people an hour on each line. Expressways can manage only about 2,000 cars an hour in each lane. If the average number of passengers in each car is 1½, the total number of people moved is only 3,000 an hour in each lane. Rapid transit systems, then, can move 20 times more people in the same amount of space.

a. More and more people are riding subways.
b. Many cities are encouraging people to join car pools in order to cut down on traffic.
c. Rapid transit systems are more efficient than express-ways in moving great numbers of people.

2. Breaking the Sound Barrier

On October 14, 1947, test pilot Chuck Yeager was ready to fly a new jet to see if it could travel faster than the speed of sound. Until then many people had believed that a plane would be destroyed if it tried to go faster than the speed of sound. Yeager took off confidently. Before long a thunderous blast was heard. The sound barrier had been broken, and Yeager brought the plane down safely.

a. The day the sound barrier was broken was a milestone in aviation history.
b. When a plane accelerates beyond the speed of sound, a loud roar can be heard.
c. High-speed jet transport is taken for granted today.

EXERCISE 3 On Your Own

Write one other possible topic sentence for each paragraph in Exercise 2.

Supporting Sentences

Supporting sentences make up the *body* of a paragraph. Their purpose is to back up the main idea in the topic sentence with specific information.

20d ▶ **Supporting sentences** explain or prove a topic sentence with specific details, facts, examples, or reasons.

Supporting sentences also provide answers to questions that readers might have about the topic sentence. Read the following topic sentence. Think of questions that you would expect the supporting sentences to answer.

People who lived in pioneer days would never have believed that world news could be received as quickly as it is today.

Most readers would probably want to know how news traveled during pioneer days and how news travels today. The supporting sentences answer these questions. They provide facts and examples that relate to the main idea.

Changes in News Communication

TOPIC SENTENCE
People who lived in pioneer days would never have believed that world news could be received as quickly as it is today. In early days newspapers were often several months old by the time they reached a settlement. Letters were

SUPPORTING SENTENCES
carried by travelers who happened to be going in the right direction and often were received months after they were sent, or not at all. Today by radio, television, newspapers, and computers, we get world news almost at once. Airmail letters are carried to distant countries in

CONCLUDING SENTENCE
just a few days. It is hard to believe that such changes have taken place in less than one hundred years. —STUDENT WRITER

326

Unity

A paragraph has *unity* when all of the supporting sentences relate directly to the main idea. Paragraphs without unity include unrelated ideas that distract readers from the main point.

20e Achieve **unity** by making sure all the supporting sentences relate to the topic sentence.

In the following paragraph about the benefits of the Medic Alert bracelet system, two sentences that wander off the point are crossed out. Read the paragraph twice—once with the sentences that stray and once without them. Notice how much easier the paragraph is to follow with those sentences removed.

Medic Alert Saves Lives

The Medic Alert bracelet was designed to help people with medical problems in emergency situations. If the wearer of the bracelet is unconscious or otherwise unable to talk, the bracelet can tell medical workers what they need to know about the patient. On the back of the Medic Alert bracelet are listed the patient's medical problem, an identification number, and an emergency number. ~~The Red Cross offers classes in emergency techniques.~~ By dialing this telephone number, the medical workers can find out about the patient's special condition from a computer. ~~Computers are also used by doctors to help make diagnoses.~~ Knowing the patient's medical background can help the workers decide which treatment to provide and what kind of medication to give. In an emergency a Medic Alert bracelet can become a lifesaver.

Although the two crossed-out sentences are about the general subject of medicine and emergencies, they do not relate specifically to the Medic Alert bracelet system. Only sentences relating directly to the main idea should be included in a paragraph.

E*XERCISE 4* *Identifying Related Supporting Sentences*

Write each topic sentence. After each one write the numbers of the sentences that relate to each main idea.

Topic Sentences

A. When a bear hibernates, its bodily functions slow down and its chemistry changes.
B. Scientists are eager to unlock the mysteries of hibernation and apply them to human situations.

Supporting Sentences

1. A bear can go without food or water for 3 months.
2. During hibernation a bear's heartbeat slows down.
3. Hibernation techniques could be applied to medicine, especially in the preparation of humans for surgery.
4. A hibernating bear's temperature is almost normal.
5. Hibernation research could help people survive in cold climates.
6. A bear's blood chemistry changes radically during hibernation.
7. Bears, in essence, have learned to adapt to starvation.
8. Knowledge of a bear's adaptation techniques could help people endure long journeys in space.
9. A hibernating bear slows down so much that a person can safely enter its den.
10. Research on hibernation may help people survive long periods without food.

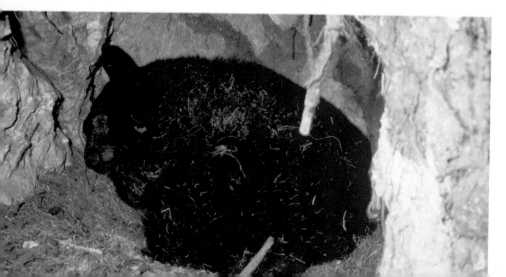

Coherence

Coherence in a paragraph is the quality that makes each sentence seem connected to all the others. One way to achieve coherence is to present ideas in a logical order. Another way is to use transitions. Transitions are words and phrases that show how ideas are related.

20f ▶ Achieve **coherence** by presenting ideas in logical order and using transitional words and phrases.

The following chart shows some common types of logical order and the transitions often used with them.

Chronological Order
This type of order is used with events or stories to tell what happened first, second, third, and so on. It is used when giving directions for telling the steps in a process.

TRANSITIONS	first	before	on Tuesday
	second	after	later
	third	next	finally

Spatial Order
This type of order is used in descriptions to show how objects are related in location.

TRANSITIONS	left	in front of	next to
	right	behind	to the south

Order of Importance, Interest, or Degree
This type of order is often used in paragraphs that explain or persuade. It presents ideas in order of least to most (or most to least) important, interesting, or sizable.

TRANSITIONS	first	the smallest
	finally	the largest
	furthermore	more important
	in addition	most important

EXERCISE 5 *Identifying Types of Logical Order*

Number your paper 1 to 3. Then write the type of logical order used in each paragraph.

1. The Legend of Excalibur

According to legend, King Arthur came by his famous sword Excalibur in a strange and mysterious way. One day, Merlin the magician took Arthur to a magical lake in a forest. There King Arthur saw a woman's arm come out of the water, and in her hand she held the gleaming sword Excalibur. Next, a mysterious Lady of the Lake spoke to Arthur. King Arthur then went directly to Excalibur and grasped the amazing and beautiful sword in his hand. From then on, he had Excalibur to help him achieve his dream of a perfect kingdom.

2. Spotting Fire Engines

Since fire engines must rush to arrive at a fire, all possible warning measures must be used to alert other drivers. One important warning is the siren, probably other drivers' first clue that an emergency vehicle is approaching. Another warning device is the flashing light. Probably the most important factor in spotting a fire engine, however, is its color. Firefighters in Detroit, Newark, and Kansas City have lime-yellow firetrucks. Their accident rate is less than half that of firefighters in Miami, San Francisco, and other cities where red fire engines are used. Although red trucks are the tradition, lime-yellow firetrucks may ultimately prove to be safer.

3. Robin's Nest

The nest of a robin is carefully layered and built to last. On the bottom are twigs and coarse grass held together with mud. The outer sides of the nest are made of twigs and grass mixed with string, paper, and pieces of cloth. The inside of the nest is smooth and hollowed out in the shape of a cup. It is lined with fine grass. The completed nest is so sturdy that it can last for years.

EXERCISE 6 On Your Own

Write each topic sentence. Then write three supporting sentences for each one. Save your work for Exercise 8.

1. Each person in my household has his or her special jobs to do around the house.
2. The common cold has several annoying symptoms.
3. Many forms of exercise are good for the heart and lungs.
4. My favorite holiday is ———. (*Fill in the blank.*)
5. A winter landscape often looks fresh and serene.

Writing Extra

A writer needs strong powers of observation. One way to learn to see beyond the obvious is to write haiku. Haiku are 3-line poems used by Japanese poets to capture the feeling of a moment. Haiku usually have 17 syllables.

Quiet cardinal	(5 syllables)
Is like a bright red ribbon	(7 syllables)
In the snowy tree.	(5 syllables)
—BETTY MAESTRO	(17 syllables)

Write a few haiku of your own. Try to capture the feeling of a moment in words. A leaf falling, the sound of laughter, the smile of a close friend are all good subjects for haiku.

Concluding Sentence

Every good composition has a clear beginning, middle, and ending. In a single paragraph, the concluding sentence serves as the ending. It wraps up the ideas and makes the reader feel that the message is complete.

20g A **concluding sentence** adds a strong ending to a paragraph by summarizing, referring to the main idea, or adding an insight.

Avoid writing a concluding sentence that simply repeats the words and ideas of the topic sentence. Notice the weak concluding sentence in the following paragraph.

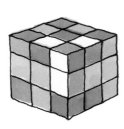

Solving the Rubik's Cube

Students at the University of Illinois have invented the final answer to solving the Rubik's Cube. Their invention is Robbie Rubik, a robot that can solve the cube in two-tenths of a second. Robbie's computer works very fast, but his mechanical hands work much slower. It takes Robbie about 5 to 6 minutes to make the 75 to 160 twists and turns needed to unscramble a cube. So you see that students in Illinois have come up with a good solution.

CONCLUDING
SENTENCE

The other problem to watch for is a concluding sentence that adds new and unrelated information.

Robots are also used on assembly lines.

The use of robots on assembly lines does not relate directly to the main idea of the paragraph. The following concluding sentence would be a good ending for the paragraph about Robbie.

Despite slow hand movements, Robbie can still solve the puzzle faster than any of its human inventors.

EXERCISE 7   Choosing Concluding Sentences

Read each paragraph. Then write the better concluding sentence.

1. Gifts from the Chinese

Many of our everyday items were first invented by the early Chinese. One of their earliest discoveries was the process of making silk. The early Chinese also invented ways to make paper from hemp, old silk, or bark. Gunpowder was another Chinese invention, as was porcelain making. The Chinese are even said to have invented the first kite.

a. Many things in our everyday world come from the Chinese.
b. These few examples show the many gifts the Chinese gave the world.

2. Automatic Trains

In San Francisco, the Bay Area Rapid Transit system (BART) is fully automatic. A computerized control system does almost all the work. It sends the trains out every 90 seconds. It also automatically opens and closes the doors. BART trains require only one human operator on board, mainly to handle any problems that may arise.

a. The automation of BART allows the efficient transportation of thousands of people each day.
b. Some other cities also have automatic trains.

3. A Cat Lover

Mark Twain's mother liked cats. Any cat down on its luck could find a home with her. At one time the family owned 19 cats. She denied that she liked cats better than children. She did, however, admit that cats had one advantage over children. She could always put a cat down when she was tired of holding it.

a. The only animals she feared were snakes and bats.
b. Although cats were sometimes a burden, she never turned a cat away.

EXERCISE 8   On Your Own

Write a concluding sentence for each item in Exercise 6.

Spotlight on Writing

A **Writing a Topic Sentence.** Write a topic sentence for the following paragraph.

Archery Safety

First of all, never point a drawn arrow at anyone. An accidental release could cause serious injury. Second, never shoot until you are sure that all other archers are behind you. Finally, let other archers know when you have gone behind the target to collect your arrows. Leaning your bow against the face of the target will alert other shooters that you are there. Observing these rules will protect you and your fellow archers.

B **Writing Supporting Sentences.** Write each topic sentence. Then write three sentences that could support each one.

1. There are several mountain ranges in France.
2. I met my friend Luisa one day when I was lost.
3. A day in the city can be an exciting experience.
4. Our neighborhood should sponsor a community theater.

C **Writing a Concluding Sentence.** Write a concluding sentence for the following paragraph.

Creative Dreaming

Dreams have long been thought to relieve tensions and help us work through emotions. For some people, however, dreams have actually provided creative ideas and solutions to problems. Elias Howe, for example, was having trouble getting his mechanical sewing machine to work. Then one night he dreamed that he was attacked by men carrying sharp spears. The spears had holes near their tips, and that image stuck with Howe when he awoke. When he placed the hole near the tip of his sewing machine needle, the machine began to work.

D **Revising a Paragraph.** The following paragraph has several weaknesses. Read the paragraph carefully and then complete the activities that follow it.

The Wolf Pack

By far the most important animal in a wolf pack is the male pack leader. His job is to maintain order, lead hunting expeditions, and protect the pack's territory. Lower than the male but still important is the female pack leader. In most cases she is mated for life to the male leader. Next in rank are unpaired males and females. When the leaders are gone, their job is to protect the territory and guard the cubs. Dogs, which are descended from wolves, also have an instinct to protect territories. Lowest on the social scale are the cubs themselves. Wolf packs are very interesting.

1. Which would be the better topic sentence for this paragraph?

   a. Wolves live in carefully structured groups called packs.
   b. Many animals live together in groups.

2. Write the sentence in the body that destroys the unity of the paragraph.
3. Which type of logical order does this paragraph use?
4. Which would be the stronger concluding sentence for this paragraph?

   a. Wolves are an endangered species in most areas.
   b. Although quarrels sometimes occur, the pack system does an effective job of maintaining order and allowing the wolves to work together for survival.

5. Write the paragraph on your paper. Begin by writing the topic sentence you chose in number 1. Remember to indent. Then write the body of the paragraph. Leave out the sentence that destroys the unity. Complete the paragraph by replacing the concluding sentence with the one you chose in number 4.

Chapter Summary
Paragraph Structure

1. A paragraph is a group of related sentences that present and develop one main idea. (*See pages 320–321.*)
2. The topic sentence states the main idea of the paragraph. (*See page 322.*)
3. The supporting sentences back up the main idea with specific details and form the body of the paragraph. (*See page 326.*)
4. Achieve unity by making sure all the supporting sentences relate directly to the topic sentence. (*See page 327.*)
5. Achieve coherence by presenting ideas in a logical order and using transitional words and phrases. (*See page 329.*)
6. The concluding sentence adds a strong ending to the paragraph by summarizing, referring to the main idea, or adding an insight. (*See page 332.*)

*S*tandardized *T*est

Directions: Decide which of the rewritten sentences best follows the direction. In the appropriate row on your answer sheet, fill in the circle containing the letter of your answer.

SAMPLE   Giant redwood trees grow in California.
          Begin with a prepositional phrase.

    A In California giant redwood trees grow.
    B Grow in California giant redwood trees.
    C Giant redwood trees in California grow.

ANSWER Ⓐ Ⓑ Ⓒ

1. The car will be ready by five o'clock.
   Begin with a prepositional phrase.

   A Will be ready by five o'clock the car.
   B The car by five o'clock will be ready.
   C By five o'clock the car will be ready.

2. Ronald called the police immediately.
   Begin with an adverb.

   A Immediately Ronald called the police.
   B Ronald immediately called the police.
   C The police called Ronald immediately.

3. A strange sight awaited them at the front door.
   Begin with a prepositional phrase.

   A At the front door, a strange sight awaited them.
   B A strange sight at the front door awaited them.
   C Them awaited a strange sight at the front door.

4. The hero's horse trudged through the mud wearily.
   Begin with an adverb.

   A Through the mud wearily trudged the hero's horse.
   B Wearily the hero's horse trudged through the mud.
   C Trudged wearily through the mud the hero's horse.

5. Her hands grew extremely cold without mittens.
   Begin with a prepositional phrase.

   A Extremely cold grew her hands without mittens.
   B Without mittens her hands grew extremely cold.
   C Her hands without mittens grew extremely cold.

Directions: Decide which sentence best combines the underlined sentences. In the appropriate row on your answer sheet, fill in the circle containing the letter of your answer.

SAMPLE <u>Roger drove the car.</u> <u>It was his father's.</u> <u>He drove it home.</u>

   A Roger drove the car, and it was his father's, and he drove it home.

   B Roger drove his father's car home.

   C Roger drove the car home, and it was his father's.

ANSWER Ⓐ Ⓑ Ⓒ

6. <u>Al spotted the dog.</u> <u>It was near the library.</u> <u>It was lost.</u>

   A Al spotted the dog, and it was near the library and lost.

   B Al spotted the lost dog, but it was near the library.

   C Al spotted the lost dog near the library.

7. <u>The judge thanked the jury members.</u> <u>She dismissed them.</u>

   A The judge thanked the jury members and them.

   B The judge thanked the jury members and dismissed them.

   C The judge and jury members thanked and dismissed them.

8. <u>It had taken months.</u> <u>Detective Sacks solved the case.</u>

   A It had taken months, but Detective Sacks solved the case.

   B It had taken months but solved the case.

   C Detective Sacks solved the case and had taken months.

9. <u>The fog lifted.</u> <u>The airport reopened.</u>

   A When the fog lifted, the airport reopened.

   B The fog lifted and reopened.

   C The fog lifted, but the airport reopened.

10. <u>He was surprised by the result.</u> <u>He repeated the experiment.</u>

   A He was surprised by the repeated result of the experiment.

   B He was surprised by the result, repeated the experiment.

   C Since he was surprised by the result, he repeated the experiment.

Composition
Part Two

The Writing Process

Picture the scene of a writer at work. What do you imagine? You probably see the writer jotting things down, stopping and concentrating, crumpling up paper and tossing it into the wastebasket, and sighing a deep sigh. Then you may see a look of relief come over the writer's face as confusion gives way to clear ideas. As the writer continues, he or she may stop again and read what has been written, then cross out words and replace them with others. Thinking, jotting, crumpling, and rereading are all part of the process of writing.

Most of the activities that go on during the writing process can be grouped into four main stages. This chapter will give you practice in all stages of the writing process.

Your Writer's Notebook

Think of a composition that you have written recently, perhaps during the past year. Choose one you particularly enjoyed writing. Write about that composition in your journal. Describe the process you followed when you wrote it. How did you think of the idea? How did you organize your thoughts? How did you choose the words? Be as thorough as possible in describing the process.

Prewriting

During the first stage of the writing process, you think of ideas to write about. You also think about your *purpose* in writing and your *audience*—the people who will read your work. Keeping these in mind, you develop a plan for your composition. All of these activities are part of the prewriting stage.

21a **Prewriting** is the first stage of the writing process. It includes all the planning steps that come before writing the first draft.

Taking Stock of Your Interests

In one way or another, nearly everything you write about will have something to do with you. You may write about your experiences, your interests, your fears, or your imaginings. Your unique personality and viewpoints will shine through everything you write.

EXERCISE 1 Taking an Interest Inventory

Make an inventory of subjects of special interest to you by completing each sentence. Write as many items as you can think of for each one. Keep the completed inventory in your writing folder for future use.

1. My personal heroes are _____.
2. The subjects I like best in school are _____.
3. My friends and I are all interested in _____.
4. I could teach someone how to _____.
5. I disagree with my friends about _____.
6. My least favorite things are _____.
7. My favorite places are _____.
8. I often dream of _____.
9. I would like to know more about _____.
10. I wish _____.

Freewriting

Freewriting is another way to think of subjects. *Free-writing* is nonstop writing that only you will see. Keep your pen or pencil moving at all times, writing whatever comes to mind. If you run out of ideas, write *I will have another idea soon* until you do have another idea. You will be surprised where freewriting can lead you.

EXERCISE 2 *Freewriting a Self-Portrait*

Look at the self-portrait of James Thurber, a comic writer. For humor Thurber chose to show himself as a dog. Choose an animal to represent you. Then draw your own self-portrait and write freely about it for five minutes.

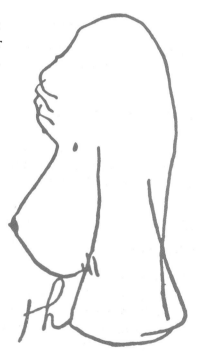

Brainstorming

Once you have thought of a subject, brainstorming can help you explore your ideas about it. *Brainstorming* means writing down everything that comes to mind when you think about your subject. Jot down your ideas as quickly as they occur to you. One idea will lead to another and then on to the next.

342

EXERCISE 3 Brainstorming

Write down everything that comes to mind when you look at the picture above.

Organizing Your Ideas

Once you have listed ideas about your subject, the next step is to organize them in a logical way. Ask yourself *What do my readers need to know first? Next? Last?*

EXERCISE 4 Choosing a Logical Order

Briefly answer each of the following questions.

1. If you were writing about the four seasons, in what order would you present them? Why?
2. If you were writing about your three favorite movies, in what order would you present them? Why?
3. If you were writing about the ages of your brothers and sisters, in what order would you present them?

EXERCISE 5 On Your Own

Brainstorm a list of interesting places you have seen. Write brief notes telling what was especially memorable. Then rank your three favorite places in the order of good, better, best. Save your work for Exercise 7.

Writing the First Draft

By the time you are ready to write your first draft, most of the hard work is over. You have already thought of a subject and have developed a plan for writing.

21b Writing the first draft is the second stage of the writing process. Use your prewriting notes to write complete, flowing sentences that would make sense to a reader.

EXERCISE 6 Writing a First Draft from Notes

Use the prewriting notes below to write the first draft of a paragraph. The first and last sentences are given.

First Sentence: One cold night last November my family decided to go to the university observatory to look through the telescope.

NOTES
- on the way, heard radio announcement that temperature was 17 degrees
- arrived and saw line of people waiting outside
- winding stairway to viewing area jammed with people waiting their turn; no heat
- so cold I wanted to forget the whole thing
- telescope fixed on Saturn; people ahead of me gasped when they saw it
- my turn finally came; could understand their excitement—Saturn a beautiful sight
- rings of Saturn looked near enough to touch
- made me wonder about all mysteries in sky

Last sentence: The wonder and beauty of Saturn on that cold night warmed me inside and out.

EXERCISE 7 On Your Own

Using your work from Exercise 5, write the first draft of your paragraph. Save your work for Exercise 9.

344

*R*evising

When asked if he ever rewrote his stories, the famous writer Frank O'Connor replied, "Endlessly, endlessly, endlessly." In some ways writing is never completely finished. It can always be improved just a little bit more.

21c **Revising** is the third stage of the writing process. Revise your draft as often as needed until you are satisfied that it is the best you can make it.

Before you revise your work, set it aside. When you come back to it, you will be able to see it with a fresh eye. You might also share your writing with a reader. A reader can often spot a weakness that you may have missed. When revising, consider the following questions.

Revision Checklist

1. Does your paper state your main idea?
2. Do any of your sentences wander off the subject?
3. Are your ideas presented in a logical order?
4. Does your composition have a strong ending?
5. Is the purpose of your composition clear?
6. Is your composition suited for your audience?
7. Are your sentences smoothly connected?
8. Did you vary your sentences and use specific words?

---

*E*XERCISE 8   *Studying a Revision*

Study the revised paragraph on page 346. Then write answers to the following questions.

1. Which sentence states the main idea?
2. Which sentence was out of order?
3. Which two sentences now start in a different way?
4. Which sentence strayed from the main idea?
5. What phrase was added to make the time order clear?

The Staff of Life

The first soft, tasty bread was made in ancient Egypt by mistake. A lazy baker in the royal palace prepared some dough one night and fell asleep. The mixture fermented, during the night, rose to the top of the bowl, and overflowed onto the table. *The next morning* The surprised baker decided to cook the spongy mass, and it turned out to be very tasty and soft. The traditional bread of ancient Egypt was hard and coarse. ~~You can easily make fresh bread at home using yeast to make it rise~~. The lucky baker received praise for his mistake, and the world received the gift of fluffy bread.

EXERCISE 9 On Your Own

Exchange papers from Exercise 7 with a classmate and comment on both the strong and the weak points in your partner's work. Then use your partner's comments and the Revision Checklist on page 345 to revise your paragraph. Save your work for Exercise 11.

Writing Extra

_____ Mark Twain once wrote, "The difference between the right word and the almost right word is the difference between lightning and the lightning bug." As you revise your work, choose words that convey exactly what you mean. Practice by completing each sentence below.

1. The _____ lights drew my admiring gaze.
2. Although the announcement _____ us, we tried not to let it show.
3. The wind _____ around the corner.
4. Feeling discouraged, Diane _____ in the armchair.
5. Overjoyed by the news, I _____ down the steps and _____ home.

Editing

Writers cannot do everything at once. At each stage of the writing process, they concentrate on something different. Through prewriting, writing, and revising, most writers do not worry about such errors as misspelled words or faulty grammar. During the editing stage, however, writers concentrate on eliminating these errors in preparation for the final copy.

21d ▶ **Editing** is the final stage of the writing process. Polish your work by correcting errors and making a neat copy.

*E*XERCISE 10 *Making a Final Copy*

Write the paragraph below, correcting errors in usage, capitalization, punctuation, and spelling. When you have finished, read your work to be sure it is free of errors.

Suprising Me

In some ways I suprise myself. Like, I enjoy having people around me but every once in a while I want to go off by myself and sometimes in the mist of a very sad moment I will think of something funny and luagh out loud. I like sports and big-mussle activety, I also like checkers and chess. I try to act self-confidenced and relaxed. When most of the time inside I am really nervous, especially in large groups. No matter how hard I try to define myself, I allways find some suprising thing that does not fit my definition.

*E*XERCISE 11 *On Your Own*

Edit your work from Exercise 9. Look carefully for errors in usage, capitalization, punctuation, and spelling. Then exchange papers with a classmate. Try to find any errors your partner may have missed.

Spotlight on Writing

A   **Prewriting: Taking Stock of Your Interests.** Write a short book about yourself.

1. On the cover draw a silhouette of your face. Think of a title for your book and write it on the cover.
2. On page 1 write ten sentences that tell how you are different from everyone else.
3. On page 2 write a paragraph about how you first became interested in some of your favorite activities. Draw a picture to go along with page 2.
4. On page 3 make a collage of your interests and personality traits. Write the words to reflect their meaning, as shown below.
5. On page 4 write about your dreams for the future. Find or draw a picture to go with your writing.

B **Prewriting: Brainstorming.** Brainstorm a list of details you could use to describe the painting shown above.

C **Prewriting: Organizing Your Ideas.** Organize your brainstorming notes about the painting in a logical way. For example, you may want to list them in one of the following ways.

    top to bottom (or the reverse)
    side to side
    the center outward (or the reverse)
    most to least important (or the reverse)
    most to least interesting (or the reverse)

349

D **Writing a First Draft.** Use your prewriting notes about the painting to write the first draft of a description. Keep the following purpose and audience in mind.

PURPOSE   To describe the painting *Backyards*
AUDIENCE   People who are thinking of going to see the painting at the art museum

E **Revising by Sharing Your Work.** Exchange descriptions of the painting with a classmate. As you read your partner's work, pretend you are a person thinking of going to the art museum. Use the following questions as a guide.

- Can you picture the painting as it is described?
- Is it described in terms you can understand?
- Does the description make you want to go to the art museum to see the painting itself?

Tell your partner what is good about the writing as well as what could be improved.

F **Revising Based on a Reader's Reaction.** If your partner has suggested changes that would improve your description, revise your work to reflect them.

G **Using a Revision Checklist.** Use the Revision Checklist on page 345 to revise your description.

H **Editing Your Work.** Check your description for errors in usage, capitalization, punctuation, and spelling.

I **Peer Editing.** Exchange descriptions with a classmate. See if you can find any errors your partner may have missed.

J **Making a Final Copy.** Copy your description neatly. Be sure to indent your paragraph and make the margins even.

Steps for Writing
The Writing Process

Prewriting
1. Think of ideas to write about by
   - taking stock of your interests. (*See page 341*.)
   - freewriting. (*See page 342*.)
2. Brainstorm for details that you can use to develop your subject. (*See page 342*.)
3. Organize your ideas in a logical order. (*See page 343*.)

Writing
4. Use your prewriting notes to write a first draft. Use complete, flowing sentences that would make sense to your readers. (*See page 344*.)

Revising
5. Look at your first draft with a fresh eye. Also share your writing with a partner.
6. Use your reader's comments and the Revision Checklist on page 345 to improve your first draft.
7. Revise your draft as often as needed to make your subject clear to your readers.

Editing
8. Polish your work by correcting any errors in usage, capitalization, punctuation, and spelling.
9. Make a neat final copy.

Expository Paragraphs

One of the most common purposes for writing is to explain something. In school you may have written a paragraph explaining an event in history or explaining how to do a science experiment. Whenever your purpose is to explain, you will be writing expository paragraphs.

22a   The purpose of an **expository paragraph** is to explain with facts and examples or to give directions.

The purpose of the following expository paragraph is to explain how a computer can "smell."

An Electronic Nose

TOPIC SENTENCE

Computers can be programmed to do many things, even tell the difference between roses and lilacs. Computers, of course, need a special kind of "nose" to do this. This electronic nose

SUPPORTING SENTENCES

samples the air and sends signals to a memory chip in the computer. The signals are compared to information stored in the memory chip. If the signals match the information for rose,

CONCLUDING SENTENCE

the computer identifies the smell. Because of clever programming, the computer nose knows!

—SEYMOUR SIMON, *COMPUTER SENSE, COMPUTER NONSENSE* (ADAPTED)

In the following expository paragraph, the writer's purpose is to give directions.

How to Take Action Photos

TOPIC
SENTENCE

Capturing an exciting moment on film requires planning and coordination. First, make sure that the lighting for your picture is suitable. Whenever possible, try to stand with your back toward the source of light. Next, try to anticipate the exact location of the action so that you can arrange an attractive frame for

SUPPORTING
SENTENCES

your picture. Finally, when the moment of action arrives, be ready to press the shutter button with your finger. Although you might be caught up in the excitement, press the button calmly and firmly. Hitting the button too hard can cause the camera to move, and the

CONCLUDING
SENTENCE

picture may come out blurred. Taking good action photos requires practice, but even beginners can capture a picture worth a thousand words if proper care is taken.

Learning how to write clear expository paragraphs can help you with present and future assignments. This chapter will take you step by step through the process of writing an expository paragraph.

Your Writer's Notebook

One way to write explanations is to show causes and effects. Try the following activity in your journal. Make a list of five of your personality traits. These traits might include generosity, stubbornness, and friendliness. Every day for the next week, pick one of your personality traits and try to explain to yourself how and why you developed that trait. In other words, try to explain the cause of each one. To help you, think back to situations and events from your childhood.

Prewriting

When you go on a trip, you do not simply walk out the door and take off. Instead, you plan the trip in advance. In the same way, when you write, you do not simply sit down and write a composition. You must first plan what you want to say. The planning stage of the writing process is called the *prewriting* stage.

Choosing a Subject

The first step in the prewriting stage is to choose a subject. Begin by making a list of ideas to write about. Then use the following guidelines to choose the best one.

22b

Choosing an Expository Subject

1. Choose a subject that interests you.
2. Choose a subject that will interest your audience.
3. Choose a subject you know enough about to explain accurately.

EXERCISE 1 Thinking of Subjects for Expository Paragraphs

Under each category write three items that are of special interest to you. Save your paper for Exercise 2.

1. sports	3. skills	5. music	7. careers
2. hobbies	4. courses	6. games	8. people

EXERCISE 2 Choosing a Subject

Using your ideas from Exercise 1, write five possible subjects for an expository paragraph. Under each one, list what you know about it. Then circle the subject that comes closest to following all three guidelines for choosing a subject.

Limiting a Subject

Some subjects are too broad for one paragraph. The subject baseball, for example, could fill an entire book. Within this general subject, however, are several smaller subjects. These include how to throw a curve ball, the meaning of the term *double play*, and the differences between the American League and the National League.

22c Limit your subject so that it can be adequately covered in one paragraph.

GENERAL SUBJECT	MORE LIMITED	LIMITED SUBJECT
nature	waterfalls	Niagara Falls
hobbies	crafts	working with clay
courses	science	using a microscope

The final step in limiting a subject is to focus your thoughts by expressing the main idea in a phrase.

LIMITED SUBJECT Niagara Falls
QUESTION What about Niagara Falls?
FOCUS where the boat *The Maid of the Mist* takes passengers at Niagara Falls

EXERCISE 3 Limiting Subjects

For each general subject, write two limited subjects. Save your paper for Exercise 4.

1. pets
2. school
3. trains
4. cars
5. movies
6. the police
7. inventions
8. George Washington
9. winter
10. dinosaurs

EXERCISE 4 Focusing Limited Subjects

Write five of your limited subjects from Exercise 3. Then write a phrase that focuses your thoughts for each one.

*L*isting Details

Once you have focused your limited subject, you can begin to list details that will help you explain it to your readers. The kinds of details you use will depend on your main idea and your purpose for writing. If your purpose is to explain, you will probably use facts and examples. If your purpose is to give directions, your details will be the steps in a process.

The following main idea is one that calls for facts and examples. The writer's purpose is to explain.

LIMITED SUBJECT	tarpits at Rancho la Brea
FOCUS	prehistoric animals trapped in pits
FACT	• rainwater gathered on surface of tar pools and gave appearance of lake
FACT	• thirsty animals came to drink and became caught in tar
FACT	• their dead bodies attracted scavenging animals who also became trapped
FACT	• tar helped preserve bones of prehistoric animals
EXAMPLES	• animals trapped include mammoths, saber-toothed tigers, and mastodons

Brainstorming. One way to create a list of details for an expository paragraph is to brainstorm.

22d **Brainstorming** means writing down everything that comes to mind when you think of your limited subject.

To guide you when you brainstorm, first make a list of questions that your readers might have about your subject. Then jot down any details that will help you answer those questions for your readers. Your final list should include three to five details.

EXERCISE 5 *Listing Details for an Expository Paragraph*

Write each focused subject. Then under each one, write a list of details that would help you explain it. Use the questions below to help you brainstorm.

1. **FOCUSED SUBJECT**   the meaning of friendship
   - What is a friend?
   - How is a friend like a family member?
   - How is a friend unlike a family member?
   - What do friends do?
   - What do friends not do?

2. **FOCUSED SUBJECT**   how to play   *(your favorite game)* .
   - What is the object of the game?
   - How do you achieve that object?
   - What special skills are involved in playing?

3. **FOCUSED SUBJECT**   ways teenagers can earn money
   - What jobs have you done to earn money?
   - What jobs have your friends done to earn money?
   - What laws affect the employment of teens under 16?

4. **FOCUSED SUBJECT**   the symbols of your school
   - What are your school colors? Why were they chosen?
   - What is your school song?
   - What are the names of your school sports teams? Why were those names chosen?

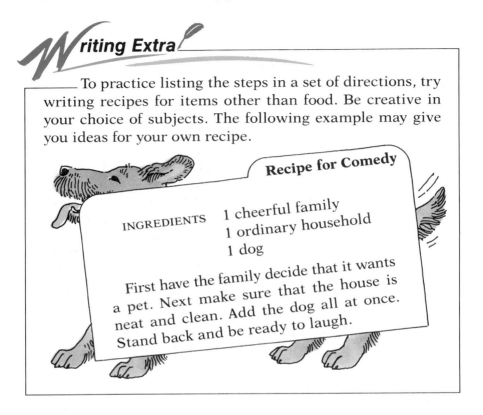

*W*riting Extra

To practice listing the steps in a set of directions, try writing recipes for items other than food. Be creative in your choice of subjects. The following example may give you ideas for your own recipe.

Recipe for Comedy

INGREDIENTS   1 cheerful family
1 ordinary household
1 dog

First have the family decide that it wants a pet. Next make sure that the house is neat and clean. Add the dog all at once. Stand back and be ready to laugh.

*A*rranging Details in Logical Order

The final step in the prewriting stage is arranging your list of supporting details in a logical order. A logical order will help your readers follow your thoughts. The guidelines below will help you organize your brainstorming notes.

22e

Organizing Details

1. Group related items together.
2. If your purpose is to explain, arrange your details in the order of importance, interest, size, or degree.
3. If your purpose is to give directions or to explain a process, arrange your details in the proper sequence.

If your paragraph calls for order of importance, interest, size, or degree, you may list your details in the order of *least to most* or *most to least*. In the following paragraph, the details are arranged in order of least to most.

Hungry Mammals

TOPIC
SENTENCE

Different animals have different food requirements depending on their body weight, activity, and chemistry. The relatively small chimpanzee, for example, eats an average of 4.5 pounds of food each day. The lion needs about 15 pounds of food, while the African elephant requires about 350 pounds. The record-holder for amount of food eaten daily is the blue whale. It eats about 1 ton of food each day.

DETAILS IN
ORDER OF
LEAST TO MOST

CONCLUDING
SENTENCE

Despite this enormous amount, the whale actually consumes a smaller percentage of its body weight than does the chimpanzee.

If you are giving directions or explaining a process, your details should be arranged in the proper sequence. This type of order, called sequential order, is similar to chronological order (*see page 329*). The following paragraph about mountain climbing uses sequential order.

Using Your Feet

TOPIC
SENTENCE

The natural tendency of beginning climbers is to look for handholds, but you must begin your climbing education by learning to look down for footholds. In the beginning tell yourself repeatedly, *"Look down; look down!"* Once you have the habit of looking down, you must learn to see footholds. They may be very small or steeply sloping. The next step is to test the foothold by trying to stand on it. While you are learning, expect to slide off holds quite a bit.

DETAILS IN
SEQUENTIAL
ORDER

CONCLUDING
SENTENCE

With more and more experience, you will learn to recognize footholds that you can stand on safely. —MICHAEL LOUGHMAN, *LEARNING TO ROCK CLIMB* (ADAPTED)

EXERCISE 6   Arranging Details in Logical Order

Write each focused subject. Then list the details in a logical order. Under each list write the method you used to organize the details. Indicate your answer by writing *least to most*, *most to least*, or *sequential*.

1. **FOCUSED SUBJECT**   how a dolphin is trained

   DETAILS
   - dolphin soon begins to connect fish reward with behavior it just performed
   - trainer waits for dolphin to do desired behavior, such as jumping into air
   - later fish reward is postponed until after a whistle signal is given
   - trainer sees desired behavior and immediately rewards dolphin with fish
   - knowing that fish reward will follow, dolphin eventually performs whenever it hears a whistle signal

2. **FOCUSED SUBJECT**   astronomical distances

    DETAILS
- Earth to nearest planet (Venus): 25 million miles
- sun to limits of Milky Way galaxy: 30,000 light years
- Earth to moon: 240,000 miles
- Earth to nearest star other than sun: 4.3 light years
- Earth to sun: 93 million miles

    (*Note: 1 light year equals 5.9 trillion miles.*)

3. **FOCUSED SUBJECT**   why many skating teams are made up of a brother and a sister

    DETAILS
- appearance when skating together is good because body types tend to be similar
- most important is ability to predict each other's movements
- more important, similar body types have similar striding motions on ice so that unison work matches

4. **FOCUSED SUBJECT**   how loran (*long-range navigation*) works at sea

    DETAILS
- time a radio message takes to travel to each station is then measured
- first a ship wishing to determine its exact location forms one point of triangle
- two radio stations form other two points
- finally the distance of the ship to each station can be determined

EXERCISE 7 *On Your Own*

Write a plan for an expository paragraph using what you have learned about prewriting on pages 354–359. Follow the steps below. Save your paper for Exercise 11.

1. Choose and limit a subject.
2. Write a phrase that indicates the focus.
3. List details that explain your focused subject.
4. Arrange the details in a logical order.

Writing

The next stage of the writing process is *writing the first draft*. Although a draft is unpolished, it should be a complete paragraph. Your first draft should contain a topic sentence, a body of supporting sentences, and a concluding sentence.

Writing a Topic Sentence

During the prewriting stage, you expressed your main idea in a phrase. Now your task is to express that idea in a complete sentence. Your final topic sentence should be broad enough to cover all of the supporting details that you plan to include in your paragraph. To make sure your topic sentence is appropriate, refer often to your prewriting notes.

If you had decided to write a paragraph about students in Japan, your prewriting notes might look like the following.

FOCUSED SUBJECT   student attitudes in Japanese classrooms
DETAILS   • students are taught to respect those with knowledge and to treat them as teachers
  • students are taught to listen carefully and to be humble when learning something
  • students are eager to ask questions to increase their knowledge
  • students believe that studying in a group can increase their knowledge

After reading over the notes, you might write the following topic sentence.

Students in Japan are humble about learning.

This sentence, however, is not broad enough to cover all the supporting details. It does not, for example, suggest anything about students working in groups. A revised, broader statement makes a better topic sentence.

Students in Japan are encouraged to respect those with knowledge and to take advantage of all opportunities to learn.

To help you think of a suitable topic sentence, complete the following steps.

Steps for Writing a Topic Sentence

1. Look over your prewriting notes.
2. Express your main idea in one sentence.
3. Rewrite the topic sentence until it covers all the supporting details you listed in your notes.

*E*XERCISE 8 *Writing a Topic Sentence*

Read each set of prewriting notes for an expository paragraph. Then write a topic sentence for each one.

1. **FOCUSED SUBJECT** the benefits of dancing
   DETAILS
   - is good exercise
   - allows you to let off steam
   - helps you fit into crowd
   - helps build confidence and coordination

2. **FOCUSED SUBJECT** types of computers
   DETAILS
   - small, portable personal computers
   - mid-sized home computers
   - large business computers
   - gigantic mainframe computers

3. **FOCUSED SUBJECT** how chess pieces can move
   DETAILS
   - on first move, pawns move two spaces forward; later one space forward or backward
   - castles can move forward and backward and side to side as far as they can
   - bishops move on a diagonal
   - knights move in an L shape
   - king can move one space in any direction
   - queen can move as many spaces as possible in any direction

4. **FOCUSED SUBJECT** safety rules for dogs
   DETAILS
   - dogs should not be left alone in yard
   - dogs should not be allowed to wander around neighborhood
   - when walking dog, owner should use leash
   - dogs should not be left in closed cars

5. **FOCUSED SUBJECT** round-trip distances covered by some migrating animals
   DETAILS
   - red bat: 2,800 miles
   - Alaskan fur seal: 6,000 miles
   - bobolink: 14,000 miles
   - white stork: 16,000 miles
   - Arctic tern: 24,000 miles

*W*riting the Body

The body of an expository paragraph is made up of smoothly connected supporting sentences. Once again, use your prewriting notes to help you with the first draft. With your organized list before you, complete the following steps for writing the body of an expository paragraph.

22g

Steps for Writing the Body

1. Write a complete sentence for each item on your list.
2. Combine sentences if necessary for variety.
3. When needed, add transitional words and phrases to help one sentence lead smoothly into the next. (*See page 370.*)

The following draft of an expository paragraph is about students in Japan. Compare the supporting sentences in the body with the prewriting notes on page 362. Notice the transitions printed in heavy type.

Student Attitudes in Japan

TOPIC
SENTENCE

Students in Japan are encouraged to respect those with knowledge and to take advantage of all opportunities to learn. **By far the most** important attitude Japanese students bring to their learning is a respect for anyone with knowledge. That person is always regarded as the teacher. **Related to** this respect is the students' humble attitude toward learning. This attitude leads them to listen carefully in class and to ask questions eagerly to increase their knowledge. **Finally,** Japanese students are taught to respect what they can learn from classmates when working together in groups.

SUPPORTING
SENTENCES

CONCLUDING
SENTENCE

These attitudes partly explain the high quality of education in Japan.

EXERCISE 9 *Writing the Body of an Expository Paragraph*

Write the body of an expository paragraph using the following notes. Include the topic sentence and the concluding sentence.

TOPIC SENTENCE	Benjamin Franklin was a man of many interests, talents, and contributions.
NOTES	• published newspaper, *Pennsylvania Gazette*, for 47 years • wrote *Poor Richard's Almanac*, popular for its common-sense philosophy and wit • believer in education; established University of Pennsylvania • served as Postmaster General of Colonies for 20 years • proved lightning is electricity by experimenting with kite in thunderstorm • invented bifocal eyeglasses • helped draft Declaration of Independence • was strong supporter of Constitution
CONCLUDING SENTENCE	Benjamin Franklin, journalist, educator, scientist, inventor, and statesman, has left his mark on the history of this country.

Writing a Concluding Sentence

The concluding sentence brings your paragraph to a strong ending. To write a concluding sentence, first read over what you have written. Then write a sentence that serves one or more of the following purposes.

Writing a Concluding Sentence

A concluding sentence may
- restate the main idea in a different way.
- summarize the paragraph, picking up key ideas or terms.
- evaluate the details.
- add an insight that shows new understanding of the main idea.

EXERCISE 10 Writing Concluding Sentences

Write two possible concluding sentences for the following expository paragraph.

Surviving in Thin Air

Most people know that astronauts and deep-sea divers need extra supplies of oxygen to survive. Even on land, however, people in certain situations need special masks and oxygen reserves to breathe normally. Mountain climbers, for example, need additional oxygen when they reach high altitudes where the air is thin. Fire fighters often need extra oxygen because flames burn up the oxygen supply in the air around them. People working with hazardous materials must also use oxygen masks to make sure they breathe pure air.

EXERCISE 11 On Your Own

Review your notes from Exercise 7. Then use your notes to write the first draft of an expository paragraph. Save your draft for Exercise 14.

Revising

If you are like most writers, your first draft will not be the best you can do. In the third stage of the writing process, called *revising*, you have a chance to improve your first draft. When revising, look at your draft as if you were the reader instead of the writer.

Checking for Unity

One way to improve your draft is to check it carefully for unity. A paragraph has unity when all of the supporting sentences in the body relate directly to the main idea stated in the topic sentence. (*See pages 362–363.*) Sentences that stray from the main idea cause readers to become confused and distracted.

In the following paragraph, the sentences that weaken the unity are crossed out. Notice that the revised paragraph is easier to understand.

Sealing a Deal

Centuries-old traditions about horses are still alive in Ireland today. As in old times, horses are still bought and sold at local fairs. The seller of a horse meets a potential buyer through a middleman. ~~One of the greatest Irish horses was a show-jumper named Boomerang.~~ The middleman helps the buyer and seller reach a fair price. In the tradition of his forebears, the middleman slaps the buyer's and seller's hands together to encourage them to make a deal. ~~Horses in western Ireland are rugged and strong.~~ When the deal is finally agreed upon, the middleman picks up a handful of Irish soil and places it on the horse's back. The horse, in true Irish tradition, then becomes an important part of its new owner's life.

22i Check your paragraph for **unity** by eliminating any sentences that stray from the main idea.

EXERCISE 12   *Checking for Unity*

Three sentences in the following expository paragraph wander off the subject. Write the sentences that break the unity of the paragraph.

Einstein's Twins

Albert Einstein developed a famous "thought experiment" to illustrate his belief that time slows down for a body traveling near the speed of light. He imagined a situation in which a twin agrees to take a space voyage in a vehicle that can travel almost as fast as the speed of light. The other twin remains on the earth. Einstein's famous equation is $E = mc^2$. The twin in space will experience a slowed-down version of time, although he will not notice anything unusual. His heartbeat will slow down. If there is a clock aboard, it will run more slowly than the clocks on Earth. Einstein first became interested in physics at a young age. When the space traveler finally returns, he will be younger than his twin on Earth. This is because his body aging time has also been slowed down. Another famous "thought experiment" involves elevators. Einstein illustrated these fascinating beliefs with a "thought experiment" because no ship of his day could travel fast enough to demonstrate this puzzling feature of time.

Checking for Coherence

Another way to improve a first draft is to make sure that it is coherent. In a paragraph with coherence, the ideas are presented in logical order with clear transitions. (*See pages 329 and 365.*)

22j Revise your paragraph for **coherence** by checking the logical order of ideas and adding transitions where needed.

The following chart shows some transitions commonly used in expository paragraphs.

22k

Common Transitions			
Order of Importance, Interest, Size, or Degree		Sequential Order	
first	also	first	next
more important	the smallest	second	after that
most important	next in size	third	last
finally	the largest	finally	as soon as

EXERCISE 13 Recognizing Transitions

List the transitions used in the following paragraph. Then tell what type of order is used to achieve coherence.

Colonists in the New World

Colonists came to the New World from Europe for a variety of reasons. First, economic conditions in parts of Europe left many people facing poverty and hunger. Second, wars and other political conflicts disrupted life in Europe. Most important, people came to the New World to escape religious prejudice and have a chance to worship as they pleased. Underlying all of these reasons was one important dream: to build a better life for themselves and their families.

Using a Revision Checklist

As a final step in revising your paragraph, rework your writing until you can answer yes to all of the following questions.

Checklist for Revising Expository Paragraphs

Checking Your Paragraph

1. Does your topic sentence state your main idea and cover all your supporting details? (*See pages 362–363.*)
2. Does your paragraph have unity? (*See page 368.*)
3. Did you use a logical order and transitions to give your paragraph coherence? (*See page 370.*)
4. Does your concluding sentence provide a strong ending? (*See page 367.*)

Checking Your Sentences

5. Did you combine related sentences to avoid too many short, choppy sentences in a row? (*See pages 302–306.*)
6. Did you vary the length and beginnings of your sentences? (*See page 309.*)
7. Did you avoid rambling sentences? (*See page 312.*)
8. Did you avoid unnecessary repetition and empty expressions? (*See pages 313–315.*)

Checking Your Words

9. Did you use clear, specific words? (*See page 295.*)

EXERCISE 14 On Your Own

Using the checklist above, revise the paragraph you wrote in Exercise 11. Ask a classmate to read your paragraph to be sure you have expressed your ideas clearly and logically. Save your paper for Exercise 17.

*E*diting

When you are satisfied with the content of your paragraph, you can move on to polishing its form. This stage of the writing process is called *editing*. The following checklist will help you check your paper for mistakes.

22m

Editing Checklist

1. Are your sentences free of errors in grammar and usage?
2. Did you spell each word correctly?
3. Did you use capital letters where needed?
4. Did you punctuate each sentence correctly?
5. Did you indent your paragraph?
6. Did you recopy your paragraph as needed?
7. Is your handwriting clear and neat?
8. Are your margins even?

When you edit your work, you may want to use proofreading symbols as a shorthand way of showing corrections. Below are some commonly used proofreading symbols.

22n

Proofreading Symbols

∧	insert	I waited for you.
℘	delete	Tomorrow is my very own birthday.
. . . .	let it stand	I recognized Sue's lilting voice.
#	add space	We made our own icecream.
◡	close up	See you to night!
∿	transpose	The clwon had a red big nose.
≡	capital letter	I was born in chicago.
/	lowercase letter	Chicago is West of Detroit.

EXERCISE 15   Using Proofreading Symbols for Editing

Number your paper 1 to 10. Next to the proper number, write the correction for each error in the paragraph below.

A Memorable Letter

Peter Rabbit is the hero of many (1) childrens books written (2) and illustrated by Beatrix Potter. The character of Peter Rabbit first (3) appearred (4) in the year 1893 in a letter she wrote to a friend's son who was ill. (5) She created a story about four rabbits named Flopsy, (6) Mopsy, Cottontail, and Peter. Ten years later her story was published. Today (7) *The Tale Of Peter Rabbit* is enjoyed by children (8) through out the world. It has been translated into thirteen languages and (9) printed also in (10) braille.

EXERCISE 16   Editing an Expository Paragraph

Write the paragraph below using the Editing Checklist on page 372 to help you correct the errors.

Sea Stunts

Training Dolphins to perform water stunts requires a great amount of pateince and a large supply of fish. first the trainor watches a paticular dolphin and waits untill it jumps into the air. Or do some other stunt? Then the trainer imediately rewards the dolphin with afish. Soon the dolphin begins to relate the fish reward with the stunt it just compleated. Later on the trainer delays the reward untill after he or she has blown a whistel. knowing that a fish reward will follow, the dolphin eventualy performs the stunt whenever it heres a whistle signal.

EXERCISE 17   On Your Own

Use the Editing Checklist on page 372 to edit the paragraph you revised in Exercise 14. Ask a classmate to look it over to see if you missed any errors.

Spotlight on Writing

A **Writing a Paragraph with Facts and Examples.** Use the following notes to write an expository paragraph.

PURPOSE   to explain the three different types of galaxies

AUDIENCE   readers of *Science Highlights*, a magazine for students

Notes
- three types of galaxies: spiral, elliptical, irregular
- spiral is shape of our own Milky Way galaxy
- spiral galaxies have mix of young, middle-aged, and old stars
- elliptical galaxies shaped like flattened pancake, slightly stretched out
- elliptical galaxies contain only old stars
- irregular galaxies have no identifiable shape
- irregular galaxies have many bright young stars and some old stars

374

B **Writing a Paragraph to Give Directions.** Use the notes that follow to write an expository paragraph.

PURPOSE   to give directions for playing the party game Chief

AUDIENCE   a friend

Notes

- choose someone to be "It" and have him or her leave room
- while person is out of room, rest of group picks Chief
- when person returns, Chief leads group in various activities, such as hand clapping or foot tapping
- the person who is "It" must figure out who Chief is
- two ways to identify Chief are: watch players to discover whom they look to for leadership; look for person who begins new activity
- to try to stump person who is "It," advise Chief to keep movements slight and to a minimum, and advise group to avoid looking directly at Chief
- when Chief has been identified, select another person to be "It"

C **Revising an Expository Paragraph.** Use the checklist on page 371 as a guide in revising the following paragraph.

A Blanket of Snow

Snow can actually help plants and animals keep warm in cold weather. The reason is on account of the fact that snow on the ground is warmer than the air above it. You can test this fact with a simple experiment. Take a reading of the temperature near the surface of a pile of snow. Borrow a thermometer from your parents. Take a reading of the temperature all the way near the ground. You will see that it is warmer there than near the surface at the top of the pile. You could also take a temperature reading in the middle of the pile of snow if you want. The temperature there will be cooler than at ground level but warmer than at surface level. So you see, snow can actually help plants and animals keep warm in cold weather.

D **Editing an Expository Paragraph.** Use the checklist on page 372 to edit the following paragraph.

Weaving History

History comes down to us in many forms besides books and old legal records. Shortly after the Normans invaded england in 1066 weavers made a large tapistry illustrating the conquest. The tapistry also shows other events of the time, one of the pictured events are Halleys comet. This woven record tells us that the comet appeared in the same year as the invasion. It also tell us about the fearfull attitudes people had toward comets. The tapistry show people pointing to the comet streaming accross the sky. Although the tapistry was made to honor the victors of the invasion. Today it is an important peice of history.

E **Ideas for Writing Expository Paragraphs.** Write an expository paragraph using one of the following subjects or one of your own. Use the Steps for Writing an Expository Paragraph on page 377 to guide you.

1. the meaning of the scout pledge
2. traditions in your family
3. popular clothing styles
4. how to stay in shape
5. parks in your neighborhood
6. popular dances
7. an unusual occupation
8. benefits of learning a second language
9. how to break a habit
10. how a computer can help with schoolwork

Steps for Writing an Expository Paragraph

Prewriting

1. Determine your purpose and think about who will be reading your work. (*See pages 352–353.*)
2. Make a list of subjects that interest you. Then choose one subject from your list. (*See page 354.*)
3. Limit and focus your subject. (*See page 355.*)
4. Brainstorm a list of supporting details. (*See page 356.*)
5. Arrange your details in a logical order. (*See pages 358–359.*)

Writing

6. Write a topic sentence. (*See pages 362–363.*)
7. Use your prewriting notes to write the body of the paragraph. (*See page 365.*)
8. Add a concluding sentence. (*See page 367.*)

Revising

9. Put your paper aside for a while. Then use the Checklist for Revising Expository Paragraphs on page 371 to improve your draft.

Editing

10. Use the Editing Checklist on page 372 to prepare a final, polished paragraph.

23

Narrative Paragraphs

An important part of planning a paragraph is knowing your purpose for writing. If your purpose is to tell a story, you will be writing a narrative paragraph. On a history test, for example, you might write a narrative paragraph telling the story of Paul Revere's midnight ride. In a letter to a friend or relative, you might tell what happened at your team's first volleyball practice. Whenever you are telling a story, you are writing a narrative.

> **23a** A **narrative paragraph** tells a real or an imaginary story.

Your Writer's Notebook

Many imaginary stories take shape when a writer asks *What would happen if . . .?* To help you think of subjects for stories, choose one of the following *What if's.* In your journal write a story answering the *What if* question.

1. What would happen if two mind readers became roommates?
2. What would happen if your dog began to talk?
3. What would happen if a person who did not speak English came to stay with you for a month?
4. What would happen if two moons rose one night?

Developing Narrative Paragraphs

The following chart shows how each part of a narrative paragraph helps to tell a story.

Structure of a Narrative Paragraph

1. The topic sentence introduces the story by making a general statement, setting the scene, or capturing the reader's attention.
2. The supporting sentences tell the story event by event and answer the questions *Who? What? Where? Why? When?* and *How?*
3. The concluding sentence ends the story by summarizing the events or making a point about the story.

In the following narrative paragraph, the topic sentence makes a general statement. The concluding sentence summarizes the events. As you read the paragraph, notice how the story unfolds event by event.

A Surprise Visitor

TOPIC SENTENCE

My nights in camp were often exciting. I could hear lions prowling around. I even came to recognize the voices of most of them. Once I awoke to hear lapping noises. Being half asleep, I listened for some time before I realized that a lioness was inside my tent drinking out of my basin. I shouted at her to go away, which finally she did. I reported this incident to the park warden. He told me that lions of the Serengeti were known occasionally to go into tents and take a look around to see what was going on.

SUPPORTING SENTENCES

CONCLUDING SENTENCE

I shall never forget the night that nothing but a table stood between me and Africa.

—JOY ADAMSON, *FOREVER FREE*

EXERCISE 1 *Writing Topic Sentences*

Write a topic sentence for each narrative subject. The story may be real or imaginary.

1. encountering a wild animal
2. finding a long-missing possession
3. going out on the lake in a boat
4. witnessing an accident
5. attending a memorable family gathering
6. the day everything went wrong
7. winning a contest
8. breaking a tradition
9. camping out in autumn
10. meeting someone for the first time

Chronological Order and Transitions

Most narrative paragraphs are arranged in chronological order. In chronological order each event is presented in the order in which it occurred. Transitions show how the events are related in time.

23c In **chronological order** (time order), events are arranged in the order in which they happened. **Transitions** show how the events are related in time.

The following paragraph is in chronological order.

Anything but Trotting

TOPIC
SENTENCE

I had often dreamed of riding a horse, of sailing smoothly as if horse and rider were one. **Today** was my day. Here I was, perched on top of a huge gray horse, patting him as I had seen experienced riders do. **At first** everything was fine. The horses in my group were walking slowly down the forest path, and holding on was easy. **Before long** we came to a clearing and the horses broke into a canter, a smooth and easy-to-ride gait. **Then** the lead horse sped into a gallop, a thunderous gait that was surprisingly easy to ride. Everything went fine **for the rest of the morning until** the lead horse started to trot. **With the first** trot, my dream of horse and rider as one came to an abrupt end. I was bouncing wildly and could hardly catch my breath. **After** minutes that seemed like hours, we **finally** headed back to the stable at a slow walk. **By then** I knew very well what it meant to be saddle sore. The only place I wanted to be **for the next** few days was in a very soft chair.

STORY TOLD
EVENT BY
EVENT

CONCLUDING
SENTENCE

When writing narrative paragraphs, use transitions to show how events are related in time.

Transitions for Chronological Order			
after	during	afterwards	immediately
before	at last	finally	after a while
later	at noon	just as	in December
next	first	meanwhile	last night
when	second	suddenly	the next day
while	until	on Monday	by evening
then	early	as soon as	throughout the day

EXERCISE 2 *Arranging Events in Chronological Order*

Write each subject. Then list the events in chronological order.

1. **SUBJECT**   being locked out of the house
   EVENTS   • remembering with relief that my neighbors had a set of keys to my house
   • assuring my parents in the morning that I would remember to take my house keys to school with me
   • arriving home that night and realizing I had left my keys in my school locker

2. **SUBJECT**   auditioning for the school musical
   EVENTS   • being called to audition
   • rehearsing for weeks to master the songs for the part I wanted
   • signing up for the audition
   • searching for my name on the list of people who made the cast
   • seeing my name next to the part I wanted

EXERCISE 3 *Adding Transitions*

As you write the following paragraph, replace each blank with a transition. Use the transitions listed below.

after	the next morning	last summer
until	before they left	for two hours

My Gardening Days Are Over

I will never be a gardener again. I was a gardener for two days _____ when my parents went away on vacation. _____, they told me to water the fruit trees every morning without fail. _____ I was about to water the trees when I had a great idea. I pushed the hose down into the ground so the water would reach the roots more quickly. My idea worked _____ I tried to pull the hose back out. It would not budge. _____ tugging at it _____, I had to cut it off. I ended up spending my whole allowance on a new hose.

First Person and Third Person Narratives

In some narrative paragraphs, the person telling the story is in the story. The first person pronouns *I, we, me, us, my,* and *our* are used. These stories are called *first person narratives.*

Seasick

FIRST PERSON NARRATIVE

Mike and **I** were just packing away **our** gear after a successful day of fishing when the trouble began. As storm clouds started to gather, Mike's dad headed for shore. Suddenly the boat started going in circles. After Mike's dad turned the engine off, **we** quickly discovered that **our** rudder had fallen off the boat! The only way back now was to find a tow. **We** waved **our** hands at the passing boats. No one noticed **us** at first, and **we** just rocked back and forth, back and forth, until **we** were all seasick. Finally someone heard **our** calls, and **we** hitched a ride back to shore. That night, though, **we** were all too seasick to enjoy **our** fine catch of the day.

Some narrative paragraphs do not involve the writer at all. Writers telling a story about other people will refer to them with third person pronouns. (*See page 31.*) These stories are called *third person narratives.*

A Cherokee Alphabet

THIRD PERSON NARRATIVE

Sequoya, a citizen of the Cherokee nation, spoke no English. **He** did, however, admire the way some English-speaking people could make marks on paper and make the marks talk back. In 1809, **he** began making a set of symbols for the sounds in the Cherokee language. When **he** was finished, **he** had an alphabet of 85 characters. Within a few months, several thousand Cherokee had learned to read and write **their** language and were teaching others.

—CLARENCE L. VER STEEG, *AMERICAN SPIRIT*

23d ▶ Use the **first person narrative** style if you are a character in the story. Use the **third person narrative** style if your story is about what happened to others.

EXERCISE 4   *Recognizing First and Third Person Styles*

Read each story beginning. Then write *first person* or *third person* to tell what style is used.

1. My last birthday was truly a day to remember.
2. Edison proposed to his wife in an unusual way.
3. Mary hoped that the important letter would come today.
4. I had to admit it: I was lost.
5. Martin, a sailor, wearily stood his turn at watch.
6. Ruth missed her family, but she was excited about beginning her first dancing lessons in New York.
7. I sometimes have to learn lessons the hard way.
8. I was 11 years old when I met Dory for the first time.
9. Luis nervously practiced his lines.
10. Patches came into my life on a rainy October day.

EXERCISE 5   *On Your Own*

One way to find ideas for a first person narrative is to sketch an autobiography, a story of your life. Divide your notes into three parts: early childhood, grammar school days, and teenage years. Save your paper for later use.

Writing Extra

In addition to determining their purpose, writers also consider their audience, or readers. Practice writing for different audiences by doing the following activities.

1. Assume your readers are your own age or older. Write a paragraph retelling a legend, such as George Washington and the cherry tree.
2. Assume your readers are third graders. Rewrite your paragraph to suit this younger audience.

Writing Narrative Paragraphs

Stories are taking place around you all the time. To record those stories in writing, think back to the time when the story began. Then ask yourself the following questions.

- What incident set the story in motion?
- What problem faces the people in the story?
- What was the high point of the story?
- What was the outcome?

EXERCISE 6   *Writing a First Person Narrative*

STEP 1: **Prewriting**

Think of times when the unexpected happened. These may include winning something, receiving a surprise gift, or being part of a strange coincidence.

- Write down as many unexpected events as you can.
- Review your ideas and choose the one that would make the most interesting story.
- Brainstorm a list of details by asking yourself *Who? What? Where? Why? When?* and *How?*
- Arrange your details in chronological order.

STEP 2: Writing
Use your notes from Step 1 to write your first draft using first person narrative style.

STEP 3: Sharing Your Work
Exchange papers with a classmate. Cover all but the first sentence in your partner's paper. Read the first sentence and tell your partner what you expect the rest of the paragraph to be about. Then read the rest of the paragraph. Tell your partner what you like about it and what could be improved.

STEP 4: Revising
Use your partner's comments and your own judgment to revise your paragraph as needed.

EXERCISE 7 *Writing a Third Person Narrative*

STEP 1: Prewriting
Think of two or three of your favorite jokes. Be sure they are story jokes and not riddles or one-liners. Tell your jokes to a partner. Ask your partner to choose the joke that he or she likes best.

STEP 2: Writing
Write a draft of your joke. As you write it, be sure to use the third person style of storytelling.

STEP 3: Sharing Your Work
Give your draft to a new partner. Ask your partner to tell you if any part of the story is not written in third person style. Also ask if any of the events seem to be out of order. Finally ask for comments about how strong your punch line is and whether it could be improved.

STEP 4: Revising
Use your partner's comments to make any changes that would improve your paragraph. Then read it over again and trim away any unnecessary words. Try to tell your joke in as few words as possible.

386

EXERCISE 8   *Revising a Narrative Paragraph*

Choose one of the paragraphs you wrote in Exercise 6 or 7. Then use the checklist below to do a thorough revision.

Checklist for Revising Narrative Paragraphs

Checking Your Paragraph

1. Does your topic sentence introduce the story by making a general statement, setting the scene, or capturing attention? (*See page 379.*)
2. Do your supporting sentences tell the story event by event and answer the questions *Who? What? Where? Why? When?* and *How?* (*See page 379.*)
3. Does your paragraph have unity? (*See page 327.*)
4. Did you use chronological order with appropriate transitions to give your paragraph coherence? (*See pages 380–381.*)
5. Did you use first person if you are a character in the story? Did you use third person if your story is about what happened to others? (*See pages 383–384.*)
6. Does your concluding sentence end the story by summarizing the events or making a point about the story? (*See page 379.*)

Checking Your Sentences

7. Did you combine related sentences to avoid too many short, choppy sentences in a row? (*See pages 302–306.*)
8. Did you vary the length and beginnings of your sentences? (*See page 309.*)
9. Did you avoid rambling sentences? (*See page 312.*)
10. Did you avoid unnecessary repetition and empty expressions? (*See pages 313–315.*)

Checking Your Words

11. Did you use specific words? (*See page 295.*)
12. Did you use words that appeal to the senses? (*See page 299.*)

EXERCISE 9   *Editing a Narrative Paragraph*

Use the Editing Checklist on page 372 to edit your work from Exercise 8.

*S*potlight on *W*riting

A **Developing Narrative Paragraphs.** Choose one of the following topic sentences. Use your imagination to list at least five events that could make up a story. Write these events in chronological order.

1. After two back-breaking weeks cutting through the dense forest, we finally saw it standing in a sunlit clearing.
2. Today was one of those days when I should have stayed in bed.
3. The boys stood at the top of the cliff, trying to coax Jason to take his turn jumping into the cold lake water.
4. One night when the stars were bright, I saw an orange flash streak across the sky.

B **Using Transitions.** Write the topic sentence you chose in Part A. Then use the events you listed to write a draft of a narrative paragraph. Be sure to add transitions to show the relation of events in the passing of time.

C **Writing a First Person Narrative Paragraph.** Draw on your experiences to write a first person narrative paragraph to suit the following purpose and audience.

PURPOSE   to tell what happened when you were careless one time

AUDIENCE   a person younger than you who could benefit from your experience

D **Writing a Third Person Narrative Paragraph.** Use the notes that follow to write a third person narrative paragraph.

PURPOSE   to tell what happened when a storm shut down the power in your neighborhood

AUDIENCE   Readers of *Town News,* a local paper

NOTES
- last Tuesday a severe thunderstorm occurred at 9:20 P.M.
- power out in six-block area near Wadsworth Park
- workers from Commonwealth Power and Electric Company began tracing the problem immediately
- located a power line that had been hit by lightning
- worked for three more hours to repair damage

E **Writing a Story about a Picture.** Look at the picture above. Then use your imagination to write a narrative paragraph telling the story behind the picture.

PURPOSE   to tell what happened in a rescue
AUDIENCE   readers of the magazine *Heroes of Our Time*

F **Writing Ideas.** Write a narrative paragraph on one of the following subjects or on one of your own. You may want to use the ideas you wrote in your writer's notebook or in Exercise 5. Use the Steps for Writing a Narrative Paragraph on page 391 as a guide.

1. going downtown
2. taking a trip
3. a narrow escape
4. running something
5. your first job

6. a surprise victory
7. a misunderstanding
8. planning a surprise
9. a memorable holiday
10. meeting your best friend

Steps for Writing a Narrative Paragraph

Prewriting

1. Use your own experiences or your imagination to think of possible stories. (*See Your Writer's Notebook and On Your Own on pages 378 and 384.*)
2. Make a list of subjects and choose one that interests you and your readers.
3. Limit your subject so that it can be covered in one paragraph.
4. Write down everything that comes to mind when you think about your subject. (*See page 342.*)
5. Arrange your notes in chronological order. (*See pages 380–381.*)

Writing

6. Write a topic sentence. (*See page 379.*)
7. Use your prewriting notes to write supporting sentences with transitions where needed. (*See pages 379–381.*)
8. Add a concluding sentence. (*See page 379.*)

Revising

9. Put your paper aside for a while. Then use the Checklist for Revising Narrative Paragraphs on page 387 to improve your first draft.

Editing

10. Use the Editing Checklist on page 372 to prepare a final, polished paragraph.

Descriptive Paragraphs

Sometimes your purpose for writing will be to describe. In school your teacher may ask you to describe the view through a microscope or the pyramids in Egypt. In a letter, you may describe some scenery you saw on your vacation. Whenever your purpose is to help your reader see what you have seen, you will be writing description.

24a A **descriptive paragraph** creates a vivid picture in words of a person, an object, or a scene.

Your Writer's Notebook

Read the following passage about a wolf pup's birth. Then in your journal try to describe something you have never actually experienced.

> The world he entered was bare and cold. He lay on sand; a cool breeze passed over him. Somewhere in the darkness of the cavern his mother's panting came to his ears. He opened his mouth and whimpered a tiny, high-pitched whine. A large tongue sloshed across his face as his mother began to wash him. Fore and aft, belly and back, the tongue slobbered over him.   —ROBERT GRAY, *THE NATURAL LIFE OF NORTH AMERICAN WOLVES* (ADAPTED)

Developing Descriptive Paragraphs

Like other paragraphs that stand alone, a descriptive paragraph has a topic sentence, a body of supporting sentences, and a concluding sentence. The following chart shows how each part helps paint a word picture.

Structure of a Descriptive Paragraph

1. The topic sentence introduces the subject, often suggesting an overall impression of it.
2. The supporting sentences supply specific details and words that appeal to the senses to bring your subject to life.
3. The concluding sentence summarizes your overall impression of the subject.

In the following paragraph, the writer's purpose is to describe part of a National Preserve in Texas.

The Jack Gore Baygall

TOPIC SENTENCE

The Jack Gore Baygall is a junglelike region about three miles wide and four miles long. Sunlight filters through one-hundred-foot-tall tupelos and cypresses, reaching the thick undergrowth in eerie green shafts. By night the sounds of animals moving, calling, warning others of their kind, fill the recesses of the baygall. It is the home of alligators, otters, beavers, hawks, owls, roadrunners, snakes, fox squirrels, and whitetail deer. Oaks growing out of the muck to heights of 135 feet sprouted from acorns in the days when America was only a British colony. The Jack Gore Baygall is a wild piece of the Big Thicket National Preserve.

SUPPORTING SENTENCES

CONCLUDING SENTENCE

—HOWARD PEACOCK, *THE BIG THICKET OF TEXAS* (ADAPTED)

The author gives the reader a clue about the kind of place this is in the topic sentence by using the word *junglelike*. His description of the eerie shafts of sunlight and the night-time sounds of animals supports the overall impression. The concluding sentence summarizes the impression by calling this area a wild piece of land.

EXERCISE 1 *Writing Topic Sentences*

For each descriptive subject, write a topic sentence that suggests an overall impression.

EXAMPLE   a swimming pool
POSSIBLE   The empty pool looked forsaken with the dead
ANSWER   leaves and branches lying at its bottom.

1. a wolf
2. the night sky
3. a carnival
4. an aunt or an uncle
5. a forest
6. a pet
7. a hayride
8. your kitchen
9. a fancy telephone
10. a spaceship

Specific Details and Sensory Words

In a descriptive paragraph, your topic sentence tells your readers your overall impression of the subject. Your supporting sentences should then help them see what you see.

24c   Use **specific details** and **sensory words** to bring your description to life.

As you read the following descriptive paragraph, look for specific details and words that appeal to the senses. (*See page 299.*)

The Square Dance

TOPIC
SENTENCE

Stepping into the school auditorium on Tuesday nights is like traveling through time to the colorful days of the frontier barn dance. On the stage at the front of the hall, musicians in overalls and red bandanas stomp out the tunes for the dances. The middle of the floor creaks under the weight of the twirling dancers in their squares. The colors of the women's full skirts blur into a mosaic as partners swing around and around. From the back of the hall, the smells of popcorn being made in the kitchen tell the dancers that a break is coming up. Within minutes the tables set up along the back of the hall will be brimming with pitchers of ice-cold lemonade and bowls of popcorn. For a few short minutes, the dancers will cool off, but before long they will be back on the floor, reliving the fun of old time dancing.

SENSORY
DETAILS

CONCLUDING
SENTENCE

EXERCISE 2 Identifying Sensory Details

Answer the following questions about the paragraph above.

1. What details appeal to the sense of sight?
2. What details appeal to the sense of sound?
3. What details appeal to the sense of taste?
4. What instruments do you picture the musicians playing?
5. Do you think the hall is warm or cool? Why?

EXERCISE 3 Listing Sensory Details

Choose five of the following subjects. Under each one write five sensory details you could use in a description.

1. Thanksgiving
2. a wedding
3. a football game
4. an old book
5. a horse

6. a workshop
7. a mountain lake
8. a newborn kitten
9. a run-down car
10. a pickle

*S*patial Order and Transitions

One way to organize the details in a description is spatial, or location, order. Transitions used with spatial order tell how the details are related in space. They are like pointers that lead a reader's eye from spot to spot.

24d **Spatial order** arranges details according to their location. **Transitions** show the relationship of the details.

As a writer of description, you can decide the direction in which you want to lead your reader's eye. In the following descriptive paragraph, the details are arranged in spatial order from top to bottom. The transitions are printed in heavy type.

Yoda's Face

TOPIC
SENTENCE

Every detail in the face of Yoda, the Jedi teacher in *The Empire Strikes Back*, suggests his wisdom and intelligence. His green body is dwarfed by his huge head. His high forehead gives the impression of a large, busy brain. **Beneath** his forehead his expressive eyes show both disappointment and hope at his young pupil's progress. His huge pointed ears that reach **the same level** as his eyes show his ability to take in sounds that others would miss. **Below** his eyes, a smallish nose twitches in response to events around him. **At the bottom** of his face, a mouth that knows how to stay shut reveals his ability to concentrate. At first sight, Yoda may appear ugly, but as you see his great intelligence at work, his face begins to show the wisdom of the Jedi masters.

SPATIAL ORDER
FROM TOP TO
BOTTOM

CONCLUDING
SENTENCE

The chart on the next page shows four directions commonly used with spatial order and the transitions associated with each one.

Spatial Order	Transitions
near to far (or reverse)	close by, beyond, around, farther, across, behind, in the distance
top to bottom (or reverse)	at the top, in the middle, lower, below, at the bottom, above, higher
side to side	at the left (right), in the middle, next to, at one end, to the west
inside to outside (or reverse)	within, in the center, on the inside, the next layer, on the outside

EXERCISE 4   Identifying Types of Spatial Order

Identify the type of spatial order used by writing *bottom to top, side to side, near to far,* or *outside to inside.*

1. The Animal Shelter

As I looked at the row of puppies at the shelter, I wanted to take all of them home. In the cage to my left was a single black puppy peacefully curled up with her nose warmed by her tail. Next to her was a litter of twelve-week-old beagle puppies, playfully pawing the cage and yelping with excitement. In the cage directly in front of me were two white, fluffy pups with wildly wagging tails. To my right, in the biggest cage, were a mother dog and her litter of four-week-old puppies who would stay with her for another month before being adopted. How would I ever choose which puppy to take home!

2. View from the Pier

The view from the pier on Mirror Lake is tranquil but full of life. Directly in front of the pier, quiet waves wash easily against the wooden pier. Delicate insects dance across the top of the water. Further out on the lake, a fish jumping in the air catches the sun's rays, and its splash sends out round ripples of water. Across the lake, bluffs rise from the water's edge. Trees growing out of the bluffs bend toward the water, forming an arched canopy. Although life is going on all around, time seems to stand still in the quiet of the scene.

3. The Piñata

Piñatas are a tradition at birthday parties in my family. The piñata is a papier-maché form, often in the shape of a burro, that is colorful on the outside and filled with surprises inside. The outside of the piñata is covered with brightly-colored short strips of paper to suggest a burro's hair. Inside the piñata is a hollow space filled with small presents such as yo-yo's, balls, twirlers, and other trinkets. The piñata is hung by a string from the ceiling at the beginning of the party. Near the end of the party, guests take turns hitting the piñata with a stick, eagerly waiting for the papier-maché to split and the presents to come tumbling down.

EXERCISE 5   On Your Own

To help you think of subjects for a descriptive paragraph, take a guided tour of your memory. The following questions will be your tour guide. In your writer's notebook, write down as many answers as come to mind when you think about each question.

1. Where have I been that stands out in my memory?
2. What unusual objects or things have I seen that I could describe to others?
3. Who do I know that has a distinctive appearance?

Writing Extra

Imagine you are a scientist living in the year 3508. Your job is to dig up the buried remains of an ancient city of the twentieth century and write a report of your findings. You have just uncovered a household item, such as an iron, a telephone, or a television. You have no idea what the item is or what it was used for. Write a paragraph describing the item. Now read your paragraph to your classmates and see if they can guess what item you have described.

Writing Descriptive Paragraphs

Writing a descriptive paragraph is like making a movie. Like a set designer, you must create striking visual images. Like a sound operator, you must include sounds that go along with the scene. Finally, like a director, you must put all the details together to create an overall impression. The following activities will give you practice with creating pictures in words.

EXERCISE 6 Describing a Person

STEP 1: **Prewriting**
Look through some photographs and choose a picture of a member of your family. Then make a list of details, such as facial features, facial expression, hair, clothing, and posture. Arrange your details in a logical order.

STEP 2: **Writing**
Without mentioning your subject's name, write a description of the family member exactly as he or she appears in the photograph. Your purpose is to describe the person's appearance so well that other members of your family will be able to guess who it is.

STEP 3: **Sharing Your Work**
Show your paragraph to other family members. See if they can figure out who your subject is. Then show the photograph to them and ask if anything in your description could be improved. Make any changes that seem necessary.

EXERCISE 7 *Creating and Describing a Scene*

STEP 1: Prewriting

The items below appeal to the sense of smell. Think of a scene that goes along with each one. Then write freely about each item using the questions that follow.

pine   popcorn   campfire

hay   soap

1. What sights go along with this smell?
2. What sounds would I hear when I smell this?
3. What tastes, if any, go with this smell?
4. What might appeal to my sense of touch?

Complete your plan by drawing a sketch of each scene.

STEP 2: Writing

Choose one item from Step 1. Use your notes and sketch to write a descriptive paragraph that creates your scene in words. Be sure to include details that appeal to at least four of the five senses.

STEP 3: Sharing Your Work

Exchange papers with a classmate. Tell your partner·what you liked about his or her paragraph and what could be improved. Make any necessary changes in your own paragraph.

EXERCISE 8   Revising a Descriptive Paragraph

Choose one of the paragraphs you wrote in Exercise 6 or 7. Use the checklist below to make a thorough revision.

Checklist for Revising Descriptive Paragraphs

Checking Your Paragraph

1. Does your topic sentence introduce the subject and suggest your overall impression of it? (*See pages 393–394.*)
2. Do your supporting sentences supply specific details and sensory words that bring your subject to life? (*See pages 394–395.*)
3. Does your paragraph have unity? (*See page 368.*)
4. Did you arrange your details in spatial order (or another logical order) with transitions to give your paragraph coherence? (*See pages 396–397.*)
5. Does your concluding sentence summarize your overall impression of the subject? (*See pages 393–394.*)

Checking Your Sentences

6. Did you combine related sentences to avoid too many short, choppy sentences in a row? (*See pages 302–306.*)
7. Did you vary the length and beginnings of your sentences? (*See page 309.*)
8. Did you avoid rambling sentences? (*See page 312.*)
9. Did you avoid unnecessary repetition and empty expressions? (*See pages 313–315.*)

Checking Your Words

10. Did you use fresh, specific words? (*See pages 295–299.*)

EXERCISE 9   Editing a Descriptive Paragraph

Use the checklist on page 372 to edit the paragraph that you revised in Exercise 8.

EXERCISE 10   On Your Own

Clip striking pictures from magazines or draw them. Put them in your writer's notebook for writing ideas later on.

Spotlight on Writing

A **Finding Transitions.** The following paragraph is from a longer work about scientists studying tornadoes. Write all of the transitions used in this paragraph.

Chasing Tornadoes

Ahead is a farmhouse, ghostly in the nightmarish light. As we turn to the right in front of it, the van slithers sideways, and we're half in a ditch. We are slammed by a gust of wind, and I see a big gray funnel dropping down behind the house. The sound is like the hollow roar of an enormous seashell. —WILLIAM HAUPTMAN, "CLOSE ENCOUNTERS WITH TORNADOES"

B **Describing to Convey Feelings.** Write a descriptive paragraph that suits the following purpose and audience.

PURPOSE   to describe the majesty of the California condor to raise funds for its protection

AUDIENCE   wildlife lovers

C **Describing an Object.** Think of an object that could serve as a symbol of yourself. Then write a paragraph that describes your symbol and its meaning.

PURPOSE   to describe a symbol and its meaning
AUDIENCE   your classmates

beauty   sturdiness

endurance   courage

D **Describing to Provide Information.** Use the following notes to write a descriptive paragraph.

PURPOSE   to describe poison ivy so people can avoid it
AUDIENCE   campers and others who spend time outdoors

Notes
- remember this saying: "Leaves of three, let them be!"
- leaves grow in cluster of three leaves
- leaves have one big vein down middle
- five smaller veins branch from each side of big vein
- leaves may be any shade of green from dark to pale
- texture varies from hairy to smooth
- edging around leaves can be smooth, notched, or saw-toothed
- leaves vary in size from less than an inch to about six inches across

403

E **Revising a Descriptive Paragraph.** Use the checklist on page 401 to revise the following paragraph.

My Little Sister

My five-year-old sister Gwen looks as mischeivous as she usually is. Her blue eyes always flash with humor when she tells a joke. A stubborn colick rises out of her sandy-colored hair. It imitates Gwen's own strong will. Her long curly eye-lashes give her an innocent look that she sometimes hides behind. Her delicate lips are often turned up in a tricky smile. Gwens cheeks are usually flushed on account of her energetic dashing around the house and yard. Once she put my mother's make-up all over herself and her favorite doll. Her bangs are cut straight across her forhead, but somehow they always seem to part in a funny spot on the left side. Gwen looks like one of the family but her own sly person-ality always shines through.

F **Editing a Descriptive Paragraph.** In the paragraph titled "My Little Sister," there are three spelling errors and two punctuation errors. Did you catch them? If not, go back and correct them now.

G **Writing from Your Writer's Notebook.** Choose an idea for a descriptive paragraph from your journal. Then write your paragraph using the Steps for Writing a Descriptive Paragraph on page 405.

H **Writing Ideas.** Write a descriptive paragraph on one of the following subjects or on one of your own. Use the Steps for Writing on page 405 as a guide.

1. your dream car
2. your favorite outfit
3. a beach
4. a museum exhibit
5. a costume
6. a party
7. band practice
8. the library
9. a clown
10. your homeroom

404

Steps for Writing a Descriptive Paragraph

Prewriting

1. Think of possible subjects by looking at pictures and searching your memory. (*See the exercises called On Your Own on pages 398 and 401.*)
2. Make a list of subjects and choose one that interests you and your readers.
3. Limit your subject so that it can be covered in one paragraph.
4. Write down all the sensory details that come to mind when you think about your subject. (*See pages 394–395.*)
5. Arrange your notes in spatial order or some other logical order. (*See pages 396–397.*)

Writing

6. Write a topic sentence that suggests an overall impression. (*See pages 393–394.*)
7. Use your prewriting notes to write supporting sentences with transitions where needed. (*See pages 393–397.*)
8. Add a concluding sentence that summarizes the overall impression. (*See pages 393–394.*)

Revising

9. Put your paper aside for a while. Then use the Checklist for Revising Descriptive Paragraphs on page 401 to revise your paragraph.

Editing

10. Use the Editing Checklist on page 372 to prepare a final, polished paragraph.

Persuasive Paragraphs

Why are some laws passed while others are voted down? Why do some products sell while others sit on store shelves? Why are some people awarded desirable positions while others are left behind? One important factor in all of these situations is the power of persuasion. The ability to persuade others is important in many areas of life. It also plays a part in sharpening thinking skills. This chapter will help you build your powers of persuasion through writing persuasive paragraphs.

25a A **persuasive paragraph** states an opinion and uses facts, examples, and reasons to convince readers.

*Y*our Writer's Notebook

Use the following starter line to write freely in your journal. Fill in the blanks as you see fit.

I used to think that _____, but now I think that _____.

Explain your responses as completely as possible. Be sure to explain why you changed your mind. Then repeat the activity several times, completing the blank spaces in the starter line with other ideas.

Developing Persuasive Paragraphs

When you write a persuasive paragraph, you assume that your audience does not agree with your opinion. To convince your readers, your topic sentence, supporting sentences, and concluding sentence must work together logically and forcefully. The purpose of the following paragraph is to persuade readers to have fire drills at home. Notice how each sentence works toward this goal.

Fire Drills at Home

TOPIC
SENTENCE

Fire drills should be conducted in homes as well as in schools and other public buildings. First of all, having regular fire drills at home would allow all family members to practice what to do in an emergency. This practice would reduce panic during a fire and perhaps make the difference between escaping safely and being trapped. Second, having home fire drills would set a good example in the neighborhood. Nearby families may be encouraged to have their own drills. Most important, having fire drills at home would probably lead people to be more safety-conscious so that fires would not get started in the first place. A few minutes a few times a year can help save lives.

SUPPORTING
SENTENCES

CONCLUDING
SENTENCE

The role of each part of a persuasive paragraph is summarized in the following chart.

25b

Structure of a Persuasive Paragraph

1. The topic sentence states an opinion.
2. The supporting sentences use facts, examples, and reasons to back up the opinion.
3. The concluding sentence makes a strong point or a final appeal to persuade readers.

EXERCISE 1   *Writing Persuasive Topic Sentences*

For each subject write a topic sentence that states an opinion.

1. eating habits
2. grades in school
3. television news
4. city life
5. endangered species
6. commercials
7. good books
8. school sports
9. curfews
10. popular music

Facts and Opinions

If you intend to change someone's mind, you must provide a convincing argument. Sticking to the facts is essential to building a strong case. Opinions have their place,
but they cannot be used as proof. Learn to recognize opinions by watching for words such as *should, must, ought,
better, best,* and *worst.*

> **25c**   **Facts** are statements that can be proved. **Opinions** are
> judgments that vary from person to person.

> **25d**   Use **facts** and **examples** to convince readers. Do not use
> opinions to support your position.

EXERCISE 2   *Recognizing Facts and Opinions*

Number your paper 1 to 10. For each statement write *F* if
it is a fact or *O* if it is an opinion.

1. Schools should allow students more say in which classes
   they take.
2. In July of 1985, musicians donated their talents to the
   Live Aid concert to raise money for hungry Africans.
3. Dolphins are beautiful creatures.
4. Dolphins use sonar to locate objects underwater.
5. Many companies in the United States now use recycled
   paper.
6. Everyone should use recycled paper.

7. The movie ratings should include more categories.
8. The rating PG-13 means that parts of the movie may be unsuitable for viewers under the age of 13.
9. Old science fiction movies are better than recent ones.
10. Some guitars have six strings.

EXERCISE 3 *Revising a Paragraph with Facts*

The following persuasive paragraph uses only opinions to support its position. Read the paragraph and the facts that follow it. Then use some of the facts to revise the paragraph.

A Throw-away Culture

The people of the United States should learn to use things over and over instead of simply throwing them away. First of all, too much trash could harm the environment. Second, disposing of things so easily might lead to an overall throw-away attitude. Perhaps the reason that so many dogs and cats are put to sleep in animal shelters is that we have a throw-away attitude toward them too. Finally, throwing away so many things is expensive. Why not spend a little more money to buy a pen that could last a lifetime instead of buying many cheaper pens that you throw away after a month? This fairly new throw-away attitude has become the worst problem of our time.

Facts to Use in Revision

- Plastics in disposable items remain in the environment for many years after the items have been thrown away.
- Americans throw out 3 to 5 pounds of items per day; this is more than half a ton of garbage per person each year.
- Each year 15 million dogs and cats are put to sleep in humane societies.
- Americans spend about 2 billion dollars each year on disposable plastic and paper plates.
- Americans spend nearly 3 billion dollars each year on disposable diapers.
- Other disposable items, such as pens, lighters, and razors, cost another 2 billion dollars.

*O*rder of Importance and Transitions

A logical presentation of ideas helps you convince your readers. Placing the most important point at the end of a paragraph can give you a special advantage. For one thing, the last point tends to stick longer in a reader's mind. For another, placing your most persuasive point last gives your argument more impact.

25e | Arrange **supporting points** in the order of least to most (or most to least) important. Use **transitions** to show the connection between the points.

Transitions for Order of Importance

also	another	for example	more important
first	besides	furthermore	most important
second	moreover	similarly	to begin with
third	finally	in addition	in conclusion

The paragraph on page 411 was written by a student to persuade readers that Jack London's book *Call of the Wild* is more than just a story about a dog named Buck. Read the paragraph. Notice that the writer has arranged the supporting points from least to most important.

*E*XERCISE 4   *Using Order of Importance*

Complete the topic sentence. Then follow the steps below.

TOPIC
SENTENCE   If you could see only one movie in your life, you should see _____.

- List three reasons to support your opinion.
- Arrange your reasons in order of importance.
- Write a draft of a paragraph recommending the movie.
- Underline all the transitions you use.

410

Lessons from *Call of the Wild*

TOPIC
SENTENCE

Although many people look at *Call of the Wild* as a fast-moving adventure story about a dog, I think of it as something more. **One reason** I do is that it shows how it is possible to adapt to a new environment even when conditions are extremely bad. Buck changed his habits and a way of life in order to survive. Along with exciting action, I **also** saw how inhuman and uncivilized people can be, not only to dogs but also to each other. Men stole from one another, fought one another, and killed one another. **The most important reason** for considering this more than just an ordinary action story is the lesson I learned from the way the story ended. Buck went off to become the leader of a pack of wolves because civilization in the Klondike was worse than life in the wild. More than just an adventure story, *Call of the Wild* presents worthwhile lessons for us today.

ORDER OF
LEAST
TO MOST
IMPORTANT

CONCLUDING
SENTENCE

—STUDENT WRITER

411

EXERCISE 5 *Editing a Persuasive Paragraph*

Use the Editing Checklist on page 372 to edit the following persuasive paragraph.

A Flying White Elephant?

The supersonic commersial airplane known as the SST presents many difficult, and unusaul problems. First, it consumes huge amounts of expensive fuel just to save a few hour's of flying time, and second, the plane is so noisey that they are not allowed to fly over certian populated areas, these restrictions limit the number of traffic lanes that it can use. Finely, it's development, production, and maintainance costs is extreamly high. In the future Commersial Airlines should concentrate on improveing conventional airplanes; instead of pouring more money into these noisey expensive aircraft.

EXERCISE 6 *On Your Own*

Read the editorial page of your school or local newspaper. In your journal write responses to each editorial, agreeing or disagreeing and adding your own reasons and insights.

*W*riting Extra

Imagine that you are entering a contest to choose a theme song for your class. The song will be played at all school dances and at graduation. Think of an appropriate song from popular music. Then write a persuasive paragraph convincing the contest judges of your choice.

Writing Persuasive Paragraphs

Think of a time when you won an argument. What finally convinced the other person? From time to time, you have probably used all of the following tools of persuasion.

Tools of Persuasion

1. Use solid reasons and examples that are based on fact.
2. Refer to experts who agree with you.
3. Think about other viewpoints and offer strong counter arguments.
4. Use polite, reasonable language.

EXERCISE 7 Persuading with Facts

STEP 1: **Prewriting**

Imagine that your science teacher has asked you to write a prediction based on current scientific knowledge. You have decided to write about athletes of the future. From your reading you have learned the following facts about athletes of today. Use these notes to form an opinion about athletes of the future.

- continue to break records
- use scientific studies to increase athletic ability
- use latest knowledge of nutrition to develop sound bodies
- use scientific training techniques

STEP 2: **Writing**

Use the facts provided and the opinion you have formed to write your first draft.

STEP 3: **Sharing Your Work**

Exchange papers with a classmate. If the opinion in your partner's topic sentence differs from yours, are you convinced by the facts provided? Tell your partner what you like about the paragraph and what could be improved.

EXERCISE 8   Persuading with Reasons

STEP 1: Prewriting

Use the picture below to help you think of subjects for a persuasive paragraph. As you look at the picture, make a list of as many subjects as you can. Then ask yourself *What is my opinion about each subject in my list?* Express your opinion in a phrase and jot down reasons that would back it up. Arrange your notes in order of importance.

STEP 2: Writing

Use your notes to write your first draft. Be sure to use transitions between ideas.

STEP 3: Revising

Look again at the picture above. What feelings does it stir in you? Review your paragraph and try to communicate some of those feelings in your writing.

EXERCISE 9   Revising a Persuasive Paragraph

Choose one of your paragraphs from Exercise 7 or 8. Use the checklist on page 415 to make a thorough revision.

Checklist for Revising Persuasive Paragraphs

Checking Your Paragraph

1. Does your topic sentence state an opinion? (*See pages 407–408.*)
2. Did you use facts and examples instead of opinions to support your topic sentence? (*See pages 407–408.*)
3. Did you think about other viewpoints and offer strong counter arguments?
4. Does your paragraph have unity? (*See page 327.*)
5. Did you use order of importance with clear transitions to give your paragraph coherence? (*See pages 410–411.*)
6. Does your concluding sentence make a strong point or a final appeal? (*See page 407.*)

Checking Your Sentences

7. Did you combine related sentences to avoid too many short, choppy sentences in a row? (*See pages 302–306.*)
8. Did you vary the length and beginnings of your sentences? (*See page 309.*)
9. Did you avoid rambling sentences? (*See page 312.*)
10. Did you avoid unnecessary repetition and empty expressions? (*See pages 313–315.*)

Checking Your Words

11. Did you use specific words? (*See page 295.*)
12. Did you use polite, reasonable language?

EXERCISE 10 *Editing a Persuasive Paragraph*

Use the Editing Checklist on page 372 to edit the paragraph you chose in Exercise 9.

EXERCISE 11 *On Your Own*

In your journal find ideas for persuasive paragraphs by answering questions about different audiences.

1. What do my friends and I disagree about?
2. What do my sister or brother and I disagree about?
3. What do my neighbors and I disagree about?

*S*potlight on *W*riting

A **Developing Persuasive Paragraphs.** Review the tools of persuasion on page 413. Then decide which tool is being used in each example below. Indicate your answer by writing *facts,* *expert opinion,* or *counter argument.*

1. Mr. Sawyer, the tennis coach at school, recommends this type of racket. This is the type you should buy.
2. At the southern end of our street, not a single accident has occurred since the traffic light was installed two years ago. At the northern end, where no traffic light is operating, there have been five accidents during the same two-year period. We need a traffic light at the northern crossing.
3. Some people may be opposed to having uniforms for the softball team because they are unwilling or unable to pay for them. With the following plan, however, the team can raise enough money to buy the uniforms so that no one would have to buy his or her own.

B **Writing Persuasive Paragraphs.** The following notes describe qualities of two candidates for class treasurer, Marla and Abdul. Think carefully about the qualities that a good class treasurer should have. Then write a persuasive paragraph endorsing one of the candidates. Be sure to give the reasons for your choice.

PURPOSE   to recommend a candidate for class treasurer
AUDIENCE   your classmates

Marla's Qualities	**Abdul's Qualities**
• respected leader	• shy personality
• good athlete	• good with numbers
• good grades	• member of Junior Achievement
• warm personality	• committed to fairness
• good with numbers	• good grades; all A's in math

416

C **Writing to Judge a Contest.** You are a judge for the school poster contest. The theme of this year's contest is Keeping Your Neighborhood Clean. The final contestants' posters are shown below. Choose the one that you think deserves to win. Write a persuasive paragraph explaining your choice.

PURPOSE   to recommend a winner for the contest
AUDIENCE   everyone who entered the contest

D **Writing Ideas.** Write a persuasive paragraph on one of the following subjects or on one of your own. You may use your journal or any previous exercises for ideas. Follow the Steps for Writing a Persuasive Paragraph on page 418.

1. staying well
2. movies
3. homework
4. books
5. school events
6. protecting endangered species
7. attitudes that should be changed
8. how services could be improved
9. what is right about television
10. high salaries in sports today

417

Steps for Writing a Persuasive Paragraph

Prewriting

1. List opinions on subjects you feel strongly about. (*See the exercises on pages 406, 412, and 415.*)
2. Choose a subject that interests you and that suits your purpose and audience.
3. Limit your subject so that it can be adequately covered in one paragraph.
4. Brainstorm a list of facts or examples that support your opinion. (*See page 342.*) If necessary, find additional facts and figures in the library.
5. Arrange your notes in order of importance. (*See pages 410–411.*)

Writing

6. Write a topic sentence that states an opinion. (*See pages 407–408.*)
7. Use your prewriting notes to add supporting sentences with transitions. Remember to stick to the facts. (*See pages 407–411.*)
8. Add a concluding sentence that makes a final appeal or a strong point. (*See page 407.*)

Revising

9. Put your paper aside for a while. Then pretend you disagree with your own opinion as you read the paper over. Use the Checklist for Revising Persuasive Paragraphs on page 415 to make your paper more persuasive.

Editing

10. Use the Editing Checklist on page 372 to prepare a final, polished paragraph.

Standardized Test

Directions: Decide which order is best for the sentences in each group. In the appropriate row on your answer sheet, fill in the circle containing the letter that indicates the best order.

SAMPLE (1) A distinguished gentleman led us to our table.
(2) On the table were soft pink menus printed in silver.
(3) A little nervously, we walked into the elegant room.
(4) "I want a hamburger!" declared my little brother.

A 4 - 2 - 1 - 3   **C** 2 - 3 - 4 - 1
B 3 - 1 - 2 - 4   **D** 1 - 4 - 3 - 2

ANSWER Ⓐ Ⓑ Ⓒ Ⓓ

1. (1) The machine cuts the wire into small lengths.
(2) The other end is shaped into a point, and a straight pin has been formed.
(3) One end of each length is flattened into a head.
(4) Wire is fed into a machine from a reel.

A 2 - 3 - 1 - 4   **C** 4 - 1 - 3 - 2
B 3 - 1 - 4 - 2   **D** 1 - 2 - 3 - 4

2. (1) Sweat glands are distributed all over the body's surface.
(2) Instead, their main function is to reduce body heat.
(3) When sweat evaporates, it has a cooling effect.
(4) They play almost no role in ridding the body of waste.

A 1 - 4 - 2 - 3   **C** 3 - 2 - 1 - 4
B 4 - 1 - 3 - 2   **D** 2 - 1 - 3 - 4

3. (1) The opposite wall was covered by a huge, colorful mural.
(2) From the doorway we looked into the entrance hall.
(3) Between us and the statue lay a tiled marble floor.
(4) In front of the mural stood a bronze statue of two men.

A 3 - 1 - 2 - 4   **C** 4 - 1 - 3 - 2
B 1 - 3 - 4 - 2   **D** 2 - 1 - 4 - 3

Directions: Choose the sentence that does not belong in the paragraph. Fill in the appropriate circle on your answer sheet.

SAMPLE   (A) A line had formed at Gate 6. (B) Each passenger showed a ticket before walking through. (C) The flight took two hours. (D) At the end of the ramp, a jet waited.

ANSWER   Ⓐ Ⓑ Ⓒ Ⓓ

4.   (A) Most pets keep themselves clean. (B) Cats wash themselves frequently. (C) Birds clean their feathers with their beaks. (D) Flying birds need cages large enough to fly in.

5.   (A) Oil is often called black gold. (B) Oil is found in different parts of the world. (C) The Middle East has about half the world's oil. (D) North America supplies one fourth.

6.   (A) I loved my grandmother's long hair. (B) Every day she braided it. (C) She wound the braids around her head like a silver crown. (D) Her face wrinkled only in a frown or smile.

7.   (A) Records used to be played at 78 RPM. (B) They held only single songs and were breakable. (C) People collect old 78's. (D) In 1948, unbreakable long-playing records were introduced.

8.   (A) Today is a good day for pollen but a bad day for me. (B) Yesterday I felt fine. (C) My eyes are itchy and watery. (D) I sneeze approximately every 82 seconds.

9.   (A) Potatoes originated in South America. (B) The potato is related to the tomato. (C) It is also related to tobacco. (D) Surprisingly, however, it is not related to the sweet potato.

10.   (A) Jill loves to use puns. (B) She is always cheerful too. (C) One of her favorite puns is "My poetry is bad, but it could be verse." (D) Another is "The cemetery workers' strike is a grave situation."

Composition

Part Three

26

Essays

In the last few chapters, you learned the process of writing single paragraphs. Sometimes, however, your ideas will need more space than a single paragraph. In history class, for example, you may be asked to write a composition about the checks and balances built into the government of the United States. In science class you may be asked to write a composition explaining the life cycle of a star. A paragraph is too short to contain these ideas. An essay would be more suitable.

26a An **essay** is a composition of three or more paragraphs that presents and develops one main idea.

Like paragraphs, essays have three main parts. In the following essay, the three main parts are labeled at the left.

Messages into Space

MAIN IDEA

> Two space missions from recent years are carrying our messages into interstellar space.

INTRODUCTION: PROVIDES BACKGROUND INFORMATION AND CAPTURES READER'S ATTENTION

Pioneer 10 is carrying a plaque with a drawing of a man and a woman plus some information about Earth and its inhabitants. Voyager is carrying a "cosmic LP," a 2-hour phonograph record. Encoded on the record are photographs, diagrams, and drawings that represent life on this planet. It also contains greetings from Earth spoken in 53 languages, musical selections, sounds of our animal life, the roar of the surf, the cry of a baby, and the soft thump of the human heartbeat.

BODY: PROVIDES SPECIFIC INFORMATION

Thirty-two thousand years will pass before Pioneer 10 draws close to a star. After that approach a million years will go by before there is another close approach, and still another million years will elapse before a third occurs. Because of the emptiness of interstellar space, the spacecraft's ancient hulk will probably never be seen by alien eyes. In fact, the messages aboard the Pioneer and Voyager spacecraft were composed with little hope that anyone would ever discover them. They were only bottles thrown in a cosmic ocean, a symbol of our deep desire to communicate with a civilization other than our own.

CONCLUSION: ADDS A STRONG ENDING

Millions of years from now, those messages will still be journeying through the universe. They may never be found. They will, however, be a solid piece of evidence that a tiny inhabited planet exists, or once existed, in the suburbs of a small galaxy with the odd name *Milky Way.*

—MARGARET POYNTER AND MICHAEL J. KLEIN, *COSMIC QUEST* (ADAPTED)

*Y*our Writer's Notebook

You have probably heard the expression, "Beauty is in the eye of the beholder." It means that beauty can be found in even the ugliest places if you know how to look for it. Think of places where you see beauty even if others do not. Then every day for one week write about these places in your journal. In the process, you will discover several subjects to write about in an essay.

Prewriting

Finding a good subject is an important part of the prewriting stage of the writing process. If you write about a subject that you are not genuinely interested in, your writing will show your lack of enthusiasm. If you choose a subject you care about, however, your writing will sparkle with interest and hold the reader's attention. The following activities will help you think of subjects that you will enjoy writing about.

EXERCISE 1 Thinking of Subjects by Listing Interests

Complete each sentence with as many items as you can.

1. I often talk or read about . . .
2. The school subjects that I am most interested in are . . .
3. I have taken (or have wanted to take) lessons in . . .
4. Over the years my hobbies have included . . .
5. I am really good at . . .
6. Reports I have written in the past were about such subjects as . . .
7. In the last month, I have learned the following interesting things: . . .
8. The most interesting places I have been to are . . .
9. Memorable times with family and friends include . . .
10. Of all the presents I have received, the ones that mean the most to me are . . .

EXERCISE 2 Thinking of Subjects by Writing Freely

Using the starter below, write continuously for five minutes. One idea will lead to another. If you run out of ideas, write *I can't think of anything* until another idea comes to mind. Keep your pen or pencil moving the whole time and do not worry about mistakes.

I want to explain to you . . .

Choosing and Limiting a Subject

After exploring your interests, the next step is to choose one that would be a suitable subject for an essay.

Choosing an Essay Subject

1. Choose a subject you are really interested in.
2. Choose a subject that will interest your readers.
3. Choose a subject that you know enough about now or can learn enough about later to develop well in at least three paragraphs.

Next limit your subject to suit your purpose.

DETERMINING YOUR PURPOSE
- Do I want to describe?
- Do I want to explain or give directions?
- Do I want to persuade my readers?

Once you have decided on a purpose, consider your audience.

DETERMINING YOUR AUDIENCE
- Who are my readers?
- What do my readers already know?
- What background information will they need?

As a final step in limiting your subject, list several possible focus points. Focus points are specific aspects of your general subject. In the example below, the subject of snorkeling is too large for a short essay. Any of the focus points, however, would be a suitably limited subject.

SUBJECT   snorkeling (underwater exploring)
PURPOSE   to explain
AUDIENCE people who may have tried snorkeling once but who do not know much about it

FOCUS POINTS
- equipment needed
- how to control breathing and clear snorkel
- things to do while snorkeling
- different kinds of surface dives

425

Steps for Limiting an Essay Subject

1. Decide on the purpose of your essay: to describe, to explain or give directions, or to persuade.
2. Think about who your audience will be and what they need to know.
3. List focus points that suit your purpose and audience.
4. Choose one focus point as your limited subject.

EXERCISE 3 *Limiting a Subject*

List four possible focus points for each subject.

1. SUBJECT   taking a risk
   PURPOSE   to persuade
   AUDIENCE   people who are afraid to take risks

2. SUBJECT   attending sports events
   PURPOSE   to describe
   AUDIENCE   people who have been to some events

3. SUBJECT   bicycling
   PURPOSE   to explain
   AUDIENCE   people who know how to ride

4. SUBJECT   volunteering
   PURPOSE   to persuade
   AUDIENCE   people who want to volunteer

5. SUBJECT   what you learn in school besides facts
   PURPOSE   to explain
   AUDIENCE   people younger than you

Listing Supporting Details

The writing process moves back and forth between controlling your thoughts carefully and letting them run freely. In the last step, you narrowed your subject and brought it under control. The next step, listing supporting details, calls for letting your ideas run freely. The kinds of supporting details you should use will depend on your purpose for writing.

26d

Listing Supporting Details

Purpose	Kinds of Details
to describe	details that appeal to the senses
to explain	facts, examples, reasons
to give directions	steps in a process
to persuade	facts, examples, reasons

Brainstorming. One way to think of supporting details is to brainstorm. Brainstorming means writing down everything that comes to mind when you think about your subject. One idea will lead to another.

LIMITED SUBJECT   things to do while snorkeling

BRAINSTORMING
IDEAS
- collecting shells
- feeding fish
- mastering basic snorkeling techniques
- shells are on the seafloor, sometimes hidden in sea grasses
- fish will eat bread or cheese
- carry the food in a bag you can close
- taking pictures
- need waterproof camera equipment
- take an extra supply of flashcubes
- if collecting shells, watch for dangerous animals that could be hiding nearby

EXERCISE 4 Listing Supporting Details

Brainstorm a list of at least five supporting details for each subject. Be sure your details suit the writing purpose.

1. how to make friends if you change schools
   (purpose: to explain)
2. how to study for a test
   (purpose: to explain)
3. my favorite holiday
   (purpose: to describe)
4. fall is the best season
   (purpose: to persuade)
5. why dancing is fun
   (purpose: to explain)

Arranging Details in Logical Order

After brainstorming, the next step is to arrange your ideas in a logical order that readers can easily follow.

26e

Types of Order	
CHRONOLOGICAL	Items are arranged in time order.
SPATIAL	Items are arranged in location order.
IMPORTANCE OR DEGREE	Items are arranged in order of least to most or most to least important.
SEQUENTIAL	Steps in a process are arranged in their proper sequence.

As you put your ideas in order, you may find that some do not fit neatly into the pattern. Save these ideas for possible use in your introduction or conclusion. Notice the order of the notes about things to do while snorkeling.

LEAST
DIFFICULT

- feeding fish
- fish will eat bread or cheese
- carry the food in a bag you can close

NEXT IN DIFFICULTY	• collecting shells
	• shells are on the seafloor, sometimes hidden in sea grasses
	• if collecting shells, be on the lookout for dangerous animals that could be hiding near them
MOST DIFFICULT	• taking pictures
	• need waterproof camera equipment
	• take an extra supply of flashcubes
INTRODUCTION	• mastering basic snorkeling techniques

EXERCISE 5 *Arranging Details in Logical Order*

The notes below are for an essay on becoming an Eagle
Scout. Write them in a logical order. List the note that does
not fit separately. Save your work for Exercise 8.

• lowest rank is simply called Boy Scout
• Boy Scouts must be between 10½ and 18 years old
• level above Tenderfoot is Second Class Scout
• First Class Scout comes after being a Second Class Scout
  for at least two months
• Tenderfoot is the first level above Boy Scout; requires at
  least two month's activity in troop
• a Tenderfoot must also take part in a personal growth-
  agreement conference
• the level above First Class Scout is Star Scout
• the level just below Eagle Scout is Life Scout
• to reach each level of scouting, you must demonstrate
  certain skills and scout spirit
• you cannot become a Star Scout until you have been a
  First Class Scout for at least four months
• boys who have been a Life Scout for at least six months
  can begin to work on highest level—Eagle Scout

EXERCISE 6 *On Your Own*

Choose and limit a subject for an essay. Then brainstorm
a list of supporting details and arrange those details in
logical order. Save your work for Exercise 11.

Writing

When your notes are organized, you are ready to begin the second stage of the writing process—writing the first draft. Your goal in writing is to turn your prewriting notes into smoothly connected sentences and paragraphs.

The following diagram shows how the three main parts of an essay are similar to the parts of a paragraph.

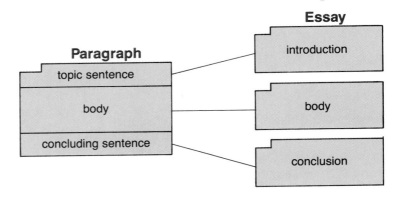

Writing the Introduction

The introduction to an essay must accomplish two main goals. The first is to arouse your reader's interest and make him or her want to read on. The second is to state clearly the main idea of the essay.

In the following introduction on the subject of snorkeling, the sentence stating the main idea is boxed.

INTRODUCTION   Imagine the feeling of suddenly having all of your weight lifted from you. You glide along almost without effort. You feel the coolness of water around you. You see the brilliant colors of fish swimming past you, and the sounds of the world outside are muffled. These are just a few of the pleasures of snorkeling. For those who have mastered the basic techniques,

MAIN IDEA

however, the pleasures are even greater. Instead of simply gliding and observing, an experienced snorkeler can keep busy underwater with several interesting activities.

Use the checklist below when writing an introduction.

Writing an Introduction

A strong introduction
1. captures the reader's attention with an interesting fact, detail, incident, or description.
2. gives background information if needed.
3. includes a sentence expressing the main idea of the essay.
4. does not include such empty expressions as *In this essay I will . . .* or *This essay will be about . . .*

E*XERCISE 7   Improving a Weak Introduction*

The following introduction is for an essay about becoming an Eagle Scout. (*See Exercise 5 on page 429.*) Rewrite it so that it follows the guidelines on page 431.

> Scouting is kind of an interesting subject. This essay will be about what it takes to become an Eagle Scout. To stress the importance of progress, the founder of the Boy Scouts created different levels of scouts. Each new level requires mastering new skills and gaining new experience. The path to becoming the top-level scout, the Eagle Scout, is clear for any boy ready to meet the challenges.

*W**riting the Body*

As you write the body of your essay, keep your reader in mind. Try to make your message as clear as possible. Your prewriting notes will help you focus your thoughts as you write.

26g | Use your notes to write complete, varied sentences with vivid words. Use transitions to connect your thoughts smoothly.

Compare the following essay body with the prewriting notes on pages 428–429. The transitions are printed in heavy type. (*See page 329 for a list of transitions.*)

BODY

One of the easiest and most enjoyable underwater activities is feeding fish. Fish particularly like bread or cheese. If you want to feed fish, carry the food in a bag you can close. **In that way** you can keep hungry fish from swimming inside your food bag. **Another** activity, shell collecting, requires slightly **more** skill. A good shell collector must know where to look for shells that might be hidden in grasses on the seafloor. He or she must **also** recognize dangerous animals that might be hiding near the shells. **A third activity,** taking pictures underwater, requires the **most** skill and equipment. The camera and gear must all be made specially for working underwater. Flashcubes float, so bring along an extra supply of cubes.

EXERCISE 8 Writing a Body Paragraph

Using your work from Exercise 5, write the body paragraph for an essay about becoming an Eagle Scout. Underline each transition that you use.

Writing the Conclusion

A conclusion to an essay is like a farewell. It wraps up the ideas in the essay and provides a strong ending. Notice the feeling of completion in the following conclusion to the essay on snorkeling.

CONCLUSION   Almost anything you do while snorkeling is a pleasure. The nearness to sea creatures, the beauty of a coral reef, and the feel of the water all add up to an unforgettable experience. When you actually interact with the life below by feeding fish, collecting empty shells, or taking action pictures, you will feel even more a part of the mysterious sea.

Use the checklist below when writing a conclusion.

26h

Writing a Conclusion

A strong concluding paragraph
1. emphasizes the main idea without restating it exactly.
2. may refer to ideas in the introduction to round out the essay.
3. does not introduce a completely new idea.
4. does not use such empty expressions as *I have just told you about* . . . or *Now you know about* . . .

433

EXERCISE 9 *Improving a Weak Conclusion*

Read the conclusion to the essay about becoming an Eagle Scout. Then revise it using the guidelines on page 433.

> To advance to each new level, boys must pass certain skill tests and earn certain merit badges. Boys must also demonstrate scout spirit. The challenge of reaching each new level helps keep boys interested in the program. Girl Scouts also have different levels to achieve. Now you know the steps involved in becoming an Eagle Scout.

Writing a Title. When you are satisfied with your first draft, think of a title for your essay. The title should give the reader an idea of what the essay will be about. It should also make your reader curious enough to want to read the entire essay. The following are possible titles for the essay on snorkeling.

TITLES Meeting the Undersea World
Activities for Snorkelers
Underwater Fun

EXERCISE 10 *Writing Titles*

Write three possible titles for the essay about becoming an Eagle Scout.

EXERCISE 11 *On Your Own*

Review what you have learned about writing a first draft. Then using your work from Exercise 6, write the first draft of an essay. Save your work for Exercise 12.

Revising

Once your ideas are down on paper, you can stand back and look at them to see how they can be improved. The following checklist will help you improve your essay.

Checklist for Revising Essays

Checking Your Essay

1. Do you have an interesting introduction that states the main idea of the essay? (*See pages 430–431.*)
2. Do your sentences relate to the main idea? In other words, does your essay have unity? (*See page 327.*)
3. Are your ideas arranged logically with transitions? In other words, is your essay coherent? (*See page 329.*)
4. Do you have a strong conclusion? (*See page 433.*)

Checking Your Paragraphs

5. Does each paragraph in the body of your essay have a topic sentence? (*See page 322.*)
6. Is each paragraph unified? (*See pages 327 and 368.*)
7. Is each paragraph coherent? (*See pages 329 and 370.*)

Checking Your Sentences and Words

8. Did you eliminate short, choppy sentences by combining related sentences? (*See pages 302–306.*)
9. Did you vary the length and beginnings of your sentences? (*See page 309.*)
10. Did you eliminate rambling sentences? (*See page 312.*)
11. Are your sentences free of repetition and empty expressions? (*See pages 313–315.*)
12. Are your words fresh and vivid? (*See pages 295–299.*)

*E*XERCISE 12 *On Your Own*

Use the Checklist for Revising Essays above to improve the first draft of your essay from Exercise 11. Save your work for Exercise 13.

Writing Extra

Some essays need to be revised because they do not include enough supporting details. Essays that lack numerous supporting details are thin and weak.

The following paragraph forms the body of a weakly developed essay about what an alien from outer space might look like. First, list the few details it *does* include. Next, add at least five more details of your own to fill out the list. Finally, rewrite the paragraph to include your new ideas.

The alien's head is huge and pointed. Its eyes are on the sides of its head instead of on the face. Its body is short and squat. The arms and legs of the alien are very different from those of a human. It has seven toes on each foot.

Editing

When you are satisfied with your ideas and organization, you are ready to check your paper carefully for errors. Use the proofreading symbols on page 372 when you edit.

26j

Editing Checklist

1. Are your sentences free of errors in grammar and usage?
2. Did you spell each word correctly?
3. Did you use capital letters where needed?
4. Did you punctuate sentences correctly?
5. Did you indent each paragraph?

The appearance of your composition can be almost as important as its content. A neat paper makes a positive impression on your reader. The following guidelines will help you prepare your final copy.

26k

Correct Form for a Composition

1. Use 8½- by 11-inch paper. Use one side only.
2. Use blue or black ink. If typing, use a black typewriter ribbon and double-space the lines.
3. Put your name, course title, the name of your teacher, and the date in the upper right-hand corner of page 1.
4. Leave a 1½-inch margin at the left and a 1-inch margin at the right. Also leave a 1-inch margin at the bottom.
5. Starting on page 2, number each page in the upper right-hand corner.

EXERCISE 13 On Your Own

Use the Editing Checklist to edit your work from Exercise 12. Then make a final copy of your essay using the proper form.

Spotlight on Writing

A **Writing an Expository Essay.** Use the following notes and illustrations to write an essay.

PURPOSE   To give directions for a magic trick that uses static electricity

AUDIENCE   A younger brother or sister

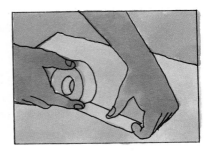

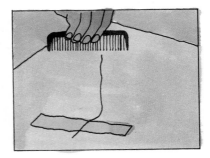

Materials Needed
- 6-inch length of dark thread
- transparent tape that is sticky on both sides
- pocket-sized comb

How to Do the Trick
- stick tape on top of table that will not be damaged when tape is removed
- show thread to audience; tell audience trick will be like Indian rope trick where rope rises in air

- attach one end of thread to top side of tape
- tell audience you need magic wand but all you have is comb; tell them your hair needs combing anyway and run comb through your hair a couple of strokes
- hold comb over free end of thread and say, "Rise, rope!"
- draw up end of thread as high as possible

How the Trick Works

- comb was charged with static electricity when pulled through hair
- thread had no charge
- thread attracted to comb's charge and pulled up by it

—NED ARNOLD AND LOIS ARNOLD, *THE GREAT SCIENCE MAGIC SHOW* (ADAPTED)

B **Writing a Descriptive Essay.** Imagine that you have been on a whale watch with your class. Then write an essay that describes the experience. Include sights, sounds, and smells that will create a vivid picture in the mind of your reader.

PURPOSE   To describe whales seen on a whale watch
AUDIENCE   A classmate who was unable to go on the class trip

C Writing a Persuasive Essay. Imagine that you are the owner of a movie theater in your town. Business has been slow lately because many people in your town have VCR's (video cassette recorders) and are renting movies to watch at home. The VCR's are expensive, but the movies are very inexpensive to rent. Write a persuasive essay to be printed in the local newspaper.

PURPOSE   To convince people to go out to the movies rather than rent a movie to watch at home

AUDIENCE   The people in your town

D Writing a Personal Experience Essay. Think of something you were afraid of recently or in the past. Tell how you started being afraid and how your fears bothered you. Then write down how you overcame that fear. Use your notes to write your essay.

PURPOSE   To explain how you overcame a fear
AUDIENCE   A young child who is afraid of the same thing

E Writing from Your Writer's Notebook. Choose one of the places that you wrote about in your writer's notebook. Then write an essay describing this place for your readers. Also explain to your readers why this ugly place seems beautiful to you.

F Writing Ideas. Write an essay on one of the following subjects or on one of your own. Use the Steps for Writing an Essay on page 441 as a guide.

1. strange coincidences
2. how to do something you are good at
3. things you are looking forward to in the next few years
4. a person you admire and why
5. a place you were afraid of as a child
6. special gifts you have given
7. your first time performing in front of an audience
8. a team effort you took part in
9. three things about yourself you would like to change
10. your favorite pastime

Steps for Writing an Essay

Prewriting

1. Make a list of possible subjects by exploring your interests. (*See page 424.*)
2. Choose one subject from your list. (*See page 425.*)
3. Limit your subject by deciding on your purpose, audience, and focus point. (*See pages 425–426.*)
4. Brainstorm a list of supporting details. (*See pages 426–427.*)
5. Organize your list into a logical order. (*See pages 428–429.*)

Writing

6. Write an introduction that includes a sentence stating the main idea. (*See pages 430–431.*)
7. Use your notes to write the body of your essay with transitions between ideas. (*See pages 432–433.*)
8. Add a concluding paragraph. (*See page 433.*)
9. Add a title. (*See page 434.*)

Revising

10. Put your first draft aside for a while. Then use the Checklist for Revising Essays on page 435 to improve your first draft.

Editing

11. Use the Editing Checklist and the guidelines for correct form on page 437 to polish your essay and make a final copy.

27

Narratives

People of all ages enjoy stories. Through stories people can experience places and situations they might otherwise never know. You have already practiced telling stories in narrative paragraphs. (*See Chapter 23.*) In this chapter you will learn how to write longer stories called narratives.

27a A **narrative** is a well-developed, true or fictional story about characters resolving a conflict or problem.

Your Writer's Notebook

Think of your two favorite television shows. Choose one character from one show and one character from the other show. In your journal write several different stories about what would happen if the two characters met. Use the following questions to help you think of story ideas.

- What would happen if one character stumbled onto the set of the other character's show?
- What would happen if both characters were to come to a party at your house?
- What would happen if the two characters decided to go into business together?

Structure of a Narrative

All narratives have three main parts. The *beginning* of a narrative introduces the characters, the location, the time of the story, and the problem or conflict. The *middle* of the story tells the events in the order in which they happened. The *ending* of the story shows how the problem was finally resolved.

Narratives also have other elements. The following chart shows the other elements in a narrative.

27b

Elements in a Narrative	
NARRATOR	the person telling the story; may be **first person** (if he or she is in the story) or **third person** (if he or she is telling what happened to others)
SETTING	the time and place in which the story takes place
CHARACTERS	the people involved in the story
CONFLICT	the problem at the heart of the story
TRIGGERING EVENT	the event that starts the story rolling
CLIMAX	the point in the story where the conflict or problem is most serious
RESOLUTION	how the problem or conflict is solved
OUTCOME	the way the story ends
DIALOGUE	words spoken by the characters
DESCRIPTION	writing that helps the reader see, hear, feel, taste, or smell what is happening

The parts of the following narrative are labeled at the left. First read the story through. Then go back and study its parts.

The Sleepwalking Pilot

There used to be an excellent pilot on the Mississippi River, a Mr. X, who was a sleepwalker. Late one night, his boat was approaching a dangerous part of the river. Since the night was dark, the other pilot, George Ealer, was thinking about asking Mr. X to help. Suddenly the door to the pitch black pilothouse opened. The undefinable shape that now entered had Mr. X's voice. It said, "Let me take her, George. I've seen this place since you have, and it is so crooked that I reckon I can run it myself easier than I could tell you how to do it."

"It is kind of you, and I swear *I* am willing. I haven't got another drop of perspiration left in me. I have been spinning around and around the wheel like a squirrel."

So the black phantom took over the wheel without saying anything, steadying the waltzing steamer with a turn or two. Then he stood at ease, coaxing her a little to this side and then to that, as gently and sweetly as if the time had been noonday. Ealer, panting and breathless, finally said, "Well, I thought I knew how to steer a steamboat, but that was another mistake of mine."

X said nothing but went serenely on with his work. He rang for the sounding lines, he rang to slow down the steam, and he worked the boat carefully and neatly. As the water became more and more shallow, he stopped the engines entirely, and the dead silence and suspense of drifting followed. When the most shallow water was struck, he cracked on the steam, carried her handsomely over, and then began to work her for the next shallow spot. The same patient, heedful use of sounding lines and engines followed. Then, under a tremendous head of steam, the boat went swinging over the reef and away into deep water and safety!

DESCRIPTION

Ealer let his long-held breath out in a great, relieving sigh. "That's the sweetest piece of piloting that was ever done on the Mississippi River!" There was no reply, and he added, "Just hold her five minutes longer, partner, and let me run down and get a cup of coffee."

A minute later, Ealer was comforting himself with coffee. Just then the night watchman happened in and noticing Ealer exclaimed, "Who is at the wheel, sir?"

"X."

"Dart for the pilothouse, quicker than lightning!"

CLIMAX

The next moment both men were flying up to the pilothouse, three steps at a jump! Nobody there! The great steamer was whistling down the middle of the river at her own sweet will! The watchman shot out of the place again. Ealer

RESOLUTION

seized the wheel, set an engine back with power,

445

and held his breath while the boat reluctantly swung away from a sandbar.

By and by the watchman came back and said, "Didn't that lunatic tell you he was asleep?"

"No."

OUTCOME

"Well, he was. I found him walking along on top. I put him to bed."

"Well, I think I'll stay by next time he has one of those fits. But I hope he'll have them often. You just ought to have seen him take this boat through that crossing. And if he can do that kind of piloting when he is asleep, what *couldn't* he do if he was dead!"

—MARK TWAIN, *LIFE ON THE MISSISSIPPI* (ADAPTED)

EXERCISE 1   *Analyzing a Narrative*

Reread the narrative on pages 444–446. Then write answers to the following questions.

1. What is the setting of this narrative? (Where and when does the story take place?)
2. List all the characters in the story.
3. Is the narrator a character in the story or does he only tell what happens to other people?
4. What is the conflict or problem in this story?
5. In your own words, summarize the events in this story.
6. How can you recognize which parts are dialogue?
7. Choose one sentence of description from the story and write it on your paper.

Prewriting

Narratives can be true or imaginary. They can be about what happened to you, to your friends or family, to people in history, or to imaginary characters.

Choosing a Subject

Many good stories tell about events that are out of the ordinary. Unusual happenings, such as a sleepwalking pilot, keep readers interested. When choosing a subject, search your memory and imagination for experiences that stand out as unusual or especially important.

27c Choose a subject that includes unusual, memorable events.

EXERCISE 2 Thinking of Subjects for Narratives

Answer each question with as many items as you can.

1. What has happened to me in the last year that I will probably never forget?
2. What experiences have taught me a valuable lesson?
3. What events in history would I like to have witnessed?
4. Who are my personal heroes? What have they done that would make a good story?
5. At what times in my life have I overcome a problem?
6. What funny things have happened to me?
7. At what times in my life have I felt in danger?
8. What embarrassing moments have I experienced?
9. What stories do my family members like to tell?
10. What unusual things have happened to me when I have been away from home?

EXERCISE 3 Choosing a Subject

Circle the incident in Exercise 2 that is most memorable or unusual. Save your work for Exercise 8.

Determining Point of View

Every story has a narrator, the person whose written "voice" is telling the story. Readers see the story unfolding through the eyes, or *point of view*, of the narrator. If the narrator takes part in the story, the narrative is said to have a *first person* point of view. If the narrator tells what happens to others and is not a character in the story, the narrative has a *third person* point of view.

Compare the two paragraphs below. Both introduce the same narrative. They are each told from a different point of view, however. Notice the different pronouns that are used in each one.

FIRST PERSON POINT OF VIEW
Last year, on an early spring evening, **I** was looking forward to having the house to **myself.** **My** parents were going out to dinner, and **my** younger sister was staying overnight at a friend's house. For about four hours, **I** would be alone in the house. **I** could play **my** records as loud as **I** wanted, or **I** could lounge around in **my** comfortable clothes and put off **my** chores until the next day. Little did **I** know what was in store for **me!**

THIRD PERSON POINT OF VIEW
Last year, on an early spring evening, Mark was looking forward to having the house to **himself. His** parents were going out to dinner, and **his** younger sister was staying overnight at a friend's house. For about four hours, **he** would be alone in the house. **He** could play **his** records as loud as **he** wanted, or **he** could lounge around in **his** comfortable clothes and put off **his** chores until the next day. Little did **he** know what was in store for **him!**

27d ▶ Use **first person point of view** if you are a character in the story. Use **third person point of view** if you are writing about what happened to others.

E*XERCISE 4* *Writing from Different Points of View*

1. Write a short paragraph telling how you met your best friend. Use first person point of view.
2. Write a short paragraph telling about something unusual that happened to a friend or family member. Use third person point of view. Call the person by name and use third person pronouns.
3. Write a short paragraph telling what a mannequin in a store would see if it were alive. Pretend you are the mannequin and use first person point of view.

*S*ketching Characters

To help you write your story, make a list of all the characters who play a part in the events. Then describe each one in a brief character sketch. Suppose, for example, that you were writing a story that includes yourself, your younger brother, and your father. Your character sketches might be as follows. Notice that they include personality traits as well as physical descriptions.

myself:	age 13, shy, a loner, tall for age
my younger brother:	age 7, outgoing, mischievous, clumsy, red curly hair
my father:	age 38, piercing eyes that tell you when you've done something wrong, impatient, good sense of humor

27e Write a brief **character sketch** for each of the people who appear in your story.

E*XERCISE 5* *Sketching Characters*

Write a brief character sketch of the following people.

1. yourself
2. a friend
3. an older relative
4. someone you just met

449

Creating a Setting

Once you have chosen a subject and a point of view, you can plan the details of your story's setting. First determine the location and time of your story. Then add details that will bring the setting to life. Notice how the following details give the setting a vivid mood.

WHERE at home
  • house is on a quiet street
  • lights were on in most of the house
  • open windows let cool breeze come in

WHEN early spring evening
  • drizzling rain outside
  • parents left at 6:30 P.M.
  • trees outside my bedroom window were rustling

27f ▶ Create a **setting** by determining the time and location of your story. Add details to bring the setting to life.

EXERCISE 6 *Creating Settings*

Use your imagination to add at least three details to the following locations and times for stories.

EXAMPLE   Location: school
Time: early Monday morning in winter

POSSIBLE   Location: • school empty
ANSWERS   • modern building
                     • locked classrooms
         Time: • first day after winter vacation
               • snowstorm raging
               • 6:30 A.M.

1. Location: a big city   Time: autumn
2. Location: a zoo   Time: night
3. Location: a hospital   Time: morning
4. Location: school cafeteria   Time: noon
5. Location: an amusement park   Time: summer

Writing Extra

Some stories are timeless. Fairy tales, for example, have been told and retold for hundreds of years. One way to add freshness to a familiar story is to cast it in a different, modern setting. Think of what would happen, for example, if the story of sleeping beauty were set in New York City. Practice creating new settings for old stories by doing the following activity.

1. Choose a fairy tale and create a fresh, modern setting for it.
2. Write a paragraph telling how the story would change and develop in the new setting.

Listing Events in Chronological Order

The last step before writing your narrative is listing all the events that make up the story. When listing events, use the questions below. Your list will then be in chronological order, the order in which the events occurred. This order will help your readers follow the story as it unfolds.

- What happened to start the story rolling?
- What happened next? Next? Next?
- What is the climax of the story?
- What finally happened to resolve the conflict?
- How does the story end?

27g List all the events in your story in **chronological order.** Include the event that starts the story in motion, the climax of the story, the resolution of the conflict, and the outcome.

EXERCISE 7 Listing Events

Choose two of the following subjects. Then use the questions above to list the events that make up each story.

1. a surprisingly painless visit to the dentist
2. a time you won (or lost) something
3. a time when you had to eat something you hated
4. your proudest moment
5. the day everything went wrong

EXERCISE 8 On Your Own

Using your work from Exercise 3, write a plan for your narrative. Include the following information. Save your work for Exercise 12.

Conflict or problem:
Point of view:
Characters, with brief descriptions:
Setting, with brief description:
Events:

Writing

Good stories draw readers into the action and make them feel involved. As you work on the first draft of your narrative, keep your readers in mind. Add details that will make your narrative more interesting but leave out unnecessary details that slow the story down.

Writing the Beginning

The opening scenes of a movie show viewers where and when the story takes place, who the main characters are, and what the story will be about. The beginning of a narrative must accomplish the same purposes. In addition, it must capture the reader's attention. While movies can use stirring music and pictures, a narrative must capture interest through words.

Notice how the following narrative beginning accomplishes all of these purposes.

BEGINNING

THIRD PERSON
NARRATOR

It was hot on June 28, 1778. Even at daybreak the air was still. Later in the day the temperature climbed to 100 degrees in the shade. Molly Hays, though a strong, sturdy woman, sometimes felt as if the Revolutionary War would never end. Even before the Declaration of Independence was signed, she had gone into battle with her husband. Along with other wives, she did washing and cooking. She worked as a nurse during the fighting, and she also learned about cannons. John Hays, who had been a gunner before he joined the infantry, turned to his wife and said, "Get your things together, Molly. We're moving." The Battle of Monmouth had begun.

—ELIZABETH ANTICAGLIA, *HEROINES OF '76*

(ADAPTED)

453

When writing your narrative beginning, include all of the following elements.

27h

Beginning a Narrative

1. Set the time and place of the story, adding details that capture the reader's attention.
2. Introduce the characters in the story.
3. Provide any background information needed.
4. Include the event that starts the story in motion.

EXERCISE 9 Writing Story Beginnings

Think of a time when you were helped by a friend or family member (when you were sick, when you broke your leg, or when you needed help studying for a test, for example). Then use the guidelines above to write a beginning for your story. Use first person point of view.

Writing the Middle

The middle of your narrative tells the story, event by event. As you read more of the narrative about Molly Hays, notice how the events are told in chronological order.

MIDDLE

CHRONOLOGICAL ORDER

DESCRIPTION

The burst of muskets never stopped. The air was cloudy with gunsmoke, and the heat smothered everyone. Molly Hays found a cool spring. Grabbing her pitcher, she scooped up water for the soldiers. One by one, soldiers dropped from gunshots or heat. "Chew on this cold rag," Molly said as she bent over a hurt soldier. Pitcher after pitcher she carried, until the soldiers began to call her Molly Pitcher. She swabbed blood, cleaned out wounds, wrapped cloths around arms and legs. Running through musket fire, Molly Hays looked down at a young soldier.

DIALOGUE

"Mam," he gasped, "get away. You will be shot." Gently she swung him on her strong shoulders and carried him out of the line of fire.

TRANSITIONS

She ran from stream to soldier, from soldier to stream. Then she spotted her husband loading a cannon.

"John! Why aren't you with the infantry?"

John Hays pointed to the ground where a soldier lay dead.

"I am taking his place."

BUILD-UP OF CONFLICT

Molly was filling her pitcher again when she saw her husband fall, badly wounded. She ran to him, when an officer spoke.

"Please move on, mam. We are going to move this gun away."

CLIMAX

"Give me that rammer staff!" cried Molly. She swabbed, loaded the cartridge, and charged the cannon. "Aim! Fire!" Through the sweltering afternoon, she swabbed, loaded, and fired.

Use the guidelines below when writing your narrative.

Writing the Narrative Middle

1. Tell the events in chronological order, using transitions to show the passing of time. (*See page 452.*)
2. Build on the conflict, or problem, until the action reaches a climax, or high point.
3. Use dialogue to show what the characters are thinking.
4. Use description to bring the events to life.

EXERCISE 10 *Adding Transitions*

The following short narrative lacks transitions. Rewrite the story, adding transitions where you see a blank. Choose the transitions from the following list.

later that evening	finally
as soon as I was dressed	soon
after lunch	about an hour

When Saturday arrived, I woke up with a heavy feeling. This was the day that my best friend, Katy, was moving away. _____, I walked the familiar steps down the block to Katy's house. The moving van was filling up. I stayed for

_____ and then went back home. _____ I heard Katy's knock at the door. She said she had to come by for one last look at the house she had spent so much time in. _____ we walked back to her house for a final goodbye. When the van _____ pulled away, I could no longer hold back my tears. _____ I pulled out the photo album and looked at all the pictures of Katy and me growing up together. I knew we would always be friends.

EXERCISE 11   Writing Dialogue

Write about ten lines of dialogue between you and a friend. Choose a subject for your conversation, such as whether or not to try out for the school play. Review the rules for writing dialogue on page 273.

Writing the Ending

The ending of the story must tell the reader the *resolution of the conflict* and the *outcome of the events*. Notice how the brief ending to the story about Molly Hays completes the action and brings the story to a close.

RESOLUTION
AND OUTCOME

After the battle, General Washington asked Molly, "Madam, who are you?"

"Mary Ludwig Hays, sir," she replied. "They call me Molly."

"You are now *Sergeant* Molly," he replied.

—ELIZABETH ANTICAGLIA,

HEROINES OF '76 (ADAPTED)

27j   End a narrative by telling how the conflict in the story was **resolved.** Tell the final **outcome** of the events.

EXERCISE 12   On Your Own

Review what you have learned about writing a first draft on pages 453–457. Then use your work from Exercise 8 to write your narrative. Save your work for Exercise 14.

Revising

The following checklist will help you revise your narrative.

27k

Checklist for Revising Narratives

1. Does the beginning of your story give the setting, capture attention, introduce characters, and include the triggering event? (*See pages 443–444 and 453–454.*)
2. Does the middle tell the events in chronological order with transitions? (*See pages 452 and 454–456.*)
3. Does your narrative build on the conflict until the action reaches a climax? (*See pages 443–445 and 455.*)
4. Did you use dialogue and description to bring your narrative to life? (*See pages 443–445 and 454–455.*)
5. Does the ending show how the conflict was resolved and bring the story to a close? (*See pages 445–446 and 457.*)
6. Did you choose the appropriate point of view and stick to it throughout the story? (*See page 448.*)

EXERCISE 13 *Revising Titles*

A title should capture your reader's attention. Revise the titles below to make them specific and colorful.

EXAMPLE   A Summer Adventure
ANSWER   Seaside Safari

1. A Camping Experience
2. The Big Game
3. Embarrassing Moments
4. My First Plane Ride
5. The School Dance
6. Another New Diet
7. My Clumsy Brother
8. Our Funny Neighbors
9. Lunch in the Cafeteria
10. A Cooking Disaster

EXERCISE 14 *On Your Own*

Write a title for the narrative you wrote in Exercise 12. Then use the Checklist for Revising Narratives above to revise your first draft. Save your work for Exercise 16.

*E*diting

Using dialogue calls for special attention in the editing stage. The following checklist will help you polish your final draft. Use the proofreading symbols on page 372 as you edit.

Editing Checklist

1. Is your story free of errors in grammar and usage?
2. Did you punctuate and indent dialogue correctly? (*See page 273*.)
3. Did you spell and capitalize words correctly?
4. Is your handwriting clear? Are your margins even?

*E*XERCISE 15 *Editing Dialogue*

The folk song "Arkansas Traveler" tells of a traveler who comes upon an old man sitting on his front porch in the rain playing a fiddle. Rewrite the following narrative version of this song, adding punctuation and capital letters where needed. Remember to indent each time there is a change of speaker.

Sir, your roof is leaking like a waterfall the traveler said. Why don't you mend it? The old man, still playing his fiddle, answered I couldn't mend it now. It's a rainy day. Well said the traveler that's quite true. This is what I think you should do. On the first nice day, get busy. Patch up your roof until it's good and tight. Get along said the old man for you give me a pain! If you're so smart, you should know that my roof never leaks when it doesn't rain.

*E*XERCISE 16 *On Your Own*

Use the Editing Checklist above to edit your work from Exercise 14.

Spotlight on Writing

A **Writing a First Person Narrative.** Imagine yourself in each scene below. Then choose one and write a first person narrative. Use the Steps for Writing on page 463 as a guide.

B **Writing a Third Person Narrative.** Each of the characters shown below could be the main character of a narrative. Write a brief character sketch of each one. Include personality traits as well as physical descriptions. Then choose one and write a third person narrative starring that character. Use the Steps for Writing on page 463 as a guide.

C **Writing a Suspense-Filled Narrative.** The picture above shows the climax, or high point, of a story. Use your imagination to list the events leading up to this point, the resolution, and the outcome. Then write your narrative.

D **Writing from Your Writer's Notebook.** Choose one of the stories that you wrote in your journal. Then write a dialogue between the two television characters.

E **Writing Ideas.** Use your work from Exercise 2 or one of the subjects below to write a narrative. Use the Steps for Writing on page 463 as a guide.

Subjects for Nonfiction Narratives
1. the first time you stayed away from home
2. a dangerous experience
3. a story of friendship between you and an animal
4. the time you were left in charge

Subjects for Fiction Narratives
1. a close encounter with an alien from outer space
2. finding a lost treasure
3. a car that could talk
4. meeting someone who looked exactly like you

Steps for Writing a Narrative

Prewriting

1. Drawing on your own experiences, make a list of events that include memorable or unusual happenings. Then choose one subject. (*See page 447.*)
2. Determine the point of view. (*See page 448.*)
3. Write a brief character sketch for every person in your story. (*See page 449.*)
4. Create a setting for your story. (*See pages 450–451.*)
5. List all the events in your story in chronological order. (*See page 452.*)

Writing

6. Write the beginning of your story. Be sure to capture attention, introduce characters, give the setting, and include the triggering event. (*See pages 453–454.*)
7. Write the middle of your story. Tell the events in chronological order with transitions. Use dialogue and description to bring the events to life. Build on the conflict at the heart of your story, bringing the action to a climax. (*See pages 454–456.*)
8. Write the ending. Tell how the conflict is resolved and bring the story to a close. (*See page 457.*)
9. Add a title that will capture your reader's attention.

Revising

10. Use the Checklist for Revising Narratives on page 458 to check all the elements of your narrative.

Editing

11. Use the Editing Checklist on page 459 to polish your final draft.

28

Reports

One way to learn about a subject is to write about it. When you try to put your thoughts into words, you discover new ideas in the process. By the time you have finished your work, you have become something of an expert on your chosen subject.

Because writing is a learning process, you will be asked to write often in school. One common assignment is the research report. It requires that you read sources carefully and then use your best thinking and writing skills to understand and explain them.

Your Writer's Notebook

Subject ideas for reports can come from many different places. To help you think of ideas for reports, answer each question below with at least three items. Then in your journal write down everything you already know about each subject. Also write any questions that come to mind.

- What television shows or movies have you seen recently that involved subjects you would like to read more about?
- What have you read about lately (in textbooks or other books and magazines) that you would like to learn more about?

Research Reports

When you write essays, you often draw on your own knowledge and experience for ideas. When you write research reports, on the other hand, you draw on the knowledge and experience of others. You acquire this knowledge by doing research—reading books and magazines and sometimes talking to experts.

28a A **research report** is a composition of three or more paragraphs that uses information from books, magazines, and other expert sources.

The three main parts of a report are the introduction, the body, and the conclusion. In addition, a report ends with a page that lists your sources of information.

Structure of a Report

TITLE	• suggests the subject of the report
INTRODUCTION	• captures the reader's attention • provides any background information that your reader may need to know • contains a sentence expressing the main idea of the report
BODY	• supports the main idea stated in the introduction • follows the order of your outline • includes specific information from your sources
CONCLUSION	• brings the report to a close • summarizes the main idea • includes a comment that shows the importance of your subject
SOURCE PAGE	• lists your sources of information • appears at the end of the report

*P*rewriting

Planning a research report requires some detective work to find the library materials you need. (See Chapter 34 for information about using the library.) The right supplies will help you keep track of your information as you collect it. These include a folder with pockets, index cards, paper clips, and rubber bands.

*C*hoosing and Limiting a Subject

A subject for a research report must pass two tests. The first is *Are you genuinely interested in learning more about the subject?* The second is *Does your subject require research in books and magazines?* Compare the subjects below. Those in the first column are not suitable for research reports since they do not require research.

PERSONAL EXPERIENCE	RESEARCH
how I spent Memorial Day	the history of Memorial Day
how I trained my dog	training guide dogs
summertime activities	why summers are warm

To find a subject, brainstorm a list of subjects that require research. Then use the following guidelines to choose one.

28b

Choosing a Subject

1. Choose a subject you would like to know more about.
2. Choose a subject your readers might like to know more about.
3. Choose a subject on which there will be enough information in the library.

Once you have chosen a general subject, the next step is to limit it. Your subject should be limited enough to allow you to cover it thoroughly in a short report.

28c

Ways to Limit a Subject

1. Divide the subject into its smaller parts.
   EXAMPLE   training guide dogs for the blind
   PARTS   basic obedience training
             training for crossing streets
             training for around the house
2. Limit the subject to a certain time, place, or person.
   EXAMPLE   training guide dogs for the blind
   TIME   how the first guide dogs were trained
   PLACE   how dogs are trained at San Rafael, California
   PERSON   how Dorothy Eustis helped found the guide
             dog program in the United States

EXERCISE 1   Identifying Subjects That Need Research

Decide whether each subject is suitable for a research report. Indicate your answer by writing *personal experience* or *research* after the proper number.

1. robots
2. popular spots in your neighborhood
3. the history of your neighborhood
4. efforts to protect the wildlife in the Everglades
5. your trip to the Everglades
6. differences among wide-body airplanes
7. clubs at your school
8. packing a picnic lunch
9. what causes thunder and lightning
10. how to keep safe in a thunderstorm

EXERCISE 2   Limiting a Subject

For each general subject, write two limited subjects that would be suitable for a short report.

1. trains
2. music
3. deserts
4. police
5. the moon
6. the Grand Canyon
7. polar bears
8. the circus
9. telephones
10. volleyball

Gathering Information

After you have limited your subject, think about what you need to learn to write a report. A good way to plan your research is to jot down some questions that you want your report to answer. Suppose you had chosen the subject of sightings of UFO's (Unidentified Flying Objects). Your research questions might appear as follows.

- What different kinds of sightings are there?
- How do scientists classify these sightings?
- What is a close encounter?
- How many kinds of close encounters are there?

The guidelines below will help you find the answers.

28d

Steps for Gathering Information

1. Begin by checking an encyclopedia. This will give you an overview of your subject. It may also contain a list of books with more information.
2. Use the card catalog in your library to find more books on your subject. (*See pages 577–580.*)
3. Check *The Readers' Guide to Periodical Literature* for magazine articles on your subject. (*See pages 585–586.*)
4. Make a list of all your sources. For each source, record the author, title, publisher's name and location, date of publication, and call number.

Following is a list of sources about UFO sightings.

ENCYCLOPEDIA   J. Allen Hynek, "Unidentified Flying Objects," *World Book Encyclopedia*, 1985 ed.

BOOKS   *The UFO Handbook* by Allen Hendry, New York, Doubleday & Company, 1979, 523 HE

The UFO Experience by J. Allen Hynek, Chicago, Henry Regnery Company, 1972, 523 HY

MAGAZINES *Newsweek,* July 25, 1983, p. 21, "E.T. Phone Your Lawyers Immediately" *Science Digest,* November 1981, pp. 86–88, "Scientists Who Have Seen UFOs" by P. Huyghe

EXERCISE 3 *Gathering Information*

Choose two of the subjects below. Then list five sources for each one. Include at least one magazine. Follow the Steps for Gathering Information on page 468, including step 4.

1. the intelligence of dolphins
2. submarines
3. how dinosaurs became extinct
4. careers in television
5. computers used in medicine
6. ghost towns in the West
7. experimental aircraft
8. how Sacajawea guided Lewis and Clark
9. what Diane Fossey learned about gorillas
10. how NASA names its spacecraft and missions

Taking Notes

Once you have found your sources, check the table of contents and the index to find the information you need. If you are working with a magazine article, skim it quickly. Then carefully read the sections that relate to your subject and take notes in your own words on note cards.

The following excerpt is from one of the books about UFO's. Read it carefully. Then study the sample note card and the guidelines that follow it.

> **Close Encounter (CE): a sighting of a UFO within 500 feet of the witness.** With the introduction of Close Encounters, we arrive at some of the most convincing reports—those sightings that are so close to the witness that the possibility of misinterpretation is reduced. *Close Encounters of the First Kind (CE I's)* are those encounters in which the UFO does not influence the environment in any way. Following are some common features of UFO's as described in accounts of CE I's.
>
> Appearance: variety of shapes; many discs, ovals, footballs; some domes and other appendages
> Behavior: hovering; rotation; rapid acceleration; very steep ascent/descent; silence even though near observer

Sample Note Card

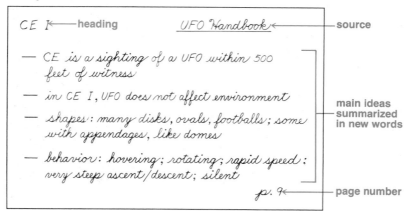

CE I ←—heading   *UFO Handbook* ←——— source

— CE is a sighting of a UFO within 500 feet of witness
— in CE I, UFO does not affect environment
— shapes: many disks, ovals, footballs; some with appendages, like domes
— behavior: hovering; rotating; rapid speed; very steep ascent/descent; silent

main ideas summarized in new words

p. 9 ←——— page number

28e

Taking Notes

1. Write the title of your source in the upper right-hand corner of your index card.
2. Identify the part of the subject being discussed with a heading in the upper left-hand corner.
3. Begin a new card for each new part of your subject.
4. Summarize main points in your own words.
5. Record the page number containing the information.
6. Clip together all cards from the same source.

EXERCISE 4 *Taking Notes*

Using an index card, take notes on the following information from page 109 of the *World Book Encyclopedia*.

A giant panda eats chiefly bamboo shoots, though it also eats some other plants and occasionally feeds on fish and small rodents. Two species of bamboo make up most of the animal's diet. About every 100 years, all the plants of these 2 species produce seeds and then die. This event occurred most recently in the late 1970s. It takes several years for the seeds to grow into plants that can provide food for pandas. By 1980, Chinese scientists reported that at least one fourth of the giant-panda population had starved to death.

Writing Extra

The ability to summarize will help you take notes. When you summarize, you use your own words to record the writer's most important points, leaving out unnecessary details. Read the paragraph below. Then summarize it by completing the activities that follow it.

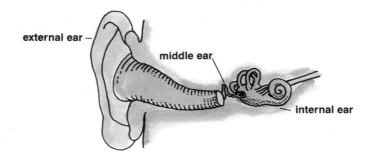

external ear

middle ear

internal ear

The Human Ear

The human ear consists of three parts—the external ear, the middle ear, and the internal ear—each of which performs different functions. The *external ear* receives sound waves traveling through the air and directs them toward the middle ear. The *middle ear* concentrates sound waves and conducts them to the internal ear. The *internal ear* converts sound vibrations to nervous impulses that are then carried by the acoustic nerve to the brain. Only when nervous impulses reach the brain do we hear sound.

—JOAN ELMA RAHN, *EARS, HEARING, AND BALANCE*

1. Look up the meaning of any unfamiliar words and write definitions for them in your own words.
2. Write the main idea of this paragraph in your own words. (State the main idea in one sentence of no more than nine words.)
3. Write 3 more sentences summarizing the rest of the paragraph. (The 3 sentences should contain a total of no more than 27 words.)

*O*utlining

Once your research is completed, you can begin to outline your report. First, use the headings on your note cards to organize your information into categories. Next, arrange your categories in a logical order. (*See page 428.*) Assign a Roman numeral to each category, or main topic. Finally, add subtopics under the Roman numerals by finding related ideas in your notes. Notes that do not fit into the categories can be saved for possible use in your introduction or conclusion.

28f ▸ Convert your note card categories into the main topics of an **outline.** Use your note cards to add subtopics.

The categories on UFO sightings can be arranged logically in order of degree.

SUBJECT	types of UFO sightings
MAIN TOPIC	I. Distant sightings
SUBTOPICS	A. Nocturnal lights
	B. Daylight discs
	C. Radar-Visuals
MAIN TOPIC	II. Close encounters with UFO's
SUBTOPICS	A. First type
	B. Second type
MAIN TOPIC	III. Close encounters with alien creatures
	A. Third type
	B. How scientists view third type

28g ▸

Outline Form

1. Use Roman numerals for main topics.
2. Use capital letters for subtopics.
3. Always include at least two subtopics under each main topic.
4. Indent as shown in the model above.
5. Capitalize the first word of each entry.

EXERCISE 5 Outlining

Use the notes below to complete the following outline.

SUBJECT   developments in police technology

   I. Ancient forerunners of police technology
     A.
     B.
  II. Advances in the 19th century
     A.
     B.
     C.
III. Modern developments
     A.
     B.
     C.
     D.

Notes

- Use of fingerprints, handwriting, and detailed word descriptions by ancient crime fighters
- Adoption of fingerprint classification system by Scotland Yard in 1901
- Telegraph first used by British bobbies in 1849
- Use of unscientific lie detector tests in ancient societies
- Telephone first used by Washington, D. C. police in 1878
- 1950 invention of transistor and police transmitter-receivers
- Automobile first used by Ohio police in 1899
- Bugs and wiretaps introduced after World War II
- Use of computers currently on the rise

EXERCISE 6 On Your Own

Choose one of the subjects listed in Exercise 3 on page 469 or one of your own. Then use what you have learned about prewriting on pages 468–473 to plan a research report. Save your work for Exercise 11.

*W*riting

After outlining your report, you are ready to write the first draft. Your first draft should include all three parts of a report—introduction, body, and conclusion.

*W*riting the Introduction

Think about your readers as you write the introduction. Remember that they have not done the research you have just completed. They do not even know what your report is about until they begin reading. Use the following guidelines to write a strong introduction.

Writing an Introduction

A strong introduction
1. captures the reader's attention.
2. provides any background information needed.
3. contains a sentence expressing the main idea of the report.

The following introductions show the difference between a focused beginning and an unfocused beginning. Both introduce the subject of UFO sightings. Only the second, however, clearly focuses on the main idea.

UNFOCUSED INTRODUCTION   Have you ever noticed something unusual in the night sky? If so, you are not alone. Thousands of people have reported seeing unidentified flying objects (UFO's) over the years. Some have even taken pictures of these objects. Many of the pictures have proved to be touched up or faked in some other way. Scientists are collecting many records of UFO sightings. They doubt, however, that any UFO was ever a spacecraft from another intelligent culture. UFO's continue to baffle astronomers and other scientists.

FOCUSED
INTRODUCTION

Have you ever noticed something unusual in the night sky? If so, you are not alone. Thousands of people have reported seeing unidentified flying objects (UFO's) over the years. One expert, J. Allen Hynek, has devised a way to classify the thousands of sightings that are regularly reported to the authorities. His system is based on the distance between the UFO and the witness.

MAIN IDEA

EXERCISE 7 Writing Main Idea Statements

Read each of the following simple outlines. Then write a sentence that clearly expresses the main idea of the report.

1. SUBJECT   how television commercials attract attention
   I. Loud, irritating ads
   II. Humorous ads
   III. Fantasy ads

2. SUBJECT   household aids for deaf people
   I. Close-captioned television programs
   II. Special telephones
   III. Hearing-ear dogs

3. SUBJECT   climate extremes in the United States
   I. Desert heat in Southwest
   II. Frigid cold in Alaska
   III. Tropical climate of Hawaii

4. SUBJECT   nutritional value of milk
   I. Protein
   II. Calcium
   III. Vitamins

5. SUBJECT   three branches of government
   I. Legislative branch that makes laws
   II. Executive branch that carries out laws
   III. Judicial branch that interprets laws

*W*riting the Body

When you are satisfied with your introduction, you can use your outline to help you draft the body of your report. Follow the order of your outline and write complete sentences and paragraphs. Use transitions to guide your reader from idea to idea. (*See page 329.*)

Compare the following body of a report on UFO sightings to the outline on page 473.

FROM ROMAN
NUMERAL I
IN OUTLINE

The first main category of UFO's in Hynek's system may be called distant sightings. Any sighting in which the witness is more than 500 feet away from the UFO falls into this group. Within this group there are three main types of sightings. One is the nocturnal light, which is any light seen in the night sky that cannot be explained. A second is the daylight disc. Into this group fall any unidentified objects of any shape seen during the daytime. The last type

FROM ROMAN
NUMERAL II

of distant sighting is the radar-visual. This group includes UFO's that are seen by a witness and recorded on radar at the same time.

The second main group of UFO sightings is made up of those that occur within 500 feet of a witness. These are called close encounters. This group is also divided into three smaller groups. The Close Encounter of the First Kind is a sighting in which the witness sees a UFO but feels no effects from it. No trace of the UFO is left after a Close Encounter of the First Kind. A Close Encounter of the Second Kind, however, does involve evidence of the encounter. The evidence may include scorch marks on the grass, footprints, odors, headaches, or electrical disturbances.

FROM ROMAN
NUMERAL III

All UFO sightings are controversial. None is more so than the last type of close encounter, the Close Encounter of the Third Kind. In this kind of sighting, a witness reports seeing occupants in the UFO. Sometimes the occupants are short; sometimes they are human-sized. Some people claim to have been taken aboard the craft. Because their accounts are often fantastic, many scientists disregard these reports.

28i ▶ Use your outline to write the paragraphs in the **body** of your report. Write a paragraph for each main topic.

EXERCISE 8 Recognizing Transitions

List the transitions used in the body of the report on pages 477–478.

1. Write five transitions that have been used in the first paragraph.
2. Write four transitions that have been used in the second paragraph.
3. Write two transitions that have been used in the third paragraph.

Writing the Conclusion

Use the guidelines below to write a strong conclusion.

28j

Writing a Conclusion

1. Restate your main idea in new words.
2. Add a comment that shows the importance of your subject or an insight about it.
3. Round out the report by referring to an idea in the introduction without repeating it exactly.
4. Avoid introducing a new, unrelated idea.
5. Avoid such phrases as *Now you have seen . . .* or *I have just told you about . . .*

The following conclusion to the report on UFO sightings reinforces the main idea and shows its importance.

CONCLUSION

Many distant UFO sightings can eventually be explained as weather balloons, comets, meteors, or even hoaxes. Close encounters are more difficult to explain, since the nearness of the witness leaves little room for mistaking the object. Some scientists dismiss all close encounters as figments of the witnesses' imaginations. Others are keeping an open mind. With the help of Hynek's system of classifying UFO's, they continue to collect reports. They hope someday an explainable pattern will emerge.

Once you have finished your first draft, give your report a title. Your title should catch your reader's interest and indicate what the report is about.

EXERCISE 9 Writing a Title

Write two possible titles for the report on UFO's. (*See pages 476–479.*)

*L*isting Sources

The final page of your report should contain a list of your sources. Center the word *Sources* at the top. Then list each source in alphabetical order according to the author's last name. If the name is not given, use the first word in the title. The following examples show the correct form and punctuation for different kinds of sources.

28k

Correct Form for Sources Page

BOOKS	Hendry, Allen. *The UFO Handbook.* New York: Doubleday & Company, 1979.
MAGAZINES	Huyghe, P. "Scientists Who Have Seen UFOs." *Science Digest* November 1981: 86–88.
ENCYCLOPEDIAS	Hynek, J. Allen. "Unidentified Flying Objects." *World Book Encyclopedia.* 1985 ed.

---

*E*XERCISE 10 *Preparing a Sources Page*

The following sources are on the subject of theatrical make-up. Prepare a sources page in correct form.

1. an article in *Horizon* magazine by Donald Chase called "The Godfather of Movie Make-Up," appearing in the May-June issue of 1982 on pages 14–19
2. a book called *The American Movies: A Pictorial Encyclopedia* by Paul Mitchell, published in 1979 by Galahad Publishing Co. in New York
3. an article called "Motion Pictures" by Arthur Knight in the 1985 edition of *World Book Encyclopedia*

*E*XERCISE 11 *On Your Own*

Use your outline from Exercise 6 to write the first draft of your report. Save your work for Exercise 12.

Revising

A report should flow smoothly and be easy to follow. Before revising, set your report aside for a while. Later imagine you are a reader seeing it for the first time. Then use the checklist below to improve your first draft.

Checklist for Revising Reports

Checking Your Report

1. Does your introduction contain a statement expressing the main idea of the report? (*See pages 475–476.*)
2. Does the body support the main idea with specific information and examples? (*See pages 477–478.*)
3. Did you use your own words?
4. Does your report have unity? (*See page 327.*)
5. Does your report have coherence? (*See page 329.*)
6. Does your conclusion add a strong ending? (*See page 479.*)
7. Does your report have a title? (*See page 479.*)
8. Does your report have a sources page? (*See page 480.*)

Checking Your Paragraphs

9. Does each paragraph in the body have a topic sentence?
10. Is each paragraph unified and coherent?
11. Does one paragraph lead smoothly into the next?

Checking Your Sentences

12. Did you vary the length and beginnings of your sentences? (*See pages 302–309.*)
13. Did you avoid rambling sentences? (*See page 312.*)
14. Are your sentences free of repetition and empty expressions? (*See pages 313–315.*)
15. Did you use specific, vivid words? (*See pages 295–299.*)

EXERCISE 12 On Your Own

Using the checklist above, revise the report you wrote for Exercise 11. Save your work for Exercise 14.

Editing

The final stage in preparing a report is editing. Use the Editing Checklist and the guidelines for Correct Form on page 437. You may also want to use the proofreading symbols on page 372.

*E*XERCISE 13 *Editing*

Edit the following paragraph from a report about bicycles.

The high wheel bicycle first attracted the attention of americans at the 1876 philadelphia centennial exposition. They featured a large wheel in the front and a much more smaller wheel in the rear. Because of the large wheel, a rider could pedal faster. And go farther with less effort. Sitting atop the big wheel, the bicycle provided a surprisingly plesant and comforable ride, a few riders even acheived a speed of 20 miles an hour. Between 1883 and 1890 the bicycle reached it's peek of popularity. Two years later however american manufacturers ended production for safty reasons during a sudden stop the light rear wheel would fly upward. Throwing the rider over the handelbars. The need for a safer bicycle eventualy led to the developement of the modern safty bicycle. With the end of production in 1892. A period in bicycle history comes to a close.

*E*XERCISE 14 *On Your Own*

Using the Editing Checklist on page 437, edit your report from Exercise 12.

*B*ook Reports

Another kind of report is the book report. Book reports can be written about works of fiction or nonfiction. In either case the purpose of the book report is the same.

28m ▶ A **book report** offers a brief summary of the book and an opinion about the quality of the book.

Like other compositions a book report has an introduction, a body, and a conclusion. The following chart shows the kinds of information that you should include in each part of a book report.

28n ▶

Structure of a Book Report	
INTRODUCTION	• gives the title and the author's name • tells the subject of the book • may give background information about the author • identifies the time and location of the story in a fictional book
BODY	• expresses your opinion of the book • offers specific reasons and examples from the book to support your opinion • includes highlights from the book
CONCLUSION	• restates your opinion in new words

When giving your opinion of a book, avoid offering only a simple statement of like or dislike. Instead, be specific and support your opinion with examples from the book.

When you summarize the story, remember that your readers may not be familiar with the book. Avoid retelling the whole story, however. When telling the highlights, use the present tense and avoid shifting into the past tense.

As you read the following book report, notice the purpose each part of the report serves.

INTRODUCTION: TELLS TITLE, AUTHOR, AND SUBJECT

A Wrinkle in Time by Madeleine L'Engle is a novel about a young girl's voyages through space and time to find her father. Along the way she also finds appreciation of her true self. The girl, Meg, and her brother, Charles Wallace, are accompanied by their friend, Calvin O'Keefe. They are aided by three magical spirits, Mrs. Whatsit, Mrs. Who, and Mrs. Which. These three loving spirits transport the young people through wrinkles in time, called tesseracts.

OVERALL OPINION

The suspenseful story, the variety of interesting characters, and the theme of individuality make *A Wrinkle in Time* a very enjoyable book.

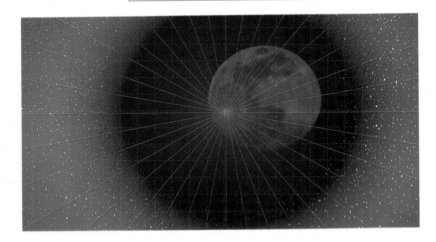

BODY: PROVIDES SPECIFIC HIGHLIGHTS

At the beginning of the book, Meg is a troubled girl. She becomes angry and belligerent in school, and she dislikes her plain appearance and her inability to control her feelings. As the story progresses, she is put to test after test. On the evil planet of Camazotz, where everyone is a carbon copy dominated by a single brain called IT, Meg learns the value of

USES PRESENT TENSE TO SUMMARIZE EVENTS

individuality, of just being herself. Later, on a gray planet called Ixchel, she learns the enormous power of love from a sightless, tentacled creature named Aunt Beast. Meg uses her power to love in a daring rescue of Charles Wallace, who is trapped by the evil power of IT on Camazotz.

CONCLUSION: SUMS UP AND RESTATES OVERALL OPINION The interesting characters in the book reinforce the theme of individual differences. Charles Wallace, believed to be dim-witted by some of the neighbors, is actually gifted with special mind-reading powers. Calvin, a popular boy in school, learns that he has been denying an important, different part of himself. The three spirits, Aunt Beast, and a soulful character called the Happy Medium are each unique. When you finish reading *A Wrinkle in Time*, you feel glad that people are as different as they are from one another. You also feel that the powers of love and goodness are strong enough to keep IT and other evils in check.

EXERCISE 15   On Your Own

Write a book report on one of the following books or on one of your own choice. Use the Steps for Writing a Book Report on page 489 as a guide.

Fiction

1. *So Far From Heaven* by Richard Bradford
2. *My Side of the Mountain* by Jean Craighead George
3. *Trapped* by Roderic Jeffries
4. *Journey Home* by Yoshiko Uchida
5. *The Tombs of Atuan* by Ursula K. Le Guin

Nonfiction

1. *The Fire Came By: The Riddle of the Great Siberian Explosion* by John Baxter and Thomas Atkins
2. *Biorhythm: Discovering Your Natural Ups and Downs* by Pauline C. Bartel
3. *Monster Dinosaur* by Daniel Cohen
4. *Assignment: Sports* by Robert Lipsyte
5. *Monarchs of the Forest: The Story of the Redwoods* by Anne Ensign Brown

$\mathcal{S}$potlight on Writing

A **Taking Notes.** The following passage is from a source about the Loch Ness monster. Assume you are preparing a report on whether the creature exists. Use as many note cards as needed to take notes on all the important information. Be sure to prepare the cards according to the model on page 470.

For a long time, there were no photographs of the monster. That is because, said people who had seen it, Nessie is nocturnal; that is, it eats and moves mainly at night and can be seen either at night or at daybreak. Then, in 1951, a man named Lachlan Stuart made a picture with a box camera that showed three dark humps above the water—the animal's back. Stuart said he had seen the thin neck and small head, but they had gone beneath the surface before he snapped the shutter.

"Could be a fake," the scoffers said. The expert who developed Stuart's negative and made his prints said, "No, they are genuine." He kept a negative to prove it.

Two earlier pictures had been made back in 1934 by a London surgeon. They showed the head and neck, sticking like a periscope above the loch (lake).

Not until 1960 was a careful study of one of these pictures made. The analysis was made by T. K. Dinsdale, an aeronautical engineer in the study of photographs. The analysis was reported by Dr. Maurice Burton of the British Museum (Natural History) in the *Illustrated London News*.

Mr. Dinsdale discovered that in the photograph there were 2 sets of ripples on the water that would be almost impossible to fake. One set was made by the head and neck as they pushed above the surface. The other set was apparently made by some part of the body, such as a hump on the back, well behind the neck. Mr. Dinsdale estimated the creature to be 25 to 30 feet long overall.

In 1962, Dr. Burton published another thought about this photograph. Instead of the head and neck of a monster, it might be the tail of a diving otter. In this case the otter would have been much closer to the camera than the monster supposedly was.

Early in the morning of May 27, 1960, Peter O'Connor, a fireman of Gatehead and an ex-navy frogman, was at the loch. "I saw something riding high," he said. "I took a closer look and realized it was the legendary monster. I grabbed my camera . . . and waded into the water within 25 yards of the monster." He got a picture of a large, blackish body *and* neck—indistinct but the best photograph yet. It looked something like a plesiosaurus, which is a sea serpent that lived during the age of dinosaurs.

—GARDNER SOULE, *THE MAYBE MONSTERS*, PP. 19–20

B **Outlining.** Use the notes that follow to complete the outline below. Place each item in its proper position in the outline.

I. Animal monsters
   A.
   B. Godzilla, a dinosaur-like creature
   C.
II.
   A.
   B. Bride of Frankenstein, created to keep Frankenstein company
III. People who undergo a change
   A. Dr. Jekyl and Mr. Hyde: one man with two personalities—one good, one bad
   B.

Notes
- Frankenstein, created by a scientist from used parts
- King Kong, gorilla
- Werewolf, man who grows hair and fangs during full moon
- Human-made monsters
- Rodan, prehistoric birdlike creature

487

Steps for Writing a Report

Prewriting

1. Choose and limit a subject requiring research. (*See pages 466–467.*)
2. Gather information from encyclopedias, books, and magazines. (*See pages 468–469.*)
3. Take notes on note cards. (*See pages 470–471.*)
4. Organize your notes into categories and use them to outline the body of your report. (*See page 473.*)

Writing

5. Write an introduction that includes a sentence expressing the main idea. (*See pages 475–476.*)
6. Use your outline to write the body of your report in your own words. (*See pages 477–478.*)
7. Add a concluding paragraph. (*See page 479.*)
8. Add a title.
9. Prepare a list of sources as your final page. (*See page 480.*)

Revising

10. Put your first draft aside for a while. Then use the Checklist for Revising Reports on page 481 to improve your first draft.

Editing

11. Use the Editing Checklist and the guidelines for correct form on page 437 to polish your report and make a final copy.

Steps for Writing a Book Report

Prewriting

1. If you are writing about a nonfiction book, briefly summarize the author's main point in your own words. If you are writing about fiction, briefly summarize the story in your own words.
2. Describe in a sentence or two the book's overall effect on you. How did you feel when reading it?
3. Skim the book, jotting down specific details that lead to your overall feeling about the book.
4. Consider whether you would recommend the book to someone else. Write a sentence or two explaining why or why not.

Writing

5. Write an introduction that tells the title, the author, and the subject. Include a sentence that expresses your overall opinion of the book.
6. Write the body. Include specific details from the book that support your opinion of it.
7. Write a conclusion restating your opinion of the book in new words.

Revising

8. Did you summarize the book briefly? If the book is fiction, did you use present tense consistently?
9. Did you avoid a simple statement of like or dislike and instead offer a specific opinion?

Editing

10. Use the Editing Checklist and the guidelines for correct form on page 437 to polish your book report and make a final copy.

29

Letters

One way to keep in touch with friends and relatives is through writing letters. Letters can also be used to contact companies or to request information from organizations.

The form of your letter and the words you choose will depend on your purpose for writing and your audience. For example, if you were writing to a company, your letter would be in the form of a business letter. Since a business letter requires formal language, you would avoid conversational expressions and follow the grammar and usage rules in this book. If, on the other hand, you were writing to your favorite uncle, your letter would be in the form of a friendly letter and your language would be less formal. You might, for example, use contractions and the latest popular expressions. Whatever your purpose or audience, create letters that make a good impression on your reader.

Your Writer's Notebook

Every day for a week, write in your journal the name of a friend or relative that you have not seen for a while. After each name write specific things about the person. Then write information about yourself that would be of particular interest to him or her.

Friendly Letters

What kinds of letters do you write to your friends and relatives? Sometimes you write just to keep in touch and share news. Other times you may write to thank someone for a gift or for the hospitality you enjoyed during a visit. You may write notes to invite people to your house, to congratulate someone, or to express sympathy. All of these kinds of letters are called friendly letters.

Friendly Letter Form

The letter on page 492 shows the correct form for a friendly letter. All friendly letters have five main parts.

29a The parts of a friendly letter are the **heading, salutation, body, closing,** and **signature.**

HEADING   The heading includes your full address with ZIP code. Use the full name of your state or the abbreviation. (*See page 498.*) Always include the date after your address. Remember to follow the rules for capitalizing proper nouns and using commas.

SALUTATION   The salutation is your friendly greeting. Always capitalize the first word and all nouns. Use a comma after the salutation.

Dear Aunt Sally,   Dear Dad,

BODY   Your conversational message makes up the body. Remember to indent each paragraph.

CLOSING   End with a brief closing followed by a comma. Capitalize the first word only.

Your nephew,   Love always,

SIGNATURE   Your signature should be handwritten below the closing.

491

Correct Form for a Friendly Letter

heading   113 Hitchcock Road
Battle Ground, IN 47920
May 5, 1987

salutation
Dear Linda,

body   I can hardly believe that graduation is only three weeks away. Are you as excited about high school as I am? I have to admit I'm a little nervous too, but I suppose that's natural.

After graduation I'm going to camp in a beautiful area in southern Indiana called Brown County. The camp has swimming, sailing, and other outdoor activities.

Please write and let me know what your summer plans are. Is there any chance you could come for a visit? I hope we can get together.

closing   Your friend,
signature   Camela

NOTE: The envelope for a friendly letter may be handwritten. It should contain the same information as that on the envelope for a business letter. (*See pages 498–499.*) Be sure both addresses are complete and clear.

Thank-you Notes

When thanking someone for a gift, mention the specific item in your note. Tell the giver how you intend to use it. Remember to use the friendly letter form when writing a thank-you note.

Thank-you Note

heading   4211 Dawes Street
Hastings, PA 16646
October 14, 1987

salutation
Dear Grandma,

body   Thank you very much for the sweatshirt with Sosha's picture on it. Mom explained to me how you found a place that prints special pictures on sweatshirts. I've already worn it to obedience class, where Sosha is doing better than the other dogs. When I start entering Sosha in dog shows, maybe the sweatshirt will be my lucky charm!

Thanks again for the perfect gift. I am looking forward to seeing you at Thanksgiving.

closing   Love,
signature   Tania

Bread-and-butter Notes. If you stay overnight or longer with a friend or relative, you should write a special thank-you note called a bread-and-butter note. Using friendly letter form, express your appreciation to your host or hostess and tell why you enjoyed the visit. Write the bread-and-butter note as soon as you return home.

EXERCISE 1 Writing a Friendly Letter

Write a letter to a friend or relative. Tell him or her about what is going on in your life.

EXERCISE 2 Writing a Thank-you Note

Imagine that you have just received a gift from a friend who lives in a foreign country. Write a thank-you note to your friend. Be sure to use friendly letter form.

EXERCISE 3 Writing an Envelope

Choose one of the letters you wrote in Exercise 1 or 2. Then prepare an envelope for it. (*See pages 498–499.*)

EXERCISE 4 On Your Own

Imagine that your favorite television star invited you to spend a day watching a show being taped. Write a bread-and-butter note telling him or her how much you enjoyed the visit.

Writing Extra

Imagine that you have been asked to write a letter that will be carried aboard a spacecraft. The spacecraft will travel for hundreds of thousands of years until it reaches another intelligent civilization. Write a message telling what you think are the three most important things about life on Earth. Use friendly letter form.

Business Letters

Most of the business letters you write will ask the receiver to do something. You may, for example, order merchandise from a catalog, asking the receiver to send the desired items. To guarantee results, state your point directly in as few words as possible. Make sure the receiver knows exactly what he or she should do.

Business Letter Form

Business letters have six main parts. The extra part is called the inside address. The inside address includes all the information about the receiver that you would include on the envelope.

> **29b** The parts of the business letter are the **heading, inside address, salutation, body, closing,** and **signature.**

The model on page 497 shows the correct form for a business letter.

HEADING   The heading of a business letter is the same as the heading of a friendly letter. Include your full address followed by the date. Remember to follow the rules for capitalizing proper nouns and using commas. You may use the full name of your state or the abbreviation. (*See page 498 for a list of state abbreviations.*) If you choose to use the abbreviation, be sure to abbreviate the state in the inside address too.

INSIDE ADDRESS   Start the inside address two to four lines below the heading. Write the name of the person who will receive the letter, if you know it. Use *Mr., Ms., Mrs., Dr.,* etc., before the name. If the person has a title, such as *Personnel Director* or *Manager,* write it on the next line. Then write the receiver's address, following the rules for capitalizing proper nouns and using commas.

SALUTATION Start the salutation, or greeting, two lines below the inside address. In a business letter, use a colon after the salutation.

Dear Mrs. Walters: Dear Sir or Madam:

BODY Two lines below the salutation, begin the body or message of the letter. Skip a line between paragraphs and indent each new paragraph.

CLOSING In a business letter, use a formal closing. Start the closing two or three lines below the body. Line up the closing with the left-hand edge of the heading. Capitalize the first word only and use a comma.

Sincerely,   Yours truly,
Sincerely yours,   Very truly yours,

SIGNATURE In the signature of a business letter, your name appears twice. First type (or print if your letter is handwritten) your name four or five lines below the closing. Then sign your name in the space between the closing and your typed name. Do not refer to yourself as Mr. or Ms.

There are many styles for writing business letters. The *modified block style* is one of the most popular. In this style the heading, closing, and signature are on the right. The inside address, salutation, and body start at the left margin. Paragraphs are indented. All business letters in this chapter use the modified block style.

Use white stationery when you write a business letter,

preferably 8½- by 11-inch size. Leave margins at least 1 inch wide on all sides. Be sure to keep a copy of every business letter you send. You can make a copy with carbon paper or use the copying machines available in most libraries.

Correct Form for a Business Letter

heading   562 Harper Road
La Grange, GA 30240
September 1, 1987

inside address
Chamber of Commerce
P. O. Box 465
Solvang, CA 93463

salutation
Dear Sir or Madam:

body   My family is planning a trip to Santa Barbara in December. We have been told that Solvang is an interesting community well worth visiting. Would you please send some information about the attractions in Solvang?

We would also appreciate receiving a list of nearby hotels and motels where we might stay. Thank you very much.

closing   Sincerely,

signature   *Charles De Fotis*

Charles DeFotis

Correct Form for Business Envelopes

29c

Charles DeFotis   your name
562 Harper Road   your address
La Grange, GA 30240

        receiver's   Chamber of Commerce
        address   P. O. Box 465
                        Solvang, CA 93463

State Abbreviations

Alabama	AL	Montana	MT
Alaska	AK	Nebraska	NE
Arizona	AZ	Nevada	NV
Arkansas	AR	New Hampshire	NH
California	CA	New Jersey	NJ
Colorado	CO	New Mexico	NM
Connecticut	CT	New York	NY
Delaware	DE	North Carolina	NC
District of Columbia	DC	North Dakota	ND
Florida	FL	Ohio	OH
Georgia	GA	Oklahoma	OK
Hawaii	HI	Oregon	OR
Idaho	ID	Pennsylvania	PA
Illinois	IL	Puerto Rico	PR
Indiana	IN	Rhode Island	RI
Iowa	IA	South Carolina	SC
Kansas	KS	South Dakota	SD
Kentucky	KY	Tennessee	TN
Louisiana	LA	Texas	TX
Maine	ME	Utah	UT
Maryland	MD	Vermont	VT
Massachusetts	MA	Virginia	VA
Michigan	MI	Washington	WA
Minnesota	MN	West Virginia	WV
Mississippi	MS	Wisconsin	WI
Missouri	MO	Wyoming	WY

*T*he Envelope

The model on page 498 shows the correct form for an envelope. Preparing the envelope correctly will make sure that your letter reaches the right address. If you type your letter, type your envelope also. Place your own name and address in the upper left-hand corner. In the center of the envelope, write the receiver's name and address. Use the same information you used in the inside address. Use the postal abbreviation for the state and always include the ZIP code.

The way you fold your letter depends on the size of your envelope. If you use envelopes that are as wide as your stationery, fold the letter in thirds as shown in the diagram below.

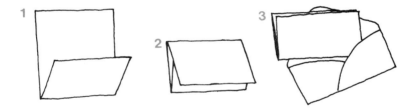

If your envelopes are narrower than your stationery, fold the letter into sixths.

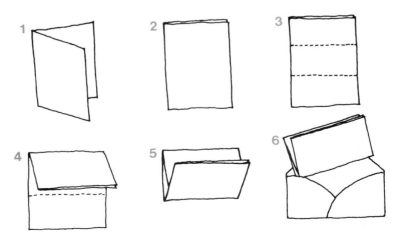

EXERCISE 5 *Writing a Business Letter*

Using the following information, write a business letter in the proper form.

Heading: your address and today's date

Inside address: Mr. Elmer Branch, President, Family Trees, Inc., 5 Oak Street, Maplewood, MO 63143

Salutation: Dear Mr. Branch

Body: I have been told that your organization can help people who want to trace their family trees. I would like to find out about my ancestors, but I do not know where to begin. Please send me any material that will help me learn more about my family. If there is any cost involved, I will be happy to send the money. Thank you very much.

Closing: Yours truly

Signature: your name

Letters of Request

One of the most common purposes for writing a business letter is to request information. A letter of request should be specific but brief. You are more likely to receive a prompt response if the receiver does not have to sift through unnecessary details. Always revise and edit your first draft until your request is clear and free of errors. Then make a neat final copy.

EXERCISE 6 Correcting Errors in a Letter of Request

In the following letter, each line preceded by a number contains an error. Rewrite the letter correcting each mistake. Then underline the corrections you made.

1 Martin O'Leary
2 635 Oakdale street
   Bellwood, IL 60104
3

4 Cynthia Peters
  Manager of Public Information
  Healthy Oats Company
  56 Miller Road
5 St. Paul, Minnesota 55111

6 Dear Ms. Peters,

7 I am a student at Roosevelt Junior High. My
  science class is writing a report on safety
  measures used in the processing of foods. I
  am particularly interested in how cereals are
8 checked for foriegn substances. Please send
  me any information on the methods your
  company uses. Thank you very much.

9 Sincerely Yours,

10

   Martin O'Leary

Order Letters

If you want to order merchandise from a catalog, you can use a business letter. An order letter includes six important pieces of information. The model on page 503 shows the correct form for an order letter.

Information to Include in Order Letters

1. description of item
2. size (and color when specified)
3. order number
4. price for each item
5. quantity (number of each item that you want)
6. total amount of order

EXERCISE 7 Writing an Order Letter

Use the following information to write an order letter.

ADDRESS   Order Department, Sports City, 1789 Juneway Place, Scranton, PA 18510

ORDER   1 baseball jacket, blue, size medium, Order # 880-3G, $22.00; 1 medium-weight Home Run King baseball bat, Order # 670-2F, $8.00; $3.75 for shipping and handling

Order Letter

4333 W. Silvestre Avenue
Bluff Dale, TX 76433
December 2, 1987

Hollywood Heaven
643 Baker Road
Detroit, MI 48222

Dear Sir or Madam:

Please send me the following items from your 1987 winter catalog:

1 poster (36 × 24) of Paul Newman
  and Robert Redford from <u>The Sting</u>,
  Order # 45–H–112 $ 4.25

1 <u>Wizard of Oz</u> T–shirt, blue, size
  small, Order # 41–T–33588   <u>$ 7.95</u>

                        TOTAL $12.20

I have enclosed a check for $14.70 to cover the cost of the merchandise plus $2.50 for shipping and handling.

Sincerely,

Raphaela Martinez

Raphaela Martinez

EXERCISE 8 *On Your Own*

Pretend you are going to Antarctica for a year. Write a letter ordering five items you will need to help you pass the time. Use your imagination to make up the company you are ordering from and the price of the merchandise.

*B*usiness Forms

You will need to fill out business forms for a variety of reasons. Subscribing to a magazine, selecting courses for ninth grade, applying for a library card, or joining a book club are just a few. Following are some guidelines for filling out business forms.

29d

Completing Business Forms

1. Read all of the directions carefully before you begin to fill out the form.
2. Check both sides of the form to make sure you do not miss any questions written on the back.
3. Do not leave blanks. If a question does not apply to you, write N/A (not applicable) in the space provided.
4. Always use blue or black pen.
5. Be sure to print neatly and clearly.
6. Remember to sign the form.
7. Read over the form when you are finished to be sure your answers are accurate and complete.

If the form you are filling out is long, you may want to write the answers on a separate sheet of paper first. Then copy the answers onto the form in ink.

The form used to open a savings account and the savings deposit slip used to put money into the account are shown on page 505. Both of these forms can be obtained and filled out at your local bank. Since each bank has its own special forms, read each one carefully before you fill it out.

*E*XERCISE 9 *Requesting Business Forms*

A bank has a number of different savings accounts to suit the various needs of its customers. Write a letter to a bank near you. Request information about savings accounts. Remember to use correct business letter form.

The form below is used when you are opening a savings account at the bank.

Savings Account Application Form

Tri-Town Savings Bank

Type of Account: _Savings_

Customer's Name: _Karen Kelly_

Home Address: (Street) _16 River Drive_

(City) _Hanover_ (State) _NH_ (Zip) _03755_

Phone #: _646-1212_ Date of Birth: _4/24/75_

Social Security #: _184-45-4380_

Initial Deposit: _$10.00_ Branch: _Hanover_

Signature: _Karen Kelly_ Date: _2/28/88_

When you want to put money into your account, you will need to fill out a savings deposit slip.

Deposit Slip

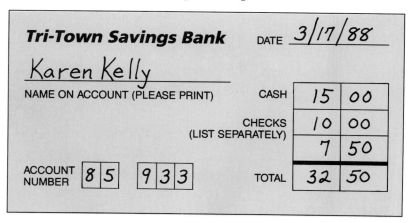

Tri-Town Savings Bank DATE _3/17/88_

Karen Kelly

NAME ON ACCOUNT (PLEASE PRINT)

CASH	15	00
CHECKS (LIST SEPARATELY)	10	00
	7	50

ACCOUNT NUMBER: 8 5 9 3 3

TOTAL	32	50

Spotlight on Writing

A **Writing a Friendly Letter.** Imagine that you have been chosen as the grand prize winner in the Celebrity Sweepstakes contest. As the winner you will be able to meet your favorite celebrity. Below is a list of prizes for you to choose from. Write a friendly letter to the celebrity whom you would like to meet explaining why you chose him or her.

- tickets to a game to meet your favorite athlete
- dinner with your favorite movie actor or actress
- tickets to a rock concert to meet your favorite group
- an appointment to meet the President at the White House
- dinner in London with Prince Charles and Lady Diana

B **Writing a Bread-and-butter Note.** Imagine that the snapshots below are from your recent trip to California. During this trip you stayed with your Aunt Eleanor, Uncle George, and cousins Tommy (age 13) and Rhoda (age 8). Write a bread-and-butter note to thank them for their hospitality and to send them copies of the pictures.

C **Writing a Note of Congratulations.** Write a friendly letter to suit the following purpose and audience.

PURPOSE   to congratulate a cousin who has just been chosen as a starting player on the state university football team

AUDIENCE   your cousin Robbie

D **Writing a Letter of Request.** Write a letter to a major zoo in the United States requesting general information. Also request any free materials the zoo might have. Below are the addresses of two well-known zoos.

- Education Department, San Diego Zoo, P.O. Box 551, San Diego, CA 92112
- Publicity Manager, Cincinnati Zoo, 3400 Vine Street, Cincinnati, OH 45220

E **Writing an Order Letter.** Imagine that you are in charge of the decorations for the school's Winter Wonderland holiday dance. You have $125.00 to spend. Choose from the items below advertised in the *Designer Decorations* winter catalog. The address is 1225 Evergreen Street, Canyon Creek, MT 59633. Add $5.50 for shipping and handling.

Item	Number	Price
artificial snow	#55-S	$25.00
tinsel (silver or gold)	#27-T	$ 9.00 a box
paper snowflakes	#46-F	$ 1.00 each
old-fashioned sleigh	#71-O	$72.50
jingle bells	#13-J	$12.50 a box
rolls of crepe paper	#89-C	$ 6.50 a dozen
gingerbread house	#38-G	$45.00
cardboard snowman	#99-M	$17.50 each

F **Writing from Your Writer's Notebook.** Write a letter to one of the people that you wrote about in your writer's notebook. Be sure to include questions about what they are doing now as well as information about yourself.

Steps for Writing a Letter

Friendly Letter

1. Use the proper form for a friendly letter. (*See pages 491–492.*)
2. Edit your letter for errors in usage, capitalization, punctuation, and spelling.
3. Recopy your letter if necessary for neatness.
4. Include a return address on the envelope. (*See pages 498–499.*)

Business Letter

1. Gather the information you need to explain your request or order accurately and completely.
2. Use the proper form for a business letter. (*See pages 495–497.*)
3. Use a salutation and closing proper for a business letter. (*See page 496.*)
4. Express your message briefly and politely in the body of the letter.
5. Use the correct form for the signature. (*See page 496.*)
6. Edit your letter for errors in usage, capitalization, punctuation, and spelling.
7. If possible, type the letter on white 8½- by 11-inch stationery, leaving margins at least 1 inch wide.
8. Keep a copy of your letter.
9. Fold your letter properly. (*See page 499.*)
10. Address the envelope correctly. (*See pages 498–499.*)

Standardized Test

Directions: Decide which sentence best supports the topic sentence. Fill in the appropriate circle on your answer sheet.

SAMPLE   Saturn is the farthest planet visible to the eye.
  A It is not as large as Jupiter.
  B It looks like a bright star.
  C Uranus is twice as far from the sun.

ANSWER   Ⓐ Ⓑ Ⓒ

1. Sewing a button back on requires very little skill.
  A Some buttons fall off rather easily.
  B I am always misplacing my needle and thread.
  C Threading the needle is the hardest part of the job.

2. Montreal is the largest city in the province of Quebec.
  A Montreal has approximately three million people.
  B Many stores and restaurants there are built underground.
  C Its subway system is efficient, clean, and attractive.

3. President Harrison served the shortest time in office.
  A F. D. Roosevelt served the longest time, 12 years.
  B Harrison died in 1841 after only one month as president.
  C President Zachary Taylor also died in the White House.

4. Jay's compositions always have something to do with dancing.
  A His last essay was called "Give Dancing a Whirl."
  B I have never been interested in dancing.
  C Jay is also the best pitcher on our baseball team.

5. The Pilgrims probably did not step on Plymouth Rock.
  A The rock has the date 1620 carved on it.
  B It may, however, have lain near their landing spot.
  C Today the rock lies under an imposing stone structure.

6. A potter prepares clay by pressing and squeezing it.
  A Potters have been using clay since ancient times.
  B Pottery is made from baked clay.
  C When the clay is softened, the potter can shape it.

Directions: On your answer sheet, fill in the circle of the line in each group that contains an error. If there is no error in the group, fill in the circle containing *4*.

SAMPLE   1)   327 Grand Concourse
           2)   Bronx, NY 10453
           3)   January 26, 1986
           4) (No error)

ANSWER   ① ② ③ ④

7. 1)   183 Delmar street
   2)   Mobile, AL 36619
   3)   March 30, 1986
   4) (No error)

8. 1)   Bentley Products
   2)   876 Bell Boulevard
   3)   Texas, 78756
   4) (No error)

9. 1)   Dear Sir or Madam:
   2)   Please send me a copy of your 1986
   3)   catalog of sports items. Thank you.
   4) (No error)

10. 1)   Sincerely Yours,

    2)   *Raymond Hurwitz*

    3)   Raymond Hurwitz
    4) (No error)

Directions: You have 20 minutes to write a brief essay on the topic below. Do not write on any other topic.

It is better to have a good enemy than a bad friend.

Related Language Skills

30

Speaking and Listening

Stop for a moment and think about each time you talked to someone yesterday. What was your purpose? Who was your audience? On the school bus, for example, you may have tried to persuade a friend to go to basketball tryouts with you. Later, in science class, you may have given an oral report to explain the life cycle of a frog.

Now think about your use of language during each occasion. When talking with a friend, did you use slang expressions and fad words? When you spoke in front of your class, did you avoid such informal language? Certain words and expressions may be acceptable in one situation but not in another. The language you choose should always depend on your purpose for speaking and on your audience.

Informal Speaking

Have you ever given someone directions to your house? Maybe you have told your friend about an exciting weekend you had or given your parents a play-by-play account of an exciting basketball game. These and similar situations are considered *informal speeches* because they are short and require no formal planning or preparation. When speaking informally, however, it is important to organize your thoughts so that you are clear and to the point.

Giving Directions

Giving directions is an important type of informal speech. Clear directions require organized thinking. As you read the two sets of directions below, determine why the second set is clearer.

UNCLEAR   The football stadium. Yes, follow this road for a while until you come to a light. Then go west. The stadium should be near there.

CLEAR   To get to the football stadium, continue on Maple Street until you come to the second traffic light. That is Spring Street. You will see a gas station on one corner and a medical building on another corner. Turn left on Spring Street and go a half mile. The stadium will be on your right.

The second set of directions is clearer because it gives a specific distance, street names, and landmarks. Keep the following guidelines in mind when you give directions.

Giving Directions

1. Use *right, left,* or *straight* rather than *north, south, east,* or *west.*
2. Use names of streets if you know them.
3. Mention landmarks whenever possible.
4. Include the approximate number of miles if you know this information.
5. If possible, draw a map.
6. Do not give directions for a difficult shortcut.
7. If you are unsure of the correct directions, direct the person to someone who might know.
8. Repeat the directions or have the other person repeat the directions to you.

*E*XERCISE 1 *Improving Directions*

Read the following set of directions. Then rewrite the directions to make them more specific. Use the guidelines on page 513 and your imagination to help you include necessary details. After you have written the directions, draw a map to accompany them.

I think the aquarium is near the river. To get there, go north for several miles. You will come to a railroad crossing. Before the crossing take a right. Soon you'll see a big building. Take another right and you should come to the river in a little while. Down the road a bit, you will see the aquarium.

*E*XERCISE 2 *Giving Directions*

Write directions from your classroom to the following places in your school. Include as many specific details as possible. If time permits, read some of the directions aloud. Then have other students list ways the directions could be improved.

1. the library
2. the office
3. the baseball field
4. the cafeteria

*F*ormal Speaking

A *formal speech* is different from an informal speech in two basic ways. A formal speech is prepared in advance and is usually longer than an informal speech. A formal speech may be anything from a science or book report, given in front of your class, to a guided tour of the school for parents at an open house.

The preparation of a formal speech is similar to the preparation of a written report. (*See Chapter 28.*) The main difference is that you will practice your speech and deliver it orally rather than write it.

*K*nowing Your Audience

Before selecting a subject for your speech, think about who your audience will be. In most situations your audience will be classmates who share your interests and experiences. At other times, however, your audience might be teachers, parents, families in your community, or students from another school.

When choosing a subject for a speech, ask yourself the following questions about your audience. The answers to these questions will help you decide upon a subject that will suit your audience. The answers will also help you determine what information you should include in your speech to make your subject clear to your listeners.

Knowing Your Audience

1. What are the interests of my audience? Are they similar to mine?
2. What will my audience already know about the subject I would like to talk about?
3. Is my audience coming to learn, to be persuaded, or to be entertained?

---

*C*hoosing and Limiting a Subject

To choose a subject, first make a list of subjects that you know something about. Then choose one that both you and your audience will be interested in. For example, if you were speaking to parents about your school's need for new athletic equipment, you might inform them about your school's athletic programs and explain the need for new equipment. If, however, you were speaking to your classmates, you could persuade them to help raise money for the new equipment.

After deciding on a subject, you need to consider the amount of time you have to deliver your speech. If you have only ten minutes, you may not be able to cover all the athletic programs your school offers. Instead, you could limit your subject to the athletic programs that attract the largest number of participants.

EXERCISE 3 *Choosing and Limiting a Subject*

Number your paper 1 to 6. Write the subject of a speech that could be included under each area below. Then limit each subject so that it is suitable for a ten-minute speech.

EXAMPLE	plants
POSSIBLE ANSWER	trees
	the giant redwoods in California

1. inventions
2. sports
3. television

4. famous people
5. wonders of the earth
6. the solar system

Understanding Your Purpose

Once you have chosen and limited your subject, you should think about the purpose of your speech. Most speeches have one of the following three purposes.

Purposes of Speeches

PURPOSE	EXAMPLES
TO INFORM	• to explain about the effect of the moon on ocean tides
	• to explain the structure of icebergs
TO PERSUADE	• to encourage students to join after-school volleyball games
	• to encourage the school administration to sponsor a school newspaper
TO ENTERTAIN	• to tell about the first time you made Thanksgiving dinner for your family
	• to tell about the first and only time you tried to ice-skate

EXERCISE 4 Determining a Purpose for a Speech

Number your paper 1 to 10. Read each of the following limited subjects for a speech. Then label the purpose of each one *to inform, to persuade,* or *to entertain.*

1. to explain a solar eclipse
2. to tell about a picnic involving 25 people and the rainstorm
3. to encourage students to try out for the school play
4. to explain the difference between a marathon and a triathlon
5. to tell about the first time you tried to sail a boat
6. to explain how penicillin was discovered
7. to trace the history of the National Football League
8. to encourage your school to plan more field trips
9. to explain how Sacajawea helped Lewis and Clark explore the Far West
10. to tell about the time squirrels got into your attic

Gathering and Organizing Your Information

Gathering information and then organizing it are the next two steps in the preparation of a formal speech. These two steps are similar to those you follow when writing a research report. (*See pages 468–473.*) The two boxes that follow contain guidelines that will help you gather and organize your information.

Gathering Information

1. List what you already know about your subject.
2. Gather more information in the library or through an interview. (*See pages 572–586.*)
3. Find interesting examples and quotations to include in your speech.
4. Write your information on note cards. (*See pages 470–471.*)

Organizing Information

1. Make an outline of your speech. (*See page 473.*) Unlike an outline for a report, an outline for a speech should include your introduction and your conclusion.
2. The introduction should capture your audience's attention and present your main idea. (*See page 475.*)
3. The body of your speech should include the supporting points arranged in a logical order. Use transitions to connect your ideas. (*See pages 329, 428, 477.*)
4. The conclusion of your speech should summarize your main idea. (*See page 479.*)

EXERCISE 5 *Gathering and Organizing Information*

Choose and limit a subject for a ten-minute speech. Write what you know about it on note cards. Next go to the library and find information for at least four more note cards. Then organize your cards and write an outline of your speech. Save your outline for Exercise 6.

Practicing Your Speech

Practicing aloud is a necessary step in delivering a successful speech. Use the suggestions below as a guide.

Practicing Your Speech

1. Study your outline until you are familiar with all the information. Then make a few notes to use during your speech so you can speak to, not read to, your audience.
2. Practice in front of a long mirror so that you will be aware of your facial expressions and gestures, such as clenching your hands or biting your lips.
3. Practice looking around the room as you talk. Good eye contact is important.
4. Time the length of your speech. Then add or omit information as necessary.

You may want to use a tape recorder to hear yourself. Then practice in front of a friend and ask for suggestions. Each time you practice, you will feel more confident. The more confident you feel, the less nervous you will be when you deliver your speech to an audience.

EXERCISE 6 *Practicing Your Speech*

Team up with another student in the class. Practice the speech you prepared for Exercise 5 and ask your classmate for suggestions. Then listen to and discuss your classmate's speech. Save your notes for Exercise 7.

Delivering Your Speech

It is important to be well prepared before a speech. Following are some helpful suggestions.

Delivering Your Speech

1. Be well prepared and have all the necessary materials.
2. Wait until your audience is quiet and settled.
3. Take a deep breath and begin.
4. Stand with your weight evenly divided between both feet. Avoid swaying back and forth.
5. Speak slowly, clearly, and loudly enough to be heard.
6. Use rehearsed gestures and facial expressions to emphasize your main points.
7. Look directly at the people in your audience, not over their heads. Try to make eye contact.
8. Use pictures and other audio-visual aids to increase the attention of your audience.

EXERCISE 7 *Delivering Your Speech*

Present the speech you prepared for Exercise 6 before a group. Afterward, write a brief evaluation of your speech. List things that you did well and things you want to improve.

Listening

Listening is more than just hearing words. It involves understanding and evaluating what a speaker is saying. Listening, like speaking, is a skill that can be practiced and improved upon. This section will help you sharpen your listening skills.

Listening for Information and Taking Notes

To improve your ability to receive and understand a speaker's message, focus your attention on the main idea and supporting ideas of the speech.

Listening for the Main Idea.   In a well-planned speech, the main idea, along with the speaker's purpose, will be expressed in the introduction. Most often both will be stated directly in a single sentence. For example, if you heard the sentence *Walking is better for your health than jogging*, then you would know that the speech will be about the benefits of walking as a form of exercise. You would also know that the speaker's purpose will be to persuade you to walk rather than jog.

Be alert during the introduction, however, because the main idea is not always stated directly. In some cases the main idea may be suggested by the introduction as a whole. In others the speakers may introduce the main idea in the form of a question, a quotation, or a personal example.

Listening for Supporting Ideas.   Once you have identified the speaker's main idea and purpose, listen carefully to the supporting information the speaker offers to explain or defend the main idea. Sometimes the speaker will tell you how many major supporting ideas he or she will present. For example, the speaker may begin the body of the speech with *There are three main reasons why* or *I will explain the four main causes of.* Then, to ensure that none of the major supporting ideas will be missed, he or she may signal each one with a transitional expression like *first, second, third, moreover, most important of all,* or *finally.*

As each major supporting idea is introduced, listen to the supporting details that the speaker provides to clarify or drive home the point. Supporting details are often in the form of facts and examples, such as statistics, a quotation from an expert, or an anecdote. In some cases a speaker will alert you to an important detail by introducing it with a phrase such as *for example, studies show that,* or *according to one expert.*

Keep in mind that not all ideas are important. Focus on the major supporting ideas and supporting details that help you understand and evaluate the speaker's main idea.

Taking Notes While Listening.   Taking notes is an effective way to focus your attention while listening to a speech. Writing the information down requires you to listen carefully for important points and to organize the information. The following guidelines will help you take clear notes while listening to a speech.

Taking Notes on Speeches

1. Write the main idea presented in the introduction of the speech.
2. Write the main topics, using Roman numerals (I, II, III).
3. Under each main topic, write the subtopics, or supporting points, using capital letters (A, B, C).
4. In the conclusion of the speech, write the restatement of the main idea.

When you take notes, do not write everything down. If you do, you probably will miss important points. Write only the information that is necessary to remember accurately. Your notes will then help you remember the other details. Following are notes in outline form of a ten-minute speech about the development of gymnastics.

MAIN IDEA   Gymnastics, a sport in which physical feats are performed in an artistic manner, has a long history.

MAIN TOPIC
SUBTOPIC

I. Originally begun in ancient Greece
   A. Greeks had gymnasiums with field for throwing discus and javelin
   B. Romans adopted Greek ideas; added them to their military training
II. Died out between A.D. 392 and the 1700s
   A. Revived in Germany by Frederick Jahn
   B. He added side bar with pommels, horizontal bars, parallel bars, balance beam, jumping standards
III. Brought to the U.S. in the 1800s by immigrants
   A. Americans participated in first international competition in 1881
   B. Four Americans won first gold medals in gymnastics for USA in 1904 Olympics

Summary statement: Gymnastics started in ancient Greece but died out for many centuries until it was revived in the 1700s. Americans did not become involved in gymnastics until the 1880s. They have participated in international competition since then.

EXERCISE 8   Listening and Taking Notes

Prepare a brief explanation on how to do something, such as how to make a puppet or how to perform a science experiment. Then take notes as each student presents an explanation to the class. Later compare notes to see if you have included the same main topics.

Listening Critically

When listening and taking notes, it is important to listen carefully and evaluate what is being said.

Fact and Opinion. A *fact* is a statement that can be proved, but an *opinion* is a personal feeling or judgment. Because opinions are often stated as facts, you must listen carefully to tell them apart.

FACT   Dogs belong to the canine family.
OPINION Dogs are people's best friends.

EXERCISE 9 *Understanding Fact and Opinion*

Number your paper 1 to 10. Then label each statement *fact* or *opinion.*

1. All books by Mark Twain are interesting.
2. Halloween is always the last day in October.
3. Tiger gasoline is the best gasoline to buy.
4. My sister is three years younger than I am.
5. *Rumble Fish* was written by S. E. Hinton.
6. Baseball is the best sport in the world.
7. My sister should be an artist.
8. Gasoline is more expensive than it was 20 years ago.
9. Betsy's costume was the most unusual one.
10. Pete Rose broke Ty Cobb's record for base hits.

Bandwagon. Commercials and advertisements sometimes include a bandwagon statement. A bandwagon statement is one that leads you to believe that everyone is using a certain product. In other words, everyone is "jumping on the bandwagon." A bandwagon statement can be misleading because it suggests that, if you do not jump on the bandwagon, you will be different from everyone else.

Don't be left out. Join the healthy generation and take Peak-of-Health vitamins.

Testimonial. In a testimonial a famous person encourages you to buy a certain product. A testimonial can be misleading because it suggests that, if a famous person uses the product, it must be worth buying.

> Hi! I'm baseball star Bob Mose. Every morning Bran Buds gives me the energy I need to hit the ball out of the park!

Loaded Words. Another type of misleading statement is one that contains loaded words. These are words that are carefully chosen to appeal to your hopes or fears rather than to reason or logic. In the following advertisement, the word *embarrassment* was chosen to stir up the listener's emotions.

> When standing close to that special person, avoid embarrassment by using Whyworry antiperspirant.

EXERCISE 10   *Understanding Misleading Information*

Number your paper 1 to 10. Then label each statement *bandwagon, testimonial,* or *loaded words.*

1. All beautiful people wear Glow cosmetics.
2. A hardworking basketball player like me, Dan Dunk, needs Hi-Jumps on his feet to win the game.
3. Eliminate unsightly blemishes with Freshface.
4. All cats, even a gourmet like André, prefer Kaviar Katmeal.
5. I'm Gloria Glitter, the star of *Life Goes On.* I drink only No-Cal juice. You should too.
6. Successful people always choose Executive Airlines.
7. Everyone with good taste has Regal Rugs.
8. I'm Mitchel Judson. A star like me knows that Sparkle works better than any other toothpaste.
9. Lose those ugly pounds with our Stream-line weight-loss program.
10. Everyone is joining the Fabulous Fitness Club. Don't be alone. Come join too.

Chapter Review

A **Giving Directions.** Choose a place of interest in your city or town. Write directions to that place from your school. Be sure to include specific details. Your teacher may ask you to read your directions to the class and ask your classmates to try to repeat them. If time permits, discuss why some directions are better than others.

B **Giving a Speech.** Prepare a ten-minute speech about one of the following subjects or one of your own. Your teacher may ask you to deliver your speech to the class.

1. heart transplants
2. glaciers
3. alternative sources of energy
4. the history of the Inca civilization in South America
5. books by Judy Blume
6. the career of Jim Thorpe
7. how dolphins communicate
8. John F. Kennedy
9. life in the future
10. color photography

C **Listening and Taking Notes.** As students deliver their speeches for Exercise B, listen carefully and take notes in outline form. Use your notes to write a short quiz on a speech of your choice. Then give the quiz to several of your classmates.

D **Listening for Misleading Information.** Write an advertisement for a new product called Zesty Sportswear. Include misleading information such as a testimonial or a bandwagon statement. Your teacher may ask you to read your advertisement to the class and direct your classmates to identify the misleading information in it.

31

Vocabulary

If someone called you *persistent*, would you be flattered or insulted? If a teacher asked you to *elaborate* after answering a question, what would you do? If a book you are reading describes a character as *meek*, what image would come to mind? In conversation, in school, and in your reading you are likely to come across many unfamiliar words. If you take the time to learn them, you will gradually build your vocabulary. The more words at your command, the more precisely you will be able to express your meaning in speech and in writing.

EXERCISE 1   Previewing the Vocabulary List

Turn to the vocabulary list on page 539. Choose ten words and write a sentence using each. If you do not know the meanings of the words you chose, look them up in a dictionary before writing your sentences.

Word Meaning

In your reading and during your conversations, you may come across words that are new to you. If this happens, what do you do? For example, suppose you came across this sentence.

Mario was indecisive when it came to choosing which hat to wear.

Perhaps you already know that *indecisive* means "prone to indecision" or "hesitant," but more likely it is a new word to you. One way to learn its meaning is to look it up in a dictionary. In this chapter you will learn several additional ways to unlock the meaning of an unfamiliar word.

Context Clues

One of the ways you can learn the meaning of a word is through context clues. The *context* of a word is the sentence, the surrounding words, or the situation in which the word occurs. The following examples show the three most common kinds of context clues.

DEFINITION   Objects in space that emit strong radio signals are **quasars.** [The word *quasars* is defined within the sentence.]

EXAMPLE   **Fossil fuels,** such as coal, oil, and natural gas, are nonrenewable resources. [The words *fossil fuels* are followed by examples that are known to readers and listeners.]

SYNONYM   Much of our knowledge about Norse explorers comes from **sagas.** These long stories were recited and passed from one generation to the next. [A synonym for the word *saga* is used in the following sentence.]

EXERCISE 2 Using Context Clues

Number your paper 1 to 10. Then write the letter of the answer that is closest in meaning to the underlined word.

1. The doctor was pleased to announce that the patient had made a complete recovery, for no signs of illness were present.
   (A) setback   (B) operation   (C) diagnosis
   (D) return to normal   (E) reversal

2. The exterior of the house was run-down, but the inside was beautifully kept up.
   (A) roof   (B) paint   (C) outside
   (D) porch   (E) basement

3. Something is missing in the egg salad; I must have omitted an ingredient.
   (A) doubled   (B) left out   (C) mixed up
   (D) chopped   (E) added to

4. Deep-sea divers keep warm by wearing suits that water cannot penetrate.
   (A) shrink   (B) make wet   (C) loosen
   (D) stretch   (E) come into

5. To avoid being scalded while taking a shower, always use your hand to test the water before entering the shower to make sure it is not too hot.
   (A) burned   (B) wet   (C) punished
   (D) cold   (E) surprised

6. Sheryl was meek and shy, while her sister Tanya was proud and outgoing.
   (A) humble   (B) tired   (C) talkative
   (D) honest   (E) slow

7. After paying all of our expenses, our club has a surplus of $45, which we are going to donate to charity.
   (A) unpaid bill   (B) extra amount   (C) surprise
   (D) prize   (E) loss

8. Animals often mimic humans; most are great copycats.
   (A) understand   (B) copy   (C) oppose
   (D) dislike   (E) recall

9. I try to <u>retain</u> my sense of humor even in hard times; those are the times a sense of humor really helps!
(A) give up   (B) lose   (C) relax with
(D) restore   (E) keep

10. Sylvester became frustrated and gave up quickly, but Ben was <u>persistent</u> and, after hours of work, finally solved the brainteaser.
(A) lucky   (B) clever   (C) determined
(D) lazy   (E) grateful

EXERCISE 3 *Using Context Clues*

Number your paper 1 to 10. Write each underlined word and its meaning. Use the context of the paragraph to help you. Then check your answers in a dictionary.

The explorers found themselves in a <u>barren</u> land, with no signs of life anywhere. The hot desert sun <u>parched</u> the earth. Water was nowhere to be found. Suddenly they heard the frightening rattle of a snake. The snake was so well <u>camouflaged</u> that the men could not see it against the rocks, stumps, and sand. They fled quickly for safety, hoping that the snake would not <u>pursue</u> them. During the long, hot weeks of exploration, snakes were only one kind of <u>hazard</u> these newcomers would have to face. One day they <u>misjudged</u> the difficulty of the trail and did not <u>exceed</u> one mile. On another day an explorer began to <u>falter</u>. He stumbled as he walked, having been <u>deprived</u> of nourishment for too long. Soon the weary travelers began to <u>yearn</u> for the cool shade and the safety of their homes far away.

Prefixes and Suffixes

In addition to using context clues, you can also unlock the meanings of unfamiliar words by breaking words down into their parts.

A word may have as many as three parts: a prefix, a root, and a suffix. For example, you might come across the word *rename*. You probably recognize one part of this word, *name*.

This part is called the root. A *root* is the part of the word that carries the basic meaning.

ROOT   mis**read**   un**touch**able   re**appear**ance   **wish**ful

EXERCISE 4 *Finding Roots*

Number your paper 1 to 20. Then write each word and underline the root.

1. unlawful
2. cartoonist
3. fearless
4. semicircle
5. react
6. disappear
7. preview
8. restless
9. coworker
10. displeasure

11. unteachable
12. independence
13. submarine
14. persistence
15. unnaturally
16. irresistible
17. speechless
18. disagreement
19. interstate
20. bimonthly

Prefixes.   The part of the word that comes before the root is called a *prefix*. A prefix can be one syllable or more than one. In the word *rename*, the prefix is *re-*. If you know that *re-* means "again," you can figure out that *rename* means "name again." Following are some common prefixes.

Prefix	Meaning	Example
bi-	two	bi + weekly = biweekly
co-	together	co + author = coauthor
de-	remove, from	de + plane = deplane
in-	not	in + secure = insecure
il-	not	il + legal = illegal
mis-	incorrect	mis + place = misplace
pre-	before	pre + historic = prehistoric
re-	again	re + gain = regain

EXERCISE 5 Using Prefixes

Number your paper 1 to 10. Write the prefix that has the same meaning as the underlined word. Then write the complete word defined after the equal sign.

EXAMPLE before + view = to see beforehand
ANSWER pre-, preview

1. together + operate = work together
2. remove + fog = to clear away the fog
3. not + logical = lacking clear thinking
4. before + determine = to figure out beforehand
5. incorrect + pronounce = to use the wrong pronunciation
6. two + annually = twice a year
7. again + organize = to set up a new order
8. not + appropriate = not appropriate
9. remove + forest = to clear away trees
10. not + legible = unreadable

EXERCISE 6 Using Prefixes

Make four columns on your paper, one for each prefix listed below. Then write as many words as you can by combining each prefix with as many roots as possible. Use a dictionary to be sure you have made real words.

PREFIXES	ROOTS		
co-	trial	heat	name
mis-	exist	star	worker
pre-	test	judge	count
re-	print	pilot	match

Suffixes. The part of the word that comes after the root is called a *suffix*. Suffixes, like prefixes, can have one or more syllables. Unlike prefixes, however, many suffixes can change a word from one part of speech to another. In the following list, notice how suffixes can create different parts of speech.

Noun Suffixes	Meaning	Example
-ance, -ence	state of	correspond + ence
-ment	state of	govern + ment
-ist	one who or that	art + ist
-ness	state of	well + ness

Verb Suffixes	Meaning	Example
-en	make, become	bright + en
-ize	make, cause to be	material + ize

Adjective Suffixes	Meaning	Example
-able, -ible	capable of	flex + ible
-less	without	pain + less

Adverb Suffix	Meaning	Example
-ly	in a certain way	careful + ly

EXERCISE 7   Using Suffixes

Number your paper 1 to 10. Write the suffix that has the same meaning as the underlined word or words. Then write the complete word defined after the equal sign.

EXAMPLE   fear + <u>without</u> = free from fear

ANSWER   -less, fearless

1. resent + <u>state of</u> = state of displeasure
2. nervous + <u>in a certain way</u> = in an anxious way
3. work + <u>capable of</u> = likely to work
4. gruff + <u>state of</u> = rough quality
5. journal + <u>one who</u> = a newspaper writer
6. cloud + <u>without</u> = clear
7. jubilant + <u>in a certain way</u> = with great joy
8. weak + <u>make, become</u> = to lose strength
9. persist + <u>state of</u> = able to stick with something
10. capital + <u>make</u> = to make big letters

EXERCISE 8 Using Suffixes

Number your paper 1 to 20. Write each word with two different suffixes. Then write the part of speech of each one.

EXAMPLE   light
POSSIBLE ANSWERS   lighten—verb, lightly—adverb

1. deep
2. depend
3. firm
4. weak
5. final
6. rough
7. plain
8. mean
9. motor
10. rapid
11. employ
12. accept
13. visual
14. light
15. vocal
16. respectful
17. manage
18. youthful
19. irritable
20. hopeful

EXERCISE 9 Using Prefixes and Suffixes

Number your paper 1 to 10. Then write the letter of the answer that is closest in meaning to the word in capital letters. Use the prefixes and suffixes to help you.

1. INFORMAL   (A) formal beforehand   (B) not formal   (C) without form
2. REASSURE   (A) not assure   (B) without assurance   (C) assure again
3. COINCIDENT   (A) happening together   (B) not happening   (C) happening again
4. INDEFINITE   (A) certain before   (B) removal of certainty   (C) not certain
5. MISJUDGE   (A) judge incorrectly   (B) judge beforehand   (C) without judgment
6. PREFERENCE   (A) prefer in a certain way   (B) one who prefers   (C) state of preferring
7. VOCALIST   (A) one who sings   (B) singing in a certain way   (C) state of singing
8. VOCALIZE   (A) one who sings   (B) to make vocal   (C) singing in a certain way
9. PRECISELY   (A) state of being exact   (B) in an exact way   (C) condition of exactness
10. HEIGHTEN   (A) make higher   (B) high in a certain way   (C) one who makes higher

Synonyms

When you write or speak, you want to express your meaning exactly. English is so rich in words that you can often choose among words with similar meanings to find just the right one. A word that has nearly the same meaning as another word is called a *synonym*.

Although synonyms mean *about* the same thing, they often convey slightly different shades of meaning. In the following sentences, for example, the word *padded* paints a more precise picture.

The wolf **walked** through the deep forest.
The wolf **padded** through the deep forest.

Dictionaries often include synonyms for words. (*See page 567.*) A special dictionary called a *thesaurus* lists only synonyms. When you write, use both a dictionary and a thesaurus to help you choose words that convey your meaning exactly.

EXERCISE 10   Recognizing Synonyms

Number your paper 1 to 10. Write the letter of the answer that is closest in meaning to the word in capital letters. Then check your answers in a dictionary.

1. NOURISH   (A) restore   (B) punish   (C) feed
   (D) fill   (E) disappear
2. DESOLATE   (A) quiet   (B) barren   (C) teeming
   (D) angry   (E) ordinary
3. EVIDENT   (A) sad   (B) harmful   (C) proud
   (D) weary   (E) obvious
4. ABUNDANT   (A) repetitious   (B) plentiful
   (C) ripe   (D) glorious   (E) scarce
5. FORETELL   (A) spy   (B) reveal   (C) predict
   (D) guess   (E) refuse
6. OBLIGATION   (A) duty   (B) celebration
   (C) ritual   (D) penalty   (E) fine

7. FALTER (A) accuse (B) interrupt (C) stumble
   (D) release (E) dismiss
8. RARITY (A) eagerness (B) oddity
   (C) healthfulness (D) fairness (E) honesty
9. IMPOSE (A) relax (B) enclose (C) capture
   (D) force (E) pry
10. BAN (A) call (B) prohibit (C) recommend
    (D) follow (E) win

EXERCISE 11 Choosing the Better Word

Number your paper 1 to 10. Then write the synonym in parentheses that fits the meaning of each sentence. Use a dictionary for help.

EXAMPLE Everyone in the room admired Stephen's (persistence, stubbornness).

ANSWER persistence

1. What (disguise, camouflage) are you going to wear to Jenna's party?
2. By counting calories, Kitty was able to (lessen, reduce) her weight by 12 pounds.
3. What shall we do with the (leftover, surplus) mashed potatoes?
4. While we're on vacation, our next-door neighbor will (nourish, feed) the fish.
5. Bill went home to (change, modify) his clothes before going out to play softball.
6. Here is a joke that everyone in the audience is sure to (scoff, laugh) at!
7. When the glass hit the floor, it shattered into hundreds of tiny (fractions, fragments).
8. Michael's older brother got a ticket for (outdoing, exceeding) the speed limit.
9. All the (residents, occupants) on my block worked together to plan the Fourth of July party.
10. Proofread your papers to make sure you have corrected all (oversights, errors).

Antonyms

An *antonym* is a word that means the opposite of another word. Dictionaries list antonyms for many words.

ANTONYMS   abundant:scarce   ban:allow
negative:positive   drab:colorful
precise:inexact   exterior:interior
descendant:ancestor   effect:cause
temporary:permanent   meek:bold

Exercise 12   *Recognizing Antonyms*

Number your paper 1 to 10. Write the letter of the answer that is most nearly opposite in meaning to the word in capital letters. Then check your answers in a dictionary.

1. ELABORATE   (A) fancy (B) complicated (C) untruthful (D) simple (E) long
2. ANXIETY   (A) fearfulness (B) eagerness (C) satisfaction (D) shyness (E) calmness
3. DEPRIVE   (A) give (B) cry (C) take (D) withhold (E) punish
4. PACIFY   (A) calm (B) relax (C) upset (D) hinder (E) touch
5. MYSTIFY (A) evaporate (B) clarify (C) confuse (D) scare (E) startle
6. ISOLATE   (A) separate (B) warm (C) boil (D) return (E) group
7. DONOR   (A) receiver (B) giver (C) charity (D) gift (E) money
8. PARCH   (A) moist (B) dry (C) flood (D) cool (E) scorch
9. ENDORSE   (A) oppose (B) ignore (C) support (D) vote (E) campaign
10. INABILITY   (A) weakness (B) handicap (C) skill (D) capacity (E) energy

EXERCISE 13 Thinking of Words between Antonyms

Number your paper 1 to 10. Then write at least two words
that lie between each pair of antonyms.

EXAMPLE   hot:cold
POSSIBLE ANSWERS   warm, cool

1. love:hate
2. freeze:burn
3. laugh:cry
4. wet:dry
5. skinny:fat

6. tardy:early
7. happy:sad
8. meek:bold
9. enormous:tiny
10. cling:relinquish

Analogies

Vocabulary is often a measure of how much a person
knows. For this reason your knowledge of words will be
tested several times throughout your years in school. There
are many types of vocabulary tests. One type of vocabulary
test asks you to identify relationships between pairs of words.
These relationships are called *analogies*. The following
example is an item from a test of analogies.

DRAB:DULL :: (A) wealth:poverty   (B) joy:sorrow
(C) wisdom:intelligence

The first step in answering this test item is to identify
the relationship between the two words in capital letters.
In this item the words are synonyms, since *drab* and *dull*
have similar meanings. The next step is to find the other
pair of words that have the same relationship. The first pair
of words, *wealth* and *poverty*, have opposite meanings, so
they are antonyms. The next pair of words, *joy* and *sorrow*,
are also opposites, or antonyms. The final pair, *wisdom* and
intelligence, is the correct answer. Like *drab* and *dull*, *wisdom* and *intelligence* are synonyms.

The capitalized words may also be words with opposite
meanings, as in the following test item. As you study it, see
if you can choose the other pair of antonyms.

LATTER:FORMER :: (A) old:ancient
(B) handsome:attractive   (C) close:open

The first two pairs are both synonyms, so they are not correct. The correct answer is (*C*), since *close* and *open*, like *latter* and *former*, are antonyms.

EXERCISE 14   *Recognizing Analogies*

Number your paper 1 to 10. Write *synonyms* or *antonyms* to tell how the words in capital letters are related. Then write *A, B,* or *C* to tell which pair of words are related in the same way.

EXAMPLE   WHISPER:SHOUT :: (A) foretell:predict
(B) lessen:increase   (C) wish:desire
ANSWER   antonyms—B

1. SHIMMER:SHINE :: (A) smile:grin   (B) cry:laugh
   (C) walk:ride
2. CUNNING:SLYNESS :: (A) beauty:ugliness
   (B) bravery:courage   (C) emptiness:fullness
3. FLEXIBLE:RIGID :: (A) black:white
   (B) similar:alike   (C) reliable:trustworthy
4. CONFIDENTIAL:SECRET :: (A) nervous:calm
   (B) rainy:dry   (C) lifeless:dead
5. MAXIMUM:MINIMUM :: (A) far:distant   (B) ill:sick
   (C) youthful:mature
6. INQUIRY:QUESTION :: (A) cup:saucer   (B) cup:mug
   (C) cup:milk
7. JUBILANT:SAD :: (A) gruff:rough   (B) drab:dull
   (C) tall:short
8. CONSUMER:SELLER :: (A) student:teacher
   (B) boy:male   (C) animal:pet
9. ABOLISH:RESTORE :: (A) leave:depart
   (B) come:arrive   (C) go:come
10. PHASE:STAGE :: (A) television:radio
    (B) photograph:picture   (C) record:phonograph

Increasing Your Vocabulary

Every day you come across new words. Take the time to learn them. Look them up in the dictionary and use them in your speaking and writing. Before long they will be part of your vocabulary.

You can also increase your vocabulary by keeping a notebook of new words. Enter each new word you find and write out a short definition. Review your list from time to time to refresh your memory.

Vocabulary List

The following list contains words that you are likely to find in your reading. All the words have appeared earlier in the chapter. If you are unsure of any of these words, add them to your vocabulary notebook.

Vocabulary List

abolish	elaborate	latter	persistence
abundant	endorse	lessen	phase
anxiety	evident	maximum	precise
ban	exceed	meek	preference
barren	exterior	mimic	preview
camouflage	falter	minimum	pursue
coincident	flexible	misjudge	rarity
confidential	foretell	modify	realm
consumer	fragment	mystify	reassure
contrast	gruff	negative	recovery
correspond	hazard	nourish	retain
cunning	impose	obligation	scald
deprive	inability	occupant	scoff
descendant	indefinite	omit	shimmer
desolate	informal	oversight	surplus
donor	inquiry	pacify	temporary
drab	isolate	parch	vocal
effect	jubilant	penetrate	yearn

*C*hapter *R*eview

A **Context Clues.** Number your paper 1 to 4. Then write the letter of the answer that is closest in meaning to the underlined word.

1. The new cars are very <u>efficient</u>: They burn no more fuel than they absolutely need.
   (A) expensive   (B) comfortable   (C) quiet
   (D) effective   (E) safe
2. The cloud <u>enveloped</u> the mountain like a shawl around giant shoulders.
   (A) rained on   (B) darkened   (C) hid
   (D) brushed against   (E) wrapped
3. Her long illness left Maria thin and <u>frail</u>.
   (A) weak   (B) ruddy   (C) alert   (D) joyful
   (E) tall
4. The twins were <u>identical</u> in every way, from the dimples in their cheeks to the color of their hair.
   (A) different   (B) well behaved   (C) alike
   (D) shy   (E) unusual

B **Prefixes and Suffixes.** Number your paper 1 to 10. Write the prefix or suffix that has the same meaning as the underlined word or words. Then write the complete word defined after the equal sign.

1. <u>before</u> + caution = care taken beforehand
2. <u>incorrect</u> + interpret = to take the wrong meaning
3. <u>again</u> + apply = to make application a second time
4. <u>two</u> + monthly = every two months
5. <u>together</u> + pilot = partner in the cockpit
6. guitar + <u>one who</u> = someone who plays the guitar
7. heart + <u>without</u> = cruel
8. human + <u>make</u> = to give human qualities to
9. still + <u>state of</u> = calm
10. drink + <u>capable of</u> = safe to drink

C **Synonyms.** Number your paper 1 to 10. Write the letter of the answer that is closest in meaning to the word in capital letters.

1. EXCEED   (A) reduce   (B) surpass   (C) please
   (D) achieve   (E) resent
2. PURSUE   (A) lead   (B) assist   (C) wait
   (D) try   (E) follow
3. MINIMUM   (A) least   (B) tiny   (C) delicate
   (D) most   (E) greater
4. MODIFY   (A) address   (B) restore   (C) change
   (D) err   (E) regret
5. HAZARD   (A) safety   (B) danger   (C) hope
   (D) denial   (E) expert
6. ABUNDANT   (A) barren   (B) large   (C) scarce
   (D) plentiful   (E) empty
7. MEEK   (A) sad   (B) small   (C) wholesome
   (D) eager   (E) humble
8. YEARN   (A) expand   (B) desire   (C) deprive
   (D) weaken   (E) exert
9. FRAGMENT   (A) piece   (B) stem   (C) item
   (D) candy   (E) stick
10. OVERSIGHT   (A) viewfinder   (B) error   (C) quest
    (D) vision   (E) reversal

D **Antonyms.** Number your paper 1 to 15. Then write an antonym for each of the following words.

1. exterior
2. informal
3. inability
4. drab
5. negative
6. maximum
7. indefinite
8. lessen
9. effect
10. precise
11. ban
12. temporary
13. endorse
14. abundant
15. meek

32

Studying and Test-Taking Skills

Athletes who perform well use more than just natural ability. They also use skills they have worked to develop. You also need to develop skills for studying and test-taking. When you learn these skills, you can use them to improve your performance in all your subjects.

EXERCISE 1 *Studying and Test-Taking Skills*

Number your paper 1 to 10. Read the list of studying and test-taking skills below. On your paper write *Yes* if the skill is helpful to practice. Write *No* if it would not be helpful to practice.

1. Study in a place that is quiet and free from distractions.
2. Take notes on your textbook assignments.
3. Study only when you feel like it.
4. Take notes during class lectures.
5. Review unit and chapter summaries before a test.
6. Ask your teacher beforehand what the test will cover.
7. Stay up late studying on the night before a test.
8. Read all test directions carefully.
9. Study hard without taking a break.
10. Budget your time during a test.

Studying Skills

Much of the information you need to learn comes from your textbooks. Before beginning to use a new textbook, take a few minutes to review the table of contents and the index. Also become familiar with other sections at the beginning or the end, such as a glossary of terms. These sections will help you use your textbooks more efficiently.

Reading a Textbook

To remember the material in a textbook, you must do more than just pick it up and read it. One way to help you learn and remember what you read is the SQ3R method. *SQ3R* stands for Survey, Question, Read, Recite, and Review.

Steps for Reading a Textbook

SURVEY	First get a general idea of what the selection is about. Begin by reading titles, subtitles, and words set off in a different type or color. Look at maps, tables, charts, or other illustrations. Then read the introduction and summary.
QUESTION	Decide what questions you should be able to answer after reading the selection. Look at any study questions in the book. Also think of your own questions, based on your survey.
READ	Now read the selection. As you read, try to answer your questions. Find the main idea in each section. Look for important information that is not included in your questions. Then review the selection and take notes.
RECITE	Answer each question in your own words by reciting or writing the answers.
REVIEW	Answer the questions again without looking at your notes or the selection. Then check your answers. Continue reviewing until you can answer each question correctly.

EXERCISE 2   Reading a Textbook

Use the SQ3R method to study the passage below.

1. **Survey** the passage. What tells you the general idea?
2. Write **questions** that you can answer later.
3. **Read** the passage and take notes.
4. **Recite** the answers to your questions.
5. **Review** your answers by writing them without looking at your notes. Then check them against the passage.

A Natural Force of Change

One important force for change comes from inside Earth. Hot, melted rock sometimes pushes up from deep within the ground. When the melted rock finds a crack in Earth's surface, it flows out and forms a **volcano.**

Volcanoes can cause dramatic changes in the land around them. If the melted rock, called **lava,** bursts up like a great fountain, it forms a steep, cone-shaped mountain. As the lava cools, it hardens into many different kinds of rocks.

Taking Notes

Another way to understand and remember what you read is to take notes. Taking notes helps you decide which points are important. It also helps you remember the material you hear or read and provides a study guide for review.

Taking Notes

1. Read the selection first. Then review it, taking notes in your own words.
2. Include only the main ideas and important details.
3. Write key words and phrases, not complete sentences.
4. Look for key words set off in different type.
5. Look for words that mark main points, such as *first, next, then, one, another,* and *finally.*
6. Review your notes soon after you write them.

EXERCISE 3 *Taking Notes*

Following the directions below, take notes on the passage about the earth's movement.

1. Read the passage once.
2. Write the title of the passage.
3. Write the words that appear in dark type.
4. Write two phrases that mark important points in the passage.
5. Write three abbreviations or symbols that you might use in your notes.
6. Using the guidelines on page 544, take notes on the passage.

Earth's Movement and the Sun

The amount of the sun's energy a place receives varies because of the way the earth moves in space. In many places, including most of the United States, winters are colder than summers. Other places may have hot or cold weather all year round. The differences are caused by changes in the earth's position in relation to the sun. That position changes in two ways—rotation and revolution.

Rotation: Day and Night. As it travels through space, the earth spins like a top. This spinning motion is called **rotation.** The earth rotates on its **axis.** The axis is an imaginary line through the center of the earth from one pole to the other. It takes 24 hours for the earth to make one complete turn on its axis. When your part of the earth turns toward the sun, it is daytime. As the earth continues to rotate, your part of the earth turns away from the sun. Then it becomes dark. The earth's rotation is the reason for day and night.

Revolution: The Seasons. In addition to spinning on its axis, the earth travels around the sun. In this motion, called **revolution,** the earth follows a nearly circular path, or **orbit,** around the sun. The earth takes 365¼ days to make one complete revolution around the sun.

Test-Taking Skills

If you have kept up with your classwork, used the SQ3R method to read assignments, and taken careful notes, you are well on your way to being prepared for a test. Even when you know the material, however, you may be confused by the test questions. The skills of test-taking or knowing *how* to answer a test question can be as important as knowing the answer.

Classroom Tests

There are two basic types of test questions—objective and essay. An objective question has only one correct answer, and the answer is short. True-false and multiple-choice are common objective questions.

True-False Questions.   A true-false question is in the form of a statement. You are asked to decide whether the statement is true or false. Every word of the statement is important.

F	Winters are colder than summers in all places. [In *many* places, but not in *all*.]
T	Some places have hot weather all year.

Strategies for True-False Questions

1. Read each word very carefully. Just one word can make the statement true or false.
2. Look for words such as *always, never, all, none, no.* They mean the statement can have no exceptions.
3. Look for words like *many, some, sometimes, usually, may.* They mean the statement can have exceptions and still be true.
4. Think carefully about each part of the statement. If any part is false, then the entire statement is false.

EXERCISE 4   *Answering True-False Questions*

Number your paper 1 to 10. Then write *T* if the statement is true and *F* if it is false. You may look in other parts of this book for the answers.

1. Proper nouns are always capitalized.
2. Abbreviations of proper nouns are not capitalized.
3. Every sentence ends with a period.
4. Some sentences end with question marks.
5. Sentences can end with periods or commas.
6. All pronouns are personal pronouns.
7. Some pronouns show possession.
8. All adverbs end in *-ly.*
9. An action verb tells what the subject does.
10. An interjection expresses strong feeling.

Multiple-Choice Questions.   A multiple-choice question gives you several possible answers. You are asked to choose the best one. Try to choose the best answer to this multiple-choice question.

The first syllable of *rotund* rhymes with which of these words?

  a. lot   b. write   c. trot   d. low

If you are familiar with the word *rotund,* you may know the correct answer immediately. If you are not certain, however, you may be able to eliminate some of the choices. *Lot* and *trot* look as if they might rhyme with the first part of *rotund,* but they rhyme with each other. A multiple-choice question has only one right answer. These two choices, then, can be eliminated. Of the two that remain, *write* seems far less likely to rhyme with *ro-.* The more likely—and correct—answer is *d, low.*

The following example shows another type of multiple-choice question. This type asks you to complete a sentence.

The capital city of Italy is _____.

  a. Rome   b. San Francisco   c. Paris   d. Austria

Begin by reading all of the choices and eliminating those you know are wrong. You may know that San Francisco is a city in the United States. Paris is a city in Europe, but it is located in France, not Italy. Austria is not a city but a country. Choice *a*, *Rome*, is the only possible answer.

Strategies for Multiple-Choice Questions

1. Read every word of the question carefully.
2. Read every choice before you answer the question.
3. Eliminate choices that you know are wrong.
4. Choose the best answer from the remaining choices.
5. Try to find a reason for your choice. Do not guess wildly.

EXERCISE 5 *Answering Multiple-Choice Questions*

Number your paper 1 to 10. Then write the letter of the correct answer to each question.

1. What is the capital of North Carolina?
   a. Virginia   c. Chicago
   b. Raleigh   d. Montreal

2. Find the pair of antonyms.
   a. hurl, throw   c. talent, ability
   b. heard, herd   d. compliment, insult

3. How many sides does an octagon have?
   a. 5   c. 8
   b. 7   d. 10

4. Find the word that is spelled incorrectly.
   a. releive   c. foreign
   b. design   d. their

5. Which word would be listed first in a dictionary?
   a. relinquish   c. rehabilitate
   b. replenish   d. remnant

6. What is another way of writing 95?
   a. 90 + 5   c. 90 + 50
   b. 9 + 50   d. 9 + 5

7. Which American president was in office during World War II?
   a. Winston Churchill c. Abraham Lincoln
   b. John Adams   d. Franklin Delano Roosevelt
8. Which planet is closest to Earth?
   a. the moon   c. the Big Dipper
   b. Venus   d. Alpha Centauri
9. Which animal is not a reptile?
   a. lizard   c. goldfish
   b. snake   d. crocodile
10. Which is the best description of lava?
   a. melted rock   c. black rock
   b. volcano   d. volcanic explosion

Essay Questions. An essay question requires you to write a full answer. The answer may be a paragraph or more. Your answer will be judged not only on how many facts you include but also on how well you understand the facts and organize them.

EXERCISE 6 *Understanding Essay Questions*

Number your paper 1 to 5. Read the Steps for Writing an Essay Answer on page 550. Then read each essay question below. Write the key word and one sentence that explains what the question requires you to do.

EXAMPLE Explain the formation of volcanoes.
ANSWER Explain—Tell what volcanoes are and how and why they are formed.

1. Describe the way in which volcanoes change the land.
2. Summarize the plot of Charles Dickens's novel *A Christmas Carol.*
3. Compare the alligator and the crocodile.
4. What are the important contrasts between the rotation and the revolution of the earth?
5. Write a paragraph that defines the term *vertebrate.*

549

EXERCISE 7   *Answering an Essay Question*

Choose one of the questions in Exercise 6 and write an answer for it. Follow the steps listed below.

EXERCISE 8   *Writing and Answering Your Own Question*

Write an essay question based on a subject you have studied in one of your courses this year. Then answer the question, following the steps below.

Steps for Writing an Essay Answer

1. Plan your time and strategy. Spend more time on questions that are worth more points. Begin with the questions you find easiest to answer. If you have a choice of questions, read each one carefully before you choose.

2. Read the directions carefully. Be sure you understand what the question is asking before you write your answer. Look for key words such as the following.

Compare	Point out similarities and differences.
Contrast	Point out differences.
Describe	Give details.
Define	Make clear the meaning.
Discuss	Examine in detail.
Explain	Tell how, what, or why.
Summarize	Briefly review the main points.

3. Organize your answer. Write a simple outline by jotting down your main points and supporting details.

4. Write the essay. Use the strategies below.

   - State the main idea of the essay in your introduction.
   - Follow the order of your simple outline.
   - Be specific. State each main point in a complete sentence. Then back up each main point with facts, examples, and other supporting details. Be sure all your details relate to the main point.
   - Write a conclusion that summarizes the main idea of your essay.
   - Edit your answer, correcting any errors.

Standardized Tests

Classroom tests are used as a measure of what you have just learned in a course. Standardized tests are used to measure your overall knowledge and abilities in various subject areas. These standardized tests are given to large numbers of students in different schools across the United States.

There are two ways to prepare for a standardized test. First, keep up with your schoolwork. You cannot study years of schoolwork just before the test. Second, become familiar with the test forms and the types of questions asked. This part of the chapter will show you how to take standardized tests.

Hints for Taking Standardized Tests

1. Listen closely to the examiner's instructions.
2. Fill in your name on the answer sheet.
3. Read the directions and sample questions carefully. Be sure you understand them before you begin.
4. Begin working when the examiner tells you.
5. Read each question carefully. Be aware of details.
6. Do not spend too much time on any one question.
7. You may write on the test form, but always mark your answers on the separate answer sheet. Most tests ask you to shade the circle that contains the letter of your answer.

   ANSWER SHEET   1. Ⓐ Ⓑ Ⓒ Ⓓ

8. Most standardized tests are scored by machine. Mark only one answer for each question. Make your marks dark. To change an answer, erase it fully.
9. Be sure the number on the answer sheet matches the number of the question.
10. Stop when you reach a stop signal on the test or when time is called.
11. If you have time, check your work.

Vocabulary Tests. One kind of question appears often on standardized vocabulary tests. This kind asks you to recognize a *synonym*. Following is one example.

felt <u>drowsy</u>
   A ill   **B** content   **C** sleepy   **D** lively

Although all the words make sense when used with *felt*, only one word is close in meaning to *drowsy*. Notice that you might feel drowsy because you are ill, but *ill* does not mean the same thing. Notice that *content* and *lively* are not synonyms of *drowsy*. The answer is *C, sleepy*. You would fill in the circle with the letter *C* on your answer sheet.

ANSWER SHEET   Ⓐ Ⓑ Ⓒ Ⓓ

***E*XERCISE 9** *Answering Vocabulary Questions*

Number your paper 1 to 5. Then write the letter of the synonym of the underlined word.

1. <u>enormous</u> crowd
   A huge   **B** noisy   **C** quiet   **D** waiting

2. <u>fortunate</u> person
   A happy   **B** lucky   **C** desperate   **D** familiar

3. his <u>responsibility</u>
   A property   **B** duty   **C** behavior   **D** family

4. <u>artificial</u> flowers
   A silk   **B** colorful   **C** faded   **D** fake

5. <u>benefit</u> from
   A escape   **B** rescue   **C** gain   **D** arise

Tests on Mechanics and Usage. These examples show the most common kinds of questions on tests of mechanics and usage. The correct answers are shaded.

CHOOSE THE CORRECT ANSWER.

She _____ the green sweater.

Ⓐ choose   Ⓑ chosen   Ⓒ choosed   Ⓓ chose

CHOOSE THE BEST WAY TO WRITE THE UNDERLINED PART.

Which of the three kittens is smallest?

Ⓐ smallest Ⓑ smaller Ⓒ more small Ⓓ most small

FIND THE ERROR IF THERE IS ONE.

Aren't you leaving for ohio tomorrow? No error
　Ⓐ　　　　　　　　　Ⓑ　　　　　Ⓒ　Ⓓ

EXERCISE 10 Answering Questions on Mechanics and Usage

Number your paper 1 to 10. Then write the letter of the best choice for the underlined part.

1. Maria seen that movie last night.
   A seen **B** seed **C** saw **D** see

2. Has anyone lost a yellow sneaker?
   A ? **B** . **C** ! **D** ,

3. Harry hasn't said nothing since breakfast.
   A nothing **B** no word **C** none **D** anything

4. Of the three jackets, which is best?
   A best **B** better **C** more best **D** most best

5. Everyone has ate supper already.
   A ate **B** eaten **C** eat **D** eated

6. The first person off the plane was aunt bea.
   A aunt bea **B** Aunt Bea **C** Aunt bea **D** aunt Bea

7. The weather was much gooder yesterday than it was the day before.
   A gooder **B** better **C** good **D** more better

8. Last night I finished reading the story "Today".
   A " **B** ?" **C** ," **D** ."

9. Is that beautiful bouquet of flowers for hers?
   A hers **B** she **C** her's **D** her

10. All of the boys carried theirs own suitcases.
    A theirs **B** his **C** their **D** him

EXERCISE 11 Answering Questions on Mechanics and Usage

Number your paper 1 to 5. Then write the letter of the part that has an error. If there is no error, write *D*.

1. Her <u>mother</u> and <u>father</u> were born in <u>iowa</u>. <u>No error</u>
        A   B   C   D

2. Ben <u>didn't</u> know <u>nobody</u> at the <u>party.</u> <u>No error</u>
         A   B   C   D

3. We <u>ate</u> grapes<u>,</u> peaches<u>,</u> and plums. <u>No error</u>
        A   B   C   D

4. Karen and <u>I</u> <u>is</u> <u>leaving</u> early. <u>No error</u>
                A B   C   D

5. Please <u>dont</u> <u>come</u> home <u>too</u> late. <u>No error</u>
              A   B   C   D

Tests of Writing Ability.   Writing well is one of your basic goals as a student. At some point in your education, you will probably be asked to take a standardized test that measures your writing skills. One of these skills is how well you put sentences together to form a paragraph. Some questions ask you to find a sentence that does not belong in the paragraph. Others ask you to select the best supporting detail for a topic sentence. Another type of question asks you to select the best order for the sentences in a paragraph. Notice in the following example that the sentences are numbered. The numbers below the sentences show the various ways the sentences can be ordered.

(1) Here is an easy way to prepare it.
(2) Spread tuna on bread slices and top with cheese.
(3) A toasted tuna-and-cheese sandwich is delicious.
(4) Put the slices under the broiler for four minutes.

    A 1 - 4 - 2 - 3   **c** 2 - 4 - 1 - 3
    B 4 - 3 - 1 - 2   **D** 3 - 1 - 2 - 4

The answer is *D*. Choice *D* shows the steps for making a toasted tuna-and-cheese sandwich in the correct order.

EXERCISE 12 Answering Questions on Writing

Write the letter that shows the best order.

1. (1) Just pat some ground meat into the right shape.
   (2) Finally, put it on a bun and eat it.
   (3) Then cook it on both sides in a hot frying pan.
   (4) It is not difficult to make a hamburger.

   A 1 - 4 - 2 - 3   **C** 2 - 4 - 1 - 3
   B 4 - 1 - 3 - 2   **D** 3 - 2 - 1 - 4

2. (1) As a result, the river was rising dangerously.
   (2) It had been raining hard for three days.
   (3) Would this barrier hold back the rising water?
   (4) So volunteers piled sandbags along the riverbank.

   A 4 - 1 - 3 - 2   **C** 3 - 1 - 2 - 4
   B 2 - 1 - 4 - 3   **D** 1 - 2 - 3 - 4

3. (1) I woke up just before dawn this morning.
   (2) Suddenly pink rays streaked the walls.
   (3) Soon the entire room shone with a rosy glow.
   (4) My eyes opened to a shapeless world of gray.

   A 1 - 4 - 2 - 3   **C** 2 - 4 - 3 - 1
   B 3 - 2 - 4 - 1   **D** 4 - 1 - 2 - 3

4. (1) "Mending Wall" and "Road Not Taken" are favorites.
   (2) Robert Frost was a well-known American poet.
   (3) Frost wrote several well-loved poems.
   (4) Most famous is "The Gift Outright," written for John F. Kennedy's presidential inauguration.

   A 4 - 1 - 3 - 2   **C** 3 - 4 - 1 - 2
   B 1 - 2 - 4 - 3   **D** 2 - 3 - 1 - 4

5. (1) These tests of knowledge try to judge how much a student has learned about a particular subject.
   (2) Other standardized tests measure ability.
   (3) Some standardized tests measure knowledge.
   (4) These tests try to judge a student's general ability to solve intellectual problems.

   A 1 - 4 - 3 - 2   **C** 3 - 1 - 2 - 4
   B 2 - 3 - 4 - 1   **D** 4 - 2 - 3 - 1

Chapter Review

A **Answering True-False Questions.** Number your paper 1 to 10. Then write *T* if the statement is true or *F* if it is false.

1. All changes on the earth's surface are from volcanoes.
2. Volcanoes sometimes change the land around them.
3. Volcanoes are formed from hot, melted rock.
4. Lava hardens into many different kinds of rocks.
5. The line of the earth's axis can sometimes be seen.
6. In all places, winters are colder than summers.
7. The earth's rotation is the reason for day and night.
8. A rotation of the earth may take more than 24 hours.
9. The earth's path around the sun is a perfect circle.
10. One revolution of the earth takes exactly 365 days.

B **Answering Vocabulary Questions.** Number your paper 1 to 10. Then write the letter of the synonym of the underlined word.

1. different <u>pattern</u>
   A clothing **B** design **C** person **D** story

2. interesting <u>notion</u>
   A idea **B** story **C** event **D** tale

3. <u>imitate</u> the style
   A copy **B** discuss **C** create **D** change

4. avoid <u>panic</u>
   A crowds **B** sadness **C** unhappiness **D** terror

5. <u>source</u> of the river
   A flow **B** length **C** beginning **D** end

6. slight <u>gesture</u>
   A dance **B** chance **C** movement **D** figure

7. <u>apparently</u> finished
   A totally **B** seemingly **C** completely **D** already

8. <u>accurate</u> map
   A incorrect **B** large   **C** colored   **D** correct

9. happy <u>occasion</u>
   A birthday **B** person   **C** ending   **D** event

10. <u>crude</u> drawing
    A rough   **B** lovely   **C** pencil   **D** amusing

C Answering Questions on Mechanics and Usage.

Write the letter of the underlined part that has an error. If there is no error, write *D*.

1. <u>Will</u> we have <u>Sunday</u> dinner at your <u>house.</u> <u>No error</u>
     A   B   C   D

2. Is <u>Fluff</u> or <u>bingo</u> the <u>bigger</u> dog? <u>No error</u>
       A   B   C   D

3. <u>Him</u> and Meg <u>went</u> there this <u>morning.</u> <u>No error</u>
     A   B   C   D

4. In <u>New York</u> we visited the <u>Museum of Natural</u>
        A   B
   <u>History</u> and <u>heard</u> a concert in the park. <u>No error</u>
       C   D

5. Many of the <u>students</u> <u>is</u> taking <u>French.</u> <u>No error</u>
                 A   B   C   D

6. <u>Mr.</u> Ames, we like <u>your</u> garden. <u>No error</u>
     A   B   C   D

7. Pedro and <u>I</u> haven't <u>never</u> <u>seen</u> a real cow. <u>No error</u>
              A   B   C   D

8. The <u>childrens</u> dragged <u>their</u> stuffed animals with
        A   B
   them <u>everywhere.</u> <u>No error</u>
         C   D

9. My <u>uncle</u> <u>bought</u> a new hat for <u>hisself.</u> <u>No error</u>
        A   B   C   D

10. The teacher asked, <u>"Which</u> of the three stories was
                         A B
    the <u>goodest</u>?" <u>No error</u>
         C   D

The Dictionary

Many writers work with a dictionary close at hand. They use it most often to check spellings and meanings of words. In addition to these uses, a dictionary can tell you how to pronounce a word, where to divide it into syllables, and how the word developed through history.

SPELLING — **cap il lar y** (kap′ə ler′ē), *n.*, *pl.* **-lar ies**, *adj.* —*n.* a blood vessel with a very slender, hairlike opening. Capillaries join the end of an artery to the beginning of a vein.

WORD ORIGIN — [< Latin *capillaris* of hair, hairlike < *capillus* hair]

Cap i tol (kap′ə təl), *n.* **1** the building at Washington, D.C., in which Congress meets. **2** Also, **capitol,** the building in which a state legislature meets.

CAPITALIZATION —

ABBREVIATIONS — **caps.,** capital letters.
Capt., Captain.

PRONUNCIATION — **care ful** (ker′fəl, kar′fəl), *adj.* **1** thinking what one says; watching what one does; taking pains; watchful; cautious. See synonym study below. **2** showing care; done with thought or effort; exact; thorough. **3** full of care or concern; attentive: *She was careful of the feelings of others.* **4** ARCHAIC. anxious; worried.
PART OF SPEECH —

DEFINITIONS —

RELATED — —**care′ful ly,** *adv.* —**care′ful ness,** *n.*
FORMS

Syn. 1 Careful, cautious, wary mean watchful in speaking and acting. **Careful** means being observant and giving serious attention and thought to what one is doing, especially to details: *He is a careful driver.* **Cautious** means very careful, looking ahead for possible risks or dangers, and guarding against them by taking no chances: *She is cautious about making promises.* **Wary** emphasizes the idea of being mistrustful and on the alert for danger or trouble: *He is wary of overly friendly people.*
SYNONYMS —

From SCOTT, FORESMAN ADVANCED DICTIONARY by E. L. Thorndike and Clarence L. Barnhart. Copyright © 1983, 1979, 1974 by Scott, Foresman & Co. Reprinted by permission.

Word Location

All dictionaries list words in alphabetical order so you can find the information you need quickly. Guide words tell you at a glance which words are on each page.

Guide Words

Guide words are the words printed in heavy type at the top of each dictionary page. They show you the first and last words defined on that page. The guide words **pinball** and **pirate,** for example, tell you that *pioneer* and *piranha* appear on that page. The words *Pittsburgh* and *pizza,* however, would appear on the next page.

EXERCISE 1   *Using Guide Words*

Make two columns on your paper. Write the guide words **glider—gnaw** at the top of the first column and **gnome—golf** at the top of the second column. Then write each word in the proper column.

gold	gluey	globetrot	golden eagle
gobble	gnat	go-cart	glory
glimpse	goatskin	glutton	gnarl
goalie	glowworm	glitter	goggles
glossary	goblet	goldfish	goal post

Alphabetical Order

A dictionary includes many different kinds of entries. Notice the strict letter-by-letter alphabetical order.

SINGLE WORD	**valentine**
TWO-WORD COMPOUND	**vampire bat**
HYPHENATED COMPOUND	**Venus's-flytrap**
PREFIX	**vice-**
PHRASE	**vice versa**
ABBREVIATION	**V.I.P.**

A compound word is alphabetized as if there were no space or hyphen between each part of the word. An abbreviation is alphabetized letter by letter, not by the word it stands for.

EXERCISE 2   Alphabetizing Words

Following are the first lines of famous poems. Arrange the underlined words in each line in alphabetical order.

EXAMPLE   When to the sessions of sweet silent thought
          (Shakespeare)

ANSWER   sessions, silent, sweet

Famous Firsts

1. A slumber did my spirit seal (Wordsworth)
2. Booth led boldly with his big bass drum (Lindsay)
3. Full fathom five thy father lies (Shakespeare)
4. I sing of brooks, of blossoms, birds, and bowers (Herrick)
5. O western wind, when wilt thou blow (Anonymous)
6. The soul selects her own society (Dickinson)
7. As I was walking all alone (Anonymous)
8. She told the story and the whole world wept (Dunbar)
9. He clasps the crag with crooked hands (Tennyson)
10. Do not go gentle into that good night (Thomas)

EXERCISE 3   Alphabetizing Different Kinds of Entries

Make three columns on your paper. Then write the words in each column in alphabetical order.

1.	2.	3.
Labor Day	jackpot	nickname
ladyfinger	janitor	New Jersey
Lab.	Japanese	numero uno
labor-saving	jack-o'-lantern	no-show
labor	javelin	N.Y.C.
lady-in-waiting	January	non-
ladybug	jack rabbit	news conference
La.	Jack Frost	Nobel Prize
lacemaking	Jan.	N.J.
laboratory	jackknife	nitty-gritty

*I*nformation in an Entry

The dictionary presents a wealth of information about each word. All of the information for each word is called the *entry*. The four most important parts of the entry are the entry word, pronunciation, definitions, and word origin. The entry for *penguin* shows these four parts.

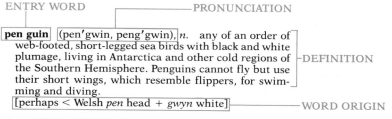

ENTRY WORD   PRONUNCIATION

pen guin (pen′gwin, peng′gwin), *n.* any of an order of web-footed, short-legged sea birds with black and white plumage, living in Antarctica and other cold regions of the Southern Hemisphere. Penguins cannot fly but use their short wings, which resemble flippers, for swimming and diving.
[perhaps < Welsh *pen* head + *gwyn* white] —WORD ORIGIN

—DEFINITION

From SCOTT, FORESMAN ADVANCED DICTIONARY by E. L. Thorndike and Clarence L. Barnhart. Copyright © 1983, 1979, 1974 by Scott, Foresman & Co. Reprinted by permission.

*T*he Entry Word

A quick glance at the entry word will give you three pieces of useful information. It shows you (1) how to spell a word, (2) whether a word should be capitalized, and (3) where a word should be divided into syllables.

Spelling. The entry word shows how to spell a word correctly. Some words have more than one correct spelling. The most common spelling is called the *preferred spelling*. The second spelling is called the *variant spelling*. Always use the preferred spelling in your writing.

PREFERRED SPELLING

yo · gurt, *also,* **yo · ghurt.**

VARIANT SPELLING

A dictionary also shows you how to spell the plurals of nouns, the principal parts of verbs, and the comparative

561

and superlative degrees of adjectives and adverbs. These are given only if the form or spelling is irregular.

mul·ti·ply   (mul′ tə plī), *v.*,   -plied, -ply·ing.── PRINCIPAL PARTS

mus·ty   (mus′ tē), *adj.*,   -ti·er, -ti·est.── ADJECTIVE FORMS

mys·ter·y   (mis′ tər ē), *n. pl.*,   -ter·ies.── NOUN PLURAL

Words formed by adding a prefix or a suffix to the entry word are often shown at the end of the entry. These related forms are called *derived words.*

mys ter i ous   (mi stir′ē əs), *adj.* **1** full of mystery; hard to explain or understand; secret; hidden. **2** suggesting mystery: *a mysterious look.*
   —mys ter′ i ous ly, *adv.*   **—mys ter′ i ous ness,** *n.*── DERIVED WORDS

From SCOTT, FORESMAN ADVANCED DICTIONARY by E. L. Thorndike and Clarence L. Barnhart. Copyright © 1983, 1979, 1974 by Scott, Foresman & Co. Reprinted by permission.

EXERCISE 4   *Correcting Spelling Errors*

The following words are misspelled. Number your paper 1 to 20. Then, using a dictionary, write the correct spelling for each of the following words.

1. oxes	11. thiner
2. sopranoes	12. whinnyed
3. qualifyed	13. choosen
4. friendlyest	14. growed
5. acquited	15. shelfs
6. hoofs	16. prefered
7. proceing	17. blury
8. dazzleing	18. happyest
9. harmonise	19. sillyness
10. skiming	20. patrioticly

Capitalization.   The entry word will be printed with a capital letter if a word should be capitalized. If a word is not always capitalized, the word will be shown with a capital letter near the appropriate definition.

southwest (south′west′), *adj.* **1** halfway between south and west. **2** from the southwest. **3** in the southwest. —*adv.* toward the southwest. —*n.* **1** a southwest direction. **2** place that is in the southwest part or direction. **3 the Southwest**, the southwestern part of the United States, especially Texas, New Mexico, Oklahoma, Arizona, and, sometimes, S California.

Statue of Liberty, a colossal statue of the goddess of liberty holding aloft a lighted torch, on Liberty Island in New York Bay. It was given to the United States by France in 1884.

From SCOTT, FORESMAN ADVANCED DICTIONARY by E. L. Thorndike and Clarence L. Barnhart. Copyright © 1983, 1979, 1974 by Scott, Foresman & Co. Reprinted by permission.

Syllables. Sometimes when you are writing a composition, you need to divide a word at the end of a line. The dictionary shows you where each syllable ends.

hel·i·cop·ter   par·a·chute   sky·div·ing

If you must divide a word, always do so between syllables. (*See rules for dividing words on page 285.*)

EXERCISE 5 *Dividing Words into Syllables*

Number your paper 1 to 10. Then find each word in a dictionary and write it with a dot between syllables.

EXAMPLE   patriotic
ANSWER   pa·tri·ot·ic

1. dishonor
2. loyalty
3. twentieth
4. hypnotic
5. audacity
6. regrettable
7. regularly
8. sandpiper
9. nationally
10. intriguing

Pronunciation

A phonetic spelling is shown in parentheses after each entry word. The phonetic spelling shows how to pronounce the word correctly.

bal·let (bal′ ā)   Fris·bee (friz′ bē)

A complete pronunciation key at the beginning of the dictionary explains all the symbols used in the phonetic spellings. In addition, most dictionaries provide a shortened form of the key on every other page for easy reference.

PARTIAL PRONUNCIATION KEY

a hat	i it	oi oil	ch child	⌈ a in about
ā age	ī ice	ou out	ng long	e in taken
ä far	o hot	u cup	sh she	ə = ⟨ i in pencil
e let	ō open	u̇ put	th thin	o in lemon
ē equal	ô order	ü rule	ᴛʜ then	⌊ u in circus
ėr term			zh measure	< = derived from

From SCOTT, FORESMAN ADVANCED DICTIONARY by E. L. Thorndike and Clarence L. Barnhart. Copyright © 1983, 1979, 1974 by Scott, Foresman & Co. Reprinted by permission.

Diacritical Marks. In the pronunciation key above, there are marks over some of the vowels. They are called diacritical marks. Diacritical marks are used to show the different sounds a vowel can make. For example, the different sounds of the vowel *e* are shown in the following ways.

DIACRITICAL MARKS

e as in let   **ē** as in equal   **ėr** as in term

The Schwa. Sometimes vowels are pronounced like the sound *uh*. Dictionaries use the symbol ə to represent this sound. This symbol is called a schwa.

pan·da (pan′ də)   **o·cean** (ō′ shən)   **gal·lop** (gal′ əp)

EXERCISE 6 *Marking Pronunciation*
Number your paper 1 to 10. Then find each word in a dictionary and write the pronunciation. Include all of the diacritical marks.

EXAMPLE   ahead
ANSWER   (ə hed′)

1. take   3. circus   5. evil   7. approach   9. lemon
2. find   4. please   6. lit   8. tapestry   10. petty

Accent Marks. An accent mark (') in a phonetic spelling tells you which syllable should be pronounced with the most stress.

fu·ture (fyü′ chər)   **con·fet·ti** (kən fĕt′ ē)

Some words have two accent marks. The darker one, called the *primary accent*, receives the most stress. The lighter one, called the *secondary accent*, receives slightly less stress.

but·ter·fly (but′ tər·flī′)   ⎯PRIMARY ACCENT
    ⎯SECONDARY ACCENT

Exercise 7 *Placing Accent Marks*

Number your paper 1 to 10. Using a dictionary, write the pronunciation of each word. Leave space between syllables and mark both primary and secondary accent marks.

EXAMPLE   recreation
ANSWER   (rek′ rē·ā′ shən)

1. influential
2. googol
3. democratic
4. exploration
5. conservatory
6. reservation
7. marshmallow
8. pliability
9. subplot
10. impossibility

Definitions

Many words have more than one definition. Look at the entry for the word *cast* on page 566. Notice that 11 definitions are given. When looking for the meaning of a word, be sure to read all of the definitions and examples carefully. Then decide which meaning makes sense in your sentence.

Part of Speech Labels. To indicate what part of speech a word is, most dictionaries use the following abbreviations.

PART OF SPEECH	*n.*	noun	*pron.*	pronoun
LABELS	*v.*	verb	*prep.*	preposition
	adj.	adjective	*conj.*	conjunction
	adv.	adverb	*interj.*	interjection

Many words may be used as more than one part of speech. Notice that the word *cast* can be used as either a verb or a noun. Be sure to find the right part of speech when searching for the definition of a word.

EXERCISE 8 *Identifying Different Uses of a Word*

Number your paper 1 to 10. Then, using the entry for *cast* below, write the number of the definition and the part of speech used in each sentence.

EXAMPLE I practiced my <u>cast</u> for hours, but all I caught was some seaweed.

ANSWER 1, n

> **cast** (kast), *v.*, **cast, cast ing,** *n.* —*v.* **1** throw, fling, or hurl. **2** throw one end of (a fishing line) out into the water. **3** throw off; let fall; shed: *The snake cast its skin.* **4** direct or turn: *He cast a glance of surprise at me.* **5** deposit (a ballot); give or record (a vote). **6** in the theater: select (an actor) for a part. **7** calculate astrologically: *cast a horoscope.* —*n.* **1** act of throwing a fishing line. **2** a plaster cast used to support a broken bone while it is mending: *I had my arm in a cast for more than a month.* **3** the actors in a play. **4** a slight amount of color; tinge: *a white dress with a pink cast.*

From SCOTT, FORESMAN ADVANCED DICTIONARY by E. L. Thorndike and Clarence L. Barnhart. Copyright © 1983, 1979, 1974 by Scott, Foresman & Co. Reprinted by permission.

1. On Tuesday I will <u>cast</u> my vote for Debbie.
2. During an eclipse, the moon takes on a copper <u>cast</u>.
3. Rhonda has to wear the <u>cast</u> on her arm for six weeks.
4. The teacher <u>cast</u> her eyes on the whispering students.
5. We <u>cast</u> our lines into the trout-filled lake.
6. Many magazines <u>cast</u> horoscopes each month.
7. Steven Spielberg <u>casts</u> many young people in his films.
8. Reindeer <u>cast</u> their antlers yearly and grow new ones.
9. Bruce and Eddie <u>cast</u> the rope across the stream.
10. The <u>cast</u> of the play received a standing ovation.

Synonyms. At the end of some entries, the dictionary will list synonyms. Synonyms are words that have similar definitions.

fun ny (fun′ē), *adj.*, **-ni er, -ni est. 1** causing laughter; amusing. See synonym study below. **2** INFORMAL. strange; odd. **3** INFORMAL. questionable or underhanded: *There is some funny business going on there.* **—fun′ni ly,** *adv.* **—fun′ni ness,** *n.*

SYNONYM ———

Syn. 1 Funny, laughable mean such as to cause laughter or amusement. **Funny** implies almost any degree of amusement from a hearty laugh to a faint smile: *The clown's antics were funny.* **Laughable** implies laughter, often scornful laughter: *Their fine airs are laughable.*

From SCOTT, FORESMAN ADVANCED DICTIONARY by E. L. Thorndike and Clarence L. Barnhart. Copyright © 1983, 1979, 1974 by Scott, Foresman & Co. Reprinted by permission.

***E*XERCISE 9** *Using a Dictionary for Improving Writing*

Using your dictionary, rewrite the following paragraph according to the directions below.

Weather Watch

(1) Meteorologists are sceintists who study the weather. (2) Part of the job is to predict wether the sky will be blue or grey by studying the layer of air that surrounds the Earth. (3) Meteorologists have a veriaty of instruments desined to help them determine weather patterns. (4) A anemometer measures wind speed, a barometer measures air pressure, and a hygrometer measures the amount of moisture in the air. (5) Altho meteorologists are well trained and experienced, the forecasts are not allways acurrate. (6) Changes in weather happen suddenly and unpredictablety.

1. Correct the misspelling in sentence 1.
2. Correct the misspelling in sentence 2.
3. Use the preferred spelling of *grey* in sentence 2.
4. Correct the capitalization error in sentence 2.
5. Correct two misspellings in sentence 3.
6. Correct the article in sentence 4.
7. Use the preferred spelling of *altho* in sentence 5.
8. Correct the hyphen error in sentence 5.
9. Correct two misspellings in sentence 5.
10. Correct the misspelling in sentence 6.

*W*ord Origins

Over the centuries the English language has gone through many changes, from Old English to Middle English to Modern English. The following examples show how the words we use today have changed over time.

Old English	Modern English
moder	mother
faeder	father
weorold	world
eage	eye
buttorfleoge	butterfly

The dictionary provides information about the history of words in the English language. This information, called the *word origin*, is usually found in brackets at the end of an entry. The following entry shows that the word *tadpole* comes from two Middle English words.

tad pole (tad′pōl′), *n.*   a very young frog or toad in the larval stage when it lives in water and has gills, a long tail, and no limbs; polliwog.   [Middle English *taddepol* < *tadde* toad + *pol* poll (head)]

WORD ORIGIN

tadpole

From SCOTT, FORESMAN ADVANCED DICTIONARY by E. L. Thorndike and Clarence L. Barnhart. Copyright © 1983, 1979, 1974 by Scott, Foresman & Co. Reprinted by permission.

*E*XERCISE 10   *Matching Old and New Words*

Number your paper 1 to 10. Then write the Old English word in group 2 that matches the Modern English word in group 1.

GROUP 1		**GROUP 2**	
1. book	6. answer	eorpe	sweoster
2. chill	7. sister	fleoge	steorra
3. earth	8. watch	scofl	waecce
4. fly	9. shovel	beech	freondlic
5. star	10. friendly	ciele	andswaru

Words from Other Languages. The English language is constantly growing as well as changing. Although there are many different sources for new words, over half of the words in the English language have been borrowed from other languages. Many come from Greek and Latin, while others have been adopted from a wide variety of sources. Following are some examples.

Words from Other Languages

GREEK	astronaut	ocean	comedy
LATIN	colony	missile	senate
SPANISH	breeze	poncho	mustang
SCOTTISH	clan	glen	slogan
FRENCH	cartoon	dentist	liberty
DUTCH	buoy	landscape	skipper
IRISH	bog	leprechaun	shamrock
ITALIAN	zero	spaghetti	violin
ARABIC	algebra	candy	magazine

*E*XERCISE 11 *Finding Word Origins*

Number your paper 1 to 10. Then use the dictionary to write the origin of each of the following words.

1. confetti
2. loafer
3. tornado
4. pirate
5. zebra
6. routine
7. yacht
8. boomerang
9. tea
10. alien

Words with Unusual Origins. Borrowing words from other languages is only one way our language grows. New words come into our language in a variety of other ways. Some words, called compounds, are formed by combining two words.

COMPOUNDS   fingerprint   raincoat   houseboat

Some words are a blend of two words.

BLENDS television + broadcast = telecast
squirm + wiggle = squiggle
fry + sizzle = frizzle

Some words are shortened forms of longer words.

SHORTENED FORM
ad advertisement
lunch luncheon
sitcom situation comedy

Some words imitate sounds.

SOUNDS crunch plunk strum yap whiff

Some names of people have also become words.

PEOPLE'S NAMES
Adolf Sax: Belgian inventor of the **saxophone**

Earl of Sandwich: English creator of the first **sandwich**

Rudolf Diesel: German inventor of the **diesel** engine

Some words are acronyms. Acronyms are words that are formed by the first letters or syllables of other words.

ACRONYMS
SAT **S**cholastic **A**ptitude **T**est
sonar **so**und **na**vigation **r**anging
loran **lo**ng-**ra**nge **n**avigation

EXERCISE 12 Finding Unusual Origins

Number your paper 1 to 20. Then tell how each of the following words came into the English language by writing *compound, blend, shortened form, sound, person's name,* or *acronym.* Use a dictionary to help you.

1. fizz
2. ACT
3. fan
4. gym
5. smog
6. deli
7. watt
8. radar
9. NASA
10. gurgle
11. whoosh
12. birdseed
13. VISTA
14. brunch
15. downtown
16. moonbeam
17. guesstimate
18. pasteurize
19. motorcycle
20. Ferris wheel

Chapter Review

Using the Dictionary. Answer each question below.

calm (käm, kälm), *adj.* **1** not stormy or windy: *a calm sea.* **2** not excited; peaceful. —*n.* absence of wind or motion. —*v.* become calm. — **calm'ly,** *adv.* —**calm'ness.,** *n.*

cal o rie (kal' ər ē), *n., pl.* **-or ies.** the quantity of heat energy necessary to raise the temperature of a gram of water one degree Celsius. Also, **calory.** [< French < Latin *calor* heat]

cap., **1** capacity. **2** capital. **3** capitalize. **4** *pl.* **caps.** capital letter.

castle in the air, something imagined but not likely to come true.

cat e go rize (kat'ə gə rīz'), *v.,* **-rized, -riz ing.** put in a category; classify. —**cat'e go ri za'tion,** *n.*

cel e bra tion (sel'ə brā'shən), *n.* the observing of a feast, day, or special season.

CIA, Central Intelligence Agency.

con do (kon'dō), *n., pl.* **-dos.** INFORMAL. condominium.

con gress (kong'gris), *n.* **1** the lawmaking body of a nation, especially of a republic. **2 Congress,** the national lawmaking body of the United States.

cour age (kėr'ij), *n.* meeting danger without fear; bravery; fearlessness. **Syn. Courage, bravery** mean fearlessness. **Courage** applies to moral strength that makes a person face any danger without showing fear. **Bravery** applies to a kind of courage that is shown by bold, fearless, daring action in the presence of danger.

From SCOTT, FORESMAN ADVANCED DICTIONARY by E. L. Thorndike and Clarence L. Barnhart. Copyright © 1983, 1979, 1974 by Scott, Foresman & Co. Reprinted by permission.

1. When should *congress* be capitalized?
2. Which entry word has two accepted spellings?
3. What are the principal parts of the verb *categorize*?
4. What does the abbreviation *CIA* stand for?
5. What is a synonym for *courage*?
6. Which word is the shortened form of a longer word?
7. What is the word origin of *calorie*?
8. What two derived words are listed under *calm*?
9. What are the meanings of the abbreviation *cap.*?
10. Which syllable in *categorize* receives the most stress?
11. Which syllables in *celebration* contain a schwa?
12. What does the phrase *castle in the air* mean?
13. If this were a complete dictionary page, what would the two guide words be?
14. What parts of speech can *calm* be used as?
15. Which definition of *calm* is used below?
    The river was <u>calm</u> the day we tried rafting.

34

The Library

When you need to choose a biography for a social studies report or a topic for a science fair project, the library is the best place to start. The library contains a wide variety of written and nonwritten materials, and it is well organized so you can easily find what you need. For example, if your science project were about the giant panda, the information you need could be found in the following materials.

- The *Larousse Encyclopedia of Animal Life* explains that the giant panda, once thought to be a bear, is really a member of the raccoon family.
- The *Atlas of Wildlife* contains maps that show that the giant panda lives in the cold, damp bamboo forests of eastern Tibet and Szechwan, China.
- *The Guinness Book of World Records* identifies the giant panda as the most valuable zoo animal.
- The *Dictionary of Animals* explains that the giant panda is the official symbol of the World Wildlife Fund.

Library Arrangement

Most libraries contain thousands of books. Finding one among these would be impossible without a clear system of arrangement. In most libraries works of fiction are filed separately from nonfiction books.

Fiction

A book or story that is based mainly on imaginary people and events is called fiction. Works of fiction are shelved in alphabetical order according to the author's last name. For special cases most libraries follow the shelving rules listed below.

- Two-part names are alphabetized by the first part of the name.

  DeCosta   **O'**Casey   **La**Salle   **Van** Allen

- Names beginning with *Mc* or *St.* are shelved as if they began with *Mac* or *Saint*.
- Books by the same author are arranged in alphabetical order by title, skipping *a*, *an*, and *the* at the beginning.

***E**XERCISE 1* *Arranging Fiction*

Number your paper 1 to 10. Then list the novels in the order they should be placed on the shelf.

Words by Heart by Onida Sebestyen
Athabasca by Alistair MacLean
Island of the Blue Dolphin by Scott O'Dell
Great Expectations by Charles Dickens
The Riddle-Master of Hed by Patricia McKillip
David Copperfield by Charles Dickens
A Formal Feeling by Zibby Oneal
It's Crazy to Stay Chinese in Minnesota by Eleanor Wong Telemaque
Flowers for Algernon by Daniel Keyes
Grandpa and Frank by Janet Majerus

***E**XERCISE 2* *Solving Shelving Problems*

Number your paper 1 to 10. Then list the following fiction authors in the order that their books would appear on the shelves.

Duane Decker   Paula Danziger
Adele De Leeuw   Rosamund Du Jardin
Lois Duncan   Daphne Du Maurier
Theodore DuBois   Dan D'Amelio
Paxton Davis   Alexandre Dumas

Nonfiction

In contrast to fiction, nonfiction books are about real people and events. Most libraries use the Dewey decimal system to arrange nonfiction books on the shelves. This system was created more than 100 years ago by an American librarian named Melvil Dewey. In the Dewey decimal system, each book is assigned a number according to its subject. The following chart shows the ten main categories in the Dewey decimal system.

Dewey Decimal System

000–099	General Works (reference books)
100–199	Philosophy
200–299	Religion
300–399	Social Science (law, education, economics)
400–499	Language
500–599	Science (mathematics, biology, chemistry)
600–699	Technology (medicine, inventions)
700–799	Fine Arts (painting, music, theater)
800–899	Literature
900–999	History (biography, geography, travel)

Each of the ten main classes is broken up into ten smaller divisions. In the social science class, for example, the numbers 390–399 are reserved for books about customs and folklore. These smaller groups can be divided even further by using decimal points.

The number assigned to a book is the *call number*. The call number is written on the spine of the book. On the shelf, books are arranged in numerical order according to their call numbers.

Social Sciences: 300–399

Biographies and autobiographies are usually shelved in a special section. Many libraries label each book with a *B*

for biography or with the Dewey decimal number 920. They are arranged in alphabetical order by the last name of the subject, not the author.

EXERCISE 3   Using the Dewey Decimal System

Number your paper 1 to 10. Then write the range of numbers and the category each subject falls under in the Dewey decimal system.

EXAMPLE   *The Sports Medicine Book*
ANSWER   600–699   Technology

1. *Computer Games and Puzzles*
2. *The Life of Martin Luther King, Jr.*
3. *A Climber's Guide to Glacier National Park*
4. *The History of Jazz*
5. *The Philosophy of Gandhi*
6. *Algebra in Easy Steps*
7. *Religions of America*
8. *Geography of American Cities*
9. *The Poems of Robert Frost*
10. *Learning Basic Spanish*

EXERCISE 4   Solving Shelving Problems

Number your paper 1 to 10. Then write the following Dewey decimal numbers and book titles in the order that the books would appear on the shelves.

1. 535.6   *Color—From Rainbows to Lasers*
2. 560.9   *Tales Told by Fossils*
3. 549.1   *Rocks, Gems, and Minerals*
4. 522.6   *Eavesdropping on Space*
5. 530.3   *Your World in Motion*
6. 550.9   *The Earth and Its Satellite*
7. 553.8   *The World of Diamonds*
8. 542.4   *Chemistry Magic!*
9. 523.5   *Mars, The Red Planet*
10. 551.4   *Exploring American Caves*

The Card Catalog

The card catalog is a cabinet of small file drawers containing cards for every book in the library. The card catalog also has cards for filmstrips, records, movies, or other materials the library has. On the front of each drawer are letters that show what part of the alphabet that drawer contains.

There are three cards for each book, arranged alphabetically in the catalog. An *author card*, a *title card*, and a *subject card* will help you find the book you need.

Author Cards

If you know the author of the book, you can look in the card catalog under the author's last name. To find a book by Roy Gallant, for example, you would look in the file drawer containing the letter *G*.

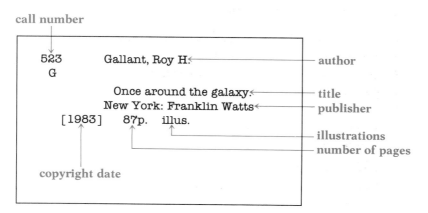

call number

523
G   Gallant, Roy H. ←——————— author

          Once around the galaxy. ←——— title
          New York: Franklin Watts ←——— publisher
    [1983]   87p.   illus.
                             illustrations
                             number of pages

copyright date

*T*itle Cards

If you know the title of a book but not its author, you can find the book by looking up the first word in the title (except *a, an,* and *the*). To find *Once around the Galaxy,* look in the drawer containing the letter *O.*

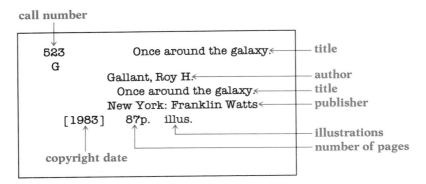

*S*ubject Cards

When gathering information for a report, you will use subject cards more than author or title cards. If your subject were astronomy, you would look under *A* in the card catalog. There you would find cards for all of the books about astronomy available in your library.

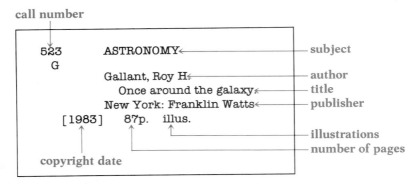

Notice that all three cards on pages 577–578 for *Once around the Galaxy* provide the same information.

Steps for Finding Books

1. Find out if the library has the book you want by finding the author card, the title card, or the subject card in the card catalog.
2. Read the card to see if the book is likely to contain the information you need. Check the copyright date to see how current the information is.
3. On a slip of paper, copy the call number, the title, and the name of the author of the book you want to find.
4. Use the call number to find each book. The first line of the call number tells which section of the library to look in.

F or FIC	fiction section
B or 920	biography section
Dewey number	nonfiction section

Then find each book on the shelves by looking for its call number, located on the spine.

EXERCISE 5 Using the Card Catalog

Number your paper 1 to 10. Then write the letter or letters of the drawer in which you would find each of the following in the card catalog.

EXAMPLE   *Old Yeller*
ANSWER   N–Ph

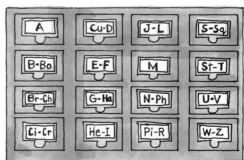

1. otters
2. caves
3. Babe Ruth
4. Mexico
5. Black Hawk
6. the meaning of dreams
7. unidentified flying objects
8. *The Cloister and the Hearth*
9. Sandra Day O'Connor
10. *The Sea Around Us*

EXERCISE 6 *Writing Catalog Cards*

Write an author card, a title card, and a subject card using the following information.

Baseball's Wacky Players, published by Dodd Books in New York City, Dewey decimal number 796.04, copyright date 1984, illustrated, written by George Sullivan, 128 pages.

Cross-Reference Cards

In addition to author, title, and subject cards, a card catalog contains "see" and "see also" cards. A "see" card will tell you that the subject you need is listed under another heading. A "see also" card will list other subjects that also have information about your subject.

```
+-----------------------------------+
|                                   |
|        PORPOISES                  |
|                                   |
|           see                     |
|                                   |
|        DOLPHINS                   |
|                                   |
+-----------------------------------+
```

```
             +-----------------------------------+
             |                                   |
             |         ASTRONOMY                 |
             |                                   |
             |          see also                 |
             |                                   |
             |     SOLAR SYSTEM, STARS           |
             |                                   |
             +-----------------------------------+
```

Guide Cards

Guide cards, like the ones shown in the file drawer on page 577, are blank cards with words or a letter printed at the top. These cards are arranged in alphabetical order in each file drawer of the card catalog. Using guide cards will help you find author, title, and subject cards quickly.

Reference Materials

The reference section of the library contains books that cannot be checked out. These include encyclopedias, dictionaries, atlases, and yearbooks. In most libraries study tables are set up so the books can be easily used.

Encyclopedias

Encyclopedias contain general information on a wide variety of subjects. The information is arranged in alphabetical order by subject. Guide letters on the spine help you find the right volume. Inside every volume are guide words at the top of each page to direct you to your subject.

Most encyclopedias provide an index in a separate volume or at the end of the last volume. The index can tell you if your subject is discussed in more than one volume or if it is listed under another name.

ENCYCLOPEDIAS *Collier's Encyclopedia*
Compton's Pictured Encyclopedia
Encyclopedia Americana
Encyclopaedia Britannica
World Book Encyclopedia

Specialized Encyclopedias

Specialized encyclopedias focus on one particular subject. They provide more information about a subject than general encyclopedias do. Specialized encyclopedias are also arranged in alphabetical order for easy reference. Following are some popular specialized encyclopedias.

SPECIALIZED
ENCYCLOPEDIAS *International Wildlife Encyclopedia*
Encyclopedia of American Cars
Encyclopedia of Card Tricks
Encyclopedia of Tropical Fish

*B*iographical References

Biographical references are books of information about the lives of famous people, past and present. Some provide only a paragraph of facts, such as birth date, education, family, occupation, and awards. Others contain long articles about each person in the volume. Following are some well-known biographical reference books.

BIOGRAPHICAL REFERENCES	
	Current Biography
	Who's Who
	Who's Who in America
	Who's Who of American Women
	Who's Who of American Politics
	Webster's Biographical Dictionary
	Dictionary of American Biography
	Dictionary of Scientific Biography
	Men and Women of Science
	American Authors 1600–1900
	British Authors of the Nineteenth Century
	New Century Cyclopedia of Names

*E*XERCISE 7 *Using Biographical References*

Number your paper 1 to 10. Then, using a biographical reference book, match the famous American cartoonists in column 1 with the comic strip character they created in column 2.

1.	C. C. Beck	Captain America
2.	Jim Davis	Peanuts
3.	Al Capp	Little Orphan Annie
4.	Jack Kirby	Captain Marvel
5.	Alex Raymond	Dennis the Menace
6.	Harold Gray	Popeye
7.	Hank Ketcham	Doonesbury
8.	Charles Schultz	L'il Abner
9.	Elzie C. Segar	Flash Gordon
10.	Gary Trudeau	Garfield

Atlases

Atlases are books of maps. They usually include many different kinds of maps, some showing climate, some showing population density. In addition, many atlases include charts with facts about mountains, deserts, rivers, oceans, and natural resources. The table of contents and the index of each atlas will direct you to the information you need. Following are some popular atlases.

ATLASES   *Collier's World Atlas and Gazetteer*
Hammond's Medallion World Atlas
Rand McNally: The International Atlas
Goode's World Atlas
Atlas of World History

Almanacs and Yearbooks

Almanacs and yearbooks are published once a year. For this reason they contain much up-to-date information. They cover a wide variety of subjects, such as famous people, unusual achievements, the economy, politics, countries, and sports. Following are some of the most popular almanacs and yearbooks.

ALMANACS
AND
YEARBOOKS   *Information Please Almanac*
World Almanac and Book of Facts
Hammond's Almanac
Guinness Book of World Records

583

Specialized Dictionaries

Specialized dictionaries contain entries about one specific subject. Some, for example, are limited to mathematics. Others may be limited to abbreviations. One kind of dictionary, called a thesaurus, includes only synonyms. The following list shows the variety of specialized dictionaries.

SPECIALIZED
DICTIONARIES
*The New Roget's Thesaurus in Dictionary
    Form*
Webster's New Dictionary of Synonyms
Grove's Dictionary of Music and Musicians
Sports Dictionary
Compton's Illustrated Science Dictionary

EXERCISE 8   Using Specialized References

Number your paper 1 to 10. Then write the best library resource for answering each question.

specialized encyclopedia   atlas
biographical reference   almanac
specialized dictionary

1. In what part of Alaska is the capital located?
2. When and where was actor-comedian Bill Cosby born?
3. What does the term *fielder's choice* mean in baseball?
4. What is a harvest moon?
5. What does the term *staccato* mean in music?
6. What river flows through the Grand Canyon?
7. What policy for naming hurricanes was adopted in 1979?
8. What sport is Martina Navratilova known for?
9. What are the chief crops grown in Indiana?
10. What does the term *Manifest Destiny* mean in American history?

EXERCISE 9   Finding Facts in Reference Books

Use the library's resources to find the answers to the ten questions in Exercise 8.

Readers' Guide to Periodical Literature

Magazines are published even more frequently than almanacs and yearbooks. For this reason they are excellent sources of current information. The *Readers' Guide to Periodical Literature* is an index that will help you find magazine articles on subjects of interest. It includes listings of about 175 magazines.

Each edition of the *Readers' Guide* has a date on its spine. The date tells you the time period covered in the volume. The following entries are from the August 1985 edition.

SUBJECT
ENTRIES

Camps
1985 camp guide and scholarship program [women's sports] il *Women's Sports* 7:39–45+ Ap '85
            Alabama
Space, the camp [U.S. Space Camp in Huntsville] A. Hollister. il *Life* 8:93–6 Je '85
Caves
Journey to the underworld [caving in national parks] J. Glover. il *Natl Parks* 59:22–7 My/Je '85
Searching for the big room [caving] A. Darling. il *Sierra* 70:48–52 My/Je '85
      Photographs and photography
Cave photography [interview with D. and J. McClurg] M. Corbett. il pors *Natl Parks* 59:34–5 My/Je '85
Characters in literature
      See
      Blacks in literature
      Moby Dick (Fictional character)
      Tom Sawyer (Fictional character)
      Women in literature
Comets
Lifetimes of comets. *Sky Telesc* 69:394–5 My '85
Was it a comet, or merely the solar wind? [Pioneer data] J. Eberhart. *Sci News* 127:278 My 4 '85

AUTHOR
ENTRIES

Corbett, Marjorie
Cave photography [interview with D. and J. McClurg] il pors *Natl Parks* 59:34–5 My/Je '85
Cousteau, Jacques Yves
"We face a catastrophe" if the oceans are not cleaned up. il *U S News World Rep* 98:68 Je 24 '85

From *Readers' Guide to Periodical Literature.* Copyright © 1985 by the H. W. Wilson Company. Material reproduced by permission of the publisher.

Each entry in the *Readers' Guide* provides all the information you need to locate articles on a particular subject. Notice how the information is listed in the following entry about eagles.

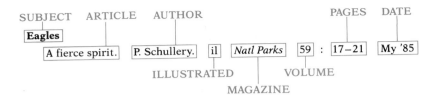

SUBJECT   ARTICLE   AUTHOR   PAGES   DATE

Eagles

A fierce spirit.   P. Schullery.   il   *Natl Parks*   59 : 17–21   My '85

ILLUSTRATED   VOLUME

MAGAZINE

EXERCISE 10   *Using the* Readers' Guide

Number your paper 1 to 10. Then, using the entries from the *Readers' Guide* on page 585, answer each of the following questions.

1. What subject is author J. Glover writing about in his article "Journey to the Underworld"?
2. On what pages in *National Parks* magazine does his article appear?
3. Under what two headings does the article "Cave Photography" by Marjorie Corbett appear?
4. What subject headings would you look under to find information about characters in literature?
5. What is the date of the magazine in which an article by Jacques Cousteau appears?
6. What volume of *Women's Sports* magazine contains the 1985 camp guide and scholarship program?
7. In what state is the U.S. Space Camp located?
8. Who is the author of the article "Searching for the Big Room"?
9. What are the titles of two magazine articles written about comets?
10. How many of the magazine articles listed in the entries contain illustrations?

The Vertical File

The vertical file is a collection of leaflets, catalogs, pamphlets, newspaper clippings, and brochures kept in filing cabinets. Inside the file drawers, items are arranged in alphabetical order according to subject.

Chapter Review

A **Finding Information.** Choose one subject. Then find two books about that subject and write their authors, titles, copyright dates, and call numbers. Next find two magazine articles on that subject. Write the name and date of the magazine, the title and author of the article, and the page numbers on which the article can be found.

1. the Coast Guard
2. China
3. earthquakes
4. polar bears
5. solar energy
6. wild mustangs
7. tidal waves
8. the Statue of Liberty
9. General Robert E. Lee
10. craters on the moon

B **Choosing Reference Materials.** Write the best library resource for answering each question.

specialized encyclopedia   atlas   *Readers' Guide*
biographical reference   almanac   vertical file
specialized dictionary

EXAMPLE   Which type of whale sings songs?
ANSWER   specialized encyclopedia

1. What is the average yearly rainfall in Death Valley?
2. How does the human heart work?
3. What movie's soundtrack won the Grammy Award for album of the year last year?
4. When did Judy Blume publish her first book?
5. What is the name of a pamphlet about hiking?
6. What are two synonyms for the word *stubborn*?
7. What magazine articles were published last year about Bigfoot?
8. What is the climate of Louisiana?
9. What lifesaving courses are offered this fall in the YMCA catalog?
10. Why is Tom Seaver famous?

35

Spelling

Misspelled words, whether in a composition for school or in a letter to a friend, are likely to distract the reader from the thought being expressed. Consequently, it is important for a writer to spell words accurately. This chapter will help you develop the skills necessary to be an accurate speller.

EXERCISE 1 *Spelling Warm-Up*

Number your paper 1 to 10. Then write the correct spelling of each underlined word.

Talking through a Puppet

When you watch a skilled ventriloquist, you may find it hard to (1) <u>beleive</u> that the voice of the puppet is actually coming from the human performer. (2) <u>Actully</u>, learning to speak without moving (3) <u>you're</u> lips is not that (4) <u>dificult</u>. Only five letters—*b, f, m, p,* and *v*—(5) <u>requier</u> lip movement. Many performers just avoid words with the (6) <u>troublsome</u> letters. In some cases a (7) <u>simular</u> sound, such as an *n* for an *m,* can be used instead. Most audiences won't (8) <u>notise</u> the difference. With (9) <u>they're</u> eyes on your puppet, most audiences won't even detect slight lip movements. If you keep a smile on your face and (10) <u>practise</u> often, you can become a ventriloquist.

Spelling Improvement

Some people are naturally good spellers. They often "see" the correct spelling of a word in their minds. Others "hear" a word, remembering how the separate syllables sound. If you are not a naturally good speller, the following suggestions will help you improve your spelling.

Methods for Improving Your Spelling

1. Start a spelling notebook. List the words you find difficult to spell in compositions, letters, and tests. By reviewing your list often, you will master each word.

2. When writing, use a dictionary to check the spelling of words you are unsure of. Do not rely on guessing to help you spell accurately.

3. Proofread your writing carefully. Writers cannot concentrate on everything at once. Take time at the end to read over your writing and correct words misspelled in haste.

4. Sound out each syllable to avoid dropping letters.

   ac ces **so** ry   bound **ary**   com **fort** able

5. Use memory tricks for words you often misspell. The most useful memory tricks are ones you think of yourself. Following are some examples.

   cemetery   A **ce**metery is **ee**rie. (3 *e*'s)
   laboratory   A **rat** is in the labo**rat**ory.

EXERCISE 2   Using a Dictionary

Number your paper 1 to 10. Write the word that is spelled correctly in each pair. Then check a dictionary and enter in your notebook any words you misspelled.

Twain's Joke

1. Mark Twain's (humorous, humerous) side shows up in his novel *The Adventures of Tom Sawyer*.
2. Twain was (allways, always) looking for a good joke.
3. On Sunday, Twain (atended, attended) church services.

589

4. He listened to the sermon of a very (famus, famous) preacher.
5. Afterward, Twain (aproached, approached) the speaker, who had a very elaborate vocabulary.
6. "I (enjoyed, enjoied) your service this morning. I welcomed it like an old friend," he remarked.
7. Then he said he had a book at home with (every, evry) word in it that the preacher had used.
8. The minister was indignant and denied that (possability, possibility).
9. Twain (promissed, promised) to send him the book.
10. The next day, Twain sent the minister a (dictionery, dictionary)!

EXERCISE 3 Recognizing Misspelled Words

Number your paper 1 to 15. Write the letter that comes before the misspelled word in each group. Then write the word correctly. Check your answers in a dictionary and enter in your notebook any words you misspelled.

EXAMPLE (A) ascend (B) defience (C) solemn
ANSWER (B) defiance

1. (A) curfew (B) circuit (C) temporery
2. (A) beverege (B) advisable (C) maneuver
3. (A) superior (B) discipline (C) disatisfied
4. (A) alliance (B) posibility (C) compromise
5. (A) accomodate (B) bazaar (C) exquisite
6. (A) pageant (B) liable (C) efficiant
7. (A) analyze (B) respectible (C) collision
8. (A) consequance (B) ingredient (C) famine
9. (A) physics (B) yield (C) occurence
10. (A) admittance (B) singulur (C) insulation
11. (A) acquaintence (B) committee (C) adjoining
12. (A) sphere (B) ambassador (C) noticable
13. (A) badger (B) regrettable (C) defendent
14. (A) capitol (B) vaccum (C) siege
15. (A) stationary (B) buget (C) vacancy

Spelling Rules

Learning a few spelling rules will help you master hundreds of words. To help you remember the rules, write them in your spelling notebook with examples. Be sure to list any exceptions. These rules will help you conquer many commonly misspelled words.

Spelling Patterns

Words with *ei* or *ie* often cause confusion. Use the following familiar rhyme to help you spell such words.

> Put *i* before *e*
> Except after *c*
> Or when sounded like *a*
> As in *neighbor* and *weigh*.

The following examples show how this rule applies.

i before *e*	except after *c*	sounded like *a*
belief	conceit	feign
brief	deceive	reins
field	perceive	veil
achieve	receipt	weigh

The words that follow are exceptions to this rule.

ancient	foreign	neither
conscience	forfeit	species
efficient	height	their
either	leisure	weird

Words ending with a "seed" sound also can cause confusion. This sound can be spelled *-sede, -ceed*, or *-cede*. Most of the words ending with the "seed" sound are spelled with *-cede*. The following chart shows the only words that are spelled with *-sede* or *-ceed*.

-sede	-ceed	-cede
supersede	exceed proceed succeed	all others

EXERCISE 4 Using Spelling Patterns

Number your paper 1 to 20. Then write each word, adding
either *ie* or *ei*.

1. r__gn	6. p__rce	11. forf__t	16. n__ghbor
2. n__ce	7. pr__st	12. rel__ve	17. front__r
3. __ght	8. h__ght	13. c__ling	18. n__ther
4. th__f	9. sl__gh	14. rec__ve	19. effic__nt
5. br__f	10. w__ght	15. for__gn	20. consc__nce

EXERCISE 5 Using Spelling Patterns

Number your paper 1 to 10. Then write each word, adding
-sede, -ceed, or *-cede.*

1. re__	3. ac__	5. pro__	7. pre__	9. inter__
2. ex__	4. se__	6. con__	8. suc__	10. super__

Plurals

There are several rules that will help you form the plurals of nouns correctly. When in doubt about an exception,
look the word up in a dictionary.

Regular Nouns.   To form the plural of most nouns, simply
add *s*. If a noun ends in *s, ch, sh, x,* or *z*, add *es* to form the
plural.

SINGULAR	moon	star	nova	planet
PLURAL	moon**s**	star**s**	nova**s**	planet**s**
SINGULAR	moss	branch	bush	fox
PLURAL	moss**es**	branch**es**	bush**es**	fox**es**

Nouns Ending in y. Add *s* to form the plural of a noun ending in a vowel and *y.*

SINGULAR	toy	bay	bu**oy**	journ**ey**
PLURAL	toy**s**	bay**s**	buoy**s**	journey**s**

Change the *y* to *i* and add *es* to a noun ending in a consonant and *y.*

SINGULAR	gala**xy**	recove**ry**	pad**dy**	par**ty**
PLURAL	galax**ies**	recover**ies**	padd**ies**	part**ies**

EXERCISE 6 Forming Plurals

Number your paper 1 to 20. Then write the plural of each noun.

1. hitch	6. ploy	11. siren	16. ax
2. loss	7. box	12. nursery	17. lady
3. factory	8. flash	13. dash	18. journey
4. tray	9. story	14. brick	19. berry
5. bundle	10. miss	15. barbecue	20. waltz

Nouns Ending in o. Add *s* to form the plural of a noun ending in a vowel and *o.*

SINGULAR	cuck**oo**	rat**io**	rod**eo**	ster**eo**
PLURAL	cuckoo**s**	ratio**s**	rodeo**s**	stereo**s**

The plurals of nouns ending in a consonant and *o* do not follow a regular pattern. Always use a dictionary to check the spelling of these words.

SINGULAR	ec**ho**	toma**to**	yo-**yo**	si**lo**
PLURAL	echo**es**	tomato**es**	yo-yo**s**	silo**s**

Add *s* to form the plural of a musical term ending in *o.* This rule applies to musical terms ending in a consonant and *o* as well as to those ending in a vowel and *o.*

SINGULAR	trio	piano	solo	piccolo
PLURAL	trio**s**	piano**s**	solo**s**	piccolo**s**

593

Nouns Ending in f or fe. To form the plural of some nouns ending in f or *fe*, simply add *s*.

SINGULAR	chie**f**	belie**f**	roo**f**	gira**ffe**
PLURAL	chief**s**	belief**s**	roof**s**	giraffe**s**

To form the plural of other nouns ending in f or *fe*, change the *f* to *v* and add *es*.

SINGULAR	hal**f**	sel**f**	li**fe**	kni**fe**
PLURAL	hal**ves**	sel**ves**	li**ves**	kni**ves**

For nouns ending in *o*, *f*, and *fe*, the rules do not always apply neatly. If you are unsure about how to form the plural of such nouns, check a dictionary for the correct spelling.

Compound Nouns. Most compound nouns form their plural the way other nouns do.

day**s**	men	hall**s**	box**es**
weekday**s**	chairmen	study hall**s**	music box**es**

Often when the main word appears first in a compound noun, that word is the one made plural.

SINGULAR	passerby	daughter-in-law	rule of thumb
PLURAL	passer**s**by	daughter**s**-in-law	rule**s** of thumb

Other Plural Forms. The following box lists examples of nouns that do not form the plural by adding *s* or *es*.

Irregular Plurals

tooth, teeth	child, children	ox, oxen
foot, feet	woman, women	mouse, mice
goose, geese	man, men	die, dice

Same Form for Singular and Plural

Chinese	sheep	scissors
Japanese	moose	headquarters
Swiss	salmon	series
Sioux	surf	politics

EXERCISE 7 Forming Plurals

Number your paper 1 to 20. Write the plural of each noun.
Then check your answer in a dictionary.

1. potato	6. elf	11. child	16. pipeline
2. igloo	7. loaf	12. woman	17. solar system
3. ego	8. sheriff	13. ox	18. grandchild
4. soprano	9. roof	14. sheep	19. son-in-law
5. taco	10. gulf	15. Sioux	20. bill of sale

Prefixes and Suffixes

A *prefix* is one or more syllables placed in front of a root
to form a new word. When you add a prefix, do not change
the spelling of the root.

    ir + regular = irregular   pre + view = preview
    dis + appear = disappear   mis + spell = misspell
    il + legal = illegal   de + frost = defrost

A *suffix* is one or more syllables placed after a root to
change its part of speech. In many cases you simply add
the suffix. In others, however, you must change the spelling
of the root. The following rules will help you spell words
with suffixes correctly.

Words Ending in e. Drop the final *e* before a suffix that
begins with a vowel.

    write + ing = writing   nerve + ous = nervous
    save + ed = saved   close + est = closest

Keep the final *e* before a suffix that begins with a consonant.

    waste + ful = wasteful   move + ment = movement
    like + ness = likeness   lone + some = lonesome

Note the following exceptions to these rules.

    courage—courageous   argue—argument
    change—changeable   true—truly

595

Words Ending in y. To add a suffix to most words ending in a vowel and *y*, keep the *y*.

boy + hood = boyhood   joy + ful = joyful

To add a suffix to most words ending in a consonant and *y*, change the *y* to *i* before adding the suffix.

grimy + est = grimiest   silly + ness = silliness

EXERCISE 8 *Adding Prefixes and Suffixes*

Number your paper 1 to 15. Then write each word, adding the prefix or suffix shown. Remember to make any necessary spelling changes.

1. mis + spell	6. goofy + ness	11. rely + able
2. re + entry	7. retire + ment	12. cozy + ly
3. im + material	8. argue + ment	13. play + fully
4. dis + appoint	9. sane + ity	14. enjoy + ment
5. cold + ness	10. strike + ing	15. true + ly

Doubling the Final Consonant. The final letter in a word is sometimes doubled before a suffix is added. Before doubling a consonant, check to make sure that the word meets both of the following tests.

- The word has only one syllable or is stressed on the final syllable.
- The word ends in one consonant preceded by one vowel.

spot + y = spotty   regret + ed = regretted

EXERCISE 9 *Adding Suffixes*

Number your paper 1 to 9. Then write each word, adding the suffix shown. Remember to make any necessary spelling changes.

1. flip + ing	4. refer + ing	7. begin + er
2. tan + ing	5. swim + er	8. contain + er
3. green + est	6. mail + ing	9. poison + ous

Commonly Misspelled Words

The following sections contain lists of words that are commonly misspelled. If you learn these words now, you will avoid many spelling errors.

Homonyms

Homonyms are words that sound the same but have different spellings and different meanings. Be sure to use each word correctly in your writing.

Commonly Confused Homonyms

all ready	completely ready
already	previously, beforehand
hear	to listen [verb]
here	in this place [adverb]
theirs	belonging to them [possessive pronoun]
there's	contraction for *there is*
to	begins infinitive [preposition]
too	excessively, also [adverb]
two	a number [adjective]
whose	belonging to whom [possessive pronoun]
who's	contraction for *who is*
your	belonging to you [possessive pronoun]
you're	contraction for *you are*

EXERCISE 10 Using the Right Word

Number your paper 1 to 10. Then write the word that fits the meaning in each sentence.

1. Sal joined the track team (to, too, two).
2. Dogs can (hear, here) sounds that humans cannot.
3. The boys are (all ready, already) to go.

4. (Whose, Who's) notebooks are these?
5. Nicholas asked why (your, you're) not swimming.
6. (Theirs, There's) a concert on Saturday night.
7. (Your, You're) locker is open.
8. It is time (to, too, two) catch the school bus.
9. (Whose, Who's) going to the game?
10. We are (all ready, already) late.

Spelling Demons

The words in the following list are often misspelled. Study the words carefully. Then ask a classmate or a member of your family to test you on each word. Enter each word that you misspelled in your spelling notebook.

Spelling Demons

accelerate	chute	forgery	possibility
accessory	circuit	furlough	precipitation
accommodate	coincidence	geyser	priest
accumulate	collision	humane	recruit
acquaintance	committee	hygiene	regrettable
adjoining	compromise	ingredient	respectable
admittance	conceit	insulation	siege
advisable	conference	liable	singular
alliance	consequence	maneuver	solemn
ambassador	convenience	masquerade	specimen
analyze	corporal	miscellaneous	sphere
appreciation	counterfeit	mortgage	stationary
ascend	curfew	noticeable	stationery
badger	defendant	occurrence	succession
bazaar	defiance	pageant	superior
beverage	delirious	paralysis	tariff
browse	discipline	pasteurize	temporary
budget	dissatisfied	penalize	toboggan
capitol	efficient	physics	vacancy
carburetor	exquisite	plague	vacuum
casserole	famine	plaque	wring
cavalry	fatigue	pneumonia	yield

Chapter Review

A **Using a Dictionary.** Number your paper 1 to 10. Write the word that is spelled correctly in each pair.

A Fable from Aesop

1. A hungry wolf who was (descouraged, discouraged) by poor hunting met up with a well-fed dog.
2. The dog seemed to be living (easyly, easily).
3. The wolf (inquired, inquiered) what the dog had to do to stay well fed.
4. The dog (replyed, replied), "I only have to guard the house, protect my human friends, and show affection."
5. The wolf (thought, thoght) carefully when he heard the dog tell of his good life.
6. The wolf's life was full of dangers, and he was never (assurred, assured) of his food.
7. After (careful, carful) thinking, the wolf decided to stay on and try the dog's life.
8. Then the wolf (noticed, notised) a bald spot on the dog's neck, and he asked about it.
9. "Oh," said the dog, "that's where I wear my (collar, coller) and chain."
10. "Chain?" the wolf said, (horrifyed, horrified), and off he trotted to his uncertain but free life.

B **Using Spelling Patterns.** Number your paper 1 to 20. Write the word spelled correctly in each pair.

1. recieve, receive
2. weight, wieght
3. consceince, conscience
4. thier, their
5. neither, niether
6. superceed, supersede
7. procede, proceed
8. secede, seceed
9. succeed, sucsede
10. preceed, precede
11. ancient, anceint
12. wierd, weird
13. believe, beleive
14. efficeint, efficient
15. field, feild
16. achieve, acheive
17. beleif, belief
18. foriegn, foreign
19. species, speceis
20. excede, exceed

C Forming Plurals. Number your paper 1 to 20. Then write the correct plural form of each word.

1. complex
2. dune
3. ambush
4. joy
5. puppy
6. veto
7. tornado
8. kangaroo
9. duo
10. fife
11. calf
12. sheriff
13. leaf
14. mouse
15. sheep
16. Japanese
17. sister-in-law
18. basketball
19. foot
20. dollar sign

D Adding Prefixes and Suffixes. Number your paper 1 to 10. Then write each word, adding the prefix or suffix shown.

1. mis + step
2. re + discover
3. crafty + ness
4. bore + dom
5. hasty + ly
6. argue + ment
7. drive + ing
8. place + ment
9. forget + able
10. plain + ness

E Using the Right Word. Number your paper 1 to 5. Then write the word that fits the meaning in each sentence.

1. (Two, Too) heads are better than one.
2. Tom has (all ready, already) left his house, so we can just meet him there.
3. Wait until you (hear, here) the news!
4. (Theirs, There's) nothing like a cool lemonade on a hot summer day.
5. Mine is finished. (Whose, Who's) will be made next?

F Spelling Demons. Number your paper 1 to 20. Then write the correct spelling of each word.

1. seige
2. acend
3. bazar
4. yeild
5. famin
6. conciet
7. phisics
8. calvary
9. allience
10. defience
11. accomodate
12. ingrediant
13. conferance
14. convenence
15. posibility
16. solem
17. cerfew
18. tarif
19. spere
20. geiser

Standardized Test

Directions: Choose the word that is most nearly *opposite* in meaning to the word in capital letters. In the appropriate row on your answer sheet, fill in the circle containing the same letter as your answer.

SAMPLE   YIELD   (a) decide (b) surrender (c) lose (d) resist

ANSWER   (a) (b) (c) (d)

1. MINIMUM   (a) maximum (b) least (c) commonplace (d) extraordinary
2. MEEK   (a) shy (b) ridiculous (c) intelligent (d) bold
3. EXTERIOR   (a) improvement (b) introduction (c) interior (d) invitation
4. TEMPORARY   (a) chilling (b) permanent (c) magnified (d) possible
5. JUBILANT   (a) joyous (b) sad (c) mischievous (d) responsible
6. DRAB   (a) yellow (b) unsatisfactory (c) colorful (d) monotonous
7. PRECISE   (a) ordinary (b) illustrated (c) displeased (d) inexact
8. ANXIETY   (a) calmness (b) nervousness (c) disappointment (d) knowledge
9. ABUNDANT   (a) doubtful (b) scarce (c) certain (d) uncomfortable
10. DESCENDANT   (a) relative (b) professional (c) climber (d) ancestor
11. INABILITY   (a) impossibility (b) separation (c) capacity (d) permission
12. PACIFY   (a) upset (b) interrupt (c) fascinate (d) discourage
13. NEGATIVE   (a) positive (b) satisfactory (c) expensive (d) cheap
14. OMIT   (a) mispronounce (b) exaggerate (c) include (d) introduce
15. FLEXIBLE   (a) unsatisfactory (b) imperfect (c) immature (d) rigid

601

Directions: Decide which word in each numbered group is misspelled. In the appropriate row on your answer sheet, fill in the circle containing the same number as the misspelled word. If no word is misspelled, fill in 5.

SAMPLE　　1) buget
　　　　　　2) toboggan
　　　　　　3) physics
　　　　　　4) casserole
　　　　　　5) (No errors)

ANSWER　

16. 1) specimen
　　2) maneuver
　　3) hygene
　　4) mortgage
　　5) (No errors)

17. 1) coincidence
　　2) occurence
　　3) succession
　　4) vacancy
　　5) (No errors)

18. 1) analize
　　2) sphere
　　3) corporal
　　4) curfew
　　5) (No errors)

19. 1) noticable
　　2) efficient
　　3) defiance
　　4) advisable
　　5) (No errors)

20. 1) geyser
　　2) cavalry
　　3) superior
　　4) pageant
　　5) (No errors)

21. 1) respectable
　　2) priest
　　3) vacum
　　4) furlough
　　5) (No errors)

22. 1) discipline
　　2) delerious
　　3) badger
　　4) tariff
　　5) (No errors)

23. 1) consequence
　　2) collision
　　3) defendant
　　4) appreciation
　　5) (No errors)

24. 1) pasteurize
　　2) exquisite
　　3) bazaar
　　4) paralisis
　　5) (No errors)

25. 1) famine
　　2) wring
　　3) alliance
　　4) misellaneous
　　5) (No errors)

Index

distinguished from possessive pronouns, 186, 279
Critical thinking, 406–413, 520–522, 523–524, 527, 537–538, 543–544

D

Declarative sentence, 3, 249
Degrees of comparison, 217–222
Demonstrative pronouns, 34, 57
Denotation, 297
Dependent clause. *See* Subordinate (dependent) clause.
Descriptive paragraph, 392–405
  sensory words, 299, 394–395
  steps for writing, 405
Dewey decimal system, 574–576
Diagram, sentence
  adjective and adverb, 65
  adjective clause, 139
  adjective phrase, 119
  adverb clause, 138
  adverb phrase, 119
  complex sentence, 138
  compound sentence, 138
  direct or indirect object, 100
  participial phrase, 120
  prepositional phrase, 119
  question, 18
  subject and verb, 18–19
  subject complement, 100–101
  understood subject, 18
Dialogue, 273, 443–446, 454–457
Dictionary, 558–570
  accent marks, 565
  alphabetical order, 559–560
  capitalization, 558, 562–563
  definitions, 558, 561, 565–567
  derived words, 558, 562
  diacritical marks, 564
  entry word, 561–563
  finding words, 559–560
  guide words, 559
  parts of speech, 558, 565–566
  preferred spelling, 561
  pronunciation, 558, 561, 563–565
  schwa, 564
  specialized, 584
  spelling reference, 558, 561–562
  syllable division, 285, 563
  synonyms, 558, 567
  variant spelling, 561
  word origin, 558, 561, 568–570
Direct address, 258

Directions, giving, 353, 358–359, 513
Direct object, 89–90, 177, 181–182, 188
Direct quotation. *See* Quotation.
Dividing words, 285, 563
doesn't, don't, 211
Double negative, 223

E

Editing, 347
  checklist, 372, 437, 459
  essay, 437
  manuscript form, 437
  narrative, 459
  paragraph, 347, 372, 376
  proofreading symbols, 372
  research report, 482
Empty expressions, 314–315
Envelope, 498–499
Essay, 422–441
  audience, 425–426
  body, 422–423, 432–433
  brainstorming, 427
  choosing subject, 425
  coherence, 435
  conclusion, 423, 433
  editing, 437
  indenting, 437
  introduction, 422, 430–431
  limiting subject, 425–426
  listing details, 426–427
  main idea statement, 430–431
  manuscript form, 437
  organization, methods of, 428–429
  paragraphing, 430–433
  prewriting, 424–429, 441
  purpose, 425, 426–427
  revising, 435–436
  structure, 422–423, 430–434
  thesis statement, 430–431
  thinking of subjects, 423, 424
  title, 434
  transitions, 432–433
  unity, 435
  writing, steps for, 424–437, 441
  writing first draft, 430–434, 441
Essay tests, 549–550
Essential clause, 128
Exclamation point, 3, 76, 249, 253
  in direct quotation, 271
Exclamatory sentence, 3, 249
Expanding sentences, 59, 103, 311
Expository paragraph, 352–377
  steps for writing, 377

610

Glossary of Terms

(See pages 341 and 515.)

A

Abbreviation   An abbreviation is a shortened form of a word. It may begin with a capital letter and end with a period. (*See page 250.*)

Action verb   An action verb tells what action a subject is performing. (*See page 39.*)

Active voice   The active voice indicates that the subject is performing the action. (*See page 171.*)

Adjective   An adjective is a word that modifies a noun or a pronoun. (*See page 53.*)

Adjective clause   An adjective clause is a subordinate clause that is used to modify a noun or a pronoun. (*See page 126.*)

Adjective phrase   An adjective phrase is a prepositional phrase that is used to modify a noun or a pronoun. (*See page 108.*)

Adverb   An adverb is a word that modifies a verb, an adjective, or another adverb. (*See page 60.*)

Adverb clause   An adverb clause is a subordinate clause that is used mainly to modify a verb. (*See page 130.*)

Adverb phrase   An adverb phrase is a prepositional phrase that is used mainly to modify a verb. (*See page 110.*)

Analogies   Analogies show the relationships between pairs of words. (*See page 537.*)

Antecedent   An antecedent is the word or group of words that a pronoun replaces or refers to. (*See page 30.*)

Antonym   An antonym is a word that means the opposite of another word. (*See page 536.*)

Appositive   An appositive follows a noun or a pronoun and renames or explains it. (*See page 259.*)

Audience   The audience is the person or persons who will read your work or hear your speech. (*See pages 341 and 515.*)

B

Brainstorming   Brainstorming means writing down everything that comes to mind about a subject. (*See page 356.*)

Business letter   A business letter has six parts: the heading, inside address, salutation, body, closing, and signature. (*See page 495.*)

C

Case   Case is the form of a noun or a pronoun that indicates its use in a sentence. In English there are three cases: the *nominative case*, the *objective case*, and the *possessive case*. (*See page 177.*)

Chronological order   This order arranges events in the order in which they happen. (*See page 380.*)

Clause   A clause is a group of words that has a subject and a predicate. (*See page 125.*)

Clichés and trite expressions   Clichés and trite expressions are worn out, overused expressions. (*See page 301.*)

Coherence   A paragraph or essay has coherence if the ideas are presented in logical order with clear transitions. (*See page 329.*)

Complete predicate   A complete predicate includes all the words telling what the subject is doing, or something else about the subject. (*See page 8.*)

Complete subject   A complete subject includes all the words used to identify the person, place, thing, or idea that the sentence is about. (*See page 6.*)

Complex sentence A complex sentence consists of one independent clause and one or more subordinate clauses. (*See page 136.*)

Compound noun A compound noun is a common noun with more than one word. (*See page 26.*)

Compound sentence A compound sentence has two or more independent clauses. (*See page 133.*)

Compound subject A compound subject is two or more subjects in one sentence that have the same verb and are joined by a conjunction. (*See page 15.*)

Compound verb A compound verb is two or more verbs in one sentence that have the same subject and are joined by a conjunction. (*See page 16.*)

Concluding sentence A concluding sentence adds a strong ending to a paragraph by summarizing, referring to the main idea, or adding an insight. (*See page 332.*)

Conjunction A conjunction connects words or groups of words. (*See page 75.*)

Contraction A contraction is a word that combines two words into one. It uses an apostrophe to replace one or more missing letters. (*See page 279.*)

Coordinating conjunction A coordinating conjunction is a single word used to connect compound subjects, compound verbs, and compound sentences. (*See page 75.*)

Correlative conjunctions Correlative conjunctions are pairs of conjunctions used to connect compound subjects, compound verbs, and compound sentences. (*See page 75.*)

D

Declarative sentence A declarative sentence makes a statement or expresses an opinion and ends with a period. (*See page 3.*)

Demonstrative pronouns Demonstrative pronouns point out persons and things. (*See page 34.*)

Descriptive paragraph A descriptive paragraph creates in words a vivid picture of a person, an object, or a scene. (*See page 392.*)

Dialogue A dialogue is a conversation between two or more persons. A new paragraph begins each time the speaker changes. (*See page 273.*)

Direct object A direct object is a noun or pronoun that answers the question *Whom?* or *What?* after an action verb. (*See page 89.*)

Direct quotation In a direct quotation, quotation marks enclose a person's exact words. (*See page 268.*)

Double negative A double negative is the use of two negative words to express an idea when only one is needed. (*See page 223.*)

E

Editing Editing is the final stage of the writing process, when writers polish their work by correcting errors and making a neat copy. (*See page 347.*)

Essay An essay is a composition of three or more paragraphs that presents and develops one main idea. (*See page 422.*)

Exclamatory sentence An exclamatory sentence expresses strong feeling and ends with an exclamation point. (*See page 3.*)

Expository paragraph An expository paragraph explains with facts and examples or gives directions. (*See page 352.*)

F

Facts Facts are statements that can be proved. (*See page 408.*)

Fiction Fiction includes partly or totally imaginary novels and short stories. (*See page 573.*)

First draft Writing the first draft is the second stage of the writing process. Writers use their prewriting notes to get their ideas on paper as quickly as possible. (*See page 344.*)

Freewriting Freewriting is a prewriting technique of nonstop writing that encourages the flow of ideas. (*See page 342.*)

Friendly letter The parts of a friendly letter are the heading, salutation, body, closing, and signature. (*See page 491.*)

H

Helping verb A helping, or auxiliary, verb and the main verb make up a verb phrase. (*See page 11.*)

I

Imperative sentence An imperative sentence makes a request or gives a command and ends with either a period or an exclamation point. (*See page 3.*)

Indefinite pronouns Indefinite pronouns refer to unnamed persons or things. (*See page 33.*)

Independent clause An independent (or main) clause can stand alone as a sentence because it expresses a complete thought. (*See page 125.*)

Indirect object An indirect object is a noun or pronoun that answers the question *To or for whom?* or *To or for what?* after an action verb. (*See page 91.*)

Interjection An interjection is a word that expresses strong feeling. (*See page 76.*)

Interrogative pronouns Interrogative pronouns are used to ask questions. (*See page 34.*)

Interrogative sentence An interrogative sentence asks a question and ends with a question mark. (*See page 3.*)

Irregular verb An irregular verb does not form its past and past participle by adding *-ed* or *-d* to the present. (*See page 160.*)

L

Linking verb A linking verb links the subject with another word in the sentence. This other word either renames or describes the subject. (*See page 41.*)

M

Misplaced modifier A misplaced modifier is a phrase or clause that is placed too far away from the word it modifies, thus creating an unclear sentence. (*See page 117.*)

N

Narrative A narrative is a well-developed true or fictional story about characters resolving a conflict or problem. (*See page 442.*)

Narrative paragraph A narrative paragraph tells a real or an imaginary story. (*See page 378.*)

Nonfiction Nonfiction books contain facts about real people and real events. (*See page 574.*)

Noun A noun is a word that names a person, a place, a thing, or an idea. A common noun gives a general name. A proper noun names a specific person, place, or thing and always begins with a capital letter. A collective noun names a group of people or things. (*See pages 25–26.*)

O

Opinions Opinions are judgments that vary from person to person. (*See page 408.*)

Order of importance, interest, size, or degree   Order of importance, interest, size, or degree is a way of organizing information by arranging details in the order of *least to most* or *most to least*. (*See page 359.*)

Outline   An outline organizes information about a subject into main topics and subtopics. (*See page 473.*)

P

Paragraph   A paragraph is a group of related sentences that present and develop one main idea. (*See page 320.*)

Participial phrase   A participial phrase is a participle with its modifiers and complements—all working together as an adjective. (*See page 114.*)

Participle   A participle is a verb form that is used as an adjective. (*See page 113.*)

Passive voice   The passive voice indicates that the action of the verb is being performed upon the subject. (*See page 171.*)

Persuasive paragraph   A persuasive paragraph states an opinion and uses facts, examples, and reasons to convince readers. (*See page 406.*)

Point of view   In first person point of view, the narrator takes part in the story. In third person point of view, the narrator tells what happens to others and is not a character in the story. (*See page 448.*)

Possessive pronouns   Possessive pronouns are used to show ownership or possession. (*See page 185.*)

Predicate adjective   A predicate adjective is an adjective that follows a linking verb and modifies the subject. (*See page 96.*)

Predicate nominative   A predicate nominative is a noun or a pronoun that follows a linking verb and identifies, renames, or explains the subject. (*See page 94.*)

Prefix   A prefix is a word part that is added to the beginning of a word and changes its basic, or root, meaning. (*See page 530.*)

Preposition   A preposition is a word that shows the relationship between a noun or a pronoun and another word in the sentence. (*See page 69.*)

Prepositional phrase   A prepositional phrase begins with a preposition, ends with a noun or a pronoun, and is used as an adjective or an adverb. (*See page 107.*)

Prewriting   Prewriting is the first stage of the writing process. It includes all the planning steps that come before writing the first draft. (*See page 341.*)

Principal parts of a verb   The principal parts of a verb are the *present*, the *past*, and the *past participle*. The principal parts help form the tenses of verbs. (*See page 159.*)

Pronoun   A pronoun is a word that takes the place of one or more nouns. (*See page 30.*)

Proofreading symbols   Proofreading symbols are a kind of shorthand that writers use to correct their mistakes while editing. (*See page 372.*)

Purpose   Writing purpose is the reason for writing. (*See pages 341 and 352–353.*)

R

Regular verb   A regular verb forms its past and past participle by adding *-ed* or *-d* to the present. (*See page 159.*)

Research report   A research report is a composition of three or more paragraphs that uses information from books, magazines, and other sources. (*See page 465.*)

Revising   Revising is the third stage of the writing process, when a writer changes a draft as often as needed to improve it. (*See page 345.*)

Root   A root is the part of the word that carries the basic meaning. (*See pages 529 and 530.*)

Run-on sentence   A run-on sentence is two or more sentences that are written as one sentence. They are separated by a comma or have no mark of punctuation at all. (*See page 148.*)

S

Sentence   A sentence is a group of words that expresses a complete thought. (*See page 5.*)

Sentence fragment   A sentence fragment is a group of words that does not express a complete thought. (*See page 145.*)

Sequential order   In a paragraph of directions, sequential order presents the details in the proper sequence. (*See page 359.*)

Setting   The setting is the location and time of a story. (*See page 450.*)

Simple predicate   A simple predicate, or verb, is the main word or phrase in the complete predicate. (*See page 9.*)

Simple sentence   A simple sentence consists of one independent clause. (*See page 133.*)

Simple subject   A simple subject is the main word in the complete subject. (*See page 7.*)

Spatial order   Spatial order arranges details according to their location. (*See page 396.*)

Subordinate clause   A subordinate (or dependent) clause cannot stand alone because it does not

express a complete thought. (*See page 125.*)

Subordinating conjunction   A subordinating conjunction is used in a complex sentence to introduce an adverb clause. (*See pages 130 and 306.*)

Suffix   A suffix is a word part that is added to the end of a word and changes its basic, or root, meaning. (*See page 531.*)

Supporting sentences   Supporting sentences explain or prove a topic sentence with specific details, facts, examples, or reasons. (*See page 326.*)

Synonym   A synonym is a word that has nearly the same meaning as another word. (*See page 534.*)

T

Tense   Tense is the form a verb takes to show time. The six tenses are the *present, past, future, present perfect, past perfect,* and *future perfect.* (*See page 168.*)

Thesaurus   A thesaurus is a special dictionary that gives several synonyms for one word. (*See page 584.*)

Topic sentence   A topic sentence states the main idea of the paragraph. (*See page 322.*)

Transitions   Transitions are words and phrases that show how ideas are related. (*See page 329.*)

U

Unity   A paragraph has unity if all the supporting sentences relate to the main idea expressed in the topic sentence. (*See page 327.*)

V

Verb phrase   A verb phrase is a main verb plus one or more helping verbs. (*See page 46.*)

Acknowledgments

The authors and editors have made every effort to trace the ownership of all copyrighted selections found in this book and to make full acknowledgment of their use. Grateful acknowledgment is made to the following authors, publishers, agents, and individuals for their permission to reprint copyrighted materials.

Page 64. "The Yo-Yo," from *Macmillan Illustrated Almanac for Kids*, by Ann Elwood, Carol Orsag, and Sidney Solomon. Copyright © 1981 by Ann Elwood, Carol Orsag, and Sidney Solomon. Reprinted by permission of Macmillan Publishing Co., Inc.

Page 125. "Field Hockey," from *Sports Firsts*, by Patrick Clark, copyright © 1981 by Facts On File, Inc. Reprinted by permission of the publisher.

Page 165. "Students Who Were Teachers," from *Significa*, by Irving Wallace, David Wallechinsky, and Amy Wallace. Copyright © 1983 by Irving Wallace, David Wallechinsky, and Amy Wallace. Reprinted by permission of E.P. Dutton, Inc.

Page 331. From *Fat Polka-dot Cat and Other Haiku*, by Betsy Maestro, copyright © 1976 by Betsy Maestro. Reprinted by permission of the publisher, E.P. Dutton, a division of New American Library.

Pages 438–439. "The Hindu Thread Trick," from *The Great Science Magic Show*, by Ned Arnold and Lois Arnold, copyright © 1979 by Ned Arnold and Lois Arnold. Reprinted by permission of Franklin Watts, Inc.

Page 486. From *The Maybe Monsters*, by Gardner Soule, copyright © 1963 by Gardner Soule. Reprinted by permission of G.P. Putnam's Sons.

Photo Credits
Photo Research: Laurel Anderson

Unit 1: **1:** Julie Habel (Woodfin Camp Associates). *Unit 2:* **157,** *Unit 3:* **231:** Nicholas Devore III (Photographers Aspen).

Unit 4: **293:** William Smith. **Chapter 19: 297l:** John Mamaras (Woodfin Camp Associates). **297r:** Hubert Schriebl (f-Stop Pictures). **303:** Courtesy of NASA. **305:** Harald Sund. **307l:** Robert Frerck (Odyssey Productions). **307r:** Richard Hutchings (Photo Researchers, Inc.). **308:** Lou Jones. **311:** Paul Johnson. **313:** Walter Frerck (Odyssey Productions). **Chapter 20: 322:** Russ Kinne (Photo Researchers, Inc.). **324tl:** E. Roth (The Picture Cube). **324bl:** Walter Frerck (Odyssey Productions). **324r:** Robert Frerck (Odyssey Productions). **325:** John Bryson (Sygma). **328:** Tom J. Ulrich (Visuals Unlimited).

Unit 5: **339:** Julie Habel (Woodfin Camp Associates). **Chapter 21: 342:** By Permission of Mrs. James Thurber/New Yorker Magazine. **343:** Peter Arnold, Inc. **349:** (Photo, Geoffrey Clements) Backyards, Greenwich Village 1914, by John Sloane. Oil on canvas 26 × 32". © The Whitney Museum. **Chapter 22: 357:** Robert Frerck (Odyssey Productions). **360:** Charles Seaborn (Odyssey Productions). **363:** Milt and Joan Mann (Camera Mann Intl.). **366:** The Bettman Archive. **369:** The Brown Bros. **374t:** The Science File (Photo Researchers, Inc.). **374c,b:** R. Royer (Photo Researchers, Inc.). **376:** R. Royer (Photo Researchers, Inc.). **Chapter 23: 380:** David Hiser (Photographers Aspen). **385:** Jerry Howard (Positive Images). **388:** Dewitt Jones (Woodfin Camp Associates). **389:** Ralph Wetmore (Photo Researchers, Inc.). **390:** Brent Jones (Gartman Agency). **Chapter 24: 394:** Cary Wolinsky (Stock, Boston, Inc.). **402:** Ted Schiffman (Peter Arnold, Inc.). **Chapter 25: 411:** Julie O'Neil. **414:** Will McIntyre (Photo Researchers, Inc.).

Unit 6: **421:** Nicholas Devore III (Photographers Aspen). **Chapter 26: 427:** Charles Seaborn (Odyssey Productions). **428:** Laurel Anderson (Odyssey Productions). **431:** David Hiser (Photographers Aspen). **434:** Tim Eagan (Woodfin Camp Associates). **439:** Ted Cordingley (Nawrocki Stock). **Chapter 27: 445:** L. L. T. Rhodes (Click/Atoz). **446:** Milt and Joan Mann (Gartman Agency). **455:** North Wind Picture Archive. **456:** Michal Heron (Woodfin Camp

Associates). **460t:** Julie Habel (Woodfin Camp Associates). **460b:** Thomas Nebbia (Woodfin Camp Associates). **461tl:** John Lazenby (f-Stop Pictures). **461tr:** Clyde Smith (f-Stop Pictures). **461bl:** Laurel Anderson (Odyssey Productions). **461br:** Richard Wood (The Picture Cube). **462:** Donald Dietz (Stock, Boston, Inc.). **Chapter 28: 469:** Thomas Hopker (Woodfin Camp Associates). **471:** Tom McHugh (Photo Researchers, Inc.). **477:** Jerry Schad (Photo Researchers, Inc.). **482:** The Bettman Archive. **484:** Robert Llewellyn. **Chapter 29: 500:** Stephanie Maze (Woodfin Camp Associates). **502:** Ted Cordingley. **506l:** Dave Anrenberg (Click/Atoz). **506r:** L. L. T. Rhodes (Click/Atoz).

Unit 7: **511:** David Hiser (Photographers Aspen). **Chapter 34: 583:** David Hiser (Photographers Aspen).

Illustration Credits

330: Leslie Evans. **332, 348, 358, 399:** George Ulrich. **400, 403:** Leslie Evans. **412:** George Ulrich. **417:** Lynn Duffy. **436:** Leslie Evans. **438:** George Ulrich. **450:** Leslie Evans. **472, 568, 573, 575, 577, 579:** George Ulrich.